Social Responsibility
in the Global Market

To John and Scott, whose love, support,

and encouragement we deeply value.

Social Responsibility in the Global Market

Fair Trade of Cultural Products

Mary Ann Littrell / Marsha Ann Dickson

SAGE Publications
International Educational and Professional Publisher
Thousand Oaks   London   New Delhi

For information:

SAGE Publications, Inc.
2455 Teller Road
Thousand Oaks, California 91320
E-mail: order@sagepub.com

SAGE Publications Ltd.
6 Bonhill Street
London EC2A 4PU
United Kingdom

SAGE Publications India Pvt. Ltd.
M-32 Market
Greater Kailash I
New Delhi 110 048 India

Printed in the United States of America

Library of Congress Cataloging-in-Publication Data

Littrell, Mary Ann.
   Social responsibility in the global market: Fair trade of cultural products / by Mary Ann Littrell and Marsha Ann Dickson.
      p. cm.
   Includes bibliographical references and index.
   ISBN 0-7619-1463-3 (cloth: acid-free paper)
   ISBN 0-7619-1464-1 (pbk.: acid-free paper)
      1. Handicraft industries. 2. Artisans. 3. Social responsibility of business.
   I. Dickson, Marsha Ann. II. Title.
   HD2341 .L58 1999
   338.4'768—dc21   99-6228

99 00 01 02 03 10 9 8 7 6 5 4 3 2 1

Acquiring Editor:	Harry Briggs
Editorial Assistant:	MaryAnn Vail
Production Editor:	Diana E. Axelsen
Editorial Assistant:	Karen Wiley
Typesetter/Designer:	Marion Warren
Indexer:	Mary Mortensen
Cover Designer:	Michelle Lee

CONTENTS

Acknowledgments   ix

I.   INTRODUCTION TO FAIR TRADE IN THE GLOBAL MARKET   I

1. Philosophy, Practices, and Organizational Culture   3

Fair Trade: Why Now?   7
How Do ATOs Conduct Business?   13
ATO Origin, Evolution, and Collaboration   16
Fair Trade in a Culture of Social Responsibility   19
Questions for Fair Trade Analysis   24
Our Fair Trade Journey   26

2. Scholarly Perspectives for Analysis of Fair Trade   29

Business Organizational Culture   30
Business Strategy   33
Small Business Performance   35
Artisanal Work and Development   39
Cultural Product Meaning for Consumers   48
Multidisciplinary and Systemic Analysis   54

II.	**INCOME, JUSTICE, AND EMPOWERMENT THROUGH FAIR TRADE**	**57**

3. **Ten Thousand Villages: A Mission-Driven Journey**   **61**

The Mission: Providing Vital, Fair Income   68
The Business: Selling Handcrafts and Telling the Story   71
Toward an Integrated, Mission-Driven, Viable Business   78

4. **SERRV: Alternative Distribution, Philosophical Considerations, and Hard Business Decisions**   **89**

Business Decision 1: Eliminating Staff Positions   96
Business Decision 2: Focusing on Product Design   97
Business Decision 3: Expanding Alternative Distribution   103
Launching the Next 50 Years   106

5. **Pueblo to People: Balancing Politics and Business**   **113**

Pueblo to People's History   114
Shared Politics, Shared Values   119
Producer-Focused Business Operations   123
An Unsustainable Business   132
Conclusions   138

6. **MarketPlace: Handwork of India "Soaring With Strong Wings"**   **143**

MarketPlace: From Mumbai, India, to Evanston, Illinois   144
Indigenous Skills and Aesthetics   150
Organizational Decentralization   154
Design and Product Development   158
Global Dialogue   160
Leadership Transition   163
Conclusions   164

7. **Focused Players With Pragmatic Approaches**   **171**

Aid to Artisans: Linking Artisans to the Market   172
PEOPLink: Using the Internet for Global Trade and
    Democracy   184
Traditions Fair Trade: Independent Retailing   190
Pragmatic Conclusions   193

III. DIVERSE STAKEHOLDERS IN THE
SYSTEM OF FAIR TRADE   195

8. Artisan Producer Groups:
   "Our Hands Are Our Future"   **199**

   ❖ Artisan Profile 1: UPAVIM   202
   ❖ Artisan Profile 2: Ruth and Nohemi   210
   ❖ Artisan Profile 3: Tejidos de Guadelupe   216
   Artisan Group Organizational Culture   219

9. ATO Consumers: Creative,
   Practical, and Concerned   **225**

   Who Are ATO Consumers?   226
   What Are ATO Consumers Looking for in a Product?   231
   Are ATOs Offering Products With the Desired Quality
       and Appearance?   238
   How Do ATO Consumers Feel About the World, Its
       People, and the Contributions ATOs Are Making?   242
   What Will Influence ATO Consumers' Future Purchasing?   244
   Conclusions   248

10. Challenges in Product Development   **251**

    Focus on Tradition   253
    Diverse ATO Approaches for Product Development   256
    Day-to-Day Factors Influencing Product Development   266
    Conclusions   282

IV. CHALLENGES AND OPPORTUNITIES FOR
MAXIMIZING SOCIAL RESPONSIBILITY
THROUGH FAIR TRADE   287

11. Strategic Appropriateness for the Global Market   **289**

    Question 1: Past Viability With an Artisan Focus   290
    Question 2: Accomplishing the Mission   302

12. The Future for Alternative Trade Organizations   **305**

    Future Viability for ATOs   306
    Core Conditions for ATO Performance   317
    Modeling the Fair Trade System   319

Appendix A: Methods   **325**

    Establishing Rapport in the ATO Community   326
    Artisan Research   327
    ATO Research   331
    Consumer Research   333
    An Assessment of 6 Years of Research   339

Appendix B   **340**

    Contact Information for ATOs and Artisan Producers   340

References   **345**

    Other Publications by the Authors on Alternative
        Trade Organizations   352

Index   **355**

About the Authors   **365**

ACKNOWLEDGMENTS

With great appreciation, we acknowledge the countless artisans, retailers, and consumers who contributed to the ideas presented in this book. Most important, we thank the many leaders in the fair trade movement who 6 years ago welcomed us to their workplaces and introduced us to "a different way of doing business." Over time they became our friends and champions in telling their story. Their frequent telephone calls to update us on their accomplishments, discuss challenges, and ask the ever-present question of "how's the book going?" were continuing inspiration. Although the interpretations offered in this book are ours, each of these individuals offered a unique and significant contribution to our analysis. More specifically, we thank Paul Myers, Joyce Burkholder, and Rachel Hess at Ten Thousand Villages; Robert Chase and Brian Backe at SERRV; Jimmy Pryor, Joan Stewart, Sandy Calhoun, and Teresa Cordón at the former Pueblo to People; Pushpika Freitas at MarketPlace: Handwork of India; Clare Brett Smith and Tom Aageson at Aid to Artisans; Dan Salcedo at PEOPLink; Dick Meyer at Traditions Fair Trade; Ron Spector at Asociación Maya; and Barb Fenske and Angela Bailon at UPAVIM.

In addition to sustained communication with the aforementioned Alternative Trade Organization (ATO) leaders, others offered important insights at various junctures along our journey. We particularly value the special contributions from artisans in Guatemala, India, and Ghana who described their work, invited us to their homes, and talked about their involvement with ATOs. Some asked that they not be named; others in

Guatemala requested that their group's name, address, and a contact person be listed in the book. We have honored this request through a listing of Guatemalan artisan groups in Appendix B. Contact information for the Mumbai, India arm of MarketPlace: Handwork of India is also included. Our opportunities to meet with artisans would not have been possible without the guidance and assistance in translation from Teresa Cordón, Jackie Arreaza, Fatima Merchant, and Bridget Kyerematen.

Still others extended details of their particular involvement in aspects of design, product development, or marketing with ATOs. Here we appreciate the perspectives of Docey Lewis, Deborah Chandler, Barb Fogle, Lynda Grose, Fran Sanders, Cathie Chilson, Lalita Monteiro, Marilyn Clark, Lee Ann Ward, Larry Lack, Kerry Evans, and Catherine Renno. Finally, more than 700 customers of ATO catalogs returned our questionnaires and as such gave of their time to the larger concern of better understanding the preferences and needs of ATO consumers.

We both feel fortunate to work in university departments that foster scholarly debate and encourage multidisciplinary work. We are indebted to our colleagues and graduate students who have encouraged our thinking and served as coresearchers on various ATO-related projects from which we have drawn. Specifically, we thank Jennifer Paff Ogle, Soyoung Kim, and Rosalind Paige. For the quantitative portion of the research, we appreciate the statistical consultation provided by Frederick O. Lorenz, Kenneth Koehler, and R. Kenneth Teas, all of Iowa State University.

Funding or in-kind contributions from a wide range of sources helped with our travel to the different ATOs and artisan groups, as well as other expenses associated with the research. We thank the following for their financial assistance: the International Textile and Apparel Association; MarketPlace: Handwork of India; Iowa State University's Professional Advancement Grant Program; the ISU College of Family and Consumer Science's Grace Olsen, Julia Anderson, and Cowan-Newbrough International Funds; the Ohio Agricultural Research and Development Center; the honor society Kappa Omicron Nu; and in-kind contributions of mailing lists, catalogs, and travel accommodations from Pueblo to People, Ten Thousand Villages, and SERRV.

To end, we want to express our immense appreciation to our editor, Harry Briggs. Throughout, Harry was just an e-mail away in answering our questions and offering valuable critique. In addition, four anonymous reviewers enlarged our thinking in helping us to consider additional perspectives on our emerging analysis.

PART I

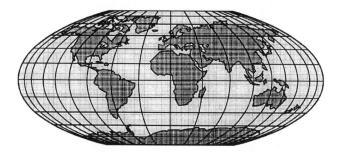

INTRODUCTION
TO
FAIR TRADE
IN THE
GLOBAL MARKET

CHAPTER 1

PHILOSOPHY, PRACTICES, AND ORGANIZATIONAL CULTURE

I am very happy that I have learned to sew. It is a more interesting and reputable occupation. It is also very consistent and I do not have to worry whether there is work or not. After starting to sew and meeting different people, I also felt the need to study and have started going to school. It is a little difficult but I think that it will help me to improve my life. I am also happy that I am able to help my brother go to school.

—Fair trade producer

In our 17 years, we have strived to offer artisans in Latin America an alternative to the exploitation they typically experience in the market. Our methods are unique, daring, and difficult. But somehow, we continue to compete in a market which is based on a very different set of goals. When you buy from us, everyone wins. And each time you use your purchase, you will share in the knowledge that it comes to you fairly, with a value that exceeds mere money.

—Fair trade retailer

Your clothes are really special. I am constantly pleased because of the excellent quality of the cloth. I continue to buy your clothing because every dress, jumper, and skirt brings continual compliments from friends and strangers alike. The attention is great fun, but what continues to be of greatest importance to me is knowing that my buying power is supporting the effort of others who are working to support themselves. Thanks so much for making the connection between us.

—Fair trade customer

Fair trade is an alternative and increasingly important way of doing business that brings together a diversity of producers, retailers, and customers in the global market. As expressed in the opening quotations, fair trade bridges artisans' needs for income, retailers' goals for transforming trade, and consumers' concerns for social responsibility through a compatible, nonexploitive, and humanizing system of international exchange.

This book focuses on businesses that market cultural products from developing countries into the United States through a system of fair trade.[1] Called Alternative Trade Organizations (ATOs), these businesses combine functions of exporters and retailers as they work directly with artisan groups on product design, quality control, management, and shipping. Products are distributed across national boundaries through mail-order catalogs, specialty stores, church sales, and other outlets in the United States. Although the majority of ATOs operate as nonprofit businesses, models of for-profit fair trade are under development.

The products traded by ATOs embody aesthetic features and production technologies that are deeply enmeshed in artisans' local traditions. Some level of handwork is common to all ATO products;[2] however, many artisans accelerate production through the use of molds, sewing and knitting machines, and a variety of other mechanized tools for processing raw materials, forming products, and finishing artisanal wares. To describe the ATO product range, we employ the terminology *cultural products* to encompass goods that are produced exclusively by hand as well as those that incorporate extensive mechanization. Using this terminology, cultural products include what are typically called *handcrafts* as well as other items on a higher ratio of machine-to-hand production.

Organizational structures of ATOs vary widely. Some, such as Ten Thousand Villages, SERRV, Pueblo to People, and MarketPlace: Handwork of India, are comprehensive (see Chapters 3-6). These organizations are involved in all phases of fair trade, including training and product development with artisans, export, and retail sales. Other organizations focus on a more limited range of functions. The following are examples:

> ➤ Asociación Maya, founded by Ron Spector, works at a grassroots level with 280 Mayan weavers in the highland Guatemalan village of Sololá.

Product design to meet aesthetic and product preferences for the U.S. market is a priority. During hands-on design workshops in Guatemala, the backstrap loom weavers experiment with new colorways, fabric weights, and surface textures. Particularly talented weavers are selected for U.S.-based study tours to augment their product development skills; upon return, these women serve as group leaders for further design inspiration.

➤ Aid to Artisans in Farmington, Connecticut, links artisan groups with wholesale buyers in the United States, Europe, and within their own countries, often through participation in the New York International Gift Fair. Under the leadership of Clare Brett Smith, president, and Thomas Aageson, executive director, services offered by Aid to Artisans include consultation on product design, technical assistance in production, market studies, merchandising and retail analysis, and business training.

➤ PEOPLink, headed by Dan Salcedo in Kensington, Maryland, promotes linkages between producers and global markets via an electronic catalog and a World Gallery on the World Wide Web. Using digital cameras and computers made available to artisans in less-developed countries, producer groups communicate with U.S. design consultants, transmit products for the Web catalogs, and educate U.S. consumers about their crafts and cultures.

➤ Traditions Fair Trade, a for-profit retail shop in Olympia, Washington, stocks products from 50 countries throughout the world. Through an extensive program of in-store musical events, speakers, public forums, and a café offering a selection of healthful entrees, owner-manager Dick Meyer positions his retail store as a shopping destination and community resource for the broader spectrum of socially responsible activities in the Olympia area.

Fair Trade Philosophy and Practice

In conducting fair trade,[3] ATOs adhere to both a philosophy and a set of practices for conducting global commerce. As a philosophy, fair trade fosters empowerment and improved quality of life for artisan producers through an integrated and sustained system of trade partnerships among producers, retailers, and consumers. With an ideological focus on paying producers "as much as possible" rather than "as little as possible," fair trade provides a dramatic contrast with mainstream business, in which attention is directed toward meeting customer demand and expanding shareholder profits. More specifically, fair trade philosophy is undergirded by three basic premises or assumptions on which members of the fair trade system operate.

Premise 1: Indigenous products can be commercialized through a process of product development that emanates from and honors cultural traditions among artisan producers.

Premise 2: Production and trade can transpire under socially responsible, nonexploitive conditions that provide a fair wage, maximize profits, and contribute to long-term, socioeconomic benefits for producers and their communities.

Premise 3: A customer base exists for culturally embedded goods produced in a socially responsible manner.

Our examination of fair trade offers readers an opportunity to consider a variety of trade-related issues. We address challenges associated with marketing products deeply embedded in one culture to consumers in a second culture for whom the products hold different meaning and serve alternative functions. We raise questions about conditions under which artisans can maintain their craft traditions as sources of family livelihood and about how consumers can use their purchasing power in a manner consistent with their values. Finally, as the book title suggests, we hope to engage our readers in contemplating the significance of *social responsibility* in the global market.

As a point of departure, we propose that social responsibility involves a systemwide range of practices for conducting business in which artisans, retailers, and consumers make decisions based on how their actions affect others within the marketplace system. More specifically, participants in the trade system consider effects of their decisions on whether

> ➤ natural resources and cultural traditions are preserved;
> ➤ workplaces are safe and conducive to the interpersonal exchange of opinions;
> ➤ workers are paid fairly so they can meet daily subsistence needs, educate their children, care for family health, and contribute to community growth; and
> ➤ artisan enterprises are sustainable across time and as customer preferences change.

Our definition of social responsibility places major emphasis on day-to-day actions within a business as related to product sourcing, employee treatment, and working conditions. As such, it differs from social responsibility as practiced by businesses that focus outside the firm into the communities where they are located in the United States. In an outward focus, a company may encourage its employees to volunteer for various community activities or set aside funds for community philanthropic projects, but it may not necessarily attend in socially responsible ways to its daily business actions. Although a firm may have both an outward and inward focus, it is the inward business decisions affecting daily work on which we center our attention in this book.

In addition to a distinctive philosophy, fair trade also embodies a singular set of business practices. In Figure 1.1, we graphically place ATOs within the larger context of fair trade. The bottom half of the figure presents fair trade as a series of practices that begin, on the left, with a focus on the workplace and expand to community-wide development and equitable trade on the right. The top half of the figure positions a series of businesses above the fair trade practices to which they are committed. One subset of mainstream businesses is dedicated to paying fair wages in the local context and to establishing safe, clean workplaces for their employees. ATOs form a second subset of fair trade businesses. ATOs go beyond attending to the immediate workplace as they collaborate with artisans to increase income, develop sustainable businesses, and ultimately foster well-being at individual, household, and community levels. Throughout the remainder of the book, we use the terms *fair trade* and *alternative trade* interchangeably to refer to this more expansive set of practices as exemplified by ATOs.

Fair Trade: Why Now?

Concerns emerging from a variety of quarters point to the need for the examination of fair trade. Artisans in less-developed countries have, in many cases, lost their local patronage to cheaper, machine-produced alternatives flooding the market. Development planners question whether artisans, when redirecting their craft traditions toward external markets with new aesthetic, product, and volume demands, can achieve sustainable employment in ways that do not erode cultural identity. Continents away, North American consumers are troubled by human rights issues; they wonder whether the products they buy may be manufactured under exploitive working conditions in less-

8

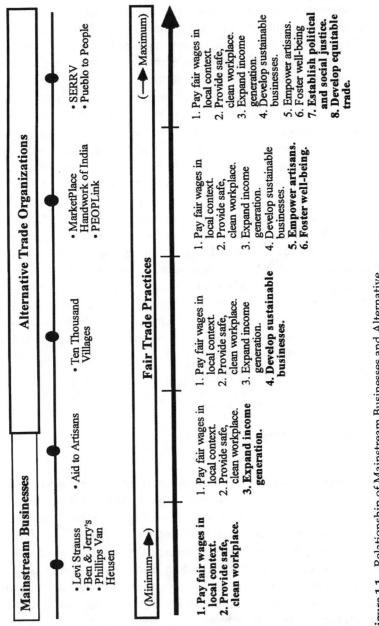

Mainstream Businesses

Alternative Trade Organizations

- Levi Strauss
- Ben & Jerry's
- Phillips Van Heusen

- Aid to Artisans

- Ten Thousand Villages

- MarketPlace Handwork of India
- PEOPLink

- SERRV
- Pueblo to People

(Minimum ——►)   **Fair Trade Practices**   (——► Maximum)

1. Pay fair wages in local context.
2. Provide safe, clean workplace.

1. Pay fair wages in local context.
2. Provide safe, clean workplace.
3. Expand income generation.

1. Pay fair wages in local context.
2. Provide safe, clean workplace.
3. Expand income generation.
4. Develop sustainable businesses.

1. Pay fair wages in local context.
2. Provide safe, clean workplace.
3. Expand income generation.
4. Develop sustainable businesses.
5. Empower artisans.
6. Foster well-being.

1. Pay fair wages in local context.
2. Provide safe, clean workplace.
3. Expand income generation.
4. Develop sustainable businesses.
5. Empower artisans.
6. Foster well-being.
7. Establish political and social justice.
8. Develop equitable trade.

Figure 1.1. Relationship of Mainstream Businesses and Alternative Trade Organizations to Fair Trade Practices

developed countries. Low employee wages in foreign countries seem out of proportion to the prices that consumers pay in their local stores. In addressing these concerns, fair trade, with its focus on social responsibility among producers, retailers, and consumers, offers a trade alternative that is timely for analysis of its past impacts, present initiatives, and future viability in the global market.

Consumer Concerns

Beginning with U.S. consumers, many were alerted in the mid-1990s to exploitive working conditions in factories operated by apparel contractors located on the East and West Coasts of the United States and in Latin American and Asian countries (Holstein, 1996; McCormick & Levinson, 1993; Mitchell & Oneal, 1994). National media coverage regarding Kathie Lee Gifford's line of apparel for Wal-Mart and of the Pocahontas, Hunchback of Notre Dame, and 101 Dalmations product lines for Walt Disney called attention to the hours, wages, and factory working conditions among Latin American workers, many of whom were young girls in their mid- to late teens. Abuses were also publicized among production contractors for major clothing labels such as Gap, Guess, and Nike.

National media coverage and rising concern from labor and consumer action groups led to a number of government, industry, and union-led initiatives. Programs included expanded in-country, independent monitoring programs for apparel manufacturing plants (U.S. Department of Labor, 1996); a "No Sweat" campaign and a presidential task force led by the U.S. Secretary of Labor (U.S. Department of Labor, 1996); and three national conferences bringing together industry officials, labor leaders, educators, and the public for purposes of exploring workable solutions. The National Labor Committee (1998) led a "People's Right to Know Campaign" that asked consumers to endorse corporate disclosure of specific factories in which their goods are produced, monitoring of factories by locally respected independent religious and human rights monitors, and payment of fair wages.

Despite some indicators toward change, polls of American consumers register their persisting concerns for workplace conditions. A *U.S. News & World Report* (Holstein, 1996) poll found that 6 out of 10 Americans express concern about workplace issues in the United States. The numbers rose to 9 out of 10 when production takes place in Asia and Latin America. Studies by market research companies and university researchers further confirm that consumers are disturbed about child labor, wage and hour violations, and hazards in the workplace (Dickson, 1999). Although consumers attest that they are more likely to buy from a socially responsible company than from a business that gives little attention to social issues, customers also affirm that products must be of comparable quality and competitively priced to gain customer acceptance (Dickson, 1999).

Artisan Issues

In addition to consumer concerns, the pressing need by the world's craftspersons for expanded markets provided another urgent point of departure for our analysis of fair trade. Longtime observers of the craft sector in developing countries assess that the escalating numbers of individuals turning to craft production are unlikely to decline significantly in the decade ahead (Herald, 1992). After agriculture, artisans constitute the second largest sector of rural employment in many regions of the world (Basu, 1995).

Shifts to craft production are closely linked with dramatic declines in access to land as a source of income. Family holdings have suffered through subdivision, overexploitation, soil erosion, and adverse climatic conditions (Nash, 1993a; Page-Reeves, 1998). In addition, income alternatives for artisans in less-developed countries are limited due to lack of access to land by women, ethnic minorities, and the very poor, as well as scarcity of other forms of employment outside agriculture for those living in rural areas. Yet, urban migration to seek employment is often discouraged as part of national planning (Herald, 1992; International Trade Centre UNCAD/GATT, 1991; Pye, 1988). In urban areas, artisans are dependent on a cash economy as they can no longer rely on their land to feed their families (Page-Reeves, 1998). In addition, artisans often must take jobs that require long hours and leave little time for attention to family members or maintenance of craft traditions.

Under this set of changing conditions for artisans, programs that provide new markets for crafts are vital. Attention to craft microenterprises has increased as government organizations and foundations have acknowledged the opportunities for employment and ensuing financial flexibility that small and microenterprises offer to households and to local and national economies (Mikkelson, Goldmark, & Hagen-Wood, 1997). Exporting crafts through ATOs provides one way of expanding cultural product enterprises beyond local markets.

International development planners and academic researchers offer a range of both encouraging stories and disquieting observations of artisan producer groups that are in the midst of developing products for new international consumer markets. On the positive side, artisan groups such as the rug weavers of Teotitlán del Valle, Mexico (Popelka, Fanslow, & Littrell, 1992; Stephen, 1991c) and the Kuna *mola* makers of the San Blas Islands in Panama (Swain, 1993; Tice, 1995) have retained a measure of control over product development and market expansion during the process of commercialization.

More common, however, are stories of producer group vulnerability from profit diversion to trading intermediaries. Due to artisans' lack of knowledge about foreign tastes, their limited experience in conducting trade beyond local or regional boundaries, and the volatile nature of foreign markets, trading intermediaries hold immense power for affecting the rate of economic return to artisans, the conditions under which the artisans work, and the products they produce (Moreno, 1995; Rosenbaum & Goldin, 1997; Steiner, 1994; Stephen, 1991c, 1993; Stromberg-Pellizzi, 1993). Yet, without outside advice or direction, artisans can quickly find themselves with an oversupply of unwanted or inappropriately designed products that fail to meet international standards for quality or aesthetics. Travel bags designed such that, when unzipped, the contents fall out; blouses with necklines that cannot be donned over larger American heads; or bookshelves that are not stable when assembled provide evidence of the need for cross-cultural assistance in understanding quality and product demand.

Erosion of cultural traditions in the process of product commercialization is a second concern voiced by development and academic observers (Cohen, 1988; Graburn, 1976; Nash, 1993a; Niessen, 1990; Popelka & Littrell, 1991; Rosenbaum, 1993; Stephen, 1991c, 1993; Swain, 1993). Invariably, production for global markets calls for larger volumes, greater repetition and exactness across products, and acquisition of new quality and aesthetic criteria. Questions have been raised concerning cultural impacts on artisan producers, their communities, and products when the organization of production is moved from households to centrally located workshops that often accompany craft commoditization.

In some cases, central workshop production favors males who, due to the seasonal nature of their agricultural work, have blocks of time available for workshop production. In contrast, workshop employment by women requires major realignment of their many household responsibilities related to daily food preparation, child care, laundry, and agriculture. Other gender issues emerge in those communities where long-standing women's crafts are targeted for expansion and where women's increased income can alter power relations in the household and community. Still other questions address what happens when techniques for producing cultural products are no longer passed down within a family but are instead taught to young workers in classroom-like settings. As production for local use is replaced by production for sales, does daily and ritual use of the products decline? How do local standards for quality and beauty evolve over time when artisans turn to products that meet outsiders' interests in the "exotic" or their perceptions of what constitutes an "ethnic" look in apparel or household products?

In summary, craft traditions have rarely been static. Artisans have long adopted new technologies and initiated new ideas in product design. However, as craft producers expand to markets outside their communities, changes in work patterns, gender roles, quality and aesthetic criteria, and methods for teaching and learning hold tremendous potential to significantly affect how artisans carry out their work and the products they produce (Basu, 1995; Dhamija, 1989; Morris, 1996; Nash, 1993a; Page-Reeves, 1998; Stephen, 1991c; Tice, 1995).

Together, perceptions and experiences from consumers and artisan producers suggest a business climate that is troubling to some and in transition for many. A sizable proportion of U.S. consumers are raising questions about ethical business practices; they hold values supportive of greater social responsibility in their consumption practices. Artisans, desperate for income, are vulnerably positioned for potential exploitation in the process of product commercialization. Against this backdrop of concern, we explore the philosophy, practices, and challenges of ATOs for their potential in providing a compatible and nonexploitive alternative for conducting international trade.

How Do ATOs Conduct Business?

ATOs engage in distinctive business operations related to the types of products produced, the conditions under which production occurs, and the approach for marketing to consumers. First, cultural products that embody indigenous colors, motifs, and designs form the ATO product core. Locally available raw materials such as clay, wood, grasses, or cotton serve as primary raw materials. Product categories include apparel and accessories, jewelry, household goods, decorative objects, toys, and musical instruments. Products convey a distinctive cultural meaning that has evolved from long-standing patterns of daily and ritual use within a community. As examples, the Ghanaian animal and figurative motifs on textiles and furniture marketed through Aid to Artisans Ghana emanate from the design motifs and proverbial stories on Ghanaian adinkra cloth and royal regalia. In a second example, the flower-surrounded necklines of the best-selling Pueblo to People blouses from Patzun, Guatemala, symbolize the linkage between a woman's embroidery skills and her overall worth as a contributing family member.

In addition to culturally embedded design, ATO cultural products are produced using dyeing, weaving, sewing, basketry, wood turning, carving, metal smithing, paper making, and painting technologies that are deeply integrated in gendered, household-based, and village-centered patterns of work. To illustrate, in India, fabric dyeing and printing is the domain of men, whereas women draw on their embroidery skills, passed down from mother to daughter, for surface embellishment of textiles. In a second example, household-based work typifies the wood carvers from several villages in Oaxaca, Mexico, where all family members are employed in carving and painting fanciful animal figures. Colorful signs over courtyard entrances signal wood carving as a villagewide craft business as well.

ATOs vary widely in the extent to which they become directly involved with producers in product design and development. For some ATOs, encouraging artisans to modify their products to meet customer preferences is viewed as neocolonial infringement by outsiders on local craft traditions. However, when limited information is provided to producers, they must rely on their observations of what is selling in tourist markets or on what other groups are making for new ideas. Without market guidance from outsiders who can serve as culture brokers between the worlds of producers and consumers, groups end up producing items that may have had minimal past success or hold little future promise. Bottlenecks from an oversupply of products with little marketability frequently occur.

In contrast, other ATOs, building on the dynamic nature of craft traditions, argue for collaboration between producers and outside design consultants in developing new products to meet changing market demand. Catherine Renno, a longtime fair trade retailer and advocate of involving design consultants as culture brokers, assesses this practice: "The market demands that you listen. You have to be knowledgeable of consumer demand if you are going to compete."

A second practice distinguishing ATOs is how production occurs. A fair trade partnership between ATO retailers in North America and producers in less-developed countries involves joint commitment to a set of guidelines for production. The guidelines include the following:

> paying a fair wage in the local context,
> offering equitable employment opportunities,
> providing healthy and safe working conditions,
> engaging in environmentally sustainable practices,
> monitoring and improving product quality,
> honoring cultural identity as a stimulus for product development and production practices,
> offering business and technical expertise and opportunities for worker advancement,
> contributing to community development,
> building long-term trade relationships, and
> being open to public accountability.

A long-term goal is that sustainable businesses evolve from a process of interaction and negotiation between an ATO and producers. Although initially the ATO may be the sole or primary customer, eventually attracting a larger group of clients at local, regional, and international levels is the desired state. Not surprisingly, ATOs receive far more requests to form fair trade partnerships than they can possibly accommodate. A producer group's commitment to fair trade guidelines and its potential for capacity building and long-term sustainability are given high priority as ATOs select new partners from the ever-expanding numbers of requests they receive each year.

A third distinguishing practice of ATOs focuses on how products are marketed to consumers. The partnership between producers and ATOs is extended to retail customers through promotional strategies that emphasize both the quality of the products and the life conditions surrounding the producers and their work. Educating customers about social, cultural, political, and environmental issues affecting artisans in developing countries is a major focus of catalog narrative, product hangtags, and in-store promotions. ATO stories and photographs may chronicle a day in the life of an artisan wife and mother from the slums of Mumbai, describe ecological practices associated with the wood logged for bookshelves from Honduras, or portray the ritual use of musical instruments in a Kenyan village. Dick Meyer, a fair trade retailer, summarizes that as customers are becoming increasingly sensitive to issues of product sourcing and questionable workplace conditions, ATO retailers have the opportunity and challenge of helping their customers understand that through their purchases of fairly traded products, "they are part of a movement of people within a community who are making a certain amount of difference in the lives of producers." As Dan Salcedo, PEOPLink founder, describes for consumers, "What and how we consume is the main way we reach out and touch people thousands of miles away whom we have never met."

Through these distinctive business operations, ATOs exhibit deep commitment to their philosophy of people-centered development; they operate from an ideological perspective that emphasizes producers' needs rather than consumer demand. ATOs measure their success in a variety of ways, all of which place emphasis on their commitment to artisans. Some ATOs cite their 30% to 45% return of the retail price to producers. For mainstream retailers, who are often dependent on a series of middlemen intermediaries to transact business, the return to producers can be as little as 10% (Benjamin & Freedman, 1989, p. 122). Dan Salcedo, an ATO movement leader, summarizes fair trade philosophy toward the commercial middleman: "The whole chain winds up squeezing the link below it. The idea of fair trade is to bypass some of these links and get the artisan a better deal" (Whitehouse, 1996, p. 33).

As a second indicator of success, other ATOs emphasize the number of producers supported through ATO sales. Producer groups that use some of their earnings for community school or health care projects are also cited as contributing to individual empowerment. Finally, among for-profit ATOs, a fair distribution of profits among producers and retailers is used as an indicator of successful fulfillment of the fair trade philosophy toward socially responsible partnerships.

ATO Origin, Evolution, and Collaboration

ATOs have a long history in Europe and North America, where they emerged after World War II in England, Holland, Germany, Canada, and the United States. Well-known European ATOs include Gepa, Oxfam, and Traidcraft. European ATOs are particularly strong in marketing coffee and other food products (European Fair Trade Association, 1998). Coffee beans bearing the quality seal of the Dutch-based Max Havelaar Foundation are widely recognized in Holland and Denmark.

In the United States, three stages mark fair trade evolution. Fair trade first emerged in the late 1940s and 1950s through the Mennonite and the Church of the Brethren churches. Field-workers involved in worldwide mission activities became aware of artisans who were in desperate need of income. Through church and home sales back in the United States, church members served as intermediaries in securing income for the artisans.

In a second stage, commencing in the 1960s and continuing through the 1980s, young, well-educated social activists visited abroad and, through person-to-person contacts with artisans, offered to assist by bringing back cultural products to sell. For many of these young Americans, their commitment to social responsibility, peace, and justice had been honed through participation in university student movements focused on the environment, civil rights, and the Vietnam War. In addition, some individuals had learned of artisan cooperatives through their Peace Corps assignments. As these young people established comprehensive ATOs or opened retail stores, they sought consumer support from a worldwide solidarity movement of like-minded individuals. Although deeply committed to social and political justice, few of these early leaders had marketing, finance, or other business-related expertise.

During the period when many ATOs originated in the 1970s and 1980s, mainstream, for-profit competitors were few. However, by the 1990s, mainstream retail competitors marketing cultural products had increased in number and importance. Accordingly, ATOs were pushed into a third stage of ATO evolution. A fair trade leader describes the sudden changes that ATOs confronted coming out of the 1970s and 1980s:

> You could have anything and people would buy it. Then the market got really saturated so that romance period ended. All of a sudden the do-gooders going into the late '80s and especially the early '90s had a heavy-duty wake-up call, and it was called market forces. Their businesses had grown, some to over $1 million. All of a sudden the bottom line, profit margins, and all of these words started having real practical meaning. As fair traders, we thought we were reinventing the business wheel, but what we really needed to do was learn the components of that wheel. We could reinvent a wheel but it wasn't going to fit on the competitive marketing vehicle. So what we are doing right now is to learn that marketing vehicle, what its components are, and *then* adapting it to our philosophy. The same market forces affect fair trade that affect Reebok. What differentiates us is we're committed to a fair distribution of the profits.

During the late 1990s (Stage 3), stiff mainstream competition comes from a variety of retailers. Pier 1 Imports, the nation's largest specialty retailer of imported decorative household furnishings and a primary ATO competitor, markets its products with a strong customer focus (Brookman, 1991; Pier 1 Imports, 1996). In addition to competition from specialty store retailers, the number of mail-order catalogs specializing in international ethnic products also has expanded in the 1990s. In the late 1990s, ATOs are at a critical crossroads in evolutionary strategic planning. In contrast to the unsaturated market of the 1970s, ATOs now face stiff competition for customers from expanding numbers of mainstream importers and mail-order catalogs promoting ethnic products.

U.S.-based ATOs, with annual sales of $46 million, are in their infancy compared to worldwide ATO sales at the $400 million level. However, a number of promising signs suggest that U.S. ATOs may be poised for growth. Marketing venues have increased significantly in the 1990s. To illustrate, Ten Thousand Villages retail stores grew from 122 to more than 200 shops between the 1980s and 1990s. SERRV's partners for church-based and catalog sales expanded to include the Christian Children's Fund in 1990 and Catholic Relief Services in 1995. As a second indicator, several of the larger ATOs have experienced steady sales growth. As examples, sales for Ten Thousand Villages grew from $5.9 million to $6.8 million, or more than 15% from 1993 to 1997. The smaller MarketPlace: Handwork of India experienced an eightfold expansion of sales, from $150,000 in 1990 to $1.2 million in 1997. Finally SERRV, after a period of declining sales, exhibited sales growth to its highest level of $4.97 million in 1997.

ATOs have joined together at international and regional levels to promote their philosophy and to expand public awareness of fair trade. Internationally, nearly 100 ATO and observer organizations from 40 countries form the International Federation for Alternative Trade (IFAT), which was founded in 1989. Members include craft and agricultural producer groups in less-developed countries and trade organizations from both Northern and Southern Hemispheres. Located in African, Asian, and Latin American nations, many IFAT producer groups work closely with individuals particularly vulnerable to exploitation, including female-headed households, displaced refugees, seasonal agricultural workers, and those living in extreme poverty.

IFAT members adhere to a code of practice related to transparency or openness in business operations, creation of ethical and effective working conditions, promotion of equal employment opportunities, concern for the environment, respect for producers' cultural integrity, and education and advocacy of fair trade. As a coalition, the IFAT has two primary goals. Through biennial conferences and regional meetings, networking opportunities, an information service database, and the Internet, IFAT provides a forum for the exchange of information and for consultation on product development, marketing, access to financing, and other forms of business training. Second, IFAT also lobbies with national governments and international trade organizations for the rights of exploited workers and for internationally recognized standards for fair trade.

After years of informal cooperation and following the lead of the IFAT, the Fair Trade Federation (FTF) was formed in 1994. Members of the FTF from North, Central, and South America are active in working with producer groups in the region and throughout the world. A national FTF consumer education campaign initiated in 1997 signaled impending potential for growth of fair trade in the United States. A 16-page publication, *Consumer's Guide to Fairly Traded Products* (Fair Trade Federation, 1997a), was the focal point for an outreach program to raise public awareness of fair trade and to inform U.S. consumers of the availability of fairly traded goods in their communities. The message to consumers—that "You can make a difference—one purchase at a time"—formed the rallying point for the promotion. Accessibility of the guide was advertised through magazines, press releases, conference and trade show participation, and coordination with allied organizations. A companion *Retailer's Guide to Fair Trade* (Fair Trade Federation, 1997b) alerted retailers to more than 50 wholesalers from which they could stock their stores.

Fair Trade in a Culture of Social Responsibility

Across our 6 years of research on fair trade, three overarching themes served to illuminate the distinctive profile of ATO organizational culture. Themes describe enduring core values, changing behavioral norms, and new ways of thinking about organizational structures. These themes point to an organizational culture of social responsibility that holds fast to core values while recognizing the need for change. Together, these themes led to the organizing questions guiding our analysis of ATOs.

Core Values

Social responsibility toward providing income for the world's poorest artisans is a widely agreed on and enduring core value. ATOs devote time, attention, and travel to the careful selection of artisan groups in need of assistance. Oft-repeated artisan success stories nourish a culture of social responsibility in which emphasis is placed on artisans and on microenterprise development. Across ATOs, the core value of assisting the world's poorest craftpersons was clearly articulated by managers, marketing analysts, purchasing assistants, warehouse stock persons, catalog customer service representatives, and retail sales associates. Comparison of mission and promotional statements between several ATOs and their mainstream competitors, as shown in Table 1.1, highlights salient differences in their approaches to marketing.

Mainstream businesses, presented at the top, achieve business success by focusing on customer demand. They attend to customers' product preferences; their interests in product quality, uniqueness, and value; and their expectations for customer service. In contrast, ATO mission statements, presented on the bottom, emphasize conditions faced by artisan producers in less-developed countries and highlight their desperate need for income. Business success is measured through economic support for artisans, worker empowerment, and community development.

That customers receive the ATOs' messages and support their mission is evidenced through the many customer letters printed in the catalogs. As an example, one customer describes her decision to provide financial support to an artisan's child:

> I was attracted to your catalog because of the beautiful clothes, but more important than that, because of your global dialogue and SHARE. So, I decided to make your catalog and programs a focus of my relationship with my friend Mae Klinger. She just turned 9 years old and we sponsor a child [in India] together. She pays 25 cents a month and I pay $11.75.

Emanating from this common value base of social responsibility toward artisans, each ATO also has cultivated a unique presence that serves to shape the specific nature of its program goals (see Figure 1.1). As examples, Ten Thousand Villages' goal of income generation for artisans is considered first when making business decisions. Managers in the company's U.S.-based office regularly communicate to producers their satisfaction or dissatisfaction with products and describe the conditions of shipments upon receipt. This communication is intended to provide producers with direction for expanding income through improved production and handling of future orders. In contrast, Pueblo to People emphasizes strong commitment to social and economic development for producer groups. Dialogue among the Houston staff, in-country directors, and producer groups focuses on developing new product ideas, understanding product quality, and developing a strong core of business and leadership skills that can be applied to social, educational, and economic development activities within the producers' communities. Finally, MarketPlace: Handwork of India's goal of empowerment through job training contributes to a culture in which communication among the Chicago- and Mumbai-based employees centers on how to produce unique, high-quality products. Creating a work

TABLE 1.1 Comparison of Mission and Vision Statements for Mainstream and Alternative Trade Organizations

---

Mainstream mission and vision statements

Our Customer Is Sovereign!

Pier 1 Imports' most important assets are the millions of customers who patronize our stores. The Company has positioned its business to exceed the expectations of every customer in product selection, merchandise value, and customer service. Pier 1 Imports has long recognized that putting the desires of customers ahead of all other considerations is the ultimate secret of successful retailing. (Pier 1 Imports)

Sundance isn't so much about what's new as a reminder of what is. What exists in the area of quality and uniqueness that may not have been seen yet—not yet experienced. Sundance has always been about artists and crafts people. It is a place where we incorporate into our daily lives the fruit of their imaginations and efforts. These things connect us to our heritage, and we believe that they enrich our lives. We try to bring the spirit of these artists to you in our catalog. We believe that by including art in everyday living we enhance and enrich the simple pleasure of ordinary routines. As much as this catalog is for the artists and craftspeople, it is, finally, for you. (Sundance)

Welcome to Reverie, the catalog of interesting and impressionable collectibles. As a part of Cheyenne Outfitters' 60 years of experience, we're always on the look-out for the most unusual, distinctively different, and out-of-the-ordinary jewelry, clothing, and gifts . . . for you and your home. And, if at any time for any reason you're not completely satisfied with your purchase, you can return it to us for an exchange or full refund. (Reverie)

Alternative trade mission and vision statements

Our mission is to relieve the suffering of the poor in Latin America. Our means is to market the products of artisans and small farmers in Latin America—paying them a good price.

Our purpose is to build bridges—to link you with the "pueblo" of Latin American women and men of meager means who are working together in cooperatives and production associations to better not only themselves, but their communities as well. When you buy something from us, you get a lot more than a finely crafted, long-lasting product at a great price—you get the community to go with it. (Pueblo to People)

Ten Thousand Villages provides vital, fair income to Third World craftspeople by selling their handcrafts and telling their stories in North America. We work with artisans who would otherwise be unemployed or underemployed. This income helps pay for food, education, health care and housing. Your purchase makes a difference.

(Continued)

TABLE 1.1 Continued

We work to increase world understanding by exploring the causes of poverty and by inviting people to be part of our international partnership. More than 7,000 volunteers in Canada and the United States help keep overhead costs low. (Ten Thousand Villages)

MarketPlace: Handwork of India is a not-for-profit organization. We offer training and employment to disadvantaged women and handicapped persons in India. While most of our artisans do not have the education and skills to be productively employed when they start, we believe that everyone can be effective if given the right job, proper training and encouragement. (MarketPlace: Handwork of India)

---

environment whereby women gain self-confidence and skills that will be transferable to future clients is a primary goal.

Behavioral Norms

In a second overarching theme, a culture of creative tension is evolving related to changing behavioral norms for ATO organizations. The long-established, producer-driven ATO culture is being nudged by an increasing awareness among ATOs of the need to devote greater attention to marketing. Major challenges related to product inventory and lack of target marketing have emerged as the international craft market has become more competitive in the 1990s. For all ATOs, long lead times of 6 to 12 months typify merchandise orders, resulting in inadequate quantities of products at crucial times during the year. Commitment to working with small producer groups and the challenges of international shipping from remote areas are among the conditions that have contributed to this delivery pattern.

Across ATOs, an atmosphere of creativity is evident as the organizations explore new behavioral norms for how they can better balance their time and energy between artisans and customers. ATOs recognize that new ways for guiding product development to meet customer demand, while also maintaining producers' cultural integrity, will be critical if ATOs are to maintain an active presence in the competitive craft market worldwide. Ten Thousand Villages director Paul Myers summarizes these challenges of the mid-1990s:

> Some would say it's a luxury to just go out there and find what you need and what fits. Plus there are those who say if you tamper with what they are producing, it no longer has integrity. We are prepared to live with those tensions. We're interested in providing as much employment as we can for those people. By starting where they are at and building on it and by recognizing that we live in an interdependent world in which we not only want to, but will, be influenced by each other.

Organizational Structures

In a final cultural theme, ATOs are intensely examining their organizational structures and models for growth as they position themselves for adapting to a more competitive market. They are envisioning a future that is different than the past. In an example of organizational analysis, Paul Myers describes the Ten Thousand Villages culture as one that was long guided by "thinking small." However, Ten Thousand Villages has adopted an expanded model of growth while also maintaining its grassroots involvement. The organization assesses that the next period of growth "will come differently than this one did" but also acknowledges the importance of addressing competition from mainstream retailers through a better understanding of customer demand and greater attention to management of retail stores at regional and corporate levels.

In summary, the ATO organizational profile of enduring core values aligned with social responsibility, behavioral norms undergirded by creative tension, and new ways of thinking about organizational structures points to an emerging paradigm shift for how ATOs will conduct business in the future. Henderson (1991) describes a new paradigm as "a pair of different spectacles which can reveal a new view of reality, allowing us to re-conceive our situations, re-frame old problems and find new pathways for evolutionary change" (p. 1). ATOs' recognition of the needs to better understand customer preferences through market research and to significantly expand collaborative product development to meet customer demand signals that the shifting paradigm is under way.

Questions for Fair Trade Analysis

How ATOs maintain their unique core philosophy of social responsibility toward artisans while adopting practices that give greater attention to consumers provides a marketing paradox ripe for analysis. Three organizing questions for our analysis of the fair trade movement evolved from this intriguing marketing paradox and from the fair trade philosophical mission.

1. How have U.S.-based ATOs developed viable organizational cultures that focus on support for producers while giving limited attention to consumers?
2. Do ATOs foster empowerment and improved quality of life for artisan producers?
3. How will ATOs continue to be viable in the increasingly competitive market for ethnic products?

In our analysis, we employ a sociocultural approach to understanding fair trade at individual, community, and organizational levels. Spradley (1979) describes culture as "the acquired knowledge that people use to interpret experience and generate social behavior" (p. 5). When studying the culture of a group of people, the meanings associated with what they do; what they know in the form of their ideas, values, and attitudes; and what they make and use are of primary concern (Ferraro, 1994; Spradley, 1980). Cultural issues related to fair trade permeate all parts of the book. More specifically, we consider culture at multiple levels, including the following:

➤ the organizational culture of ATOs, including their philosophy, values, and patterned behaviors;
➤ village culture that gives rise to the aesthetics and production techniques on which cultural products are based and that provides the immediate context for product development among artisan producer groups;
➤ the consumer culture of fair trade customers, including their lifestyles, values, and concerns for human rights, business ethics, and environmental issues.

Throughout the book, we explore how culture has (a) contributed to and impeded successful ATO operations and business sustainability among producers, (b) evolved dynamically throughout the more than 25 years of fair trade in the United States, and (c) played a part in achieving positive, challenging, and in some cases disturbing outcomes for fair trade.

In addressing this fair trade marketing paradox, we offer perspectives from all constituencies within the fair trade marketing system. Chapter 2 concludes Part I by describing the scholarly frameworks we employed for developing our arguments. Part II uses a case study perspective for appraising the varying approaches, experiences, problems, and challenges for four of the five U.S.-based comprehensive ATOs in operation at the time we began our investigation in the early 1990s (Chapters 3-6).[4] In Chapter 7, assessment of smaller, more focused ATOs provides contrasting insights on flexibility and innovativeness among ATOs involved in a more limited part of the trading system. Part III focuses on artisan and consumer constituencies. Turning first to the artisan producers, we examine their varying organizational structures and consider the challenges they face for developing products across cultural and international boundaries (Chapter 8). Next, consumers are profiled for their demographics, product preferences, and purchase intentions (Chapter 9). Motivations driving ATO consumer purchasing behavior are proposed. Chapter 10 links artisans and consumers through discussion of issues and challenges for ATO product development. In the remaining chapters of Part IV (Chapters 11 and 12), we integrate insights from ATO managers, producers, and consumers for answering the guiding questions; offer a set of fair trade "strategic implications" that we believe have broad applicability to fair trade and mainstream marketing of cultural products; propose future research; and offer a model to assist in furthering the work of ATOs.

Our presentation format varies across the four sections of the book. Chapters in Parts II and III are written from the viewpoints and voices of the artisans, retailers, and consumers who are engaged in fair trade. To emphasize this perspective, we open Chapters 3 through 10 with intimate vignettes that chronicle the daily experiences, decisions, and business transactions of specific ATO artisans, retailers, or consumers. Throughout these chapters, quotations from ATO participants are extensively employed in bringing the ATO experience to life. In contrast, the opening and concluding chapters in Parts I and IV present our analysis as we are distanced from the day-to-day practices of those involved in

ATO trade. We believe that the differential use of vignettes and quotations within sections of the book helps to clearly demark the more emic "insider" approach in Chapters 3 through 10 from our more etic and comparative analysis in Chapters 1, 2, 11, and 12.

Our Fair Trade Journey

Over the past 6 years, our journey into the organizational culture of ATOs has been guided by a host of artisans, retailers, and consumers who have informed our understanding of the mission and strategies undergirding the alternative trade movement.[5] Our journey began among founders of the fair trade movement in the United States. In Illinois, Maryland, Oregon, Pennsylvania, and Texas, charismatic founders shared their visions of a business world shaped by their grassroots experiences of working among the poor in many parts of the world. For some founders, their beliefs were molded during periods of political activism in the 1960s and 1970s, when young leaders truly believed their actions could change the world.

Typical of the visionary thinkers were early experiences of Pushpika Freitas, founder of MarketPlace: Handwork of India, which is based in Evanston, Illinois. As a young social worker in Mumbai, she met on a daily basis with women who were abused, abandoned, or widowed and who desperately needed to make a living for their children. Likewise, in Kensington, Maryland, Dan Salcedo outlined how Pueblo to People emerged following his and Marijke Velzeboer's experiences in conducting nutrition research among the poor in the Guatemalan highlands during the late 1970s. Frustrated that their actions were not helping the poor in any direct way, the two worked with a group of Guatemalan hatmakers in Quiché. The founders bought part of the artisans' production, packed their car, and drove to Texas, where the hats were an immediate success at flea markets, fairs, and festivals during the boom days of oil-rich Texas.

Continuing our journey around the world, ATO artisans further broadened our perspectives as they described impacts of their involvement with fair trade. In places as far apart as India and Guatemala, we sat on the floor of artisans' homes, often rooms no larger than 8' by 12', while women shared stories about their early marriages, loss of husbands and children during civil war, dashed hopes for education, and the long hours spent preparing food, collecting water and firewood, farming, accompanying children to and from school, and supervising homework. Children and their futures were central to the opportunities offered to the women through their work with ATOs.

Returning to the United States, ATO customers offered penetrating insights about their marketplace decisions. Consumers appeared to cross a "philosophical bridge," where the meaning that artisans experience in creating household objects is transferred to consumers who create value through owning and using the items in their homes. Making connections is difficult in a world where producers and consumers have few opportunities for interchange.

That ATOs are addressing this concern to some measure was expressed by a fair trade customer who talked about her buying decisions:

> If I had to choose only one of all the reasons why I shop at Pueblo to People, it would surely be the spirit of cooperation. Of course, even that would not keep me coming back if the products were not of such consistent high quality. In a world increasingly dominated by corporate greed, worker exploitation, and plastic everything, it comforts me to be a part of a network of real people. Although our backgrounds and cultures are so different, from the artisans to the consumers, we each provide something of value which we hope will enrich the lives of the others and bring us closer together.

Coming full circle, our journey into ATO organizational culture allowed us a panoramic view of artisans, retailers, and consumers who are joining together in a highly competitive global market. Artisans are continents away from those who use their products on a daily basis. Culture brokers and importers are introducing standards for quality control and large-scale production while seeking ways to honor local production traditions. International retailers demand timely delivery, quality control, and competitive prices.

Cultural products, as marketed by ATOs, are commodities moving through a process of decontextualization of meaning in the developing world to recontextualization in the homes of consumers many miles away. The vast distances inherent in the global market hold potential for creating anonymity and loss of meaning among producers, marketers, and consumers. How the fair trade movement counters such dehumanizing anonymity through a system of compatible trade among artisans, retailers, and consumers forms the substance for our analyses.[6] Throughout, we draw on the voices of our many guides in sharing with you our journey into the culture of ATOs. In telling their stories, we honor the fair trade philosophy of individual empowerment through socially responsible trade partnerships.

Notes

1. Although Alternative Fair Trade organizations are also active in Great Britain, Europe, Australia, and Japan, this book focuses on fair trade practices and performance in the United States.

2. Although not the focus of this book, some ATOs also market food products such as coffee, tea, dried fruit, nuts, and spices. As an example, Equal Exchange, the third largest U.S.-based ATO, markets fairly traded coffee and tea; 1997 sales were $4.5 million.

3. We assume that for many readers, the term *fair trade*, as used in this book, is new. Our use of *fair trade* should not be confused with the U.S. fair trade laws in effect from the 1930s to the 1970s. These laws allowed manufacturers to assign a minimum price to their branded products. These practices provided protection to independent retailers from price-cutting competition by large, nationwide retail chains. Our use of *fair trade* also differs from the terms *free, managed*, or *protectionist* trade, which are applied to certain global trade arrangements.

4. The fifth ATO, Equal Exchange, was not included due to its focus on marketing of food products, a topic beyond the scope of the book and expertise of the authors.

5. See Appendix A for a detailed description of the research methods used for collecting and analyzing the data on which this book is based.

6. A list of the authors' publications resulting from this research is provided in a separate section as part of the references at the end of the book.

CHAPTER 2

SCHOLARLY
PERSPECTIVES FOR
ANALYSIS OF FAIR TRADE

Five interrelated bodies of scholarship from the fields of business management, marketing, consumer behavior, anthropology, and the arts provided a lens through which to consider the work of fair trade artisans, retailers, and consumers. First, research on business organizational culture contributed business practices, core values, and behavioral norms for characterizing Alternative Trade Organizations (ATOs). Second, studies on business strategy stimulated our thinking on how competitive approaches could serve fair trade growth. In addition, small business performance research provided perspectives for defining and measuring ATO business success and sustainability. Fourth, investigations of artisan work as a strategy for Third World development suggested economic, social, and cultural considerations important for ATOs as they select and work with artisan groups. Finally, scholarship on cultural product meaning led to frameworks for understanding fair trade consumer behavior. As our analysis of fair trade evolved, we were able, in some cases, to refine these scholarly viewpoints. In other cases, we created new perspectives for the future assessment of fair trade, artisanal work, and consumer behavior.

Our use of multiple scholarly frameworks serves several purposes. First, we alert readers to some of the larger issues concerning organizational culture, artisan development, and consumer motivations as a context for considering the specific business practices outlined in the ATO case studies and in the discussion of ATO artisans and consumers. Then, as later chapters unfold, we integrate our ATO findings within the larger scholarly milieu. In some cases, we are able to refine these scholarly viewpoints. In other cases, we have created new perspectives for future assessment of fair trade, artisanal work, and consumer behavior.

Business Organizational Culture

In exploring organizational culture, we adopted Spradley's (1980) definition of culture as "the acquired knowledge people use to interpret experience and generate behavior" (p. 6). Culture encompasses a group's ideology, as well as its normative behaviors and its physical environment, artifacts, and technology. As applied to business, the study of organizational culture offers insights into a firm's unique character. Organizational culture evolves as a group learns to solve problems and conduct business (Schein, 1985). Often initiated by a strong founder, a firm's culture perpetuates itself through the telling of company stories, daily rituals, hiring practices, training, rewards, and marketing decisions (Kotter & Heskett, 1992). By understanding a firm's shared values and behaviors, dimensions of culture that are supportive of organizational goals can be encouraged, and those that are counterproductive can be identified and changed.

A glimpse at the artisan enterprise of Unique Ceramics in Accra, Ghana, illustrates the distinctive features of a specific organizational culture as well as the need to assess whether business decisions are supportive of organizational goals (Littrell, Wolff, & Blackburn, 1999). Cofounded by university-educated ceramist Happy Kufe, Unique Ceramics exports a line of bead- and raffia-embellished pottery vessels. The firm's strong profit motive is undergirded by an organizational mission of assistance to others. A visitor to the sprawling firm would find a group of women from a nearby village sitting under a shade tree where, under the tutelage of Unique Ceramics potters, they learn how to perfect the finish of their village's pots. Such training is ongoing despite impending deadlines for ever-increasing export shipments. Demands from major U.S. importers for timely deliveries have forced Happy and his coworkers to reexamine their business practices. Managers and employees are now questioning how they can speed up production while also maintaining their commitment to training for artisans with a range of production skills.

Research on organizational culture offers insights for artisan businesses such as Unique Ceramics. From disciplinary bases in business management and anthropology, organizational culture studies have progressed in two directions. One group of scholars extracted critical business practices for describing a firm's distinctive character. Other researchers explored relationships between corporate culture and performance. Whether researchers are focusing on elucidating distinctive business practices or assessing linkages between culture and performance, anthropologists argue for embedding business analysis in larger sociocultural environments and attending to the dynamic nature of organizations across time (Hamada, 1994; McLeod & Wilson, 1994). Interaction with all levels of business employees is recommended as an alternative to the almost exclusive focus on management-level employees in business studies. Exploration of the differential access that individuals have for accumulating knowledge and skills within a business system is also encouraged (Stewart, 1991).

The first group of scholars has delineated a broad range of business practices that seem to distinguish organizational cultures for large corporate firms in the United States (Baligh, 1994; Kotter & Heskett, 1992; Reynierse & Harker, 1986; Schein, 1985; Smircich, 1983a, 1983b; Willmott, 1993). Of these variables, goal orientation, risk taking, and communication patterns are particularly relevant for understanding organizational culture of smaller firms within and outside the United States. In addition, issues related to the work-family interface are salient for small firms (Fincham & Minshall, 1995; Hamerschlag, 1994; Kosters, Damhorst, & Kunz, 1996; Loker & Scannell, 1992; Popelka et al., 1992; Wong, 1987).

Small firms often have goals beyond those of profit maximization. Employee empowerment and the satisfaction of family financial needs suggest a human focus in which profits are a means toward meeting goals of individual well-being. Risk is assumed as resources are invested at the time of business initiation; day-to-day risk taking may be kept at a minimum to maintain stable work flow. In small firms, internal communication often occurs openly among employees at all levels. In other cases, communication patterns are influenced by gendered or familial authority and respect.

In attending to the work-family interface, flexibility in scheduling and the opportunity to work at or near home are important business considerations influencing day-to-day productivity and the achieving of business objectives. The workplace becomes an extension of family as workers share family matters among themselves. In some cases, the workplace becomes an extension of family in a more literal sense when, in hopes of reaching family financial goals, family members are hired regardless of their skills or abilities.

In a second direction for studying organizational culture, Kotter and Heskett (1992) propose a model that links business success with cultural strength, strategic appropriateness, and adaptability to change. The researchers argue that business success is positively influenced when organizations exhibit strong cultures in which clearly understood values, goals, and normative behavior are broadly shared. These values persist over time despite change in company personnel. Second, business is enhanced when the culture is strategically appropriate; company practices and management decisions "fit" the context in which it is operating. Fit refers both to the company's internal environment as well as the larger business context, including changing customer demand. Finally, in successful businesses, strong leaders adapt company practices to the evolving needs of customers, stockholders, and employees. Entrepreneurial and risk-taking behaviors are initiated by company leadership on behalf of the organization's constituencies. Visionary leaders have an insider's power base and an outsider's perspective that is open to new ideas.

Returning to the artisan enterprise of Unique Ceramics introduced earlier in the chapter, the challenges faced by the business illustrate the lack of strategic appropriateness in its present fit between the company's dramatically expanding export orders and its current production flow. As Unique Ceramics has expanded its workforce, little time has been spent considering the optimal positioning of workers in relation to their tasks. As a result, valuable production time is lost as employees must backtrack through workshop buildings to deliver pots to the next stage of production. Happy Kufe, company cofounder, assesses that without changes in production flow, Unique Ceramics could endanger its economic success, which would also render the company incapable of meeting its larger organizational mission of expanding artisan employment.

In summary, we drew on organizational culture scholarship in several ways to study ATOs. Kotter and Heskett's (1992) focus on centrally held values, strategic fit in the business environment, adaptability to change, and leadership seemed central for understanding ATO performance. Applying Kotter and Heskett's model was particularly intriguing as ATOs have, in the past, given limited attention to customers, one of the important constituencies in the model. Although we were attentive to previously identified business practices for understanding organizational cultures, we were also aware that additional issues were likely to emerge in a more holistic analysis that included all levels of ATO employees and that examined business behaviors across time. Placing the ATO profile within the broader sociocultural context of the international marketing of crafts allowed us to identify future challenges that ATOs may face in the competitive global marketplace.

Business Strategy

Scholars of strategic business management provided a second body of research influencing our analysis of fair trade. These researchers concentrate on relationships between a firm's management actions and its performance in the market. Porter (1980) offers three strategies by which a successful business can outperform its competitors in a fragmented industry where "no one firm has significant market share and can strongly influence industry outcomes" (p. 191). Porter's framework is considered generic in that it is applicable to many business types (Bartol & Martin, 1991). Competitive business strategies include the following:

> *Cost leadership:* Business offers a competitively lower price while attending to quality and service.

Differentiation: Business offers a unique product or service related to design, brand, technology, or promotion.

Focus: Business offers products or services to meet the special needs of a select segment of customers. The firm uses cost leadership or differentiation to focus on a specifically targeted portion of the market. Through focus, a business fulfills demand more effectively than competitors that market to a more diverse customer base.

Porter (1980) advises that businesses emphasize one, but no more than two, of the strategies. Because small business size precludes economies of scale, combining differentiation and focus is recommended (Miller & Toulose, 1986; Watkins, 1986).

Nomoda E. Djaba (Cedi), of the Ghanaian company Cedi Beads, exemplifies well the advantages of a differentiation strategy for business start-up and growth (Littrell et al., 1999). Cedi has successfully launched a rapidly expanding enterprise from the craft he learned while working alongside his parents during after-school hours as a young boy. Aware that he would have to develop new products if he were to succeed in the highly competitive domestic and international bead market, Cedi spent long hours studying his family's old beads and practicing with colorful broken glass pieces provided by his sister. Over time, Cedi perfected the technology for a product line of translucent beads to differentiate his products in a market saturated with primarily opaque varieties. Popular both in Ghana and abroad, Cedi's effervescent blue, amber, violet, and sea green beads are now produced by an expanding workforce of more than 20 workers and can be found far from Ghana in ethnic arts galleries in New York City and in the *African Market* catalog distributed throughout the United States.

In contrast to Cedi Beads, another Ghanaian enterprise, Mama Ree Textiles, offers a focus business strategy (Littrell et al., 1999). In developing her business in Tema, Mama Ree observed the intense competition among domestic producers of hand-stamped, wax-resist batik fabrics. She also assessed that lack of consistency in Ghanaian dyes precluded her entrance into the export market. Mama Ree skillfully observed the Ghanaian market, detecting that local banks and hotels might be an appropriate showcase for made-in-Ghana batik draperies, bedspreads, and table coverings. By focusing on the special needs of the local commercial market, Mama Ree carved out a targeted niche within the larger Ghanaian batik industry.

For our analysis of ATOs, business strategy scholarship offered an approach for analyzing how competition applies within fair trade. Choice of strategy is closely linked to a firm's goals. Within fair trade, artisan groups want to attract larger numbers of international wholesale clients. Retailers strive to increase market share among similar businesses selling cultural products, gifts, housewares, and apparel. At the national level, ATOs want to establish a distinctive and recognizable market presence. Consideration of competitive strategy was useful for assessing past performance and identifying future approaches for achieving fair trade goals.

Small Business Performance

ATOs, with as few as 10 artisans on up to several hundred employees, are classified as small businesses. Accordingly, research on domestic and international small business performance provided a third scholarly perspective to our fair trade analysis. In numbers and contributions to employment, small businesses are of critical importance to household income generation worldwide (Liedholm & Mead, 1987). Businesses with fewer than 300 employees make up more than 90% of all manufacturing firms (Wijewardena & Cooray, 1995). As contributors to national employment, firms with fewer than 200 employees in the ASEAN (Association of Southeast Asian Nations) 5 countries of Indonesia, Malaysia, Philippines, Singapore, and Thailand account for 40% to 52% of total employment (Hill, 1995). Strategies for small business growth and sustainability are vital as small firms are expected to provide the major source of world income well into the next millennium (Halvorson-Quevedo, 1992). Much of this income will be directed toward the world's most desperately poor, a primary focus of fair trade businesses.

U.S. Perspectives

For business performance to be measured, an understanding of how a firm defines its success is a critical first step. Financial measures figure prominently in U.S. discussions of business success and performance.

Sales figures, market share, and shareholder return are common indicators.

Delineating exemplary business practices, approaches to problem solving, and network enmeshment are advocated for their usefulness in understanding how financially successful businesses differ from their less successful counterparts (Gartner, 1985; Stevenson & Gumpert, 1985). Successful manufacturers and retailers engage in a set of distinguishing practices (AT&T, 1993; Donckels & Lambrecht, 1997; Gaskill, Van Auken, & Kim, 1994; O'Neill & Duker, 1986; Vesper, 1990). Successful firms

> ➤ participate in formal business planning;
> ➤ produce high-quality products;
> ➤ provide good service;
> ➤ apply sound management strategies;
> ➤ attend to inventory sourcing, fluctuation, and shipping;
> ➤ develop marketing plans that delineate target markets and promotional strategies;
> ➤ seek professional advice from experts;
> ➤ establish networks with colleagues; and
> ➤ use electronic tools for management and communication.

More specifically for successful craft businesses, establishing regional and tourist markets is an additional priority. Unique products are developed, and skill-oriented hiring practices are followed. In contrast, less successful firms are often formed to allow continued production of existing crafts characterized by little product originality. Personal networks are employed for local marketing (Littrell, Stout, & Reilly, 1991). As two midwestern artisans of wood and fabric crafts described for their less successful businesses, "It was a hobby then and it just got out of hand. People wanted to buy our products" and "Some asked me to make one, then someone else, and it just boomeranged" (Littrell et al., 1991, p. 36).

Because failure rates for small retail businesses are high within the first 5 years, correlates of small business failure also have been closely scrutinized. Management practices such as inadequate knowledge of pricing, ineffective promotions, lack of a personnel strategy, inflexible decision making, and failure to establish a merchandise assortment plan typify failed businesses. Poor relations with vendors, difficulty in receiving merchandise, inadequate financial records, and undercapitalization accompany poor management. Competition from discount stores, inventory control, and overexpansion further exacerbate the problems (Gaskill, Van Auken, & Manning, 1993).

Although sales and profit maximization figure prominently in the research literature on business motivations, recent studies of entrepreneurs have uncovered additional motivations for launching and sustaining a business. Along with realizing profits, entrepreneurs mention maintaining personal freedom, enjoying the excitement of new challenges, achieving personal recognition, and securing a future for their families, all of which suggest that entrepreneurs are motivated by factors in addition to money (Buttner & Moore, 1997; Kuratko, Hornsby, & Naffziger, 1997; Soldressen, Fiorito, & He, 1998). Accordingly, valid measures for assessing entrepreneurial success should include both financial and social indicators.

Perspectives From Developing Countries

In developing countries, artisans' economic needs are pressing. With limited education, their employment alternatives are few. Expectations that crafts can serve as the sole source of year-round employment are generally unrealistic. Artisans residing in rural areas with some access to farming appear to benefit the most from craft production as a financial supplement for participation in the cash economy (Ehlers, 1993; Nash, 1993a; Tice, 1995). Even a small income from crafts can make a substantial difference in day-to-day life. Morris (1996) notes, "Making a little money is a huge improvement over none at all" (p. 113). For urban artisans who are dependent on a cash economy, income from part-time craft employment provides, at a relative level, less improvement in subsistence survival. Yet, urban pottery workers at Alfadom in the Dominican Republic judge full-time craft employment not to be without its risks as well. The potters assess that long workdays leave them with little time or energy for maintaining smaller income-generating activities to which their families can turn should their full-time jobs be terminated (Morris, 1996).

If reaching economic self-sufficiency through crafts is difficult, how can craft businesses be viewed as successful? Beyond the purely economic, are there measures of artisan business success that help explain why artisans participate? When asked, artisans provide a range of individual, social, and cultural indicators for assessing performance, including acquiring transferable language, business, and computer skills; establishing credit; gaining independence and control over one's life; participating in organizational, community, and regional planning; preserving and elevating the stature of a craft tradition; investing in community institutions; and reinforcing cultural identity (Morris, 1996; Nash, 1993a; Page-Reeves, 1998; Stephen 1991a, 1991b, 1991c; Tice, 1995). For some women artisans, simply getting out of the house is a small but first step toward success. Morris (1996) assesses that "women artisans, no matter which market they enter, inevitably find a broader social purpose" (p. 139).

Documenting business sustainability in less-developed countries is difficult as craft businesses are highly decentralized. Many are scattered in difficult-to-reach rural areas. In cities, artisanal activities are virtually invisible within the informal sector. Some attempt has been made to distinguish factors contributing to business start-up from those correlated with sustainability in Peace Corps–assisted handcraft businesses (Durham, 1996). Essential to business start-up are the following:

> ➤ locally available raw materials;
> ➤ use of indigenous technologies and simple tools;
> ➤ the creative or organizational skills of a local or external facilitator;
> ➤ donations of capital, equipment, transport, or in-kind contributions; and
> ➤ skills for training, business, product development, and leadership.

Beyond start-up, project sustainability is enhanced by overcoming a variety of culturally associated challenges (Durham, 1996). First, at a conceptual level, organizational structures such as cooperatives are often unfamiliar and not always readily understood by group members. Again, using Peace Corps–assisted businesses to illustrate, women in one Guatemalan cooperative, with their third grade education, faced difficult challenges in learning the requisite accounting and record-keeping skills demanded for legal recognition of their cooperative by the Guatemalan government. Second, interpersonal relationships such as kinship alliances, authority vested in local social hierarchies, or jealousy and rumor can obstruct operations. In a small Turkish village, the fact that the Imam, the local religious leader, joined the rug weaving association provided sanction for others to become involved. Finally, gender-related challenges emerge, particularly when men are reluctant to allow new opportunities for women or when women who are unaccustomed to assuming authority accept leadership roles. Members of a second Guatemalan weaving group acquired leadership skills slowly as their husbands first allowed them to attend local meetings, then travel outside the village, and eventually participate in meetings of a federation of cooperatives some distance from their home village.

In summary, scholars of business performance provide important perspectives from which to consider fair trade success. Across the research studies among small businesses in the United States and abroad, generating income or maximizing profits and enhancing personal and family well-being through day-to-day business involvement stand out as dual indicators of business accomplishment in artisan enterprises. Balancing economic and social goals is a formidable challenge for craft organizations. Measuring business success by focusing only on economic goals negates the importance artisans place on social and cultural impacts. Differences in how businesses define success serve as an important reminder for development researchers to understand a group's goals prior to selecting measures for assessing fair trade business performance.

Each entrepreneurial venture has a unique set of circumstances under which it operates, such that generalizations about success and failure should be applied with caution. However, understanding correlates of business performance can prove useful in assessing whether chosen lines of action will lead to fair trade success or failure. In addition, characteristics for successful and failed businesses can offer new ways of thinking about fair trade decisions. Finally, although research on business sustainability is limited for the crafts sector, the interplay among local resources, internal leaders, external facilitators, and daily cultural patterns seems crucial for assessing fair trade potential and performance.

Artisanal Work and Development

To place the work of fair trade artisans within a broader perspective, research on artisanal work and development provided a fourth scholarly perspective. Several decades of top-down development programs that focused primarily on economic growth have produced limited change in many less-developed countries. Accordingly, development planners are adopting more holistic approaches for addressing human well-being. Bottom-up, grassroots programs integrate economic progress with environmental sustainability and preservation of cultural identity and continuity (Leander, 1994). Local cultural patterns, including indigenous knowledge on agriculture, commerce, and medicine, provide the context from which development occurs (Chambers, 1983; Warren, 1991). Claxton (1994) succinctly describes this symbiotic relationship:

> Development can only flourish where it is rooted in the culture and tradition of each country, since it is an all-encompassing process linked to each society's own values and calling for the active participation of individuals and groups who are the authors and beneficiaries of it. (p. 5)

Local participation and decision making, rather than paternalistic external direction and dependency, undergird grassroots approaches as they seek to achieve individual or group empowerment (Buell, 1987; Carroll, 1992; Chambers, 1983; Nyoni, 1987). External ideas or models, if applied, are reinterpreted through an endogenous, participatory process using the filter of local culture (Claxton, 1994).

Crafts as a development strategy generates intense debate. Some observers lament what they perceive to be the loss of craft traditions when artisans turn to tourist or export markets. However, artisans and scholars vehemently note that craft traditions have always been dynamic processes of accumulation, innovation, appropriation, and transformation (Berlo, 1991; Hendrickson, 1995; Moreno, 1995; Price, 1989; Stephen, 1991b).

As artisan groups shift from local patronage toward market commercialization, they face a variety of challenges, including sourcing raw materials in quantities needed for volume production, finding skilled artisans and appropriate equipment, forming organizational units to accommodate production and achieve negotiative power, and establishing fax and Internet linkages to compete in wider markets (Herald, 1992). Also, artisans often lack knowledge of market structures, credit, and business skills. Additional obstacles include the need for design innovation and quality elevation to compete in world markets (Page-

Reeves, 1998). Finally, existing infrastructures frequently do not facilitate ease of deliveries and shipments (Aageson, 1997).

The business experiences of Nanasei Opoku-Ampomsah, when expanding his wood-carving industry, African Version, in Accra, Ghana, illustrate some of the aforementioned challenges (Littrell et al., 1999). Nanasei evaluates that his greatest assets as a businessman lie in machinery design and training, particularly in a country where all of the exporters are fighting for the few available carvers. In a 3-day period in 1998, 127 men showed up at his workshop in response to a small sign announcing employment that was posted at a nearby road intersection. Nanasei's ability to train carvers for a potential large export order was critical as none of the new employees knew how to carve. In another example, Nanasei drew on his machinery design expertise when his business needed a simple piece of lathe equipment that could turn out an order for 25,000 wooden buttons in 1 week.

Under these and other challenging conditions, some development experts question the advisability of promoting crafts as a strategy for change (Dhamija, 1989). Some wonder whether the time-consuming work of craft production is the best choice for income generation, particularly among women with already heavy daily burdens. Renumeration is low, and many projects offer artisans little opportunity to upgrade skills for producing products at higher price points. Creating and managing the organizational structure for a craft project can be more complicated and require more training than other income-generating choices such as food processing for local markets (Dhamija, 1989).

However, other scholars and development planners cite evidence for craft marketing as a strategy that will realize income generation along with achieving broader social and cultural goals (Basu, 1995; Pye, 1988; Stephen, 1991a, 1991b; Tice, 1995). Morris (1996), a longtime activist in craft development, voices a pragmatic challenge: "Artisans are not going to disappear in the new millennium and neither will their contributions to our daily lives and culture. The time has come to rethink their position" (p. 150). Rosenbaum and Goldin (1997) argue further that among Guatemalan women, income from weaving, while providing for participation in the cash economy, also serves as a form of "resistance and ethnic revitalization" (p. 73) in a country struggling with creating a new identity in the postviolence in the late 1990s. Finally, Aageson (1997), an international craft marketing specialist, assesses that building strong artisan enterprises requires investment in three critical areas: business skills; creativity for innovative, market-driven product development; and marketing to diverse patrons. In the remainder of this section, we explore three major issues related to gender, organizing for production and marketing, and cultural evolution of crafts as they stand to influence artisan "positioning" and ATO enterprise development for the global market.

Gendered Behaviors

Gendered behavior and cultural product marketing are dual-directional in influence. Gender affects opportunities for participation in artisanal activities. In turn, craft participation affects gendered dynamics and empowerment at household, community, and national levels.

Year-round, day-to-day constancy typifies the lives of women artisans. Craft production occurs in and around household tasks of cooking, gathering water, caring for children, and gardening. Without other supports in place, women have limited time for traveling to and participating in artisan group meetings (Dhamija, 1989). In contrast, men's lives in rural areas are regulated by the seasonal agricultural cycle, leaving larger periods of time for uninterrupted work at central workshop locations. As artisans commercialize products for external markets, production often shifts from household to workshop venues. When such shifts occur, women are vulnerable for achieving equity in income generation. In addition, long-standing, gendered patterns of communication and leadership are frequently followed; when both genders are present, women defer authority to men (Hamerschlag, 1985; Nash, 1993a). With little experience in group leadership, women often encounter difficulty in consensus building for cooperative business management (Mayoux, 1995).

Gender effects rarely occur in isolation from other social classifications. Rather, gender interweaves with clan, class, race, and ethnicity in influencing craft participation. Among Mexican rug weavers in the community Teotitlán del Valle, women's involvement is clearly compounded by social class. In weaver households where work is done for others, women exert control over the allocation of work and negotiation of prices within the household. In contrast, in merchant households, where rugs are contracted, bought, and marketed, women are in subordinate roles for decision making. Yet through their greater earnings, women of merchant households are accorded higher status within the community due to their ability to host community and ritual events (Stephen, 1991c, 1993). In addition to social class, Tice (1995) notes that "women of different ages and generations may experience social change in different ways" (p. 14). Among Kuna *mola* producers, a division of labor evolved in which older women assumed household and child care responsibilities, and younger women sewed *molas* for sale.[1] When assessing impacts of craft participation on gendered relations, Swain (1993) cautions that the unit of analysis be clearly distinguished when assessing empowerment. The assumption by development theorists that shifting from a subsistence to a cash economy lessens women's authority has not been fully supported. Across a series of artisan groups, Swain assesses that women gain empowerment at household levels but not necessarily in larger arenas:

> Household roles change in response to sources of cash income while role options outside in the state society's prevailing patriarchal, ethnically stratified order may limit indigenous women and men to the "same old stuff." (p. 50)

At the household level, as income from craft participation increases, women shoulder responsibility for decision making and money allocation—in some cases, choosing to establish single-headed households rather than remain in abusive relationships (Eber & Rosenbaum, 1993; Nash, 1993a). In other cases, a fluid complementary between genders evolves; men in the Mexican pottery village of Amatenango del Valle gathered clay and wood for firing, leaving more time to their wives for forming the pottery that had become a lucrative commodity (Nash, 1993b). Likewise, in eight northeast Thai weaving villages, more than one third of the men began assisting with household chores, child care, and gathering of firewood and natural dyestuffs as income from their wives' weaving increased (Local Weaving Development Project, 1995).

Organizing for Production and Marketing

Quite commonly, craft production for local consumption is individually managed and household based. As external markets are developed, new organizational configurations are needed to achieve expanded economies of scale in production. Linkage with a variety of consultants offers a network for cross-group exchange and cultural brokerage related to product development and marketing. Finally, developing a diversified market can offer some measure of security during periods of fluctuating consumer demand for a group's products.

Beginning with organizational configuration, business structures that simulate indigenous organizational models within the community appear to be the most promising for transitional positioning (Dhamija, 1989; Morris, 1991, 1996). In cases in which craft production is integrated with another preexisting organization, "many-stranded" alliances evolve (Walter, 1981, p. 176).

Because of their prevalence in craft production, cooperative organizational structures warrant further attention to their advantages and disadvantages (Eber & Rosenbaum, 1993). On the positive side, cooperatives offer "safe" places for expressing opinions, particularly among women who are reluctant to speak before men; provide opportunities for intergenerational teaching and learning of craft; offer members a voice in decision making; serve as sources for credit; and provide a venue that affirms participants' language, culture, and creative work. For some artisans, women-only cooperatives may be the only venue where, because of religious practices or gendered customs, women can participate in activity outside the home. Size of the cooperative influences participatory involvement and business practices. In Guatemala, India, and Panama, artisans in smaller groups participated more actively; decision making and commercial agreements were less complex (Hamerschlag, 1985; Mayoux, 1995; Tice, 1995). In contrast, larger groups provide economy of scale for buying supplies and attracting customers with larger wholesale orders (Durham, 1996).

Cooperatives can also exhibit negative features (Durham, 1996; Eber & Rosenbaum, 1993). The many meetings associated with cooperatives can use up valuable time. When membership is open to both genders, males often assume management roles that can defeat goals of egalitarian building of business skills. Successful cooperatives can invite envy and jealousy both within and outside the organization. Such divisions among members can fracture whole communities at times when solidarity is needed. Marital tension may arise when women assume public roles and make significant contributions to household expenditures.

Beyond consideration of an organization's structure, producing and marketing goods in regional and international venues call for cross-group exchange and collaboration. Establishing a network with designers and technical consultants, advisory boards, volunteers, government agencies, religious groups, and nongovernmental development organizations (NGOs) provides a springboard for product development, culture brokerage, and collaborative action (Dhamija, 1989; Durham, 1996; Morris, 1996; Stephen, 1991a). At critical junctures, facilitators have provided a "centrifugal force from which a producer group gained collective strength and action" (Durham, 1996, p. 101). However, dependency relations can easily evolve (Page-Reeves, 1998). In particular, Morris (1991) emphasizes the importance of artisan groups refusing assistance where possible so that financial control is not transferred to outsiders.

Technical assistants offer expertise for parlaying local woods, clays, fibers, barks, gourds, grasses, and stones into salable products. Changing loom elements to weave wider fabrics, introducing kilns for higher firings, and transferring skills from clay pot manufacture to candle holders and cut work lamps have created new clientele bases among artisan groups in India, Indonesia, and Turkey (Dhamija, 1989). With technical assistance, Maya weavers in Sna Jolobil of San Cristóbal de las Casas in Chiapas, Mexico, revived natural dyes for producing upscale items that appealed to foreigners interested in traditional art (Morris, 1991). The weaver's own brightly colored acrylic yarns, although preferred for everyday clothing, commanded lower prices and stood little chance for acceptance among foreign collectors.

Design consultants serve as brokers of consumer taste between cultures. Their expertise on changing fashion and target markets provides much-needed insight for artisan groups that have little knowledge of outside markets. Experiences of W. M. Arrafin, who heads the Malaysian firm Noor Arfa Batek, illustrate well the challenges he faced as he explored marketing his batik scarves and fabrics in the United States (Kadolph, Gaskill, Littrell, & Heinicke, 1997). As Arrafin visited U.S. trade shows and consulted with designers, he learned about designing products for a society in which many consumers wore varying fabric weights to accommodate the changing seasons, organized their wardrobes around neutral colors, and fluctuated across time in their preferences for fashion accessories such as the scarves that Arrafin hoped to market. These insights provided strong contrast to Malaysian women consumers who wear lightweight fabrics due to nearly constant temperatures throughout the year and prefer pastel and bright colors in their attire.

Finally, advisory boards or boards of directors can offer professional expertise as well as link artisans with contacts at regional and national levels (Stoesz & Raber, 1994). Dedicated boards offer an outsider's perspective on implementing the mission and can ensure that resources necessary for fulfilling the mission are available. The board for the Alfadon pottery group in the Dominican Republic includes members who are well placed politically for solving governmental problems. Some members sit on other boards, such as a shipping company, that can offer additional useful connections (Morris, 1996).

Turning now to the issue of achieving sales consistency in product categories marked by fluctuating demand and rapid fashion change, market diversification offers greater security for artisan producer groups. The short-lived fashion for bleeding madras cloth from India serves as a warning. Indian weavers, seizing on an export opportunity, turned their looms to the production of outside-inspired madras designs while ignoring the long-standing local market for men's sarongs. When Western interest in madras waned, Indian weavers had large inventories and no buyers (Dhamija, 1989). Production for local markets, even if small in volume, can provide continuing income while external markets are developed. In addition, selling products in local shops that cater to tourists facilitates personal contacts useful for assessing quality, working out production details, and learning how the market works (Morris, 1991, 1996). Producing for too many target markets can, however, lead to fragmentation without success in any single market. As Morris (1996) assesses, "It is hard enough to work in one market. Trying to be equally competent in two or three compounds the problems" (p. 76).

Cultural Evolution of Crafts

As artisans engage in product development for external markets, they are confronted with balancing outsiders' preferences with their own core values and traditions. The production of crafts is one part of "that indefinable but dynamic force that constitutes the identity of a people" (Claxton, 1994, p. 8). Craft products, processes, and aesthetics contribute to how a society perceives and presents itself (Berlo, 1991; Hendrickson,

1995; Rosenbaum & Goldin, 1997; Zorn, 1987). As multivocal markers, products symbolically distinguish between the worlds of men and women, elders and youth, leaders and followers, and the sacred and profane. The potential for the transformation of self-identity during the process of craft commercialization is voiced by journalist Pico Iyer (1993), who questions whether artisans (in this case, producing for tourist markets) have "begun to see themselves through tourists' eyes, to amend themselves to tourists' needs" and are "losing a little of [their] soul with each transaction" (p. 116).

Cultural evolution of craft traditions can be considered from vantage points of producers and the communities in which they reside. Baizerman (1987) contends that producers' decisions regarding the process of production (where, when, and how something is made; who teaches and learns) have a greater impact on how a tradition evolves than decisions concerning the product itself (resources, specific techniques, aesthetics). Kuna *mola* producers, Zapotec rug weavers, Hmong textile artisans, and Indonesian weavers have each retained long-used processes while developing new products for consumption (Niessen, 1990; Stephen, 1991c; Swain, 1993; Tice, 1995). Products for outsiders frequently exhibit simpler designs and less time-consuming techniques than those for personal use or local patronage. Page-Reeves (1998) describes design changes among Bolivian knitters as incorporating " 'traditional' Andean symbols, patterns and colors to give a sweater an 'ethnic' flavor, but in a way that is contemporary and fashionable, rather than distinctly ethnic" (p. 89). The Maya weavers of the Sna Jolobil cooperative in Chiapas, Mexico, provide a contrast by "making tradition a conscious source of inspiration" as they developed a fine-arts market for their intricately woven, natural-dyed textiles (Morris, 1991, p. 418). Yet who produces the textile craft and where the work is performed have remained relatively stable.

From a broader community position, Stephen (1991a) describes how local Zapotec identity has been maintained and strengthened during the evolution of rug production in Teotitlán del Valle. Production and marketing of rugs not only contribute to expanded income, as evidenced by a flurry of multistory house construction and new model pickup trucks, but also support the maintenance of costly community-wide ritual events that reinforce Zapotec heritage. In this and other Latin American communities, Stephen (1991a) credits the evolution of self-managed craft production to several factors. An already lively production and local trading network provided valuable experience and an infrastructure for launching artisans toward new marketing opportunities available through tourism and export. Patterns of shared labor exchange and reinvestment in community life served as a base within which larger volume craft production could be integrated. Finally, craft production blended with subsistence and commercial agriculture in which artisan households were already engaged.

Studies of artisanal work as a strategy for Third World development provided guides to us for considering how ATOs go about selecting and working with producer groups to accomplish goals of empowering and improving the quality of life for artisan producers. More specifically, we directed our attention to (a) the dual-directional intersection between gendered behavior and craft participation, (b) relationships between organizational structures and artisan impacts, (c) artisans' enmeshment in broader business-related networks, (d) advantages and warnings for domestic and international market diversification, and (e) functions of product and process in the cultural evolution of a craft tradition.

Cultural Product Meaning for Consumers

The meanings that culturally embedded products hold for consumers provided a fifth and final scholarly point of view to our analysis of fair trade. Cultural products are traded in a volatile market characterized by rapid change in consumer preference. Through the choices they make, consumers hold immense potential for affecting the lives of artisans at national, village, and household levels. Entire countries can experience dramatic decline or growth in sales as wholesalers, ever mindful of the bottom line in bringing fresh products to the market-place, search the world for new ideas and cheaper sources of labor. Such change was evident in U.S. retail shops when Guatemalan *típica* (garments and accessories produced from brightly colored fabrics) was replaced by a barrage of products from Bali and Java during the late 1990s. Within a single country such as Guatemala, demand for embroi-dered vests rather than backstrap woven backpacks can leave one artisan group with few customers, whereas producers in a village 100 miles away have an oversupply of orders. At the village level, sudden increases in demand serve as catalysts for workplace reorganization. As shifts occur to accommodate large orders, artisans experience increased levels of stress related to household responsibilities, agricultural cycles, and gendered patterns of group leadership and management.

Bases of Meaning

Consumers act on a variety of motivations when selecting cultural products. Research on object attachment, craft consumers, and product authenticity provides insight on potential consumer demand for cultural products produced by ATOs. In addition, demographic analyses of the U.S. population (Ray, 1997) point to a shift in values and worldview for an emerging consumer segment to which the marketing of cultural products may be timely.

Cherished artifacts provide a continuum of opportunities for owners to create meaning in their lives (Csikszentmihalyi & Rochberg-Halton, 1981). At one end, special objects, such as trophies, sports equipment, or cars, express a person's differentiation from others through emphasis on skills and experiences unique to the owner. In contrast, objects such as family photos or heirloom quilts integrate the owner with events or persons associated with the object. Similarity to others through descent, ethnicity, or lifestyle is recalled through contemplation of the special item. Whether through differentiation or integration, objects provide a path for defining the self. As people age, their symbolic investment with objects evolves (Belk, 1986, 1988; McCracken, 1986; Wallendorf & Arnould, 1988).

Scholars hypothesize that craft consumers, through their purchases, seek linkages with indigenous lifestyles, long nostalgically for the past, or search for the exotic as a contrast to their more mundane daily lives (Basu, 1995; Graburn, 1977, 1983; MacCannell, 1976; Stephen, 1991a). Our empirical studies suggest that "ethnic linkages," "nostalgia," and "exotics" are but one component of a larger set of consumer themes. We believe that consumers' "outside appropriation of indigenous culture . . . in the 'packaging' of indigenous identity," as described by Stephen (1991a, p. 101), speaks to only a limited range of meaning behind consumer choice. Although artisans and retailers may be commodifying ethnicity, that is not necessarily what customers are buying.

Craft consumers repeatedly mention seven bases of meaning as they talk about cultural products purchased in their home communities or during their domestic and international travels (Littrell, 1990, 1994, 1996; Littrell, Reilly, & Stout, 1992; Slaybaugh, Littrell, & Farrell-Beck, 1990). Meaning evolves as crafts are acquired and used across time, as noted in quotes from the aforementioned research.

Workmanship. Through crafts, consumers reach out to and value work of the hand. Having an item of superb workmanship and using the item on a daily basis allow the patron to continually search for and delight in details of an intricate weave, well-turned pot, or wood-joining techniques. As one woman described an Indonesian textile hanging in her home, "The more I look at it, the more detail I appreciate in it."

Sensuous Appreciation. Multisensory attachment to crafts characterizes some buyers' interactions with the crafts they purchase. Using holistic expressions such as "It's the most beautiful thing I had ever seen," customers go on to talk about "colors that knock me out" or wood that "reaches out to be touched."

Functional Value. Whether a cultural product has a clearly understood functional use or is versatile across multiple settings or occasions is important to other consumers. "Easing a garment into an existing wardrobe" or being able to use a decorative vase "many places in the home" add to a product's appeal.

Daily Contrast. Acquiring cultural products under unusual conditions provokes a spark of contrast to the buyer's everyday life. "Nonordinary qualities," "a splurge," "it's so different," or "exotic" describe an aura of specialness for certain products. At home, contemplation of the crafts provides treasured moments of release from daily routine.

Cultural Linkage. Sampling a way of life different from one's own and expanding a worldview are common goals of many consumers, especially tourists. Through searching for and buying crafts, often in rural markets, tiny shops, or in craftspersons' workshops, consumers create linkages with a culture. A tourist's description of a Finnish craft souvenir typifies this theme: "I want things that are typical of how people are feeling about their work, how they are feeling about their country, and how they are feeling about their surroundings."

Artisan Interchange. Through purchasing crafts directly from artisans, consumers participate in an intimate human interchange that can transcend cultural differences between buyer and seller. Stories of how a product is made and explanations of indigenous symbolism contribute to global dialogue and a sense of commonality in pride of work worldwide. A consumer relates, "The people's story always enters in. I ask, 'Did you personally do this? Is this craft something in your family?' If I have a little empathy going, it means a lot."

Singularity (Individuality). Phrases such as "that's me," "it's something only I will have," or "a great addition to my collection" address consumers' desires for individuality, creative expression, and specialness in their lives. Crafts serve as a medium for forming a unique statement reflective of the individual. Compliments from others serve to reinforce this specialness.

For some consumers of ethnic products, issues of authenticity are of concern. As consumers discuss their purchases, it becomes clear that "authenticity is a socially constructed concept and its social connotation is, therefore, not given, but 'negotiable' " (Cohen, 1988, p. 374). Employing two broad categories, consumers judge crafts to be authentic related either to criteria of product workmanship or to the processes and materials employed in their manufacture (Littrell, Anderson, & Brown, 1993).

Consumers centering on products as the source of authenticity refer to "handmade" workmanship or "fine attention to detail" (Littrell et al., 1993, p. 205). An authentic product is "not one that you see duplicates of in every shop you visit" (p. 205). When products are similar, "they [should] still differ from each other because of size, shape, and texture" (p. 205). Other consumers find authenticity in the cultural context of the artisans and their processes. "Handmade by a person who lives in the area" (p. 206) is an essential ingredient. The cultural context of a craft's

indigenous clays or grasses, local patterns of usage and aesthetic preference, and artisans' feelings for their work are accessed through the stories
that artisans or retailers share with customers about production details.
Artisans trained in methods handed down through a family for generations is an important ingredient of authenticity as well.

Cultural Creatives

Demographers point to a shift in values and worldview for approximately one fourth of U.S. adults (Ray, 1997). Labeled *cultural creatives,*
these individuals are college educated, in their early 40s, and with
average household incomes of $52,200. Six out of 10 are women. Values
of community building, ecological sustainability, abhorrence of violence,
and attraction to the foreign and exotic guide their lives. Cultural creatives are attentive to global issues and systems. Three fourths are involved in volunteer activities. As prolific users of the print and radio
media, they want rich, holistic stories rather than bullet-point summaries
of human events and conditions.

As careful consumers, cultural creatives "want to know where a
product came from, how it was made, who made it, and what will
happen when they are done with it" (Ray, 1997, p. 32). Product integrity
and authenticity are salient consumer criteria, as compared to high
fashion, imitations, and fakes. Their homes exhibit eclectic decoration;
creating individual style with art and craft pieces is typical. Rather than
amassing more products, cultural creatives focus on consuming new or
unique experiences, including encounters during travel.

Motivations for Purchasing Cultural Products

In preparation for considering consumer behavior of ATO products,
we integrated scholarship on object attachment, craft consumers, and
authenticity (see Figure 2.1). Four motivations for selecting cultural
products are the central focus. Creating aesthetic experience, managing
daily life, and establishing self-identity are self-directed, whereas connecting with others is other-directed. On the left and right columns of
Figure 2.1, bases of meaning and authenticity that underlay the motiva-

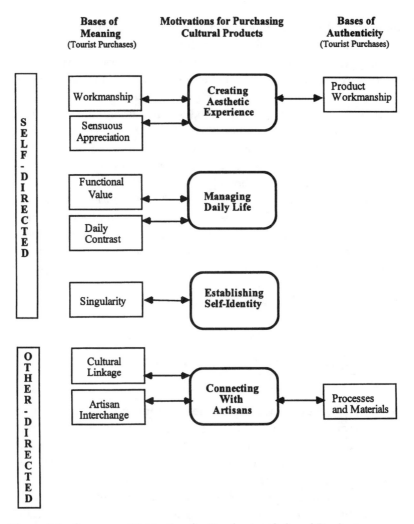

Figure 2.1. Consumer Motivation for Purchasing Cultural Products

tions are depicted. Two-way arrows suggest dual-directionality between motivations and their underlying bases.

Beginning with self-directed motivations, consumers encouraged toward *creating aesthetic experience* access meaning through the physical features of cultural products. Viewing, touching, and learning about a product's structural and aesthetic qualities provide an inward, individualistic, and affective interaction with cultural products. *Managing daily life* is facilitated for consumers through products used for eating, cooking, playing, dressing, and decorating. When products spark momentary surprise, delight, or diversion, the quality of life is enhanced. Consumers motivated toward *establishing self-identity* are attuned to the creation of a personal style through products that differentiate the owner from others. Turning to an other-directed motivation, *connecting with artisans* emerges as consumers focus outwardly to other people, their communities, and ways of life. Understanding artisan processes forms a path for making these connections.

The newly emerging "cultural creatives" appears to be a consumer segment to which fair trade philosophy, practices, and products would be particularly inviting. The final two motivations, connecting with artisans and establishing self-identity, match these consumers' interests in indigenous cultures, production origins and process, and emphasis on personal style.

Multidisciplinary and Systemic Analysis

Each body of scholarly work provided a point of departure and informed our analysis of fair trade. Summarizing, we framed our examination of fair trade from perspectives on organizational culture and success, competitive business strategy, measures of small business performance, artisan social and economic development, and consumer preference for cultural products. Although each disciplinary base offered a distinctive focus to our investigation, we recognized that the perspectives are highly interconnected within fair trade. Therefore, we integrated them rather than simply giving saliency to only one perspective for our analysis. For example, we were highly aware that competitive strategy would be linked to an ATO's shared values. Likewise, we anticipated that adaptability to the market environment and consumer preferences would be highly related to artisan development. Accordingly, our approach is purposefully multidisciplinary as we consider the individual, social, and cultural impacts when cultural products are produced and exchanged within a marketing system that places primary emphasis on artisan producers.

In addition, we adopt a systemic perspective that focuses on interactions among all members of the fair trade network—producers, ATO managers and employees, retailers, and consumers. We believe that a multidisciplinary, systemic approach contributes to a greater depth of understanding for past performance and assists in better identifying future challenges than if we were to employ a single disciplinary perspective or consider each member of the trade network alone. Alternative traders have established a very different set of goals as they learned to compete in the international market for cultural products. Drawing from business, social sciences, and the arts, we offer insight and analysis on how members of the fair trade marketing system accomplish their work.

Note

1. *Mola* textile production involves a reverse appliqué technique in which artisans begin with layers of colored cloth. In cutting and turning under edges of designs in the top and second layers, colors of lower layers are revealed. Embroidered motifs and decorative edging add final embellishment on the top layer. *Mola* designs range from birds and animals to scenes of daily life and interpretations of magazine advertisements and other media.

PART II

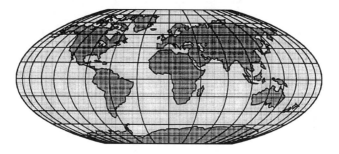

INCOME, JUSTICE, AND EMPOWERMENT THROUGH FAIR TRADE

In Part II, we present concrete examples of how seven organizations operationalize fair trade philosophy in their day-to-day business practices. Each organization illustrates a systemwide commitment to social responsibility, as defined in Chapter 1. In Chapters 3 through 6, we provide case studies of Ten Thousand Villages, SERRV, Pueblo to People, and MarketPlace: Handwork of India, respectively. All are large, comprehensive organizations involved in all functions of alternative trade, including design and product development, production, purchasing, importing, retailing, and consumer education. In contrast, the three organizations in Chapter 7—Aid to Artisans, PEOPLink, and Traditions

Fair Trade—are smaller, more focused organizations placing special attention on a more limited range of business functions.

Rather than offer expansive profiles for each organization, we highlight what we believe to be unique practices for each Alternative Trade organization (ATO). In addition, we decipher the nuances of each group's philosophical focus as they interpret the fair trade mission. Our intention in accenting each group's unique approach is threefold: (a) provide a comprehensive view of the different ways that fair trade can be conducted, (b) illuminate the multiple interpretations of the fair trade mission, and (c) learn from the organizations' successes, challenges, and failures. Our overriding message is that no single organizational model definitively describes the practice of fair trade in the global market.

Distinguishing practices for each organization include the following:

Chapter 3: Ten Thousand Villages

- ➤ Transformative approach to change in business operations
- ➤ Philosophical focus on creating employment and income opportunities
- ➤ Limited outsider intervention in product development
- ➤ Retail store structure with contract, partnership, and company stores
- ➤ Critical contribution of volunteers to warehouse and retail operations

Chapter 4: SERRV

- ➤ Diverse channels for alternative distribution
- ➤ Philosophical focus on trade-related issues of social responsibility, global business practices, and distribution of wealth
- ➤ Hard business decisions for financial exigency
- ➤ ATO-to-artisan directed design and product development

Chapter 5: Pueblo to People

- ➤ Cooperative organizational structure
- ➤ Innovative *magalog* format for retail catalog
- ➤ Philosophical focus on the politics of social and economic change in Latin America
- ➤ Priority placed on producer relations, ultimately at the expense of business viability
- ➤ Immense sadness and loss resulting from business dissolution

Chapter 6: MarketPlace: Handwork of India

➤ Philosophical focus on artisan self-esteem, dignity, and self-sufficiency
➤ Product line predicated on indigenous needlework skills, fabric printing, and India-inspired garment styles
➤ Organizational culture of flexibility, experimentation, and openness to change
➤ Workplace decentralization from single to multiple groups
➤ Global dialogue between artisans and customers

Chapter 7: Aid to Artisans

➤ Project-based structure supported by outside grants
➤ Well-designed products for mainstream markets
➤ Linkages between artisans and wholesale buyers
➤ Organizational culture of collaboration, networking, and alliance building

Chapter 7: PEOPLink

➤ Philosophical focus on the Internet as a tool for global trade and democracy
➤ Internet marketing through partner organizations, designer's studio, and educational programming

Chapter 7: Traditions Fair Trade

➤ Merchandising challenges of the independent alternative trade retailer
➤ Customer base expansion through a widely visible community presence

Each chapter in Part II follows a common format. Through an introductory quotation from an ATO leader and an opening business scenario, we first engage readers in the organizational culture unique to each ATO. Brief histories chronicle each group's organizational evolution. We then address current issues, struggles, and outcomes for the ATO. Throughout each unfolding story, we apply an emic or insider's perspective in capturing the participants' human response to alternative trade. Finally, the chapters conclude with our assessment of implications, challenges, and questions for the larger alternative trade movement that arise from each organization's unique business practices.

The chapters in Part II offer myriad examples that inform and advance our understanding of the scholarly frameworks introduced in Chapter 2. To preserve the emic flow in Chapters 3 through 7, we chose to delay a more etic discussion of scholarly linkages until the chapters in Parts III and IV. However, a few examples illustrate the range of scholarly connections to which we will return. To begin, differing core values, varying from deeply embedded Mennonite religious beliefs to passionate concern for political and commercial change, undergird the businesses' contrasting organizational cultures. Second, ATOs vary in their attention to competitive business strategies for defining market niches. In a third example, definitions of success and measures of small business performance range from establishing a diversified market to attracting wholesale clients at trade shows. Discussion of artisan- and outsider-directed product development provides a fourth set of practices for considering artisan work and development. We return to these and other scholarly linkages in Part III (Chapters 8-10), in which we focus on artisans and consumers, and in Part IV (Chapters 11-12), we address our three guiding questions concerning past performance, organizational mission, and future viability for alternative trade.

CHAPTER 3

TEN THOUSAND VILLAGES

A Mission-Driven Journey

For craftspeople in the Third World, "village" is where one's heart is: where family and tradition and culture reside. In our mass production world, villages are still a setting for the individualized creation of authentic handicrafts.

Making handicrafts is a way to pass one's culture and skills to the next generation. But as the outside world pushes at the village, taking its natural resources and often its children, it becomes more and more difficult to live the village way of life.

By selling their handicrafts, Ten Thousand Villages helps craftspeople provide food and education for their families and helps these threatened villages survive. Each village represents a unique, distinctive group of people. Multiply the village idea by ten thousand and it represents the world that our program is working to build.

—Ten Thousand Villages promotional brochure, fall 1997

Worldly Goods, a visually inviting retail store in Ames, Iowa, welcomes customers to its cornucopia of cultural products from throughout the world. Exuding the excitement of an international bazaar, merchandise displays bid customers to pick up an onyx bowl, don a necklace, try a musical instrument, play with a toy, or ponder a well-coordinated tabletop of placemats, dishes, and candles. A sign prominently announces that 108 artisan families were supported through the previous year's sales. In this town-and-gown community of 50,000, more than 80 volunteers join together in managing the store's day-to-day operations and in bringing to life the mission of their primary supplier, Ten Thousand Villages.

A typical day at Worldly Goods finds volunteers busily tending to sales, planning work schedules, placing wholesale orders for shop merchandise, training new volunteers, or arranging window displays. A paid manager and assistant offer guidance and facilitate activities. Not content to remain only in the store, volunteers hold an annual, off-site sale targeting the 25,000 students on the nearby Iowa State University campus. In turn, university student volunteers lead a sidewalk band playing the store's international musical instruments during the town's annual Ginkgo Festival. Still other community members, including two businesspersons (a retailer and banker), a multicultural education specialist, a retired university educator, the director of the YWCA, and two university professors, offer guidance as members of the board of directors. Through Worldly Goods, these volunteers, managers, and board members act on a local level to support artisans in improving the human condition worldwide.

Multiply the Worldly Goods experience in Ames, Iowa, by the more than 200 retail stores across the United States and Canada and a picture of Ten Thousand Villages' deep commitment to impoverished artisans begins to emerge. For more than 50 years, the Villages' mission of providing "vital, fair income to Third World people by selling their handicrafts and telling their stories in North America" has guided their journey. Headquartered in Akron, Pennsylvania, Ten Thousand Villages provides income for more than 60,000 artisans in more than 30 countries. In 1997, sales of $6.7 million resulted from the time and expertise contributed by 7,000 volunteers at store and warehouse levels.

The 50-year journey of Ten Thousand Villages began in 1946, when Edna Ruth Byler, a Mennonite Central Committee (MCC) volunteer, brought embroidered textiles from Puerto Rico and Jordan to sell at churches and among women's groups in the United States (see Table 3.1). Over time, artisan groups increased, product lines expanded, stores opened, and sales grew. By 1998, 40 members of the Akron headquarters staff worked in four divisions: purchasing, finance and administration, warehouse and distribution, and marketing. Figure 3.1 offers a Ten

TABLE 3.1 Ten Thousand Villages Time Line and Sales Figures

Year	Sales	Activity
1920		Mennonite Central Committee (MCC) formed to help Russian Mennonites suffering from civil war and famine.
1940s		Sewing and needlework projects initiated in Puerto Rico by MCC volunteers Mary Lauver and Olga Martens.
		SELFHELP initiated by Edna Ruth Byler in 1946 when she brought needlework from Puerto Rico to the United States to sell through churches and women's sewing circles.
1950s		Needlework project initiated in Jordan for Palestinian refugees by MCC volunteer Ruth Lederach. Products sold at Mennonite World Conference in Switzerland.
		Byler became known as the "Needlework Lady" as she initiated a craft marketing campaign called the Overseas Needlepoint and Crafts Project.
		Byler established a gift shop in her home basement for direct retail sales.
1960s		MCC assumed responsibility for the growing crafts program in 1962, with Byler as manager.
		Church-based consignment sales began.
		Overseas Needlepoint and Crafts Project renamed as SELFHELP Crafts in 1968.
1970s		First SELFHELP retail store opened in 1972, with expansion to 60 stores by decade's end.
		Crafts sourced in 20 countries.
		Edna Ruth Byler retired; Paul Leatherman assumed leadership.
1980s		Remodeled Miller-Hess building in Akron, Pennsylvania, dedicated in 1987 as SELFHELP Craft Headquarters.
		Crafts sourced in more than 30 countries.
		Paul Leatherman retired; Paul Myers assumed leadership.
		Mid-decade review reaffirmed SELFHELP focus on artisan producers and importance of nonprofit, self-supporting status.
		Retail stores expanded to 122.
1990s		Retail stores expanded to more than 200 in the United States and Canada.
1992	$5,300,000	
1993	$5,900,000	Strategic Plan developed for 1993-1998.
1994	$5,700,000	Mail-order catalog initiated.
1995	$6,100,000	Due to sales less than $40,000, retail catalog discontinued.
1996	$6,200,000	50th year celebrated with unveiling of name change from SELFHELP Crafts of the World to Ten Thousand Villages.

(Continued)

TABLE 3.1 Continued

Year	Sales	Activity
		Plan developed for Ten Thousand Villages contract stores and partner stores.
		Clothing product lines discontinued.
1997	$6,800,000	Strategic Plan developed for 1998-2003.
		First company stores opened.

Thousand Villages organizational chart showing functional relation-ships among management roles and national, regional, and local sales and store managers. National and local boards of directors are also positioned. Many among the national headquarters staff have a Men-nonite background. All commit to three employment criteria: Christian faith, adherence to nonviolence, and church membership.

Analysis of the Villages journey begins with focus on the Mennonite culture within which the Villages mission is deeply rooted. Mennonites, fleeing from Europe in the 17th century due to persecution for adherence to their beliefs, settled in North America, where they could practice their faith through lives of simplicity, discipleship, and constructive nonresis-tence. The MCC, founded in 1920, became the international develop-ment, service, and relief agency through which Mennonites responded to the needs of impoverished people throughout the world (see Box 3.1). MCC development activities center on education, health, agriculture, and job creation; the artisanal work of Ten Thousand Villages supports the latter. Mennonite cultural norms for service to others guide Villages leaders as they embrace the viewpoints, honor the lifestyles, and encour-age the work of artisans and coworkers with whom they are engaged.

Approaches to Change

Across their 50 years, Villages has approached change in varying ways. As Charvet (1997) describes in *Words That Change Minds,* some individuals prefer an *evolutionary* "sameness with exceptions" approach to change that encourages gradual improvement and growth. Others

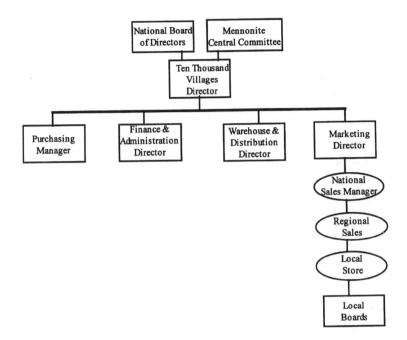

Figure 3.1. Ten Thousand Villages Organizational Chart

BOX 3.1

Mennonite Central Committee

Mennonite Central Committee (MCC) is the cooperative relief, service and development agency of North American Mennonite and Brethren in Christ churches.

MCC is built on the conviction that meeting human need and service to others is an integral part of the Christian life and that God intended all people to share the earth's resources. Volunteers work to remove barriers that separate people from each other and from God in a ministry of reconciliation.

Mennonites believe that war and violence violate the sacredness of human life, are destructive and costly and rob the poor of needed development assistance. MCC joins with those who are seeking less costly, nonviolent ways to settle disputes and to secure greater equality and justice.

—*Mennonite Central Committee informational brochure (fall 1995)* adopt a more *transformative* "difference" approach. In this second approach, change is revolutionary; current actions echo little from the past. Charvet suggests that individuals may use both strategies at various times across their life spans.

Villages' journey of the first 50 years unfolded in an evolutionary sameness with exceptions approach, as illustrated in Charvet's (1997) conceptualization. In accordance with Mennonite cultural values, change was carefully considered and implemented after deep introspection and discussion. As Villages grew and global competition expanded, organizational attention slowly shifted from a mission-directed focus on artisans to greater emphasis on running a business and meeting the needs of consumers.

In contrast to the first 50 years, Villages embarked on a more transformative approach to change as the 1990s drew to a close. Integrating "mission" and "business" was a high priority. For some individuals involved in the strategic planning process of 1997, achieving integration seemed an unworkable paradox. Director Paul Myers explained,

> Some people come down on the side of mission and some on the side of business. And some say you can't be both. Most would say you have to be both, but don't emphasize business too much or you'll be like everyone else. Others say don't become too mission or you'll be like all of the other crowd [of ATOs] who never gets it together.

As Villages enters its second 50 years, several initiatives suggest an organization in the process of embracing certain operational strategies quite different from the past.

As one dramatic indicator, in the fall of 1996, Ten Thousand Villages boldly launched its second 50 years of operation by changing its name from SELFHELP Crafts of the World to Ten Thousand Villages. Villages management explained that for some staff, particularly for potential customers unfamiliar with Villages and its mission, "SELFHELP (do it yourself) Crafts (supply store) of the World had increasingly been viewed as a barrier to bringing more people into our shops." During the process of selecting a new name, staff questioned, "Who are we and who do we want to tell people we are? What do we want to tell them we are doing?" Inspiration for Ten Thousand Villages' new name drew heavily from Mahatma Gandhi's perspective on the real and symbolic importance of village life in India (see Box 3.2). In a letter sent to all stores, the new name was further explained:

> The word village is a strong symbolic word. It implies community, traditions, and micro versus macro. Each village represents a special, unique, distinctive group of people and their way of making a life together. In our modern, mass production world, villages are still a setting for the individualized creation of authentic handicrafts expressed in visible form. The diversity that is represented by this word, VILLAGE, is something we value, celebrate and want to preserve. Multiply this village idea by ten thousand and it represents the world that our program is working to build.

By combining more transformatory approaches to change, along with past evolutionary patterns, Villages is acquiring flexibility for participating in the fast-moving, competitive market for crafts.

BOX 3.2

Villages

I have believed and repeated times without number that India is to be found not in its few cities but in its 700,000 villages. But we town dwellers have believed that India is to be found in its towns and the villages were created to minister to our needs. We have hardly ever paused to inquire if these poor folk get sufficient to eat and clothe themselves with and whether they have a roof to shelter themselves from sun and rain.

—*Mahatma Gandhi*

In the remainder of this chapter, we first examine Villages' mission-focused interactions with artisans; our discussion of their U.S.-based business operations follows. For both mission and business, Villages' many workable solutions and ensuing challenges are illustrated. As such, we chronicle Villages' evolutionary journey up through the mid-1990s. The bolder, more transformative change for achieving a "mission-driven viable business," which was under way in the late 1990s, is introduced at the chapter's end.

The Mission: Providing Vital, Fair Income

Permeating the culture of Ten Thousand Villages is its mission to provide work and income for the most economically disadvantaged craft producers throughout the world. Principles of operation guide producer group selection, pricing, and product sourcing (see Box 3.3). Frequent international trips aid Villages staff in understanding the artisans' rich craft traditions as well as the limitations and conditions under which artisans work. As delineated in the Ten Thousand Villages 1993-1998 Strategic Plan, when the diverse needs of Villages' constituent groups (craft artisans, shop personnel, and North American consumers) demand that they choose, Villages makes decisions that favor artisans.

A variety of actions provides evidence that Villages acts on its principles. Product orders take into account which producers need more

---

BOX 3.3

Principles of Operation

- We work with disadvantaged artisans.
- We purchase from craft groups that are concerned for their members and that promote member participation.
- We pay fair prices for handicrafts. We pay promptly.
- We pay up to 50 percent advance when a craft order is placed, the balance when the items are shipped to North America. This provides operating capital for artisans to purchase raw materials and for craft groups to pay workers.
- We offer handicrafts that reflect and reinforce rich cultural traditions.
- We promote fair trade.
- We use marketing strategies and messages consistent with our mission and ideals.
- Our ideals include responsible lifestyle choices, efficiency and Christian ethics. We seek integrity in all our actions and relationships.
- Whenever possible, we work with volunteers in North American operations.

—*Ten Thousand Villages promotional brochure (fall 1997)*

orders and whether new groups warrant support. When possible, orders are spread out across time to provide even work flow and steady income generation; one-time placement of large orders is avoided. So that artisans are not forced to buy raw materials under credit terms with exorbitant interest rates, artisans are advanced 50% of the value at the time an order is placed. The balance is paid when shipping documents are received. Sales success is defined in terms of how many producers are supported rather than how many products are sold. A retail sales figure of U.S.$1,200 is used for calculating the equivalent of full-time work for one artisan.

Purchasing Decisions

All purchasing is coordinated by the purchasing manager, a buyer, and a support team of three. Together, the team reviews approximately 10,000 new sample items each year. In some cases, samples arrive unsolicited at Akron headquarters. More commonly, Rachel Hess and Kristen Yoder, purchasing manager and buyer, respectively, request samples from producer groups with whom they have corresponded or previously conducted business. In addition, the buyers travel extensively to identify new products and connect on a human level with producer groups and their communities. Buyers place orders on their return from approximately 10 to 12 weeks of international travel per year. Villages buyers have long been sensitive to impacts on artisans of outside demands; they adhere to Villages' organizational tradition of limited product intervention.

Villages receives new requests weekly to work with producer groups in need. Inquiries appear from a variety of quarters, including travelers who have encountered a producer group with attractive products, charities or nongovernmental organizations (NGOs) concerned about employment creation, residents of the United States with artisan family members living abroad, and organized producer groups seeking work. Although not currently in an "expansive mode," Villages embraced a few new producer groups in the late 1990s from the African nations of Burkina Faso, Nigeria, Ethiopia, Tanzania, and the Congo. In all cases, new groups participate in employment generation programs under the auspices of the MCC. Villages collaborates closely with MCC in-country staff to facilitate these new producer interactions. Rachel Hess describes Villages' expanded African presence for sourcing crafts: "If you consider the response to human need, it was important for us to be there."

Once products arrive in Pennsylvania, they proceed to the Warehouse and Distribution Center. Orders are processed through computerized inventory control, inspected, and tagged. Receiving and checking shipments are time- and labor-intensive processes carried out by warehouse volunteers. Villages managers assess that the intensive process of unpacking and attaching labels to all products may warrant review to assess how certain steps could, in the future, be transferred to the artisans and accomplished in-country prior to shipping.

Implementing the Mission Through Fair Pricing

Defining a fair price for Villages products is carefully considered. Pricing decisions start at the producer level, with fair compensation based on local standards within the artisan's community. In-country MCC staff serve as valuable resources in assessing fairness at local levels. In arriving at a fair price, Villages personnel start by posing questions such as the following: What does the schoolteacher get? What do you get if you take this to sell in the market? What does a laborer get who sells his or her services in the community? Answers to these questions, along with costs for raw materials and labor, are considered as Villages staff determine prices judged to be fair by the people who make it and by their community. Establishing prices that contribute to dignity and sustainable employment is also part of the decision-making process. A staff member relates,

> I think of it as a very straightforward relationship. We place value on what artisans are making and then we sell it. It's a very clean relationship as opposed to when one person is donating to another. That's an important distinction to me. It's much more equal to have them creating something we value and pay for. I feel strongly about not subsidizing prices, or buying out of charity, but making sure we buy products that we can sell. Each step of the process is a viable business.

Sensitive issues can arise when the locally determined "fair wage" is not sustainable in the U.S. market. Paul Myers, Villages director, describes these difficult interchanges:

It becomes sensitive at the point where we determine what's fair, and then we add on our costs, and then the price we need to charge for it at the end is too high. At that point we have to go back to the artisans and say, "We can't buy it because we can't sell it at that price." The producer asks, "Can I lower my price?" Well, does one even entertain that question? And many times, we won't. We try to avoid that question coming up.

More likely, Villages staff will work with producers to "simplify a product so the price constraint can be removed and the producer doesn't end up having the same investment in labor and getting a lower price." After more than 50 years of working with artisans, Villages managers have discovered that when artisans believe they are paid fairly, the ultimate retail price in North American stores is of limited concern. Rather, producers declare, "Pay me fairly. I don't care what you sell it for. You know your market, your costs, just sell it, and give me another order."

The Business: Selling Handcrafts and Telling the Story

Moving to the retail-oriented path of the Villages journey, Ten Thousand Villages conducts business from a strong core of specialty shops. Although a growing number of stores operate with paid managers, the bulk of the sales function is assumed by community volunteers. Older retail stores often originated in communities with a strong Mennonite base. Today, broad-based ecumenical support is encouraged for its potential to strengthen volunteer involvement and expand the customer base. Preliminary to store start-up, a local board of directors is formed from interested community residents with business, legal, and educational interests, and funds are raised by the board for purchasing merchandise and opening the store. Board membership from a variety of religious affiliations and professional positions in the community is considered ideal for maximizing local store visibility. Once an initial board is seated, future members are commonly elected by the existing board from individuals who have been nominated or volunteered for membership. Increasingly, boards are becoming more systematic in matching board member expertise to evolving store needs.

Villages marketing and information staff reach out to communicate with the shops regularly, provide resources for business management, assist in telling the Villages story, and conduct workshops for shop managers and volunteers. However, Villages recognizes that it has little control over what happens in the shops. Sometimes, Villages feels helpless not knowing whether poorly performing stores have unattractive displays, are in a bad location, or are not advertising. Establishing and maintaining a consistent and clearly communicated "corporate" identity can be difficult under these circumstances.

During 1996, in an evolving strategy toward building a stronger corporate image and focusing resources, two store categories were designated: Villages *contract* and *partnership* stores. Existing stores selling Villages products were offered one of the two options. Villages contract stores entered into an identity agreement that involved adopting the store name of Ten Thousand Villages. Contract stores stock 100% fairly traded merchandise, with 75% of their product assortment from Villages. These stores have ready access to the many operational resources offered through regional managers and headquarters staff. Training is offered for store managers, as is specially targeted assistance with promotions and visual merchandising.

In contrast, partnership stores use names other than Ten Thousand Villages and are not obligated to source 75% of their fairly traded goods from Villages. They must, however, purchase at least $20,000 of Villages merchandise annually. Resources for promoting the Ten Thousand Villages brand name are available; however, the total range of operational assistance is not as readily accessible as for contract stores. Seasonal loans and lines of credit are also lower than for contract stores.

In contrast to their differences, several similarities exist. Both contract and partnership stores are resourced with hangtags and informational cards concerning products and producers, receive monthly newsletters as well as store and sales manuals, and are listed in the Ten Thousand Villages stores brochure. In addition, a group of shop managers and volunteers are invited to Akron each spring for a workshop focused on current issues of shop management and promotion.

Prior to and during the store option selection process, Villages gently encouraged many of its mature stores toward redefinition and a smaller number into closing. For those stores seeking revitalization, broadening their perceptions of sources for volunteers, assessing a store's life cycle, and setting sales projections were encouraged. One Villages staff member described the following:

> Store personnel often see the older volunteers who started 15 years ago, when they were in their 50s and 60s, as not able to continue. They don't quite see there are other people who are ready to take over. There are shops that are getting younger volunteers. Some of them hardly know how to handle looking for volunteers from other churches and the community.
>
> When a shop gets started, there is a lot of enthusiasm and support. In some communities they have begun to ask, "When does the saturation point arrive when customers have been buying from the store for 6 years and they all have their houses full of stuff?" At that point a store needs some remodeling, moving, enlarging, carrying a different product, reaching out to off-site sales. This year's workshop is focused on revitalizing your shop with the idea that if you don't do something to put new life into your store, it will die a slow death. You have to do things to sell.

A growth strategy of opening stores in urban locations as opposed to smaller, rural communities began in the mid-1990s. The first urban stores were organized by two young energetic "store planters" who, across the span of 4 years, went into four urban areas deemed promising from a marketing perspective, generated a board of directors for fundraising, and assisted in all phases of store start-up.

Regardless of the contract or partnership identity, wholesale buying is conducted in a similar manner. Managers or volunteer wholesale buyers make selections from a regularly updated wholesale catalog. In 1993, Villages upgraded from black-and-white to a full-color wholesale catalog to assist wholesale buyers in making decisions that would enhance the shop's stock and in conceptualizing how merchandise might be attractively displayed. A basic stock of 2,500 items is presented. New and special promotion items are added regularly. One Villages employee who develops the full-color catalog describes,

> We've always gone on the philosophy that our wholesale customers know what our products look like and they don't have to have the wholesale catalog in color. I guess what it boils down to is a wholesale

buyer has to have fun and look at the catalog and get excited and then she'll buy. Otherwise she may not buy, particularly if she can't figure out exactly what the design is.

In addition to the catalog, shops can subscribe to the "new items program" in which they automatically receive samples of all new items within a specified price range.

A cadre composed of four regional sales managers services Villages stores by providing guidance on inventory control and retail management to both store managers and the boards governing the stores. Regional sales managers also hold several yearly regional workshops for store managers to jointly problem solve and brainstorm on innovative store promotions. The regional sales managers also travel to stores in their region to meet with boards of directors and encourage and inspire volunteers to keep volunteering. As regional sales managers visit stores, they offer suggestions on how to coordinate displays that will assist customers in understanding how to use Villages products. Attention is also directed toward helping stores understand the importance of increasing inventory turns as a strategy for increasing sales.

At Villages headquarters, staff communicate across functional lines to ensure that the store perspective is considered in purchasing decisions. As national sales manager, Joyce Burkholder is a member of the product development team. In this role, she interprets store capabilities and communicates their needs for exciting, salable product lines. She describes her role and its relationship to sales:

> At this time, the relationship between purchasing and sales is very good. We've come a long way in acknowledging one another's realities, and I think our product line has grown much stronger than it was at one time. Now *product line* is a part of our language. Our promotion, our positioning of stores, how we present ourselves in the marketplace, all of that has to have a clear focus in order to promote sales.

Volunteer Participation

Unique to Villages' organizational culture is its reliance on a strong grassroots base of short- and long-term volunteer employees. Volunteers assist in managing the warehouse in Pennsylvania and are essential for operating the more than 200 retail shops in the United States and Canada.

Not only do volunteers partner with the national organization in spreading the organizational mission, but they also help maintain low overhead expenses so that more artisans can be assisted. Due to volunteers' contributions, Villages operates with only one paid employee for every $110,000 in sales (Hess, 1996, p. 20).

Warehouse volunteers are often retirees who arrive from throughout the United States and Canada, frequently as part of church-sponsored, weeklong service trips. Villages provides food and accommodations for these continuously revolving volunteer groups. At peak holiday periods, as many as 200 energetic volunteers expedite the massive shipping that occurs on a daily basis. Prior to employment, volunteers at the Pennsylvania headquarters are screened for their religious beliefs and adherence to nonviolence; employment screening does not carry over to store-level volunteers.

At the store level, volunteers perform a variety of important functions. In a long-established practice for many stores, selling is carried out by individuals who volunteer on a half-day or full-day per month basis. Other volunteers choose more focused activities related to buying, display, or education functions. Although Villages believes it receives high-quality work from volunteers, continuing to motivate and maintain a spirit of enthusiasm among volunteers is a challenge. This is particularly an issue in the shops and has prompted a move to hire paid managers in many locales. A manager questions,

> One of the things we are concerned with is what happens to the volunteer spirit after you've operated a store for 10 years. It's one thing to do it the first year and it's fun and exciting, but after you've done it for 10 years? Some of our shops are encountering this.

Most of the stores have found that transitioning from a volunteer to paid manager gives focus and direction to the store and more than pays for itself in added sales.

Villages' deep commitment to working with volunteers begs attention, particularly as related to telling the story of "how we're different." Some Villages staff question whether the volunteer who serves as a sales associate on the floor a half-day a month is in a position to be well informed on new product lines and artisan stories. Their effectiveness in communicating the Villages mission is of concern. Not surprisingly, store managers reiterate, "We're always training, always training." How to more effectively involve individuals who routinely volunteer several hours per month versus those with greater time to contribute entreats further debate.

In addition to working as store volunteers, approximately 275 groups throughout the United States host annual consignment sales, many in churches during holiday periods. Villages sends a shipment of craft products to each group; the proceeds from the sale, as well as the unsold merchandise, are returned to Villages following the event. Of the 275 off-site sales, approximately 200 generate more than $2,000 in sales annually.

As with use of volunteers at the store level, achieving greater efficiencies in off-site sales warrants attention. Although off-site sales generate income, is there a point when energy expended offsets added dollars? The dilemma is explained by Paul Myers:

> The tendency is to look at what we can sell in 3 days and not to measure what it takes to make that happen. And if one isn't careful, an off-site sale distracts from important resources that should be going into the store. The manager can't spend time in the store working at some things, whether it's inventory management or ordering for Christmas, because she's over there getting these three special sales off the ground.

Villages management is aware that it can no longer afford to conduct some consignment sales. However, criteria for making such judgments, such as a dollar figure, are not yet in place.

Education and Promotion

Educating consumers is another priority permeating the Villages organizational culture. Aware that many consumers are purchasing because they want to support impoverished artisans, Villages media and education staff have developed and are continually updating an extensive set of educational leaflets for in-store distribution to customers. Villages believes that educated consumers will be motivated by the Villages goal of empowering people who have limited opportunities for income generation. A staff member conceptualizes that Villages educational materials help customers cross a "philosophical bridge" where the meaning attached to objects by an artisan is linked with the meaning that evolves as customers own and use the objects. The educational program is further described in relation to the Villages goal of "telling the story":

> We provide our Third World brothers and sisters a spot in our marketplace. It doesn't have to be the best spot, but neither should it be on the fringe. In the process of doing that, I would like for our customers, the public, to learn as much about these people and why they need a spot in our marketplace. But I don't want people to buy out of pity. I want the customer to be able to say, "I think this craft is a beautiful piece not only for its aesthetic value but because it was made by hand by someone who has learned the skill through generations and is doing it because it's their way of feeding their family."

Media, advertising, and public relations tools are also provided to Villages shops. However, the role these play in advancing sales is not clear. The predicament is described as follows by one Villages staff member:

> Typically, store managers are very committed to this mission so we send them all this warm fuzzy material. . . . There could be things that are exciting like special events suggestions, recipes for food we would offer people, culture things—stores are doing them and they're not having people come, so there's no sales generated.

The perceived symbiotic relationship between educational and promotional materials warrants further attention due to its potential for affecting sales and providing the added value Villages hopes to offer its customers. At issue is whether educational materials and promotional activities perform similar functions. Should they be considered as separate initiatives in contributing to the added value of shopping at a Villages store? Paul Myers summarizes,

> I think most would agree that we have to provide good quality product, good price, good customer service just like anyone else. The question is what do we add to that. What is the added value? I think that question is far more important in terms of our success 10 years from now than whether we choose this particular store model or that particular marketing channel. Strategic planning will force us to find different ways, hopefully deeper ways of involving producers in what we do. That

brings back the old problem of do you listen to the consumers or the producers. Well, the answer is clear—you listen to both, but how we bring that together will be a very important issue.

Toward an Integrated, Mission-Driven, Viable Business

The organizational culture of Ten Thousand Villages in the 1990s is best described as one of "creative tensions." Following a period of rapid growth during the 1970s and early 1980s, Villages is currently at a crossroads for addressing change. Long guided by "thinking small," Villages has now assumed the challenge of adopting a more comprehensive perspective in its planning as it moves toward an integrative, mission-driven, viable business.

Villages director and managers at the national office assess that the next period of growth "will come differently than this one did." Challenges include guiding product development while maintaining cultural integrity, focusing on increased sales while continuing to work with small groups in unstable environments, working in the realm of business reality while maintaining Mennonite ideals, and delineating a new model of growth for the future while maintaining grassroots involvement. A Villages manager summarizes the tensions:

> Some would say it's a luxury to just go out there and find what you need and what fits. Plus there are those that say if you tamper with what they are producing, it no longer has integrity. We are prepared to live with those tensions. We're interested in providing as much employment as we can for those people. By starting where they are at and building on it and by recognizing that we live in an interdependent world in which we not only want to, but will be influenced by each other. There is a tension that always exists here, but I feel that most people enjoy that tension. They enjoy trying to bridge that gap between low-income producer groups and the North American buying population.

A variety of bold changes herald a transformed face for Ten Thousand Villages in certain areas of its operation. Most dramatic among these are adopting and implementing a new name (discussed earlier in the chapter), seating a Villages board of directors, commencing a new purchasing initiative, and opening company stores.

From SELFHELP Crafts of the World to Ten Thousand Villages

Reaction to the new name of Ten Thousand Villages has been overwhelmingly positive. Particularly gratifying to Villages staff have been artisans' reactions of "it's great, it's us, we like it." However, having inaugurated a new name, Paul Myers reminds staff, "Introducing a new name and logo in one year doesn't do it. We now need to imbue this new name and logo with meaning, and that gets right back to mission and business and how we're different."

Villages Board of Directors

December 1, 1996, marked what was a pivotal transition for Ten Thousand Villages with the seating of its first national board of directors (see Figure 3.1). Although Director Paul Myers still reports regularly to MCC officials, he is also directly accountable to the national Villages board, much as individual store managers are responsible to their local boards of directors. From their first meeting, national board members, many with extensive backgrounds in business and retailing, advised the director and his staff that "you must operate this [Villages] like a business, but a business of a different kind." Some of those differences are readily apparent in new types of stores, use of volunteers, and educational/promotion programs. More elusive, however, are questions regarding the added value that customers receive from patronizing Ten Thousand Villages.

Purchasing and Product Development Initiatives

Increasing marketplace competition for cultural products and flat sales in the mid-1990s forced Villages staff to reassess their product offerings, particularly their long-valued tradition of limited product intervention. In the Mennonite spirit of honoring artisans' indigenous knowledge and artistic skills, product development had become equated with objectionable outside interference. As expressed by a Villages manager, the organization has long been sensitive to not become the next "generation of colonials spreading solutions to the developing world from the outside."

However, product lines needed strengthening from previous decades. Villages buyers often found little that was new or exciting during their annual trips to visit producers with whom they had worked for many years. Updating, pizzazz, and greater product sophistication were high priority, particularly for products destined for the newer, more upscale Villages shops in urban areas. Buyers' and artisans' concerns about product development directions reached a confluence by the late 1990s. Producers, whose ATO purchases had dropped off, were asking, "What can we do?"

A three-part plan was developed for evaluating current product lines and identifying a purchasing strategy for the future. Initially, an outside consultant with extensive retailing experience was brought in, not just to "provide a report card" but to let the staff in on his thinking—to understand what he was looking for in assessing a product line. To the surprise of purchasing staff members, the consultant chose not to focus on specific products but rather directed his attention to what he perceived to be an urgent need for greater cross-product coordination in retail store presentations. Making connections between the product collection and store presentation was deemed vital. The consultant advised that customers needed help, through store displays, with how to integrate and use Villages products. Emanating out of the exercise was more focused sourcing on six well-coordinated product categories.

Other components of the three-part product development plan included systematic, in-depth assessment of domestic markets. The purchasing team regularly began to attend wholesale trade shows to monitor product trends. They also "shopped" their retail competitors for a better understanding of benchmark products that potential customers might choose over those offered by Villages. A third part of the plan brought MCC field staff from Bangladesh, Indonesia, and Kenya to Pennsylvania for briefings on product directions. The staff, with assigned responsibility for working with Villages, in turn communicated with artisans concerning implications of the new purchasing directions.

A buying strategy that looked quite different than decades past evolved. The strategy centered on six foci:

> ➤ persistent attention to mainstream market trends for line and product development;
> ➤ annual planning for coordinated product lines around color and content themes;
> ➤ use of a continually updated product development bank for assessing strengths, redundancy, and holes in product lines;
> ➤ assessment of new product samples for their contribution to and fit with a product line;
> ➤ addition of more products at upper price points; and
> ➤ guided product development to achieve balanced and integrated product lines.

A next agenda item involves translating the evolving purchasing and product development strategy into a plan that is meaningful and useful for artisans. Rachel Hess describes the situation:

What we really want to do with product development is "the least intervention with the deepest knowledge" so that people can interact with the information and use it for themselves. Ideally, if the world were perfect, people could understand enough from what we're telling them that they could take a concept and actually make an application. They would have the tools in their own thinking process so they could continue to build on it. Rather than us sending a specific sketch with Color A here and Color B there and have no real grasp of the bigger picture. So we're trying to figure out what to provide them—the least intervention with the deepest knowledge possible. We're not really there yet.

Getting at the "deeper knowledge" important to product development calls for discerning study and sensitive understanding on both sides of the buyer-producer equation. Rachel Hess states that for the purchasing staff, deeper knowledge of the producer's reality may include the following questions:

How much flexibility do they have for change? It could be technical change; for instance, how much can they control the dye? How much can they control the materials they gather? What can they do about weather changes? Those are the things that are often really hard to know, even after working with people for a while. It just takes a long time to accumulate that kind of understanding.

Understanding trends at a conceptual level so they can be translated to products for both the Villages market as well as for the artisans' more diversified client base serves as an example of deeper knowledge valuable to producers. Joyce Burkholder, national sales manager, describes a related issue of importance for communicating with artisans:

> We're sending a letter to everyone about what we're thinking regarding quality, how we're planning to upgrade product. We're trying to define for each product group those critical points that will make or break the customer appeal and then define a quality standard. We're asking, What's the one detail that if it's not up to a certain standard, it destroys the whole product?

Part of the evolving plan for working with artisans will likely include more extended "south-to-north" travel by producers. As an example, the payoff to both Bangladesh artisans and Villages was recently evident in an exciting new line of handmade paper products. The products were designed by a Bangladesh paper group following their designer's 1-month residency at Villages headquarters in Pennsylvania. Activities such as visiting retail stores, reviewing product lines, and interacting with other paper artisans served to strengthen the designer's perspective on U.S. customers and expand her technical expertise. Holding in-country or regional meetings, such as with all the producer groups with whom Villages works in India, is another approach under consideration. Bringing artisans together would encourage cross-group fertilization and collaborative planning for product development.

Committing greater resources to the purchasing department, particularly through staff expansion, appears on the horizon. A variety of approaches emerge in discussions of how to better work with artisans in defining "how we're different." Director Paul Myers speaks of "going deeper" or "renegotiating the contract" with artisans. Currently, many producers believe that if high-quality goods are delivered in a timely manner, additional orders will be forthcoming. However, in actuality, Villages holds nothing firm beyond an initial commitment to one order. Issues of capacity building would likely be central to "renegotiation" discussions. Are groups willing to invest over a 3-year period in becoming more technically efficient, increasing volume, producing more quickly, or expanding product lines? Myers believes, "We have to come to the point in the next several years where we must sit down and have that kind of conversation with every group we work with."

Outcomes of contract discussions could result in more joint ventures, expanded training, and working with producers to diversify their markets through participation in regional, national, and international wholesale trade shows. Depending on groups' readiness and commitment to capacity building, certain groups might receive intensive attention for a specified time. As their capacity expands, they would cycle out and others move forward for a period of special attention. Irrespective of the outcomes, Villages managers are sensitive that the future not find Villages working only with a few strong producer groups. Managers are mindful of undesirable directions to which greater product development or larger-scale ordering could lead. Paul Myers describes,

> We're concerned that product demand would push us to buying more from the large, sophisticated producers or concentrate too much in only one region or with just a few groups. We don't want to work with just those groups who happen to live in the most stable economic environment. We want some leeway to be able to continue to work in the Cameroon and buy those individual musical instruments where only a few people can make them and you don't know if the ship will go. Maybe it's a matter of making some choices and saying for these people we are going to reserve a certain percentage of stock.

At the same time, Villages managers acknowledge that it is unlikely that Villages will take on many new producer groups when they "renegotiate the contract" with its existing artisan partner groups.

Villages purchasing staff recognizes that not all Villages staff are on board with the transformative changes under way for product development. Framing purchasing, product development, and marketing as a means of providing more work for producers appears to enhance their palatability for those who perceive more directed product development and focused product sourcing as incompatible with Villages' focus on producers.

Company Stores

Over time, Villages realized that in certain urban areas, it would be difficult to attract a local board of directors willing to commit to the level of fund-raising required for contract or partnership stores. A new concept of a company store was developed to accommodate such urban settings deemed highly desirable in terms of sales. The first Ten Thousand Villages company stores opened in 1997. Providing full financial and staff start-up support from Villages headquarters marks a dramatic change from previous store initiation. The upscale company stores are positioned in cities where the population is at least 45,000 and the medium income above the national average. Once a city is targeted, a ZIP code analysis helps identify areas where upper-income households are located. A final locational decision draws on foot traffic assessment of several targeted sites. Coordinated store presentation is particularly salient in the visual merchandising for the new company stores. As sales margins improve, a longer-range goal is that company stores be entirely staffed by paid employees; currently, only a manager and assistant are on payroll. Remaining employees are volunteers.

Past Strengths and Future Planning

The case analysis of Ten Thousand Villages depicts an ATO moving on a path from evolutionary to transformative change. As such, the case provides a number of useful insights for consideration in advancing the fair trade movement within an increasingly competitive marketplace. Across Ten Thousand Villages' 50 years, we learn about the importance of the following:

Partnerships with artisans

> Modifying approaches for working with artisan groups as a group's skills evolve and an ATO's financial situation tightens.
> Conceptualizing the ATO product assortment as a series of lines of coordinated items that consumers can use in their homes or wear.
> Recognizing that artisan groups need ATO intervention and direction in contributing items toward a product line that may come from producer groups in geographically diverse parts of the world.
> Acknowledging that greater depth of involvement with artisan groups will likely reduce the total number of artisan groups with which an ATO can work.

Store operations

> ➤ Exploring new store operation and ownership formats for increasing an ATO's visibility in the marketplace.
> ➤ Providing ongoing, in-service training for store managers and volunteers through workshops and regional store manager meetings.
> ➤ Acknowledging that not all stores warrant the same resources for operation, as evidenced by past sales and future potential.
> ➤ Establishing a strong foundation of local volunteers while also exploring new strategies for matching volunteers' time and expertise with store needs.

Intraorganizational

> ➤ Developing sound merchandising decisions that are also compatible with Mennonite philosophical views on mission.
> ➤ Optimizing boards of directors at local and national levels.

In looking to the future, Villages' exploration of "how we're different" from mainstream businesses that market crafts strikes at the core of its strategic planning for 1998-2003. The challenge for arriving at a common answer rests deep in employees' hopes and dreams for the organization. A national manager speaks for the group in explaining that "everyone works here because it's their own personal mission, so they tend to bring a lot of different agendas. Nothing is taken lightly." The fact that there is such vigorous debate about mission and business speaks to the ownership assumed by members of the Villages organization.

In conclusion, the lives of artisans and Villages' organizational focus on increased sales are tightly intertwined as Villages continues its journey toward becoming a mission-driven, viable business. The journey began deep in Mennonite roots of working to alleviate world poverty among individuals for whom "work of the hands can provide a future." Over time, a competitive market environment for handcrafts demanded that the journey expand to giving greater attention to running a business and increasing sales. Fifty years into the journey, how Villages links "providing vital, fair income" with "selling their crafts" through a "business of a different kind" continues to gradually evolve. However, some dramatic and transformatory changes loom on the horizon.

Our analysis of Ten Thousand Villages suggests that the alternative trade movement has much to learn from closely watching the outcomes from how Villages does the following:

Purchasing and developing products

➤ Translates a focused and coordinated buying plan in ways that continue to build on artisans' traditions and provides work for a range of groups. How can a product development bank used for line planning be linked through computer software with indices of artisan skills, cultural aesthetics, and regional diversity so that work can be spread to the maximum number of artisans?

➤ Identifies parameters of artisans' indigenous knowledge useful for understanding how to carry out product development in a variety of contexts. Of the range of issues related to raw materials, production techniques, and local aesthetic practices about which Villages staff could become informed, which are better predictors than others for facilitating collaborative or artisan-initiated product development?

Selling crafts

➤ Increases efficiencies among time-honored business practices for which some employees and staff may hold particular allegiance. At what level do consignment sales offset human and financial inputs? How can labeling, packaging, and pricing be reduced to the fewest steps while maintaining accurate inventory control?

➤ Focuses store resources with the greatest potential for strengthening performance. Realizing that Villages' resources for store management, operations, and promotion cannot be shared similarly with company, contract, and partnership stores, which resources hold the most potential for contributing to sales in each type of store?

➤ Tells a consistent, timely, and accurate story of the Villages artisan mission using a staff composed almost exclusively of part-time volunteer employees. What aspects of volunteer training are most effective in providing volunteers with resources to "tell the story"?

➤ Assesses the enmeshed relationship between promotions and education. Do educational materials attract customers? Do promotional activities inform customers of the store mission? What value does each contribute to shopping at Villages stores?

Linking mission and business

➤ Renegotiates the contract with producers toward more intense involvement in building capacity. Which producer group criteria prove effective for first selecting groups and then collaboratively developing capacity?
➤ Plans and executes south-to-north training programs for artisan development. What U.S.-based activities facilitate artisan-led product development for the visiting producers and among their groups upon the leader's return home?

It is our assessment that Ten Thousand Villages has charted a compelling but resource-laden direction for working more intensely with artisans than in the past. Projected undertakings advance well beyond buying their crafts to developing artisans' human capacity for establishing sustainable trade. Garnering the human and financial resources for moving the plan into action will require that Villages carefully monitor its many other activities. Asking how various activities contribute to the retail sales that are so critical to accomplishing the mission will be increasingly important.

It appears unlikely that Villages will be able to operate with its same full plate if it is truly to interact with artisans in proposed transformative ways. However, carefully focusing its attention and resources, creatively linking the seeming paradox of mission with business, and clearly communicating its "differentness" through concrete, artisan-related impacts hold promise for helping customers understand the "value" they buy in Villages products. Outcomes of these initiatives provide Ten Thousand Villages with vibrant potential for richly endowing its new name with meaning.

CHAPTER 4

SERRV

*Alternative Distribution,
Philosophical Considerations,
and Hard Business Decisions*

*In this church we want to give people lots of different ways to learn about
people's lives and needs. The SERRV sale is one piece of the whole puzzle for
how our members can become involved in the church's mission
commitment. Some contribute canned goods for local distribution. Others
volunteer at the Salvation Army. Many members, young and old, buy crafts
at the annual SERRV sale.*

—Beth Lepinski, Memorial Presbyterian
Church, Appleton, Wisconsin

The first Sunday of Advent arrives at Memorial Presbyterian Church in Appleton, Wisconsin. Following morning worship services, church members eagerly stream to the church library for their annual SERRV holiday sale. Young boys and girls search for their parents' Christmas gifts among the enticing selection of crafts from around the world. Older church members purchase several boxes of their favorite Rainforest Crunch candy. Still others come to peruse "what's new" among global crafts. They discover last season's playful toy llamas and decorative wooden boxes replaced by new, equally appealing products for this year's gifts to family and friends.

For the remaining three Sundays of Advent, church leader Beth Lepinski and her six-member volunteer team staff the well-attended event, which annually generates between $1,500 and $2,000 in sales. In preparing for the sale, Beth carefully selects products from SERRV's biannual wholesale catalogs mailed to church constituencies. In a parish strongly committed to service, Beth explains that church members "really like to participate in this type of ministry." Many customers request SERRV's informative enclosures about artisans' lives as a way of extending the educational message to their gift recipients.

The Appleton church sale illustrates one of SERRV's distinguishing characteristics within the Alternative Trade Organization (ATO) community—its diverse "alternative" channels for product distribution. Two additional distinctive features include SERRV's deep philosophical consideration of trade-related issues and its execution of hard business decisions.

First among the characteristics, SERRV interprets *alternative distribution* to be synonymous with *alternative trade*. Approximately 3,000 Protestant and Catholic churches throughout the United States form the core of SERRV's alternative distribution channels. These annual holiday sales involve as many as 20,000 volunteers yearly; the core program accounted for 36% of SERRV sales in 1997 (see Figure 4.1). Conference sales during national denominational gatherings provide a second growing venue both for direct sales and for recruiting parishes to join the core program of holiday sales in their home churches. SERRV also partners with the Christian Children's Fund and Catholic Relief Services in distributing catalogs to its constituencies. Finally, SERRV products appear in more than 300 retail shops, many of which are associated with Ten Thousand Villages.

Second, SERRV is at the forefront of the alternative trade movement in addressing philosophical underpinnings for how and why alternative trade can and should occur. Introspective critique of alternative trade in relation to broader trade options undergirds SERRV's unwavering commitment to its position on alternative distribution. Robert (Bob) Chase, SERRV executive director, offers his perspective:

> I think the bigger issue for me is that for a while, we kidded ourselves that we could operate an alternative economic system within a larger economic system—sort of a socialist system within a capitalist system.

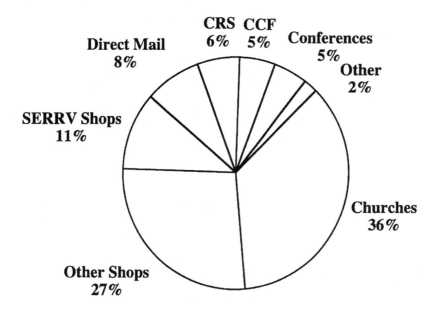

Figure 4.1. SERRV 1997 Sales
NOTE: CRS = Catholic Relief Services; CCF = Christian Children's Fund.

We've come to realize that is incredibly difficult, if not impossible. The only way it can be done is if somebody subsidizes part of it. If you're going to be competitive, either the consumer pays more, your employees or producers get less, or the volunteers do more. Something's got to give or you're not competitive. That's part of what is bringing me back to the idea that we at SERRV really have to invest a lot more effort into staying in the alternative distribution channels, which are based on volunteer sales and volunteer-run shops.

In addition, philosophical concerns about distribution of wealth, global business practices, and trade inequities guide SERRV's day-to-day business decisions. Bob Chase appeals for discussion of these important issues:

My belief is that the way most of the world is doing business right now doesn't have a great future. The whole trade construct is built on assumptions that we in the First World will live at a far better standard than people in the Third World, even adjusted for inflation of currency. For example, I assume that all my employees who work here will have health insurance, vacations, and so on. Few of the employees of the organizations we buy from have those, and probably none of the craftspeople. And so we are still in a situation where we're saying, most craftspeople make practically nothing, so if they're doing a little better than that, then that is an improvement and we want to strive for that. But that's not where I think we need to be in the long run. That's part of the educational process and it's very difficult to talk about. What we're really talking about is redistribution of wealth in the world.

Deeply committed to the belief that fair trade and alternative trade are not the same thing, SERRV continually struggles with the question of what makes alternative trade distinctive (see Figure 1.1 in Chapter 1). As an example, in a discussion with another ATO leader, Bob Chase questioned the organization's practice of purchasing products manufactured in a factory setting:

I pursued this and said, "What can you tell me about it?" They said, "Well, it's clean, well lit, they pay minimum wage, there's no worker participation, the people who own it are very wealthy, but it does provide jobs." And in the end I questioned, "What's the bottom line here?" And they said, "The bottom line is jobs. They provide jobs." And my response was, "Isn't that exactly what Reebok says when we ask them about Indonesia. They say it's clean, it's well lit, we create jobs." That's the kind of thing that we're trying to figure out. How do we remain financially viable in today's incredibly competitive world with committed customers who are much more demanding about quality— and still be true to what we see as our mission and differentiate ourselves from socially responsible businesses?

In a third distinguishing characteristic, SERRV is admired as the organization that turned its business around. In but 2 short years between 1995 and 1997, SERRV moved from being financially in the "red" to a "black" bottom line. As the 1990s unfolded, SERRV found that the higher discounts demanded from retailers and wholesale customers were gradually cutting into their revenues. Bob Chase described the pressing need for tending to business in 1995:

> We had relatively strong sales growth from 1988 to 1992. Sales were at an average of about 12% a year and we were profitable. And then we moved into the 1993 to 1995 period where we had losses. Growth masks lots of problems. We were feeling like everything is OK here and not looking deeper to see what the trends were. As the losses grew, the urgency grew. We found more and more that we needed to focus on the day-to-day business activity and come up with a plan to get out of this fix we were in.

Although 1997 profits of $289,000 from sales of $4.97 million were relatively small, SERRV was one of very few U.S. ATOs that was not currently dependent on outside support to compensate for shortfalls.

Other ATOs, many of whom are experiencing similar financial exigencies, question, "How did they do it? How did they get out of the red?" In providing answers for the business turnaround, SERRV leaders credit hard business decisions in three key areas: (a) eliminating staff positions, (b) focusing on product design, and (c) expanding alternative distribution channels. After briefly outlining SERRV's history, the remainder of this chapter explores each of these areas for details of the business decisions. Within the discussion, we also highlight philosophical issues integral to SERRV's thinking. In a final section for the chapter, we explore SERRV's continuing integration of alternative distribution, philosophical considerations, and hard business decisions as it entered its second 50 years of operation in 1999.

SERRV's Post–World War II Origins

As World War II ended, refugees desperately searched for work in war-torn Europe. Church of the Brethren members assisted in the United States by transporting handmade clocks and other crafts for sale in their home parishes and at the Brethren international gift store, adjacent to the SERRV headquarters in New Windsor, Maryland (see Table 4.1). The program of assistance assumed official status within the Church of the Brethren in 1950. The name SERRV stood for Sales Exchange for Refugee Rehabilitation and Vocations.

For the next 49 years, church support served a number of important functions. Of initial importance were headquarters offices and a warehouse from which to operate in New Windsor, Maryland, as well as a church constituency for conducting sales. In addition, working capital

TABLE 4.1 SERRV Time Line and Sales Figures

Year	Sales	Activity
1949		Crafts, including handmade clocks, made by European refugees from World War II sold through Church of the Brethren churches and in the New Windsor, Maryland, gift shop.
1950		SERRV formalized as a Church of the Brethren program.
1967		SERRV hired Bill Nyce as the first full-time director.
1960s–1970s		SERRV achieved broad ecumenical appeal through close partnership with Church World Service, the development arm of the National Council of Churches.
1989	$3,538,000	Robert Chase joined SERRV as executive director.
1990	$3,943,000	Direct-mail catalog initiated.
		Partnership established with Christian Children's Fund and Habitat for Humanity.
1991	$4,430,000	SERRV is the first to market fairly traded coffee that is produced, processed, and packaged in the developing world.
1992	$4,785,708	Conference sales initiated.
1993	$4,702,702	
1994	$4,646,660	
1995	$4,682,730	Partnership with Catholic Relief Services.
1996	$4,737,765	Product development partnership formed with design consultant, Docey Lewis.
		SERRV joined Aid to Artisans Trade Network.
1997	$4,968,000	SERRV purchased products from 100 producer groups in 40 countries.
1999		SERRV incorporated as a nonprofit organization independent from the Church of the Brethren.

buttressed periods of uneven cash flow and furnished backup resources when profit and loss statements showed negative balances. Perhaps most important was the Church of the Brethren's reputation as an institution promoting peace, justice, and nonviolent approaches to problem solving. SERRV drew strength and inspiration from these church-associated values as it carried out its mission to "promote the social and economic progress of people in developing regions of the world by marketing their crafts and other products in a just and direct manner."

Current SERRV employees express deep admiration and appreciation to the Church of the Brethren for its supportive but hands-off approach as SERRV carried out its work. In particular, SERRV credits Church of the Brethren's active involvement in the National Council of Churches with providing a conduit for developing a range of ecumenical sales channels over the years. Bob Chase assesses the partnership:

> They have been willing to allow this program to function autono-mously without any attempt to utilize the program to make their denomination grow, to generate revenue, or preach their particular perspective on anything. In the 1960s and '70s, Church of the Brethren had a close partnership with Church World Service, the development arm of the National Council of Churches, and through that partnership, a lot of Protestant denominations, like Presbyterians, United Church of Christ, and Methodists, came to feel that this [SERRV] was their pro-gram. We find when we talk to people, they thought this was owned by the Methodist church. And many Presbyterians thought the pro-gram was theirs. The program took on a very ecumenical appeal.

Broadening its sourcing options for craft products from war-torn Europe, SERRV gradually branched out across the globe. Today, SERRV works with 100 artisan cooperatives, nongovernmental organizations, and locally controlled small businesses in some 40 countries. SERRV adheres to fair trade guidelines similar to those of other ATOs. Fair pricing and encouraging producer group development are salient con-cerns. SERRV employs a marketplace perspective as it negotiates fair prices with producer groups; helping producers understand SERRV's customer base is part of the teaching/learning process. Barb Fogle, purchasing director, describes this process:

> We're very honest with them up-front and say this is a wonderful product and we would love to carry it. But at this time we just don't have the market. That's one of the things we tell people when we talk about the prices they are quoting to us. We say, "this would fit our market if it were 25 cents less, or you could probably charge 25 cents more." And then when they say, "well, this is the price we think it should be," we say, "fine, but that's not going to work for our particular market." Not to say that it won't work for someone else. We try to help them understand the middle American people we are looking for.

Assisting producer groups to upgrade their equipment, improve productive capacity, or take advantage of special training through the

SERRV Grants Program is another priority (see Box 4.1). Rather than figuring the cost of development initiatives into its front-end pricing structure, SERRV supports artisan development from funds derived after earnings are assessed. However, even in the difficult years when SERRV found itself in the red, it made special efforts to keep the grants program alive by cutting back on other initiatives so that some grants to artisans could be awarded. With this short overview of SERRV history as background, we now move to the decisions involved in SERRV's business turnaround in the mid-1990s.

Business Decision 1: Eliminating Staff Positions

First among SERRV's hard business decisions was assessing staff roles. As SERRV grew and its distribution channels expanded, each new program initiative contributed to continued staff enlargement. Yet, the financial losses of the mid-1990s demanded strident change. In what

---

BOX 4.1

SERRV Grants

SERRV offers grants to current producers to help them increase sales by investing in up-to-date equipment, building new workshops, purchasing land, or offering training courses. In 1997 . . .

- COOCAFE in Costa Rica used funds to provide a month of English language and management training for three rural youth leaders.
- The ECOTA Forum in Bangladesh sent its first full-time director to the Philippines for training in marketing and management.
- Union Progressista Artesanal in Mexico purchased a new metal cutting machine and patterns for new jewelry designs.
- The YMCA in Dhaka, Bangladesh was provided assistance from Docey Lewis on updating their product line.
- Leaders of three producer groups in Haiti, Chile, and India attended the IFAT (International Federation of Alternative Trade) conference in India.
- Emergency assistance for food was provided to the woodcarvers of Bombolulu in Kenya who suffered extensive flooding following torrential rains in Mombassa.

—*International Partnerships Newsletter (fall 1997)*

was described as an extremely painful process, SERRV asked, "Is this essential?" for everything it was doing. Each function and staff position was examined. The review was particularly stressful for an organization that had grown for nearly 50 years and that had a variety of popular programs deemed fundamental to its operations.

Between 1993 and 1996, SERRV agonizingly reduced its permanent staff by approximately 20%, going from 31 personnel to a current staff of 25 at the New Windsor, Maryland, headquarters office. In some cases, responsibilities were reconfigured. In other cases, functions were contracted out rather than retained as part of an employee's job description. In the case of design, as a staff member resigned, SERRV chose to consult with an outside designer rather than retain the in-house staff position. SERRV's much leaner staff of the late 1990s seems clearly aware of the need for downsizing. They caution that their reconfigured jobs demand integration of a range of diverse responsibilities, which can lead to feelings of fatigue and overwork in times of stress. However, Director Bob Chase summarizes that attacking the overstaffing issue was critical to "becoming better business people, which helped us to get out of hot water."

Business Decision 2: Focusing on Product Design

A second pivotal business decision emerged from careful consideration of SERRV product lines. Up through the 1980s, SERRV believed that it was selling "fair trade" more than "product." However, SERRV observed that customers of the late 1990s, although still wanting to support artisans, were also much more demanding related to product quality and design. The change in customer orientation led to three decisions: (a) hiring a design consultant, (b) focusing criteria for selecting producer groups, and (c) developing an integrated and purposeful design strategy.

Hiring a Design Consultant

Although SERRV strives for long-term social and economic progress among people in the developing world, it also is closely tuned to the realities of day-to-day needs for income among severely impoverished artisans. Meeting these long- and short-term goals creates a philosophical dilemma for SERRV when embarking on product development. For example, although SERRV encourages product development based on indigenous aesthetics and production practices, it also recognizes that locally inspired designs may have limited marketability for providing sorely needed income to the artisans. Brian Backe, marketing director, shares his personal thoughts:

> Philosophically, one of the challenges with product development is that it's a very difficult line where you've come in and imposed a design that has no reflection on that culture versus adapting a design. But the producers would say, "Forget it. We're not concerned. Give us stuff that will sell." From the short-term point of view, they want sales from us and they want product design. And they say, "You can worry about all this philosophical stuff. We want sales. And if that means new designs, great." I worry greatly that if we get too much product development going and we're too successful, we could take away what is unique about our products. It's both a long-term and a short-term issue.

With these philosophical concerns in mind, SERRV made a dramatic move to search for a designer. The job description called for a person who could combine concern for artisans with international design expertise gleaned from working with mainstream, profit-oriented businesses. It found such a person in Docey Lewis, who joined SERRV in 1996 as design consultant. Docey has extensive experience as a design consultant with Aid to Artisans, operates a fabric import business, and had previously owned a weaving production and design studio with a showroom in Manila.

Almost immediately, Docey Lewis's valuable overseas experiences allowed her to alert SERRV that, in some cases, it may have been paying too much compared to other socially responsible organizations. Situations also occurred in which SERRV not only paid a higher price but had products delivered last, as SERRV was the vendor that producers believed would not cancel an order if the products arrived late.

Because Docey Lewis's design background centered on high-end craft markets, SERRV ensured that she had travel opportunities to visit its producers and learn how production for a mid-range, alternative trade market may be different than the higher-end, commercial world in which she had previously worked. Docey returned from such trips enlightened and inspired as to the difficult circumstances under which some artisans design and produce their crafts (see Box 4.2). The value of these travel experiences for team building within SERRV is described by Barb Fogle, purchasing director:

> I remember when Docey Lewis came back from one trip, she was saying, "I see now what you mean. People have very difficult working conditions and can be very slow to get things done." When the product development team sits down around the table, it's not like it's her and us. We're a team and it feels good to all be thinking along the same lines of getting the job done.

Focusing Criteria for Selecting Producer Groups

Since Docey Lewis's arrival, several product-related guidelines have been added by the purchasing staff to direct them in selecting producer groups with whom to work. SERRV continues to apply its long-used criteria concerning fair wages, working conditions, and worker involvement. In addition, SERRV now ponders several further questions as it considers whether to add a new producer group.

> ➤ Is the producer group able to develop a single item into a line of products?
> ➤ Does the group work in a medium in which SERRV already has coverage among its existing artisan partnerships?
> ➤ Does the group produce products that can be priced to appeal to SERRV's target market?

These criteria contrast starkly with previous practices, some of which were costly to business. Bob Chase and Barb Fogle, respectively, offer explanations:

> A few years ago, if we had a producer with one product that we thought looked interesting, we probably would have placed an order. But now it's really unusual. Related to the cost of doing business, do we really want to open a relationship in order to get one item, and maybe $1,200? If it doesn't look like they have the potential to develop a line of products, it's unlikely we'll open a relationship with them.

Box 4.2

Mutual Inspiration

The SERRV design consultant describes the mutually beneficial exchange from a 1997 visit by SERRV designer Docey Lewis with Joseph Muchina at Trinity Jewellery in Nairobi, Kenya:

> Joseph Muchina is one of the most inspirational individuals I have ever met. When he was a young boy, his mother and family migrated to overcrowded Nairobi to scratch out a living there. Rescued at a young age by nuns from a life of poverty, Joseph . . . learned jewelry making and accounting, thanks to the Catholic mission. Instead of leaving the depressed area, he began Trinity Jewellery which employs about a dozen young men from the same poor area.
>
> Joseph is caring, generous, hardworking, smart, highly organized, and professional. One thing I learned from him is that you don't need a fancy office or a lot of money to support these virtues. You can just as well have your office in a tin building as he does.
>
> The artisans are hungry to know what will sell and what they might develop as alternative products. We implemented a few changes to make the jewelry more wearable for working women. I encouraged them to think of making small brass picture frames, napkin rings, etc. They want product development more than anything else. They have the ability and imagination to respond. People like Joseph Muchina make the effort workable and worthwhile.
>
> —*Docey Lewis, Partnerships Newsletter (May 1997)*

Also, we're not taking in new producers if we're already covered in that area. And that's different because before we'd just take them on and then they'd be writing and asking, "When can you order?"

Developing a Design Strategy

In addition to product-related criteria guiding with whom SERRV worked, the "how" of that work also has evolved during Docey Lewis's ongoing consultancy. The new design strategy embraced attention to five factors: production costs, adaptations, time schedules, price points, and design inspiration. Beginning with production costs, how to retain the central elements of a product while reducing costs surfaced as an early priority. In some cases, changing something as simple as painting only one side of a decorative wall plaque increased the artisans' efficiency to produce more items while also reducing the cost to SERRV.

A second change has had broader philosophical implications. In the late 1990s, when strongly ethnic products are little promoted in the housewares market, Docey guided the purchasing team to consider how "adaptation" fits with the SERRV mission. Barb Fogle assessed this design strategy:

> Ethnic products are "out" right now. But if you can take a portion of something, like a little strip of weaving, and put it on something else, or a little portion of a painting and use it in some other way that mixes nicely in your home, say on a bookcase . . . you haven't lost the dignity of the country, the ethnic part of it, but yet you've created a whole new product that can work and looks very nice and mixes in with what people have now. It's important because customers aren't going to go in and buy the whole line for their living rooms. They're going to buy one piece, so the mirror has to be nice enough that it will fit in with the things that are already in customers' homes.

A third area of focus was scheduling. New products represent from one third to as many as two thirds of the items in each wholesale and retail catalog; the product development team has developed a tight schedule for design and development of what can amount to as many as 800 new items across a single year. Docey Lewis joins the in-house staff approximately six times a year for periods of 2 days to a week. During these periods of intense activity, they (a) develop overall themes, identify product ideas, and write specifications that are then sent to targeted producer groups; (b) review, refine, and select products from among samples that have been returned from artisans; and (c) place final orders.

With little time leeway for mistakes, clear communication with artisans about design intentions via fax and e-mail is critical. When artisans are unclear about a product's intended use in households halfway around the globe, production specifications can be confusing. In an example from Bangladesh, cane producers questioned whether SERRV really wanted large cane structures that were taller than most humans. Once the product's intended use as trellises for flowering vines in an outdoor garden was explained by the SERRV staff in New Windsor, the specifications were more meaningful to the artisans.

Attention to price points was a fourth area for consideration. As costs assumed increased importance both to SERRV and the artisans, artisan groups asked for potential price points at the time when samples were requested by SERRV. Producers argued they are wasting their time if they come up with a product that is five times as much as SERRV will pay. Although SERRV staff does their best to provide such information, they also hesitate to be too precise until they see how a product turns out. As a staff member explained, "If you price it too low, they're not even going to try and if you price it too high, then unrealistic expectations about volume orders sometimes emerge."

Encouraging artisan initiative in product design was a final consideration. In an effort toward "stimulating creativity and imagination within the boundaries of market demand," Docey Lewis produces a biannual review of the New York International Gift Fair held in January and August of each year. The report, sent to 30 of SERRV's major producer groups, highlights popular themes, motifs, materials, colors, and patterns central to the products offered by more than 2,800 exhibitors and considered by the 45,000 wholesale buyers who attend the semi-annual trade shows. Storyboard collages and a sketchbook of products accompany the text of Docey Lewis's reports. How producers use the information is yet to be evaluated; however, Barb Fogle assesses that some producer groups appear to be inspired by the new design initiatives. In a few cases, producers have returned samples that surpassed the originating specifications for creativity and spirit.

In looking back over the new approach to product design, SERRV purchasing staff assessed that the new operational procedures were difficult at first. The new strategy called for a proactive and directed "SERRV-to-producer" way of thinking about product development. Formerly, SERRV operated more from a wait-and-see approach. Purchasing decisions were made by selecting from among the thousands of samples that arrived each year at SERRV's doorstep or by "shopping the market" while traveling abroad to visit producer groups. Because other ATOs such as Ten Thousand Villages also "shopped" the same market and received some of the same samples, SERRV judges that it was often working off the same products. With the new intervention-oriented design strategy, Barb Fogle now concludes:

SERRV has cornered a little piece of the market. Years ago, there weren't as many retailers offering the products we had. Now you can go in every mall in the U.S. or every street corner in a major city and find products from the Third World. People are going to Peru and bringing back jewelry and selling it. The problem is that before we had just waited for artisans to bring products to us. We were relying on them to help us get ahead. Now, we have this small, narrow niche of products that we are developing, and we hope that will grow and keep us apart and different for a while.

SERRV requests a 1-year exclusivity with artisans on their designs. However, it encourages producer groups to offer the products, perhaps in a modified form, to other clients following the year under contract with SERRV. In this way, groups are encouraged to strengthen their local and international clientele base beyond that of SERRV.

Business Decision 3: Expanding Alternative Distribution

A third business decision involved SERRV's resolution to continue expansion of its alternative distribution channels for the sale of crafts. Attracting the "nonconverted" lies at the heart of SERRV's continuing commitment. Brian Backe, marketing director, explains,

It provides a mechanism that doesn't happen in shops. A lot of the mailing lists that ATOs use, as well as people who gravitate toward a shop, are people who are interested in those issues generally anyway. But if you've got an event happening in a church or community-based organization, oftentimes those people aren't there for that purpose (craft sale) so you've got an opportunity to communicate much more broadly. Not just about producers, but some of the broader issues of alternative trade. I guess the bottom line is that we're not preaching to the converted.

Beginning with alternative church-based sales in the 1950s, SERRV gradually added new distribution channels, resulting in an increasingly complex distribution picture by the late 1990s (see Figure 4.1). Being open to partnerships in which SERRV is a key component, but not necessarily the most visible player, led to linkages with the Catholic Church and Christian Children's Fund. A recently added channel involves sales at annual national meetings of eight mainline Protestant denominations. Brian Backe assesses both the challenges and opportunities offered through such a diffused distribution system:

> It drives me crazy every day of the week in terms of the number of different markets we're in, but it does allow us, in a time of great change, to be looking at a lot of different possibilities. We're not locked in only to selling through churches. It's a variety of different marketing approaches.

Despite the challenge of developing marketing strategies for a diverse range of distribution channels, SERRV believes that the positive benefits of the model outweigh the negative. More specifically, SERRV staff conclude that the model offers them three advantages. First, by not having to pay a large number of employees, SERRV reduces overhead costs as compared to commercial craft retail counterparts. Second, SERRV's discounts to wholesale customers range from 0% for those conducting consignment sales to 20% for church distributors. Within the ATO community, these discounts provide advantages compared with other ATOs that wholesale to alternative trade retail shops, many of which command discounts as high as 50%. SERRV does, however, match the higher ATO discounts for its sales to retail stores. Finally, alternative sales through mainline churches allow SERRV to reach audiences not already knowledgeable about or yet attracted to fair trade issues. Brian Backe clarifies,

> Actually, our constituency is fairly conservative. We've got a lot of conservative people who are selling these products. The potential for them to talk with people beyond those who are already convinced about this is pretty significant. These are the wives of the bankers and the Presbyterian leaders, and that's a core base. And increasingly we're attracting very sharp, well-educated businesswomen who get it quickly. So there are some different potentials coming down the road for influencing ideas more fundamental than just the movement of crafts. People get interested in it because they like the craft and they like the story attached to it. But very quickly, we can have a different conversation about the potential for consuming in different ways.

SERRV's commitment to alternative distribution channels is dependent on a well-thought-out and successful strategy for attracting and maintaining volunteers. As the 1990s end, SERRV's volunteers are aging. Almost 60% are older than age 55, and only 3% are younger than age 35. SERRV currently faces critical decisions concerning whether to focus its attention on the maintenance of current volunteers versus recruiting new volunteers. The dilemma is outlined by Brian Backe:

> We give our volunteers a lot more stuff than they used to get such as a monthly newsletter and three new catalogs per year. We're just attracting enough new volunteers to not see that part of the pie shrinking, but it's not growing. Some would argue that the old model needs to be more intensive, requiring more of us and them. And I'm thinking, no, we need to make this very easy for someone. I say, it's not practical to do both. You've got to pick.

SERRV is currently exploring two options for volunteer recruitment. SERRV's first option, a volunteer development approach, works from the premise that SERRV can do more training and motivation within its existing core of church-based volunteers. Activities such as offering wholesale customer appreciation days, establishing producer-to-customer dialogue through letters or trips, spending more on educational materials such as videos and hangtags to tell the story, and developing a regional workshop or at-home training program call for extensive expenditure of staff resources. This strategy is based on the assumption that volunteers will commit significant time to setting up church-based sales for which they expect limited return to their parishes.

A second option, the individual representative approach, is viewed as a way of attracting new volunteers. Enhancing convenience for the wholesale representative is key to the strategy. For busy young professionals, providing them with a set of catalogs that they distribute to friends and colleagues, followed by collecting orders, may take 5 hours rather than the more than 40 hours involved in setting up a sale. The wholesale representative may repeat this activity annually or only every couple of years. Under the "rep" system, selling is quicker and easier than in the older approach. Not only is selling simpler for the SERRV representative, but it is convenient for the customer as well. SERRV's concern about convenience to the retail customer is outlined by Brian Backe:

We haven't made it easy for our retail customers. That's true of the whole ATO community. We don't have all the products people need. They have to find us. It's hard to find the stores—you may have to drive clear across town. People are too busy—they can't do three different shopping trips at one time. The convenience issue, that is terribly important.

For SERRV, the decision stands firm that alternative distribution is synonymous with alternative trade. Marketing Manager Brian Backe summarizes the tough question on the table related to the allocation of resources to volunteers: "Do we do a lot more with what we've got, or do we make it a lot easier for more people?"

Launching the Next 50 Years

Within the alternative trade movement, SERRV demonstrates in an exemplary fashion that it is possible to make hard business decisions while also continuing to raise questions about how and why alternative trade can and should occur. SERRV has developed and continues to foster an organizational culture in which business practices and philosophical questioning are continuously integrated. It is within this context that SERRV began its second 50 years of operation.

Incorporating as a Separate Nonprofit Organization

On January 1, 1999, SERRV incorporated as a nonprofit organization, independent from the Church of the Brethren. Two major reasons lie behind the decision. Foremost among these is the belief that, without a specific denominational affiliation, SERRV, as an ecumenical organization, will be able to attract new volunteers and establish additional organizational partnerships for its alternative distribution system. SERRV staff members concur that although there have been a number of very positive benefits derived from the association with the Church of the Brethren, the linkage can be a deterrent for attracting certain organizations with a more secular orientation. Possible linkages for purposes of acquiring grants from environmental or development organizations serve as examples. Director Bob Chase further elaborates that "when we go to talk to organizations like UNICEF, they're not really sure they want to talk with us."

In addition, certain issues related to Brethren organizational culture have surfaced. As part of the Church of the Brethren, SERRV follows Brethren personnel policies and work schedules. These practices do not always mesh well with SERRV's ability to conduct business. An example surfaces each year around the Thanksgiving holiday. On some of the busiest days of the year for SERRV, when shipping and receiving are at their height, Brethren policies require that employees have a work holiday. To deal with this issue, SERRV has had to hire temporary workers to keep the customer service telephones operating for taking product orders.

Finally, Church of the Brethren board members assessed that as the church declined in size and SERRV grew, there would be too much risk in owning a subsidiary that would soon be larger than the parent organization. Board members were also sympathetic to difficulties in operating a program that required different culture, personnel, and financial policies than their other programs.

Although alternative distribution and organizational culture have been central to discussions, the issue of forming a for-profit rather than nonprofit structure has not been part of the decision-making mix. Although strongly advocating a nonprofit status, Brian Backe acknowledges that being a nonprofit is not without its downside:

> From a marketing point of view, nonprofit makes some things easier. People assign some credibility to nonprofits that they don't automatically assign for-profits. Also, it holds you to a different standard. There are some downsides too. I get asked almost daily what percentage goes to the artisans and when they hear nonprofit, they want to hear 80%. I go into a long laborious explanation and in the end they go away somewhat satisfied, but never fully satisfied when we talk about 30% or 35%. Right now the terminology being adopted in the nonprofit sector is "not for profit." Our ultimate goal is not around creating profits for shareholders. It's around providing benefits to our constituencies.

Continuing to Raise Philosophical Questions

Amid an organizational culture in which hard business decisions continue to be made, SERRV also remains on the path of raising philosophical questions integral to its operations. How to better promote alternative trade, source products, and educate volunteers and customers are issues under discussion. Bob Chase describes dilemmas for promoting alternative trade to the next generation of SERRV customers:

> One part of the struggle—have we found a way to tell our message that makes sense to people today? We have this aging customer base, and they seem to find the story enticing and really get wound up in this activity. But we're having a hard time interesting young people in working with SERRV. It's difficult for us to be clear with them about what separates us from socially responsible businesses. Twenty years ago, if you wanted to buy a socially responsible gift, there weren't many options. And now there are all kinds—I go down the road to Starbucks in December and they have their CARE Christmas pack and $2 goes to CARE. And for most consumers who don't understand the fine points of fair trade versus sort of charitable giving, this seems like the same thing. That's part of the problem and we haven't quite figured out how to clarify to our consumers what the difference is.

Bob Chase clearly views ATOs as embracing a set of practices that go beyond concern for workplace conditions to embrace human empowerment, group development, and long-term business sustainability (see Figure 1.1 in Chapter 1). However, he remains challenged by describing clearly to the public how the comprehensive, systemic ATO trade approach differs from more back-end charitable contributions made by mainstream businesses.

Compared to other larger mainstream retailers, Bob Chase laments that alternative traders are faced with merchandising questions related to the nature and size of their stock:

> All of the consultants that we have had tell us, "You have way too many products." You should have far fewer products for a whole lot of reasons—focusing and marketing. Most businesses would hope to have a couple hundred products and sell a lot of each one, in which case you could afford to invest in packaging and educational materials to go along with it. And then you would try to sell those products to the 40,000 gift shops in the U.S.—there's a huge potential customer base. Well, right now our potential customer base is 2,000 to 3,000 churches and about 200 shops. And the people in the shops want to buy a huge range of products from us, but not very much of any one thing. So, we're trying to buy a hundred of this, a hundred of that. When

you're buying and marketing that low of volume, or even 500, it's not cost-effective. It's impossible. And we haven't figured out what to do about that. That's a really crucial issue for us.

In a final question, SERRV asks whether there are alternative or more effective educational programs to assist volunteers and customers in developing concern about artisans' lives and trade issues in developing countries. In searching for answers, SERRV has formed a partnership with the Center for Global Education to offer a travel program for its volunteers (see Box 4.3). Although never able to reach large numbers of individuals, SERRV hopes that face-to-face, in-country discussions among artisans and customers will lead to fundamental challenges in volunteers' thinking about artisans' lives, trade inequities, and redistribution of wealth.

BOX 4.3

Unique Travel Opportunity for SERRV Volunteers

Are you interested in an alternative travel experience that will enlarge your horizons, challenge your perceptions, and strengthen your spirit? The Center for Global Education and SERRV International are embarking on a new partnership . . . for a 2-week travel seminar that will challenge and inspire you.

Speak directly with Central Americans about their lives, their hopes, and their goals. Visit one or two SERRV artisan groups at their workplace or homes. Talk with Salvadorans who fought on both sides of their country's civil war and now together face the challenges of democratization and development. Expect intense interaction with individuals and organizations working for the betterment of the lives of their people.

Who should participate? People who care about issues of peace and justice, democracy, human rights, indigenous people and culture, spirituality, Central American history and politics, and "development" strategies.

—*Partnerships Newsletter (Christmas 1997)*

That SERRV remains dedicated to exploring new approaches for ATO-artisan collaboration was evidenced during 1998, when it and a group of collaborative sponsors committed funds to assisting Guatemalan artisan groups that had been severely affected by significantly declining sales due to the closing of another ATO, Pueblo to People, in 1997 (described in Chapter 5). At a spring workshop in Antigua, Guatemala, SERRV brought together 12 U.S. and European design and product consultants with 44 leaders of 21 artisan groups. Discussion centered on U.S. market trends and standards for quality, critique of groups' current designs, and cross-group fertilization of ideas. In particular, artisans were encouraged to give special attention to the versatility of their color palettes related to changing marketplace trends. Docey Lewis emphasized that "artisans who are prepared with color choices . . . are more likely to make a sale."

Following the workshop, Bob Chase conceptualized that information is an important commodity for the artisans when he stated, "They thirst to understand the North American and European consumer and to be informed of the trends as they develop." An artisan expressed her appreciation: "Many have come to address the human rights abuses, but few have dealt with the poverty issues and our need for marketing ideas to improve our incomes." SERRV is involved in follow-up consultations to assess the effectiveness of the workshop approach for enhancing market awareness and product design.

Considering the Past and Evaluating the Future

Across its first 50 years, SERRV's unique path provides a number of lessons applicable to the fair trade movement more broadly. Reflecting on SERRV's history, we discover the following:

Business operations

- ➢ Value of strong alliances with church constituencies for sales and for communicating about alternative trade.
- ➢ Importance of reducing and realigning staff roles in relation to changing financial resources.
- ➢ Need to continually evaluate the demographic characteristics, needs, interests, and capabilities of volunteers and to change strategies to maintain and/or expand their involvement.

Product design and producer alliances

➤ Value of taking risks in implementing new strategies for product design and development.

➤ Importance for a design consultant and ATO purchasing staff to work closely as they jointly orient each other on how a market-driven design approach and the fair trade mission can be integrated.

➤ Outcomes from selecting producer group collaborators to strengthen line development, concentrate on selected price points, and avoid overcoverage of producer groups in certain media.

Philosophical concerns

➤ Significance of SERRV's leadership in continuing to confront hard questions about ATO practices, the meaning of fair pay, worldwide distribution of wealth, and global commerce.

As SERRV continues to expand alternative distribution, implement hard business decisions, and explore philosophical questions, ongoing program evaluation will be critical for assessing outcomes. We end the chapter by posing the following questions for evaluation by SERRV and for eventual dissemination of its findings to the broader alternative trade community.

➤ How do artisans' products designed for local use change when they are encouraged to produce "adapted" products for external markets? Across time, do artisans retain a full range of indigenous aesthetic qualities (motif, color, media, etc.) in their artistic repertoire?

➤ What are the long-term social and economic impacts for artisans working within an ATO-to-artisan directed approach to product development?

➤ How do artisans use the summary reports from the New York Gift Fair? How do producers translate information about themes, colors, motifs, and materials into artisan-initiated product development?

➤ How cost-effective are product development activities in an alternative distribution environment where demand volumes for many items are low?

➤ How effective is a "rep" system for attracting a next generation of younger sales volunteers? What are their motivations for becoming involved with SERRV's alternative distribution system?

➢ What types of travel experiences or other educational opportunities challenge customers or volunteers in their thinking about artisans' lives and trade inequities?

➢ How can the energies of a downsized staff be directed to best cover the range of distribution and product development activities that SERRV desires to offer?

CHAPTER 5

PUEBLO TO PEOPLE

Balancing Politics and Business

*Pueblo was a true pioneer. Absolutely a pioneer in its efforts to work
with the urban poor, to work with the indigenous people, to introduce
their products here, to tell their story. . . . And everybody is using it now
. . . indigenous people have been romanticized and glamorized and are
very much in the forefront right now in all sorts of media marketing.
But I think Pueblo was something quite different. It was a genuine
operation which did allow for consumers here to connect directly
with people from Latin America. And to understand their lives, to
understand their culture. And those are priceless things.*

—Fran Sanders, volunteer executive
director, Pueblo to People

Pueblo to People headquarters in Houston, Texas, are buzzing with
activity in the fall of 1992. Phones ring steadily with customers ordering
Christmas gifts. In a meeting in the product development office, the
small staff sorts through samples submitted by the Latin American
artisans who hope to have their work featured in the upcoming catalog.
The work is occasionally interrupted by phone calls from Guatemala or
Honduras, where a producer needs clarification on an order or wants to
explain a shipping delay. Down the hall, catalog staff prepare editorial
commentary for the catalog that will give readers a glimpse of life in
Latin America. The writing is periodically set aside to take a phone call

from another Alternative Trade Organization (ATO) seeking how-to information and advice. The bustling office and its warehouse stacked to the ceiling with palm leaf hats and other artisan products houses a multimillion dollar catalog business that provides a retail outlet for the work of poor Latin American artisans.

Just 5 years later the phones are quiet. Customer orders have halted, and no producers in Latin America need attention since no orders are outstanding. A small staff, made up primarily of the board of directors, is clearing out file drawers and wondering what to do with photos of artisan groups and product development files outlining each group's skills and the sales success of their products. Other staff are bringing in products that remain in the large warehouse, preparing them for a sale that will close the 18-year-old business.

During October 1997, Pueblo to People (PtP) liquidated its inventory of apparel and crafts imported from Latin America and began the process of dissolving the corporation. PtP staff at least twice contemplated closing the business in the proceeding 2 years as debts mounted, but the tireless and committed staff of PtP stubbornly persevered. Ultimately, the staff was unwilling to allow 18 years of hard work and assistance to 85 worker co-ops comprising thousands of Latin America's poorest people come to an end without a fight. This chapter tells the story of Pueblo to People—an ATO uniquely positioned among other ATOs because of its intense interest in providing development opportunities and ultimately contributing to social change for the poor and politically oppressed in Latin America.

Pueblo to People's History

Dan Salcedo and Marijke Velzeboer founded PtP in 1979 when the couple was living on Lake Amatitlán in Guatemala. Dan was working as a systems planner with the United Nation's Institute for Nutrition for Central America and Panama (INCAP). Dan and Marijke were frustrated that their work in Guatemala was not directly helping those most in need. According to Dan,

> There were 200 M.D.s/Ph.D.s running around studying the balance of amino acids, and when you look at it you realize that's not why people

are malnourished. It's not for lack of gringo scientists. . . . It's for lack of food. We realized that trade was much more important than foreign aid. Every time a U.S. housewife goes to the supermarket and pulls a bunch of bananas or a can of coffee off the shelf, she puts in motion a chain of events reaching back to very poor producers, often not in their benefit [the producers may have been exploited]. But trade is the most powerful means by which the U.S. influences Central America, and we realized that, rather than ignore or reject it, we had to turn it around to work for the benefit of the dispossessed.

So Dan and Marijke began to consider other avenues of assistance they could provide, eventually coming up with the idea for PtP, a nonprofit organization focused on trade as a vehicle for helping artisans and educating North American consumers. The idea for selling the artisan crafts of Guatemalans came when Marijke came across a group of palm leaf hatmakers in a village in Quiché, Guatemala. Dan and Marijke bought 100 dozen hats, drove to Texas, and sold them at flea markets, fairs, and festivals. Sales at outdoor markets continued over the next 4 years. During their 10 years with PtP, Dan and Marijke invested $60,000 of their personal funds toward PtP's effort.

Later in 1979, with Guatemala becoming increasingly dangerous due to impending civil war, Dan and Marijke moved to Honduras and began working with producer groups there. They still traveled to Guatemala every month or two to maintain a presence in that country, but due to the civil unrest, they feared risking their family members' lives by residing in Guatemala. Work expanded to Nicaragua in 1980. Eventually, PtP ended up working with 12 Latin American countries: Bolivia, Brazil, Chile, Colombia, Costa Rica, Ecuador, El Salvador, Guatemala, Honduras, Mexico, Nicaragua, and Peru. The largest volume of products came from Guatemala.

During the first few years, PtP operated with a small staff that shared responsibilities. Dan Salcedo reminisces that it was a magical period, "characterized by chaos and creativity" and energized by "outstanding folks" who willingly accepted very low salaries to help the poor in Latin America. PtP staff made their presence known to others working in international development and in the alternative trade movement, attending conferences such as Friends of the Third World and European ATO conferences. PtP would continue as a leader, mentor, and very visible presence in the U.S. fair trade movement throughout its history.

Fast-paced change and risk taking were the norm in the early years. Employees interested in trying a new product, working with a new group, or even working in a new country were encouraged to do so, if the costs were reasonable. Dan Salcedo recalls,

> We figured out it was easier to try something out and then stop it rather than analyze it. We were constantly trying new things, new products. The broomstick bookshelves were a good example. We were teaching a group of *campesino* women to do carpentry and the first shelves were really lousy. They weren't exactly square and the pegs didn't go into the holes. . . . And we maintained that we had to stick with people in those early days, and of course the bookshelves have been a huge success.

Besides PtP's best-selling products of palm leaf hats and broomstick bookshelves, another product that became popular during PtP's early years were roasted cashews. Categories of merchandise added later included clothing and accessories, jewelry, home decor items, and musical instruments.

As PtP sales increased, Dan Salcedo realized that the organization needed more business direction. In 1983, Jimmy Pryor was hired as a general administrator to "give order to the organization." Jimmy had an M.B.A. and had worked in the international department of a large Houston bank. His philosophy toward development and politics in Latin America was compatible with the mission of PtP. Jimmy was also assigned duties for facilitating the mail-order business, which at the time had just been initiated and was very small.

PtP's mail-order business commenced in 1983 with a simple brochure featuring 16 Central American products and mailed to 5,000 people. Following the success of the initial mailing, a 16-page black-and-white catalog was produced and mailed to 25,000 potential customers the following year. The first full-color catalog, coined a *magalog* for its extensive articles and editorials, was produced in 1987. During the early 1990s, PtP maintained a catalog mailing list of more than 90,000 customers. Although sales figures were not available for each year, they continued to increase until 1989, when gross sales peaked for the 1980s at around $2.5 million. After declining a bit, PtP reached its highest sales in 1996—nearly $4 million (see Table 5.1).

TABLE 5.1 Pueblo to People (PtP) Time Line and Sales Figures

Year	Sales	Activity
1979	$ 40,000	PtP founded by Dan Salcedo and Marijke Velzeboer, who are selling palm leaf hats made by Quiché Maya Indians at festivals in the United States.
1981		Quiché hatmakers are killed.
		PtP's in-country representative in Guatemala is killed.
1983		PtP commences mail-order business with black-and-white brochure.
		Houston office adopts cooperative organizational structure.
1984	$ 531,000	Full catalog (16-page black and white) is published.
1986	$1,000,000	Houston and San Francisco retail stores are opened.
1987	$1,500,000	First full-color magalog is published (16 pages).
		Guatemala office is established.
1988	$2,100,000	
1989	$2,450,000	
1990	$2,280,000	San Francisco store is sold to Global Exchange.
1991	$2,285,000	
1992	$2,025,000	Moves to Silber Road warehouse.
1993	$1,811,000	Secured loan for $300,000 obtained from the Ecumenical Co-operative Development Society.
1994	$1,925,000	
1995	$2,417,000	
1996	$3,839,000	Ideas from design consultant are adopted—new products, higher price points, and less editorial fill the catalog.
		Outsider hired as executive director is fired 4 months later.
		Cooperative structure abandoned.
		Board of directors, including some outsiders, is elected.
1997		PtP liquidates inventory and begins process of dissolving the corporation.

Shortly after its inception, the mail-order catalog became the primary sales tool, accounting for 95% of PtP's total business; however, there were additional sources of revenue. Sales continued at flea markets and festivals. Two retail stores were opened in 1986, one in Houston and one in San Francisco. In 1990, the store in San Francisco was sold to Global Exchange, which retained PtP merchandise for the store. The Houston store remained open, not as a profitable business but more as a testing ground for new products and new producer groups. A small wholesale operation was also in place. In addition, PtP received charitable donations each year. Set up as a nonprofit organization from the start, PtP made many applications for grants over the years, but most were rejected.

Organizational Structure

From the beginning, PtP worked primarily with worker cooperatives in Latin America. Headquarters were established in Houston, Texas, but in-country offices were also maintained in El Salvador, Honduras, and Guatemala. After Jimmy Pryor's arrival at PtP, a cooperative organizational structure was implemented among the staff in Houston as well. Pryor had a love for cooperative organizations stemming from self-study and involvement in a food co-op in Austin, Texas. Under the cooperative structure, all of PtP's approximately 25 employees in Houston had equal voting rights. As told by a number of employees, consensus was required on all business decisions, and this led to lengthy meetings (5 hours was not atypical), sometimes charged with emotion. Salaries were similar across all work areas; most employees were making a modest $12,000 to $14,000 per year in 1992.

Within PtP's Houston office, the nonhierarchical management structure was a strong drawing card for its employees but also a point of contention for many. Employees describe the cooperative structure as "an ideologically compatible environment" and "a great alternative to other businesses," but many employees also wished for a leader to whom they could turn. A few changes were made in the cooperative structure during the early 1990s, when the stress of a fast-growing business was taking its toll on employees. Committees and work groups were established to deal with day-to-day decisions. However, major decisions, including hiring and firing of employees, remained at the hands of the entire group. The fast-paced changes that characterized PtP's early years slowed considerably during this period of cooperative management. This slowdown in organizational decision making contrasted markedly with the larger global marketplace with its rapidly changing retail environment that demanded business agility.

The democratic-style organization remained in place until early in 1996. As business grew and financial problems mounted, PtP's employees felt an urgent need for clear leadership, and a decision was made to hire an executive director. Jimmy Pryor and an outsider both applied for the job; the outsider was hired, and Jimmy left the organization. Shortly after Jimmy's departure, his wife, Joan Stewart, who had been a key figure in producer contact and product development, also resigned. The new executive director lasted only 4 months after PtP staff realized they had made the wrong choice; the man they had hired lacked the necessary commitment for helping solve PtP's problems. The next management team came from within PtP. Sandy Calhoun, a longtime employee who currently was in charge of the catalog, and Cathie Chilson, a relatively new addition to the producer contact staff, took a codirectorship; one of their first decisions was to replace the cooperative system with a more hierarchical organizational structure.

Shared Politics, Shared Values

From its inception, PtP was marked by a highly political focus that distinguished it from other ATOs. Along with the political emphasis came a strongly committed staff. Recalled by Dan Salcedo,

> In the early '80s, we were the only organization in the highlands of Guatemala. It was pretty hairy stuff. . . . We couldn't afford good vehicles. . . . We had an engine separate from the transmission. . . . We had a Peace Corps couple volunteer enthusiastically to spend the night with the stuff to make sure that it was OK. It was in Quiché, where it was really, really dangerous. . . . If you talk to people who were involved, they'll say those were the best years of their life.

The danger of working with Guatemalan cooperatives during this period was realized when in 1981, 23 craft producers were pulled from their huts in Guatemala and killed by Guatemalan soldiers. Outraged and saddened by the incident, PtP made its stance known to the public with a guest editorial in one of Houston's newspapers written by Monte Tidwell, then PtP's U.S. coordinator. Other incidents would bring similar reactions. In 1983, PtP's Guatemala in-country representative Celia Chet was killed. Jimmy Pryor remembers,

It scared us to death. We didn't know what they knew about us, whose names they had. [Celia] was our only link to the producers, and some of them we didn't know how to get back in touch with. The hatmakers we did, fortunately. And we were quickly able to find some other Guatemalans to pick up the work. But it did underscore that the dangers of the work were very real. And it made operations difficult in Guatemala, where we were not able to do the sort of development work that we wanted to do. We couldn't go openly to the groups and discuss the plans.

The politics of the organization were shared by those employees who followed in the founders' footsteps. PtP's employees have been highly educated persons but are generally inexperienced in their business roles. Pervading the PtP organizational culture was the employees' dedication to helping the poor in Latin America along with an anti-mainstream business, anti-government stance (see Box 5.1). The enduring philosophy is described by one employee as a "chance to address some very troubling social and cultural kinds of issues." In a letter printed in the fall 1993 catalog, Jimmy Pryor describes PtP's approach:

> I support the politics of meaning. I know there are some cynics in our midst who belittle cooperation, mutual aid and working for the common good. I invite them to spend some time at Pueblo to People. Here they could meet . . . people who find greater satisfaction in working for the good of our human community than in accumulating riches. They might meet a few people with rose-colored glasses. But mostly they would meet people whose eyes are open to environmental crisis, poverty, and cruelty. They would meet people whose minds clearly perceive the demeaned and demeaning influences of commerce, whose hearts are torn by the suffering they see. And our visitors would see these same people actively at work doing something concrete about it.

PtP's employees were strongly committed to the producers in Latin America, often making decisions in tandem with the producers. Cathie Chilson, a producer contact representative and codirector of PtP from 1996 to 1997, explains,

> I think that there was a very, perhaps unique and special relationship that was developed between the founders of Pueblo to People first and foremost, and all the subsequent staff. All the people who have worked

BOX 5.1

Pueblo to People's Political Values

When you've had all the mashed potatoes and white bread you can stand, maybe it's time for a little salsa, black beans, and handmade corn tortillas. Pueblo to People markets handicrafts from Latin America as a way of introducing the "pueblo" (people of those countries) to you—the North American consumer. Our project began not as a means of preserving indigenous cultures, nor as a way to spice-up the suffocating blandness of our overly homogenized society. It began as a project to help the desperately poor gain a foothold in their struggle to survive against the army boots of the rich—an elite made wealthy and powerful by us—our tax dollars to train their "security police" in tactics of terror and genocide. Strong language, isn't it? Will it play in Peoria? Probably not. Nor Des Moines (maybe Iowa City), nor Minneapolis, nor New York, nor Houston. In 1979, delivering up such a plateful of truth to the American public was considered, well, downright communistic—a lot of lies cooked up by Fidel Castro. But Dan Salcedo and Marijke Velzeboer had decided that merely studying the diets of the poor (as they were doing for the UN) just wasn't going to cut it. The poor already knew what was lacking in their diet— power to resist the landed elite who took the land on which they grew corn and beans to grow coffee and sugar instead, pay them $2 to work a 12-hour day, fire them when they got sick, then sell us these drugs at a handsome profit. I like espresso. Maybe you do too. But cappuccino is better—strong stuff, tempered with sweetness, and light.

Guatemalans are beautiful weavers, among the best in the world. They make great palm-leaf hats, too. "We can sell these in Houston," thought Dan and Marijke, "and make a lot of money for these people. We'll get people's attention with these fine crafts. Then we'll tell them how they're made, who made them, how they're under the gun, how we're guilty." They bought a hundred dozen hats in Quiché, Guatemala, piled them into and on top of a station wagon and drove them to Texas. They sold like hotcakes in the flea market. Young bucks and flashy lassies flush with the oil money flowing into Houston in those days snapped them up to look sharp and party with the other urban cowboys. Other craft products were soon added to the sales roster and received equal enthusiasm.

Then in January 1982, disaster struck. Two Spanish reporters sneaking around the Guatemalan countryside disguised as peasants visited a village of craft producers in Guatemala. They asked how life was under military rule. The villagers spoke their mind. On the way out of the country, the

(Continued)

BOX 5.1 (CONTINUED)

identity of the reporters was discovered. Their detailed notes pointed to the village crafts people. At 5:00 a.m. one morning, the military marched into the village, pulled 23 people from their huts and shot them in the head.

Shock, grief and guilt at Pueblo to People. Was this done because of us? Enraged, Monte Tidwell, U.S. Coordinator wrote a letter to the *Houston Post*. It was given a prominent position as a guest editorial. And he laid it out for Houston. "Thousands of these products we have sold in Houston," he said, "each one signed by the man who made it. And now they lay dead." The following weekend there was a steady stream of young bucks and flashy lassies at the flea market. They came somber, tears in their eyes. One by one they held their purchases so Monte could read the tags inside, each one signed by the man who made it, "Was this man killed?" "Was this man killed?" "Was this man killed?" All had the same question. Now Houston cared about the wretched poor, the beautiful, resourceful poor, and the war we were financing against them.

But it was too much for us. "Stop talking about it!" the craft producers said. "We've received too much publicity already." We still sell the crafts made by the poor in Guatemala. We still tell people how they're made, who makes them and how poor they are. But we don't say anything about military and the genocide. It's just too dangerous. Instead, we fill our catalog pages with messages of hope—stories about how working together democratically these same poor are building loving, caring communities—weaving a beautiful new social fabric. An inspiration to us all.

Now we sell lots of crafts and food: weavings, baskets, clothing, cashews, coffee, pottery—from eleven Latin American countries. And we still do it for the same purposes—to give the poor at the bottom of the heap a fighting chance: make money for them, strengthen their cooperatives and communicate at least some of their message to Peoria, Des Moines, Houston, Iowa City: "What's lacking in our diet is a cupful of power. We're loving, hard working, beautiful people who want to live in peace and democracy. Won't you be our friends?"

—*Jimmy Pryor, Pueblo to People, 1983-1996*
(prepared for an invited roundtable discussion on "Marketing Third World Crafts," University of Iowa, April 1994)

at Pueblo to People through the years, from shipping and customer service, producer contact . . . mainly with the buying trips that were taken . . . during those trips a tremendous connection happened. I think

I can safely say that every single person that went on a trip to Latin America with Pueblo to People . . . everyone came back feeling high about the trip, feeling very good about the work we were doing at Pueblo to People. It was rejuvenating and energizing. . . . These people are real, their lives are real, their communities are real, their struggles are real. And what we are doing makes a difference.

PtP's political orientation flavored its retail sales catalog as well. First published in 1987 and coined a *magalog* by Dan Salcedo, the part magazine/part catalog featured a mix of product offerings along with editorials and pictures aimed at educating consumers about the realities of life in Latin America. PtP's considerable editorial commentary in its catalogs provided consumers with an intimate view of producer cooperatives, the hardships of life, and the success groups were experiencing due to trade with PtP. At first, the editorials were highly critical of problems stemming from the war and the imbalance of power and wealth. Later, realizing that taking such a critical stance was putting its Guatemalan producers in danger, the staff softened their editorializing. Over the past few years, catalogs focused on themes of education, women in development, environmental concerns, and efforts toward land reform. Human rights and equality permeated the editorial commentary as a persistent theme.

Producer-Focused Business Operations

Because of its strong focus on the needs of the Latin American people, nearly all of PtP's business decisions centered on assisting the producers. PtP was very clear that it did not want to act only as a source of jobs. One of PtP's guiding principles in working with producer groups was that

> the generation of income alone is generally not a sufficient benefit for the members to justify PtP's participation. In addition we strive for these individuals to gain social and organizational skills.

This strong development-oriented culture led PtP's Houston and in-country staff to work long term with artisan groups on product development, production training, pricing, exporting, and record keeping. For example, in 1988, PtP staff and two consultants conducted a workshop for a group in Guatemala that produced clothing to teach them how to use more efficient cutting technology. An exchange program in 1991 brought two Guatemala City artisan groups together so they could share knowledge and plan for collaborative projects. Other training sessions were more impromptu.

PtP was unique among the larger ATOs in its maintenance of in-country staff in its top-producing country, Guatemala. This PtP staff person was responsible for preparing export documents, distributing orders and payment, and working with the groups on a variety of business-related activities, such as product development and quality control. Teresa Cordón, the Guatemala representative from 1987 to 1993, was well suited for the cross-cultural work that sometimes placed her in personal danger. This Guatemalan woman, who had spent several years in Southern California, was described by Ron Spector of Asociación Maya as "street smart and totally cool."

As part of her work, Teresa would conduct training in Guatemala as needed. For example, when she had to return 60 blouses to a group in Patzún because they were made of a polyester-cotton fabric rather than 100% cotton as their label indicated (a difference that would have prevented the product from passing through U.S. customs because of laws requiring clothing fiber content to be accurately labeled), Teresa showed the group how to use a burn test to determine fiber content. During her tenure with PtP, Teresa conducted a detailed price analysis, showing where money was being lost on certain products. It was sent to the Houston office but never acknowledged or implemented.

Kerry Evans, an American woman with an artistic background and experience working with a cooperative of silk growers in Colombia, joined PtP in 1993, replacing Teresa Cordón, who was retiring from PtP. Kerry continued working with the groups much as Teresa had but also used her design expertise for product development ideas. Throughout its history, PtP clothing was made from the distinctive *jaspé* fabrics[1] traditional to Guatemala. These fabrics are woven from a mix of bright colored cotton yarns that are carefully measured and dyed in intervals that create intricate patterns when woven. Realizing that the *jaspé* look was going out of style, Kerry proposed product development ideas for the fabric and styles. Numerous ideas were sent to Houston, and, as Teresa had experienced earlier, none was acknowledged by Houston staff. Although PtP was unique among ATOs by maintaining in-country staff, it may not have used the knowledge and skills of these culture brokers to the greatest extent possible.

Selection of Producer Groups

With the exception of a few groups whom Dan Salcedo and Marijke Velzeboer helped organize and train, a requirement for working with PtP was that an artisan group already be organized, preferably in a cooperative structure, and already be producing a product. PtP waited to be approached by a group rather than seeking out new producer groups with which to work. There was no shortage of groups wanting to associate with PtP. PtP's decisions to collaborate with a new artisan group were based on the products that group could make and their skills.

Production capacity was a key restraint when considering the volume of orders to place with a group; some groups had very limited production output that would create tremendous problems for PtP and its catalog customers if a product turned out to be popular. However, even when production capacity seemed adequate, problems still arose. Orders for Peruvian ceramics needed to be made 3 months earlier than orders for other types of products in other countries because the products needed sufficient drying time. A period of rain in Guatemala could slow down the entire process of dyeing yarn, which then affected weaving and sewing, causing groups to miss shipping deadlines. Occasionally, landslides and robberies interfered with the timely delivery of shipments.

An unexpectedly large order for embroidered blouses from one Guatemalan group made it necessary for the group to seek out family members and additional base fabric to complete the order. Unfortunately, the fabric the group procured was a blend of polyester and cotton, not the required 100% cotton, making shipment to the United States impossible due to labeling laws mentioned previously. Trade regulations imposed on textile products as a result of the Multi-Fiber Arrangement could also create slowdowns for receiving shipments. In Guatemala City, Teresa Cordón registered as an export broker so that she was authorized to ship products to the United States. The paperwork was tedious and sometimes required several attempts before it was done correctly. In addition, delays could occur in Houston where the products cleared U.S. customs because, again, more detailed paperwork was required. Because of quota imposed by the United States on many types of textile products from developing countries, PtP staff frequently was required to complete formal entry forms that identified the products according to the Harmonized Schedule of Tariffs, have the shipment verified, and pay duties. Several days later, by the time the proper forms were filled out and customs examined the shipment, PtP could finally pick up its shipment.

The effects of late shipments were realized when customers placed orders that included both products that were in stock along with those that were not in stock. Available products would be mailed immediately, at the customer's expense. However, the costs associated with shipping the remainder of a consumer's order when the trailing products arrived in Houston fell to PtP. Cathie Chilson reported that PtP once paid $10,000 in additional shipping costs because of just one group's late shipment of a product.

Product Development

Understanding how PtP approached product development reveals the extensive work that staff would do to realize their development goals. PtP carefully considered each group's unique skills, production limitations, and the availability of raw materials and equipment. Product development was never given a budgeted position within the organization but was done by staff in advertising and producer contact roles as their skills and time allowed. Tracy Cramer, employed with PtP from 1989 to 1995 as a producer contact representative for Honduras, spent extensive time developing food products and getting organic certification for the food-producing groups. His efforts developing products such as chocolate-covered nuts and dried fruits launched these products as top sellers for the holiday season.

Sometimes new products would be developed in Houston and a sample shipped to the producer group to re-create. Sandy Calhoun describes one committed staff person's work on product development:

> Diane Trevino was very interested in El Salvador because there was so much suffering there. A group of women who made a successful product, a stuffed parrot, wanted to break into clothing manufacturing.

So for 2 years, Diane tried to help them find marketable clothing ideas. It was very frustrating with samples and suggestions going back and forth, and very little progress. Finally they hit on a simple women's shirt cut from gauzy white cotton, which became a best-seller several years in a row. In this case, we probably recouped our product development costs.

Other times the producers were asked to submit samples. Yet, even when producers drew on their cultural traditions, product development frequently required the input of PtP staff since the Latin American producers typically did not have enough experience with their targeted North American customer to anticipate the types of products the customer would choose to buy. For example, one time PtP's product development staff sent a variety of bright and pastel colored yarns to a group in Guatemala to crochet into caps for babies. The Houston-based staff was surprised when the caps were received at their headquarters; each cap included an array of bright and pastel colored yarns rather than the separate bright caps and pastel caps that the product development staff assumed their customers would prefer.

The amount of product development performed in Houston varied by product category. Tracy Cramer and Diane Trevino worked with several Guatemalan groups to develop products using handwoven textiles, such as bags and wallets. Clothing required extensive intervention by Houston-based staff, and jewelry was designed almost entirely by the producers. Sandy Calhoun would make clothing samples periodically as the catalog production schedule allowed. However, because PtP staff was more mission-oriented and did not have extensive product development skills, the intervention and suggestions they provided may not have been most productive for the artisans.

One idea that was evident by the product offerings was the choice to develop artisan products at least somewhat based on tradition. Sandy Calhoun describes how PtP focused on traditional indigenous craft as a teaching tool:

> Traveling through Guatemala, a visitor will see different weaving patterns and colors in each village, so that every village can be identified by their weaving. The significance of weaving with being Maya cannot be discounted. So in our product development, we strove to combine the cultural reference of clothing in north and south while being respectful of each. Color, for example, carries strong life-affirming refer-

ence based on its occurrence in nature—especially flowers and birds. These references transcend mere fashion trends.

This unwritten goal caused Jimmy Pryor to question what PtP would do if it were approached by a desperately poor worker cooperative from Latin America that made plastic buckets.

Despite its involvement in product development, PtP's staff remained fearful that providing design ideas for producers would create a dependent relationship in which producers could not function without PtP's assistance. Interestingly, however, PtP almost always assumed the financial loss of unsuccessful products. In addition, merchandising decisions concerning which products to include in the catalog were sometimes made solely with the producer in mind, shielding them from the actual market conditions. As described by Sandy Calhoun, PtP would sometimes pick

> something that we bought knowing that it probably wouldn't pay for the space in the book. And we would put it on the page with something we knew would carry it, or we thought would carry it. And that was sheerly a mission-based decision, not a sound merchandising decision.

PtP also carefully considered the products included in its catalog, taking care not to drop the only product a group made because the decision would likely push the group out of business. As a result, often products remained in the catalog despite slowing sales (see Box 5.2). According to Joan Stewart, a former product development representative with PtP, the priority given to PtP's producer groups over sound business decisions "drained a lot of the organization." Joan describes the difficulties staff had making necessary changes:

> When a group wasn't managing to meet their obligations to produce good quality or their product wasn't selling well, we were very slow to change. Either come up with a new product for them or help them develop something new or no longer work with them. It was years before we ever really stopped working with anyone.

These difficulties in product development concomitantly created inventory management problems. Jimmy Pryor reported that in the early 1990s, there was probably a 10% loss in sales due to items being out of

---

BOX 5.2

Should ATOs Assume Business Risk for the Producer?

You have to recognize that the market is a tough place and if people are going to graduate from being dependent on charity or quasi-business like practices . . . they have to compete. . . . It means being hard-nosed sometimes. "The value of this product, even though it took you a long time to make it, isn't that good. You've got to accept the low price Mr. Producer, because that's all we can sell this for." Or to turn back the goods. To say, "these are not acceptable. And we're sorry, but you've got to do them over again." Those are tough lessons, but the reality is, as much as we may not like it, we are living in a market economy.

—*Doug Brunson, lender, Ecumenical Development Co-operative Society*

---

stock. In addition, unsold inventory was allowed to accumulate over several years, and much of PtP's capital was tied up in products.

Pricing Decisions

How much to pay producers was always on the minds of PtP staff who associated fair trade with fair prices (see Box 5.3). The goal was to pay as much as possible to the producers: 40 to 45 cents of each dollar spent by consumers was common. Retail prices were established with price points in mind that would make the merchandise comparable to mainstream apparel that might be purchased by a middle-income consumer; a PtP handwoven jacket sold for $67, a skirt for $38, and a men's long-sleeved shirt was priced at $40. If a product's retail price seemed too high, it would not be produced. The focus on paying producers as much as possible while maintaining certain price points provided only small margins that did not adequately cover the administrative costs of the business, particularly given the losses PtP incurred due to late shipments and product development expenses. The evidence of inadequate margins is more compelling when considering the salaries drawn by PtP employees in Houston. During 1996 to 1997, when PtP changed to a hierarchical management structure, the yearly salary for its codirectors was $14,400 to $15,600 each. In essence, PtP's staff subsidized the

BOX 5.3

What Is a Fair Price for Producers? For Consumers?

The mission is to practice fair trade, and pricing is a big part of it. Making sure that the producers participate in the decision-making as far as what they feel is fair to them. . . . There's the issue of percentage going to producers. In the last year there was a lot of discussion about what we pay the producer and have we in fact paid them too much? . . . Have we been too generous? I think we did our best to make sure we weren't being ripped off and that also the producers were getting a fair price. But in some cases we probably should have done more research . . . making sure we were pricing [a product] properly . . . and still making sure the producers are getting what they need to, in terms of covering raw materials, as well as labor, and not taking advantage of them.

—*Cathie Chilson, producer contact representative*
and codirector, 1993-1997, Pueblo to People

Fall 1996 we marked our prices up quite a lot to our customers to try and get a higher level of profitability. But it didn't really work very well. Sales slipped quite a lot.

—*Sandy Calhoun, packer, catalog director, and*
codirector, 1989-1997, Pueblo to People

workers in Latin America by personally drawing lower than market value wages in the United States.

The Forgotten Customer

Despite relatively early involvement with product development as compared with other ATOs, most of PtP's business decisions focused on producers; little time was left to give attention to the consumer. PtP did not have a clear understanding of its customer. At one time, the customer was believed to be a "solidarity" customer whose primary interest was in promoting a better life for the peasants in Latin America; marketing strategies were based on this customer profile. Yet, over the years, the needs of the solidarity customer seemed to change. The story told by PtP in its catalogs was about the poverty and suffering in war-torn Latin America. However, in the 1990s, wars ended in El Salvador and Nicaragua. Finally, in late 1996, a peace accord in Guatemala concluded the country's long-raging civil war. Media attention and, subsequently, consumer attention turned to Bosnia and other parts of the world, lessening demand for PtP's products from the solidarity customers who assumed that all was well in Central America. But PtP staff continued to support the Latin American peasants. Sandy Calhoun reflects on this paradox:

> This has so much to do with what's happening in the news—and what isn't happening in the news. And of course we assume, because there is some sort of democratization in Latin America right now, that all is well. But we know that poverty is as bad or worse than ever. . . . And it's not bad that people's attention goes to Bosnia and other places in the world where there is a lot of suffering right now. . . . But Pueblo has always worked in Latin America, so that's the story we've had to tell.

Product-wise, consumers were assumed to have the same tastes and preferences of the staff, who tended to sport a "hippie" look more indicative of the 1970s. Staff members' personal tastes and limited market exposure directed product development efforts. Only one staff person had any experience in clothing product development. Although information from consumers was collected informally on complaints and returns, and letters arrived from customers, there was never time to analyze these. However, with increasing mail-order competition, PtP realized that information on its customers was crucial if trade with Latin American craft producers was to be successful. Through experimentation with prices, PtP learned that its customers were fairly price sensitive. Sales dropped when a garment previously priced at $39 was raised to $42. We conducted a market study of PtP's customers that confirmed the importance of PtP's mission but also revealed the consumer requirements for a high-quality product (see Chapter 9).

In later efforts to address customer needs, PtP hired consultants for product development and catalog marketing ideas. Despite instincts to do otherwise, on the advice of a merchandising consultant, PtP made a number of changes in the product offerings and price points. A wider array of alpaca products was offered, including sweaters and throws that ranged in price from $150 to $350. The fashionable palazzo pant style filled the catalog. In addition, in a last-ditch effort to save the company, the editorial content of the catalog for fall and holiday 1996 was reduced to make room for more products (see Box 5.4). The efforts were unsuccessful. The products may not have been on target for the existing customers who continued to prefer the simple gray alpaca sweater that PtP had sold for years. The extent of changes seemed to go against the needs of PtP's established customer base and, in retrospect, might have been better directed to a new customer group. Yet, targeting different customers for high-price goods may have been unsuccessful as well, as it appeared by 1995 or 1996 that Guatemala, where the majority of PtP's products was made, had "gone out of style," no doubt from the saturated market in the United States for these types of products.

BOX 5.4

Using Editorials for Marketing

It was suggested to us by [a consultant] that the editorial does not sell products—but in fact it does. Because it helps the reader participate in the mission that Pueblo is trying to achieve. It really enlists their imagination in that activity.

—*Sandy Calhoun, Pueblo to People*

An Unsustainable Business

In 1997, despite achieving its highest sales ever the previous year, Pueblo to People made the decision to liquidate its inventory and dissolve the corporation. Prior to shutting down the entire organization, PtP closed its Guatemala City office. Kerry Evans, Guatemala's in-country representative at the time, expressed her sadness in a letter planned for the next PtP catalog, one that was never published:

> I feel privileged and honored to have worked with all these groups in Guatemala. I have been invited into their homes, to their weddings, and fiestas. I have seen their struggles and the harsh conditions in which they live. I have witnessed the proudness of the people and the pride

---

BOX 5.5

The Importance of Understanding ATO Failure

I think that all fair trade organizations right now are pioneers. In a sense we are stepping into new territory. And there are bound to be mistakes that are made. But I think it's so important for them to be out there because I think that this is affecting the way other businesses are thinking about doing business. But I also feel that it's important not to sweep the problems under the carpet. Honesty is the best policy—I truly believe that. I think it's a great mistake to pretend that the problems don't exist, to pretend that the model works when sometimes it doesn't. But there are always lessons to be learned in a struggle, and this is a struggle.

—*Fran Sanders, volunteer executive director, 1997, Pueblo to People*

---

they have in their work and the eagerness to learn new things. And now I see and feel the sadness in their faces as the door to the Guatemala office closes.

When the decision was finally made to close the business completely, PtP's employees grieved openly, not so much for the loss of their own jobs but for the producers in Latin America with whom they had built close relationships. Cathie Chilson expressed the feelings of many staff:

It gives me great grief to think that the many personal connections we made are going to be severed because of our closure. And I would hope that the people will be understanding.

"The people" refers to the many Latin American producers who had trusted and relied on PtP to provide an outlet for their crafts (see Box 5.5).

It is difficult to determine what factors ultimately led to PtP's demise in 1997. In retrospect, PtP's former employees pointed to many problems plaguing the organization relating to all aspects of the business, including

➤ operations (day-to-day decisions, rising costs, inexperienced staff, scope of operations in relation to available capital),

> organizational structure (confusion with being a nonprofit and a business, no outside board to oversee the business, cooperative management system),
> leadership (lack of strong leaders with good communication skills),
> mission (attention to producers over consumers and their own business viability), and
> crises (a series of multiple disruptions and setbacks).

Although PtP was aware of these problems, the staff lacked the time, money, or expertise to solve them, and all eventually took their toll.

First, the apparent growth in sales masked a truer picture of PtP's financial health that was marked by increasing costs. Increases in postage and the price of paper made producing and mailing the catalog more and more expensive over the years. Overhead greatly increased in 1992 when, in hopes of achieving further growth, PtP moved to its larger warehouse location in northwest Houston. PtP's poor financial health was well known across its staff. Even as early as 1992, every staff member interviewed reported that how PtP handled its current financial crisis would be critical for the survival of the organization.

Also during the 1990s, the general competition for mail-order sales increased dramatically. Jimmy Pryor perceived marked pressure from other catalog retailers beginning around 1992. PtP employees believed that any catalogs that arrived in their customers' mailboxes were competitors, even if the competing business did not sell the same type of product. Many referred to the beginning of PtP's mail-order history in 1983, when this type of retail sales venue was less used by other businesses and thus had provided PtP with a unique advantage.

Many of PtP's business practices were made in support of the producers and placed PtP in a high-risk situation. Paying the highest price possible to producers; not maintaining a high enough margin to cover operating expenses, including costs incurred when developing new products; absorbing the costs of shipping late-arriving products to customers; and not returning poor sellers or damaged products to producers whittled away any capital PtP might have accrued. For example, in 1990, PtP lost $35,000 when it received a shipment of moth-infested cashews. Ironically, given the many business decisions favoring the producers, at some point over the past several years of PtP's operation, it ceased paying the customary 50% upfront to the producers. Cathie

Chilson, who began work at PtP in 1993 after this practice was in place, explains the problems this causes producers:

> If you don't send any money down for them to buy raw materials, then you're putting pressure on them to scrape up the money locally to get started. . . . We got into this cycle of forcing the producers to assume a lot of debt at the beginning and wait sometimes months for payment.

Not surprisingly, the ramifications of this practice ended up hurting PtP because producers were late turning in shipments and inventory problems were created. In addition, the debt to the producers steadily rose and required PtP to take a secured loan for $300,000 in 1993. Nearly all the loan went to repaying the producers, but by 1997, the total debt to PtP's creditors had risen to nearly $500,000, with around $250,000 owed to the producers in Latin America.

Another issue that may have contributed to business closure is the scope of operations in which PtP was attempting to engage. Not only was PtP attempting to have a successful mail-order business, but it was also involved in grassroots development in 12 countries in Latin America. Given the people available and the capital to fund these operations, PtP was stretched very thin. The project was too broad for its available resources.

Having a nonprofit legal status and operating a business also seemed to confuse PtP's employees and board members. Jimmy Pryor recalls a board meeting in which one person who had been on the board for a couple of months remarked, "This looks more like a business than a nonprofit to me!" PtP had an inconsistent and unsuccessful grant-writing history. In earlier years, Dan Salcedo had some success obtaining grants but received little support from other employees and board members for doing so. Had its grant-writing efforts been better developed through the years, this aspect of being nonprofit might have supported more of the development programs with the producers. The need to charge high enough prices to cover all the organization's needs would have been alleviated and a cushion to deal with unexpected expenses and losses provided.

In addition, PtP did not make use of many of the perks of being a nonprofit, including seeking and using the help of experienced professionals on a pro bono or reduced-cost basis. Late in its second decade of operation, many volunteers were enlisted, but they primarily worked in areas such as packing and did not contribute the professional expertise most needed by PtP. Finally, fearful of outsiders' interference with their work, when a board was finally elected in 1995, it was stacked in such a way as to ensure employee control rather than to gain knowledge and experience from outside board members who might have lent a more objective perspective to PtP's business challenges.

Also related to the insufficient margins generated on the business side of the organization and limited fund-raising on the nonprofit side was the lack of investment in infrastructure and human resources. PtP never had capital to invest in the equipment that would make it more efficient. Probably most illustrative of this was its antiquated computer system that used proprietary software that few employees really understood. Catastrophe hit in July 1997, when its computers failed and PtP's operations halted. In addition, PtP's policies on staff salaries may have ultimately damaged the business. With such low salaries, PtP was unable to attract the needed expertise in areas such as product development, merchandising, and accounting. As such, PtP made mistakes that a more experienced staff may have been able to avoid. PtP realized its needs, especially after having student interns in merchandising and catalog operations. Cathie Chilson was inspired, stating that "to actually have someone who had studied it [merchandising] and could combine the theory with the practice is a lovely match."

At least some blame was also placed on PtP's cooperative organizational structure. The democratic processes used to arrive at business decisions resulted in lengthy meetings that ate up valuable time of an already lean staff. In addition, achieving consensus on business decisions was too slow and inefficient for a growing business in an increasingly competitive environment. Staff could not be fired without approval of all the members of the organization; thus, sometimes employees who did not have the needed expertise for their jobs remained in their positions. Furthermore, at least some employees and board members felt that not all major decisions were put on the table for discussion and decisions by the group as they should have been. The slow business decisions made by PtP became more notable during the latter half of the 1980s and early 1990s when mainstream apparel and related industries were focusing on speedy decisions and quick response. Ultimately, too much time and energy may have been directed toward the organizational structure itself, rather than the day-to-day business decisions. Eventually, many business decisions were turned over to subcommittees.

Leadership was also a weak point in the organization, and the issue was magnified by the cooperative organizational structure. Although a host of decisions were made by the group as a whole, Jimmy Pryor and Joan Stewart maintained control over many aspects of the business. Jimmy admits that the organization acted more like a "loose hierarchy with a lot of collegiality" and that he and Joan ended up having much responsibility for decision making due to the knowledge gained from working with the organization for so long. Many employees concurred, saying that Jimmy and Joan were essentially in charge. Jimmy seemed to want a cooperative structure with exceptions in which those who had been involved only a short time would not have voting rights.

Communication within the organization was volatile. Even though many perceived Jimmy Pryor and Joan Stewart to be in charge, the cooperative structure did not legitimize this power. One employee suggested that the organization maintained "an internal power struggle that was made more difficult by not having a clear boss." In addition, Jimmy and Joan's communication styles were not always effective for building rapport across the organization and convincing others that their ideas were best. Some employees report that the pair were unlikely to listen to others' ideas. Jimmy admits that, although he had hoped for a group of more equally committed people who would take more initiative in business decisions, his style of communication and leadership probably discouraged this. Because of the democratic style, single individuals could disrupt and virtually halt decision making. Nearly all employees recalled very difficult meetings, saying that some individuals, who adopted defensive stances or took things personally, could get the group charged up and create disharmony throughout the organization. However, most employees seemed to take the volatile and blunt communication style in stride. Nearly everyone interviewed in 1992 reported enjoying the congenial group of people with whom they worked.

Interestingly, although Jimmy Pryor was known for generously sharing ideas and information with the larger ATO community, he seemed unwilling in turn to accept assistance and advice offered by outsiders. For example, when Jimmy expressed interest in developing a Web site, Dan Salcedo, who had founded PtP but since left the organization and was very involved in the creation of these sites, offered to create one for free for PtP. Instead of accepting the offer, Jimmy hired an outside consultant to create the site, paying $2,000 for the work. Another example of the insular work environment Jimmy created within PtP is that of having a board of directors primarily made up of staff.

Despite the internal communication issues, however, staff were very well informed of PtP's mission and organizational problems. Everyone interviewed in 1992, from Jimmy Pryor to a shipping clerk and a customer service operator, could easily verbalize PtP's mission. In addition, when asked about the greatest challenge facing PtP, all reported that the financial health of the organization was by far the most significant obstacle facing PtP.

The mission to work with the poorest of the poor also may have contributed to PtP's inability to sustain business over the long term. Risks were high, especially given the large amounts of money invested in inventory each year and the commitments made for long-term relationships with untested producer groups. PtP was never certain that it would have the merchandise when it needed it or whether it would be the right merchandise for the needs of the consumer, which were not clearly known.

Finally, PtP faced multiple disruptions over the past several years—ones that a tired and struggling organization had little resources to fight. Major organizational changes saw the departure of two longtime employees, Jimmy Pryor and Joan Stewart, and the arrival of an executive director who ultimately offered little assistance and was fired 4 months later. In addition, a volunteer who had just begun to provide significant help in finance and accounting was killed in an automobile accident in 1996. Sandy Calhoun, coexecutive director at the time, was stricken with a brain tumor requiring surgery in 1996. Much time was also spent in 1996 dealing with the Internal Revenue Service's audit of PtP's nonprofit status. Fran Sanders, a volunteer executive director who joined PtP in April 1997, arrived too late to help the organization that "needed everything." After 18 years of tireless support and struggle for the Latin American producers, PtP was financially drained and too tired to continue.

Conclusions

PtP became unsustainable. Yet despite this, its history of achievement and leadership in fair trade cannot be overlooked. Every year, many businesses are started and many fail. Yet, over an 18-year period marked by economic highs and lows, PtP sent an estimated $9 million to Latin America. Numerous individuals, families, and producer groups directly benefited from the organization's help, the outlet PtP provided for its products, and the experience it gained from working as a group. Children who were born and grew up during the 18-year period attained better education and ultimately have more choices in their adult lives. As expressed by Sandy Calhoun,

> I do believe we've fulfilled our mission. I think poverty has been attacked at the root in a lot of communities in Latin America where we've been active. And also empowering women has been another very important thing that we've seen happen as a result of our work. And that's very important. Because one woman understanding her meaning in her family first, and then her community, can be a very powerful thing.

In concurrence, Sister Catherine, a nun working with a group of widows in the Tejidos Guadelupe group, stated that PtP was "there when we needed them most." She went on to describe how the women were pursuing other entrepreneurial activities to support themselves and their families since PtP no longer offered an outlet for their products.

During PtP's 18 years, founder Dan Salcedo and employees Jimmy Pryor, Joan Stewart, and Sandy Calhoun also provided leadership to other ATOs and contributed to the formation of the Fair Trade Federation. Staff from PtP were highly visible at conferences of the Fair Trade Federation, hosting workshops on catalog retailing, among other things. As Pushpika Freitas, founder of MarketPlace: Handwork of India, shares,

> For me, PtP was like a role model. When I started, I had zero experience. I would call Jimmy and say, "I don't know what to do about. . . . How are you dealing with this?" Jimmy shared helpful information on how to carry out the nitty gritty of the business. The kind of information you can't read in a book. Like how to evaluate a list, not only the response rate to the list, but also the income per book mailed. Jimmy had a lot of good ideas and he always took the time [to help].

PtP's success also supports the idea of alternative trade as a means of aiding in the development of those countries in need. The opportunities

PtP gave producers to tap the rich North American market shows the value of a system of alternative trade.

In addition, through its magalog, PtP taught many North American consumers about life in Latin America for the poorest of the poor. PtP's editorials provided a means for consumers to make connections across cultures and understand the ramifications of current events in Latin America. In a letter published in a PtP catalog, one customer writes,

> Although our backgrounds and cultures are so different, from the artisans, to the volunteers, to the consumers, we each provide something of value which we hope will enrich the lives of the others and bring us closer together. As I work in my kitchen and use my beautiful napkins, table coverings, and potholders, I often think with admiration and fondness of the women who wove them for me. I realize we are all threads woven into the same colorful piece of work and the more threads there are, the stronger the piece. My corner expands as I share with my friends and family not only the well-made attractive and unique items, but also the philosophy of cooperation.

Finally, PtP's leadership almost certainly had some impact on the business world's move toward social responsibility, although how much cannot be measured. As an early entrant into catalog retailing in 1987, PtP's catalog provided a visible example to other retailers on how business could be conducted in a socially responsible manner. Jimmy Pryor believes that PtP had a voice in the increased consciousness many businesses have assumed toward their employees by suggesting other ways for conducting business. Sandy Calhoun assesses that PtP's influence is something its employees had valued:

> This was a trend that I think Pueblo had a chance to help influence. And we tried very hard. And with a slick catalog you can get somewhere— into people's imagination. It was money well spent, truly. A lot of money!

Insights for Alternative Trade

The Pueblo to People case study provides a thorough analysis of the operations and management of a failed ATO. As such, it provides insights for the greater community of ATOs striving to sustain their businesses. In particular, PtP's example points to the following:

Operations

> ➤ The need to maintain tight financial control and quickly eliminate debt.
> ➤ The importance of hiring skilled professionals who not only provide direction on product development and other business activities but also weigh these suggestions with insights gained through business experience in alternative trade.
> ➤ The need to balance the financial health of the organization with support for artisan groups, realizing that providing temporary risk reduction may damage the ATO's own sustainability.
> ➤ The importance of maintaining a flexible and adaptable organization able to make quick changes to stay abreast of the prevailing market environment.
> ➤ The need to balance the scope of operations to the available capital and human resources.
> ➤ The importance of not imposing employees' product preferences on potential customers.

Organizational structure

> ➤ The need for maintaining an organizational structure that facilitates effective operations, rather than one that impedes efficient business operations.
> ➤ The importance of clearly understanding and making the most of nonprofit status.
> ➤ The value of having a clear leader with good communication skills.
> ➤ The importance of strategically building and using an outside board of directors.

Note

1. *Jaspé* fabrics are produced from yarns that have been resist dyed. Prior to dyeing, long hanks of white or brightly colored yarn are wrapped with plastic strips in intermittent sections along the yarn's length. When dyed, the wrapped sections "resist" the dye and retain their brilliant color, and the nonwrapped sections take on the dark blue or black dyes. As the yarns are woven into fabric, geometric and figurative motifs emerge from the carefully planned resist patterning.

CHAPTER 6

MARKETPLACE:
HANDWORK OF INDIA

"Soaring With Strong Wings"

*Late one evening a woman came over to my house and said,
"Pushpika, can I leave this stove with you because my husband
is drunk and he's going to sell it and I'll never be able to have enough
money to buy a new one, so can you keep it for me for a couple of
days?" That was when it hit me that women had so little control
over their lives. A woman is defined by her relationship to a man. And
although she may be the sole breadwinner in the family, she still has
no decision-making power to say that their daughter should go to school or
how many children they should have, nothing. It just didn't seem fair.*

—Pushpika Freitas, founder of MarketPlace

The setting is the Golibar slum of Mumbai (Bombay), India, in the
early 1980s. Densely packed, 10-foot by 10-foot, one-room homes line the
narrow dirt lanes where children play and pungent odors permeate the
air. One by one, women quietly share their stories of helplessness with
Pushpika Freitas, a young social worker who resides near the slum's
edge. Some have been abandoned by their husbands or are widows with
little status in Indian society. Others live in abusive relationships; for
many, their husbands are unemployed. That women find themselves in
situations over which they have so little control is alien to Pushpika; her
parents have reared their family of six Freitas daughters to feel a strong

143

sense of self-worth and to assume responsibility for their lives. As a social worker in a leprosy rehabilitation program, Pushpika soon finds herself deeply drawn to the women as they tell about their lives of physical and mental hardship, lack of self-respect, and desperate need for income to support their families. Pushpika remembers, "What I decided then was at least I could try to do something about the economic part of it. Maybe that would lead to other things."

Moving ahead to the spring of 1996, Pushpika sits with a group of eight women artisans on the floor of the Mumbai offices for MarketPlace: Handwork of India, the dynamic business that has evolved from the slum dwellers' early pleas. With great pride, the women show Pushpika a series of small fabric squares they embroidered to send to U.S. customers who wrote a letter to them as part of the Global Dialogue program. When asked to describe the symbolism of six in-flight birds depicted on one fabric square, a woman quickly responds, "We're the birds soaring with strong wings."

The story of MarketPlace: Handwork of India chronicles a fair trade business from its inception among artisans with intense feelings of hopelessness to an organization that today fosters artisan empowerment expressed in "soaring with strong wings." Central to the story is a flexible organizational culture supportive of innovation and open to change. With ever-present energy, Pushpika, staff, and artisans chart new territory as they repeatedly explore now models for how to organize and run a business in a socially responsible manner.

MarketPlace: From Mumbai, India, to Evanston, Illinois

MarketPlace: Handwork of India grew from roots in a modest sewing project initiated by Pushpika Freitas, Lalita Monteiro, and three women in the Mumbai slum of Golibar (see Table 6.1). Then, as now, empowerment of women and physically challenged individuals through raising their self-esteem, dignity, and self-sufficiency was a driving goal. Initial work focused on patchwork quilts, an endeavor appropriate to the women's resources and skills. Little capital investment was required; tailors and mills donated scrap fabrics. Given the

TABLE 6.1 MarketPlace Time Line and Sales Figures

Year	Sales	Activity
1980s		Initiates leprosy rehabilitation project in Golibar slum.
		Begins to focus on women's needs—leading to sewing projects. Project generates limited local sales.
1986		Founds MarketPlace as a not-for-profit organization.
1986-1988		Ships products to the United States and sells in Evanston, Illinois, area through home parties.
1988-1990		Initiates wholesale trade to retail specialty stores through participation in the Chicago Apparel Show.
1989	$ 49,000	Develops proposal for funding the first catalog.
1990	$ 149,000	First catalog mailed in fall.
1991	$ 215,000	
1992	$ 490,000	Begins participation in New York Boutique Show to expand wholesale market.
		Adds line of interiors products.
		Initiates "Global Dialogue" catalog section to encourage communication between artisans and catalog customers.
1993	$ 575,695	Initiates line of children's apparel.
		Begins Child Sponsorship Program for catalog customers to provide funds for assisting artisans in educating their children.
1994	$ 687,908	Expands catalog size (24 to 32 pages).
		Initiates theme format for each catalog issue.
		Begins participation in California Gift Show.
1995	$ 890,270	Discontinues children's apparel.
1996	$ 974,262	Adds line of packaged Indian meals, including spices, serving pieces, and recipes.
		Adds clothing "basics" produced by Southwest Creations Collaborative in Albuquerque, New Mexico.
		Adds XL sizing.
1997	$1,217,371	Begins participation in Las Vegas "Magic" Apparel Trade Show.

women's urgent need for income to support their families, lengthy training was neither feasible nor practical. Rather, the women's well-honed, handsewing skills provided an immediate opportunity for work. While working at home where they could look after their children, the women refined their skills, and production commenced. The sewing project grew quickly as the women's neighbors observed their work, inquired how much they were paid, and asked to join the group.

A limited domestic market for the quilts and mounting inventory prompted Pushpika to reflect, "We made these beautiful quilts and the reviews were excellent. The color combinations were really great and the quality was good, but we didn't sell much. That was my first lesson in marketing. You've got to look at the market and see what the customer wants to buy." Stepping back and observing that Indian people often wear their wealth in beautiful clothes and expensive jewelry, the women transferred their sewing skills to a line of traditional Indian clothing. The apparel, priced to pay the artisans a fair wage, again met with limited success, as competition was stiff from lower-priced, more finely sewn alternatives.

As with many small businesses during their start-up phases, MarketPlace took advantage of opportunities as they arose and tried various business approaches before finding ones that worked best for it. After observing domestic and international markets, production was refocused to the export of women's apparel emanating from Indian textile and design traditions. Returning in the mid-1980s to the Chicago suburb of Evanston, Illinois, where she had earlier earned a master's degree in sociology, Pushpika initially marketed the clothing at house parties where she found enthusiastic customers for the bold prints and distinctive embroidery. Likewise, wholesale customers at the Chicago Apparel Mart reacted positively as they placed orders for their retail specialty stores. These early customers served as a ready source for market research on product design and quality preferences among U.S. customers.

Growing customer demand and the impending need to establish nonprofit status for the business in the United States soon forced Pushpika and colleagues to carefully consider how the organization could be more formally structured to ensure that the primary focus remained on artisan empowerment. Officially founded in 1986 with a two-part structure, MarketPlace: Handwork of India is the U.S.-based marketing arm located in Evanston. In contrast, products are designed and produced in Mumbai at SHARE (Support the Handicapped's Rehabilitation Effort), which is the social conscience and development side of the organization. In 1996, the Mumbai organizational structure was further reorganized. A new MarketPlace Mumbai unit focuses on design and production. SHARE now oversees the many social work programs that have evolved for MarketPlace artisans and provides technical assistance in management, finance, and production.

Catalog Development

In the late 1980s, additional avenues for marketing MarketPlace clothing were sought. However, Pushpika met with repeated roadblocks from funders when trying to initiate what was eventually to become the visually distinctive and highly innovative MarketPlace catalog. Yet, attracting foundation funding was essential for launching the costly and potentially risky catalog. Pushpika describes potential funders' responses to her catalog proposal:

> Most of the foundations thought that the project was very innovative and loved the idea but they said, "We can only give you the money for training and product development in India. We cannot give you the money in the United States for marketing." By that time I had realized that if money was not invested in marketing, all the training and product development would be of no use. Many of the organizations I know, SHARE included, had trained artisans and had piles and piles of unsold inventory. If the last step of the process, namely marketing, was not developed, all the money was tied up in inventory. The foundations saw this but for some reason *marketing* was a dirty word.

Undaunted, Pushpika forged ahead by drawing together a group of energetic, like-minded individuals with creative ideas and wide-ranging expertise. Together, the group collaborated on the first catalog, which appeared in fall 1990. Funding from Catholic Relief Services in Chicago cushioned the first 2 years of catalog operations. Jane Brunette, a Chicago graphic artist with design layout expertise, expressed interest in the organization's artisan-related mission and provided her services for little or nothing for the first few years. A photographer was located in a similar manner. Finally, in a practice of open and frequent communication common among Alternative Trade Organization (ATO) leaders, Jimmy Pryor, director of Pueblo to People; Marty Paule, former owner of DEVA; and Paul Freinluch, founder of Co-op America, provided valuable information regarding mailing lists, catalog production, and evaluation indicators. The threefold increase in sales from 1989 to the catalog's launching in 1990 provided immense promise for catalog marketing to U.S. customers (see Table 6.1).

The promise was confirmed as sales continued to grow; the catalog was enlarged from its single, 18" × 27" foldout page to a 32-page 8.5" × 11" format; mailings were expanded to two per year, and new lines of interior products, children's apparel, and foodstuffs were added (see Table 6.1). Wholesale customers also increased, with more than 150 specialty stores offering the MarketPlace apparel line to their retail customers by 1997. To avoid oversaturation of the market, new wholesale customers were not accepted if a previous customer existed in the same ZIP code area.

Distinctive Focus on Clothing

Among ATOs, MarketPlace is unique for its almost exclusive focus on clothing. Across time, the signature MarketPlace "look" evolved with its strong ethnic but not uniquely Indian appearance. Fabric prints are bold, intensely colored, and visually exciting. Two to four prints are configured in a patchwork format on the fronts and backs of many vests and jackets. Embroidered surface embellishment follows the lines of fabric motifs for ease of application by artisans. Although visually striking and sometimes complicated in appearance, embellishments remain simple so that new artisans can learn the techniques in a day. Maintaining an embroidery-intense clothing line is central to the MarketPlace mission. A product development formula of providing employment to three embroiderers for each sewer gives work to a maximum number of artisans.

The standard garment styles, modeled on Indian and Western vest, shirt, jacket, and pant styles, vary little from season to season. In contrast, fabric prints, colorways, and embroidery applications undergo nearly continuous innovation. Although other ATOs eschew clothing due to sizing difficulties, MarketPlace tackles the sizing issue by offering clothing designs intended to fit loosely on bodies, small and large. Pushpika explains more fully the decision to go with clothing:

> When MarketPlace was started, the most frequent advice we were given was, "Don't try to import cotton clothes." But most women in India are comfortable with sewing and embroidery. So clothing it had

to be. MarketPlace has always been driven by the needs and abilities of artisans. We plan our orders to accommodate the production capacity of the artisans, facilitating their growth with larger orders and more complicated garment designs as skills increase. We do not regret our decision to produce apparel as a means to economic development . . . our eyes are always on the needs of the artisans.

Supportive Workplace

From its inception as a very tiny operation, the business grew to provide employment for more than 450 artisans, primarily women. Many of the women earn four times the income of a household servant, one of their only income occupational alternatives in India. In both India and the United States, creating a nonexploitive, supportive business environment in which women of different religions, ethnicities, and ages can gain energy and learn to work together is an underlying objective. In Mumbai, women of Hindu, Muslim, and Christian faiths sew and embroider together, many talking with each other for the first time. Commonalities among the women emerge during animated discussions of early marriages, dashed hopes for education, and difficult home lives. Yet, their hardships are overshadowed by the artisans' hopes and dreams for their children. Empowerment is reflected through women's expressions of heightened self-esteem and dignity (see Box 6.1).

Box 6.1

Expressing Self-Esteem and Dignity

What I value most is the fact that I have confidence in myself. I come to meetings at SHARE and everyone listens to what I have to say and I feel important. I have never felt like this before. And I see that other people in my life also respect me more. I have changed. I have new friends. I hear new ideas and think about them. It is very exciting.

—*Mehrunisa, MarketPlace artisan*
(spring/summer 1995 MarketPlace catalog)

The Evanston office finds a multiethnic group of employees overseeing day-to-day operations, taking catalog orders, and preparing boxes for shipment. Several are young, single mothers managing dual responsibilities of work and family. Finally, the global community of artisans and consumers is vibrantly portrayed in catalog pictorial content and narrative. Women of African, Asian, Hispanic, and European descent, young and middle-aged alike, model MarketPlace apparel in active poses of interaction and vibrancy. Sometimes Evanston staff members serve as models so that customers are introduced to the "real people" in customer service who answer phones and fill orders. On interior pages, artisans share their stories of daily life and their hopes for the future.

Values of creativity and innovation, goals of artisan empowerment, and normative behaviors supportive of organizational self-analysis and change permeate MarketPlace business culture. These values, goals, and behaviors undergird MarketPlace organizational thinking and response as it addresses a variety of issues related to (a) indigenous skills and aesthetics, (b) organizational decentralization, (c) design and product development, (d) artisan-customer dialogue, (e) volunteer involvement, and (f) leadership transition. Across all functional areas, ongoing experimentation with new models for meeting organizational goals pervades and animates day-to-day discussions. Although some programs grew and expanded, other approaches were phased out or replaced.

Indigenous Skills and Aesthetics

Use of locally available raw materials and application of simple technology have long been a hallmark of MarketPlace production. For apparel, Indian traditions of fabric dyeing and block printing serve as the foundation from which new products evolve. Women's and girls' long-standing practice of recycling clothing for younger family members and of using patchwork to sew household bedding filled with old sarees as batting serves as a second source for product inspiration. Third, the learning of embroidery and other sewing skills is an integral part of girls' formal and nonformal education and provides a resource for income generation, or at least income saving, later in life. Finally, the garments are based on traditional Indian garment styles for pants, vest, and jackets. Pushpika elaborates,

Partly what I wanted to do was to produce or design clothes that didn't alienate the producer. So what we've done is take traditional garments and change them around. Like the pants are very traditional but we put pockets in the pants. In India nobody wears their shirt inside or short [for pockets]. The shirt is always long. But here [the United States], people would wear them short, so pockets make a good addition.

Not content to limit product development to these traditions, MarketPlace continues, within an organizational culture of experimentation, to explore additional raw materials and indigenous technologies for their potential contribution to the ever-dynamic MarketPlace family of products (see Box 6.2). As examples, during the intense activities surrounding a 1996 design workshop in the city of Bhavnagar, India, product development for jute shoulder bags and table mats was under way. Yarns were unraveled from worn or damaged jute bags that are commonly employed for shipping and storage throughout India. The yarns were then redyed in vibrant fashion colors and crocheted into a variety of bag designs. In a second example, a line of bead-embellished products, such as votive candle holders and necklaces, was taking shape from buckets of old beads. The beads had been recycled from discarded decorative objects that could not be salvaged as household decor in Gujarath. Finally, wood and metal recycled from old ships and sold by the ton in Bhavnagar formed the raw materials for new jewelry and decorative housewares.

BOX 6.2

Recycling in India

Nothing, and I really mean nothing, is thrown out in India. Newspapers are made into bags, and these bags are used to pack fruits and vegetables at the local markets. Old bottles are sold, never thrown out. Old vessels that have holes and can no longer be used for cooking are recycled. In rural areas, where firewood is used for cooking, the ashes are used to wash the cooking utensils and the coir in the coconut is used to scrub the utensils. When I visit India, I always take back sturdy plastic bags because I know they will be used for many, many years.

—*Pushpika Freitas, MarketPlace founder*
(fall/winter 1996 MarketPlace catalog)

The commitment to use locally available raw materials and technologies is not, however, without its challenges, as witnessed in the monsoon seasons of 1993 and 1994. Summer rains arrived late, were heavy in intensity, and contributed to extensive flooding. In the region of Kutch, fabrics could be dyed but not dried. Thus, a bottleneck ensued that led to late delivery of the next season's line of apparel in Evanston. Some of the fabrics, although they eventually did arrive in Mumbai, were still sitting on warehouse shelves in 1996.

What followed from the monsoon seasons illustrates MarketPlace's commitment to use or recycle fabric made by the producers so that they do not have to undertake the entire financial burden of problems such as natural calamities and late deliveries. Rather, the responsibility is on both parties to ensure the financial viability of their businesses. The producers put in additional labor, and MarketPlace uses product development to rework the fabric into a product that will sell. For the 1993 and 1994 monsoon seasons, artisans' indigenous dyeing knowledge came to the rescue as they applied a series of overdyeings of one color on top of another to create new looks for the old fabrics. Overdyeing builds on the long-used household tradition of "tea dyeing," in which a strong tea infusion is used to tone down garish colorations in Indian textiles. A collaborative global community emerged as the artisans in India, the customers in the United States, and the staff in Mumbai and Evanston dealt with challenges stemming from the monsoons of 1993 and 1994. Pushpika testifies,

> The fabric producers worked hard to get their lives together after the rains and produced the fabric as quickly as possible. The artisans at SHARE had to make up for lost time and found creative ways to complete production. The administrative staff at SHARE had to develop many systems to track a very complex production plan. On this side, the staff at MarketPlace had the difficult task of informing customers of the late delivery, and their jobs doubled because communication with India was not always possible. Last but not least, most of the customers were remarkably understanding about these problems in particular and problems we face in running a socially conscious organization in general.

A letter from Megan Yeary, a customer in Yachats, Oregon, voices this understanding:

> You just *can't* let it not work, Pushpika! Too many people depend on
> MarketPlace—both our sisters in India and customers like me. Over
> 75% of the clothes I wear are from MarketPlace. I have probably spent
> nearly $2,000 in the past three years on your products and I'll likely
> spend another $2,000—but only if there is a MarketPlace to buy from.
> *Please* hang in there and stick with it.

Acting on its position of fostering artisan dignity, MarketPlace
strives to produce clothing that customers buy because of high quality
and distinctive styling, rather than out of charity. Pushpika turns to her
roots in India in describing this contention:

> We have put a lot of emphasis on design and quality. Coming from India
> myself, I am insulted when people buy something only because it helps
> an artisan. That kind of compassion insults the artisan. I wanted people
> to buy from MarketPlace because they liked and wanted the product.
> The fact that it helped the artisan was like the icing on the cake. Hence,
> the determination to do everything as professionally as possible be-
> cause the dignity of the artisan is the most important.

From a cultural perspective, establishing quality standards acceptable to the U.S. market has not always been easy. In addition, garment
sizing has presented special cultural challenges. The idea that each size
12 shirt of a particular style should be cut exactly the same as all other
size 12 shirts in that style was a difficult concept to grasp in a society
where individuals customarily go to tailors for individualized sewing
and fit. In addition, the fact that several one-meter tape measures sold in
the local market can vary as much as 2 to 3 centimeters in length adds to
challenges when several supervisors prepare cardboard patterns for the
clothing. Working with artisans to correct mistakes and improve quality
calls for special sensitivity in a society not accustomed to giving bad
news. When artisans were reluctant to communicate with Pushpika by
mail concerning production difficulties, one artisan explained, "We only
write and receive letters when someone dies, and we didn't want you to
be upset when you first see our letter."

MarketPlace exports its products using a "handicraft" classification
for international trade. Under these conditions, apparel styles must be
patterned after traditional Indian clothing styles. In addition, certain
garment features are closely regulated. For example, drawstring waist-
lines are acceptable; the use of elastic, zippers, or Velcro is not. Although

at one point in its earlier history, MarketPlace investigated the process of acquiring an export quota (government allotment of garments allowable for export in a year) to broaden its product designs, it made the decision to not become involved. Once a quota is achieved, failure to deliver the specified quantity within a specified time frame can have serious consequences for maintaining the export privilege in ensuing years.

For a business such as MarketPlace, working with an export quota would challenge MarketPlace's commitment to indigenous modes of production. Its work with materials and technologies easily interrupted by natural disasters, such as monsoons, could easily conflict with the need for timely deliveries of specified volume demanded under quota shipping. Overall, dealing in the quota system would place an additional burden on the whole business. Instead, MarketPlace chooses to place extra effort at the design stage in continuing to develop products that classify as handicrafts. MarketPlace believes this approach gives it more control over its business. Because it has done well under the system it uses, MarketPlace has not felt the need to investigate the quota system further because it is very hesitant about turning over to the government a portion of control of MarketPlace business. However, new opportunities may exist for MarketPlace to expand its styling as the Multi-Fiber Arrangement, with its system for restricting trade through quota, is phased out early in the 21st century.

Organizational Decentralization

Across time, MarketPlace progressed from a centralized organization in the 1980s to a decentralized organizational structure by 1996. Initially, although embroidery was carried out in artisans' homes, much of the cutting and sewing occurred at an intensely busy, central workshop near the edge of the Golibar slum. Inspection and packing took place on a mezzanine level of the large workroom. The centralized workshop served a number of important functions in MarketPlace's evolution, including establishing a unified and inspiring organizational identity, developing standards for product quality, working with cash flow, and establishing timely delivery.

The early stages of any company are characterized by repeated problem solving. For MarketPlace, each time a challenge emerged, Pushpika explained that they followed the Indian cultural practice of designating a supervisor to oversee the problem area. Soon, MarketPlace had 14 to 15 salaried supervisors overseeing subareas such as cutting, embroidery, sewing, shipping, inspection, and packaging. Each supervisor attempted to carve out a position of control, which led to competition and dissatisfaction. Slowly, a top-heavy organizational structure had emerged that had lost sight of the mission of assisting artisans at grassroots levels. A new organizational structure was in order that would take the artisans to the next step toward self-sufficiency.

During a period of transition in 1994, four working committees were formed to encourage greater artisan participation in quality control, production planning, individual and group performance evaluation, and social development. This step was intended to assist artisans making the progression from viewing the organization as one that met their individual needs to a broader view of the group's role in achieving self-sufficiency.

Full decentralization was completed in 1996 with the formation of 11 groups ranging in size from 20 to 80 members. Four groups print fabric, and 7 groups cut, sew, and embroider garments. For sewing, 6 to 10 sewing machines are housed in a leader's home; in other cases, women who own their own machines sew at home. In contrast to sewing, all embroidery and patchwork are done in the women's individual homes. For Muslim women, working at home follows religious practices of female seclusion; for all women, embroidery fits in and around their many household chores.

Two organizational models for small producer groups are in place. In one model, groups are financed and led by single individuals (all men), and in the other, groups are organized around a cooperative structure (more common for women). For all groups, the risk-taking challenges of running their own businesses have not been easy; however, the aim is for each group to independently control its decision making and production.

Irrespective of the organizational model, several problematic issues arose during the first early months of structural change. First, when working at the large centralized workplace, group members had become accustomed to receiving orders of sufficient magnitude for steady income generation across each month and over the production seasons. As necessary, SHARE subsidized the artisans when work was inconsistent. Artisans acquired little entrepreneurial spirit or skill for broadening a group's market base or for planning for continuous production through-out a year. With the new decentralized structure, MarketPlace does not guarantee each group consistent work. Yet, workers seem reluctant to attract new clients in local apparel markets, such as those in need of school uniforms. Income from sewing products for the local market does not match that offered by MarketPlace. Commitment by MarketPlace to principles of fair trade through higher wages has, in this case, fostered reluctance among artisans to develop a diversified market composed of both local and international clients. Instead, groups appear to be in a watch-and-wait mode for the next MarketPlace order to appear, which in the long run leads to dependency on MarketPlace.

A second potentially problematic issue relates to gendered patterns of work. Under the new organizational structure, group leaders meet together to review product samples and distribute MarketPlace orders. They must then procure the fabrics and other materials for production under their own business labels. Acquiring fabric involves exten-sive travel both within Mumbai and outside of the city to the fabric-producing regions in Gujarath, a day's train travel to the north. For women, being away from their households is difficult because they have daily responsibilities for the time-consuming activities of Indian food preparation, overseeing their children's travel to and from school, and supervising their after-school studies. In addition, husbands are often reluctant for their wives to travel far from home. Thus, a differential work pattern appears to be emerging in which men are more closely allied with fabric procurement, an area of power around which all manufacturing revolves. Over a longer period of time, this emerging pattern could contribute to an imbalance in the development of entrepreneurial skills that favors men over women.

A final challenging issue relates to MarketPlace's enduring commit-ment toward holistic development for artisans and their families. When under a single roof, the SHARE director was able to oversee the many development initiatives on a daily basis. To sustain the commitment to develop under the new organizational structure, the SHARE director and MarketPlace Mumbai staff conduct a monthly meeting with man-agement personnel from each group. As a group they discuss, using a problem-solving format, equitable work orders, pricing, and other issues of concern. For groups to understand the MarketPlace mission and commitment to development, new, more formalized guidelines have been established for a biannual review of a group's progress toward development goals. During reviews, points are awarded with continual improvement, rather than an absolute numerical score, as the goal. Guidelines address topics such as the following:

1. Clear understanding and implementation of the MarketPlace mission.
2. Well-implemented social programs.
3. Fair wages with earning potential of the lowest-skilled artisan not less than one fourth of the highest-paid manager.
4. Good profit (10% of earnings) with equitable distribution according to wages (profit is described as excess cash after reinvestment for developing group viability, repayment of loans, etc.).
5. Acceptable composition of skilled artisans, with the percentage of women in skilled positions higher than the percentage of female membership for the group as a whole.
6. Acceptable composition of management staff, with the percentage of women in supervisory or leadership positions higher than the percentage of female membership for the group as a whole.
7. Good decisions by the group with fair representation in decision making.
8. Accurate assessment of production capacity and timely delivery of a quality product (quality production is defined as matching sample specifications).

Despite these problematic issues, the projected advantages of a decentralized organization for fostering self-sufficiency are beginning to emerge. Women acknowledge that organizing and running their own groups is much harder than they imagined. However, they are drawing on their experiences at the former centralized workshop for developing skills to deal with intragroup delegation of tasks and to diffuse "group" tensions. As the 11 groups come together to bid for production of a season's offer, groups are learning to acknowledge and respect each other's skills. Phrases such as "you do jackets best, we do dresses" suggest a broader-based assumption of responsibility for the planning of production. Production planning was formerly in the hands of a few supervisors. Pushpika Freitas assesses the new organizational structure:

> One of the reasons that this is successful is because the producers depend on one another as well as are in competition with each other.

For example, if a group takes on too many products and is not able to produce them in time, there is group pressure and also pressure from SHARE and MarketPlace Mumbai for them to redistribute their production to other groups who may have little production at that time. Because others can also make the same products, the groups are aware that they should be good at organizing the production or they will lose an opportunity. They are also dependent because one group may have some fabric that the other group may need, for example. We are trying to develop a culture that for one group to succeed, everyone has to succeed.

In addition, as groups gain confidence, they are taking on new challenges. One group of eight women proudly told of going across the city for the first time by themselves to participate in a YWCA bazaar. To their surprise, not only did their products sell well, but their husbands offered to care for the children while they were gone and even brought them water to drink when they returned.

Design and Product Development

Each season through 1997, new MarketPlace product lines develop via the following process:

1. The season's line is initiated by Pushpika in Evanston, Illinois. Using a storyboard format with a few pictorial ideas and major color combinations, three overall concepts are introduced in a "brief" for the season. The brief is air mailed to Kirit Dave, the MarketPlace designer in Mumbai.

2. In India, Kirit further develops the line by drawing on his extensive clipping file of ideas for design inspiration. In addition, using his knowledge of Indian fabric dyes and dyeing procedures, the precise colors to be featured for the season are refined.

3. Design workshops are then organized, the first one for fabric design, household products, and jewelry, followed by a workshop for embroidery and apparel design. Pushpika usually participates in one or both of these weeklong events, depending on her biannual travel schedule to India. Prior to the fabric design workshop, basic design blocks are sent to the fabric producers outside Mumbai. The dyers prepare initial samples and bring them for review at the first work-

shop. Design workshops are highly creative, intense, and at times frantic weeks in which fabric samples are reviewed and ready-to-wear designs are selected and executed in knock-off (a practice of making garment patterns from copying existing ready-to-wear apparel). Embroidery designs are initiated followed by repeated reworking, and the final line of products is prepared for Kirit's official "sample list." Among the list are one or two garments intended as "show stoppers" for the catalog cover and frontispiece. As many as 20 group leaders and artisans may be involved in experimenting, giving ideas, and expressing their likes and dislikes. Lunch is taken communally with much visiting and sharing of family news along the way.

4. Pushpika returns to Illinois with samples for the catalog photo shoot and to work out the final order.

5. On receipt of the order, group leaders gather to review the samples, prepare a costing estimate that must include a profit, and bid for orders. Across steps 4 and 5, fax and computer spreadsheets are used extensively for communication and record keeping.

6. At the end of each sales season, MarketPlace Chicago staff conduct detailed analyses of returns and profit and loss for each garment, and they identify the five "best" and five "worst" sellers. A summary is shared with the staff and artisans in Mumbai. In this way, artisans have at their disposal a valuable tool for understanding what is happening in the market and why certain design changes are made. The information also proves useful in planning the next season's design workshops.

MarketPlace's decision to involve a designer came early in the company's history. Kirit Dave, a Mumbai resident trained as an architect, was widely recognized as a highly creative designer who had previous apparel design experience working with several ATOs. Over time, many long discussions, and with input from Pushpika on U.S. market preferences, Kirit and Pushpika developed the distinct, unified, and highly salable "look" for which MarketPlace is known. Achieving a unique and unified look is uncommon among other fair trade businesses, many of whom view a designer as someone from outside who imposes ideas on artisans.

During design workshops, Kirit's dedication to and clear focus on the MarketPlace look are salient in his frequent verbal references to the desired "handmade, ethnic" qualities versus an undesired "homemade, sweet" look. In addition to his evolution as a designer, Kirit has clearly developed valuable culture brokerage skills for design evaluation during his visits to the United States and Europe and through access to MarketPlace market analyses. As an example of his expertise at cross-cultural interpretation, Kirit was particularly attentive to the beige fabric samples under review for the spring 1997 line of apparel. Knowledgeable about the ethnic and racial diversity in the United States, Kirit offered opinions related to the varying skin tones for which he believed particular fabrics might be attractive when worn by MarketPlace consumers.

In late 1996, after their long collaboration, Kirit and MarketPlace arrived at a crossroads concerning their future collaboration. Kirit, clearly aware of his contributions toward the success of MarketPlace, wanted greater recognition and less involvement in the day-to-day operations. In addition, with MarketPlace apparel lines increasing, a full-time designer was needed. Kirit was tiring of design repetition and did not want to devote all his efforts to MarketPlace alone.

Once again, within the MarketPlace organizational culture that embraces self-analysis and change, the management teams are experimenting with new designers. During the transition since Kirit left as MarketPlace designer, an Indian woman designer is working on a contract basis, and two U.S.-based artists, one of whom is Indian, have each assumed responsibility for one season's designs. How the challenge will be resolved in the long term remains to be seen. It is possible that the next generation of designers may be Indian women who will integrate their gender-based training in needlework with formal academic design training received in India's colleges and universities.

Global Dialogue

Despite worldwide media attention devoted to political and social issues in India and the United States, the majority of Indian artisans and U.S. customers know little about the realities of each other's day-to-day lives. Educational programs for rectifying this situation figure prominently in MarketPlace's promotional materials. Since 1994 and much like the magalog approach in Pueblo to People's catalogs, MarketPlace catalogs have featured themes such as Celebrating Strong Women, Redefining Community, Transitions, Celebrating Our Differences, Choices and Changes, and Living in Harmony With Nature. Pushpika introduces each theme through a letter explaining details of Indian daily life illustrative of the theme; the theme is then elaborated on through a lively array of artisans' stories, photos, and explanation of textile traditions.

BOX 6.3

Call for Global Dialogue

It used to be that artisans created things for people living in the same village. A cobbler knew what was fashionable in the village and made quality shoes for his neighbors. He could see his neighbors wearing the shoes and could experience the sense of satisfaction that comes from knowing when the shoes he made became favorites. Now artisans work in a global village where customers live thousands of miles away. The women working in the slums of Golibar know nothing of life in Chapel Hill, NC, or New York City. They feel distant from the people they create things for, and they never experience the pleasure of seeing someone they know wear their products. We want to bring customers closer to the artisans who make the products and would like to start a dialogue between the two groups. Please send us your questions. . . . The artisans will be doing so, too.

—Pushpika Freitas, MarketPlace founder
(fall 1992 MarketPlace catalog)

In a second innovative program, MarketPlace is creating a more direct link between customers and the Indian artisan. A Global Dialogue column was introduced in a 1992 catalog (see Box 6.3). Customers are invited to send photos of themselves in MarketPlace clothing in situations of work and play. Questions about the lives of Indian artisans are encouraged. The artisans, in turn, pose their own questions. In Evanston, a volunteer reviews all "global dialogue" letters and sends a summary of themes for discussion among the artisans in India. Fatima Merchant, the executive director of SHARE, meets monthly with two women from each of the 11 groups in Mumbai to facilitate discussion, identify questions, and record answers for return to the United States. In India, women have asked, "What are some of the family traditions that make you feel connected with your past? How is your household different than the one you were brought up in? What makes women decide or have the inner strength to get divorced?" On the other side of the globe, a U.S. customer queried, "Does TV play a role in shaping the values of your children?" Another U.S. customer's question—"What do you do in your free time?"—led to intense discussion in India of what Americans mean by free time. For women who may walk several hours to collect water or take their children to school, the question of "free time" was puzzling.

In a nationwide survey of MarketPlace customers, 95% attested to regularly reading Global Dialogue letters and stories printed in the catalog (see Box 6.4). U.S. customers have begun to realize that their clothing is made by another human being who is struggling to support her family and educate her children. For the Americans, clothing production is no longer an impersonal process carried out by anonymous people in distant lands. As a MarketPlace customer commented, "My MarketPlace clothes have more soul and spunk than the rest of my wardrobe combined." The Indian women, through the letters and observations of U.S. women modeling the clothes in each season's catalog, learn about the lives of the teachers, nurses, and lawyers who wear their clothes in the United States. In their discussions with Fatima Merchant, the artisans convey dignity and self-respect from learning that customers value their artistic skills and are empathic to their lives. A MarketPlace artisan expressed, "We are really honored that our customers would be so interested in the details of our lives." To take the Global Dialogue one step further, and in keeping with the Indian custom of returning a gift with a gift, one group of MarketPlace artisans is embroidering small wall hangings to be sent as acknowledgment to U.S. customers who have devoted time and thought to writing letters.

For customers who wish to more actively commit to the MarketPlace mission, a child sponsorship program allows customers to contribute $15 per month to the education of a MarketPlace artisan's child. Eligible mothers include widows, handicapped women, or those whose husbands are not providing for the family. Fatima Merchant meets monthly with the women and their children to review how each child is progressing in school. Biannual reports are sent to the U.S. sponsors.

BOX 6.4

Global Dialogue Letter

In the Fall/Winter 1995 MarketPlace catalog you asked how my life differs from my mother's. The greatest difference between my mother's life and mine is that I've had more freedom of choice in my profession and my lifestyle. . . . I will always be grateful to women of my mother's generation who were bold enough to demand more from life. They have made it much easier for women of my generation to pursue whatever dreams their hearts hold. My dream was to earn a degree in physics. With much support and encouragement, I was able to accomplish this in 1991. I now work in a natural history museum and an observatory.

—Tracy Glomski, Hastings, Nebraska, MarketPlace customer
(spring/summer 1996 MarketPlace catalog)

Realizing that income generation alone does not adequately meet all of the artisans' needs, Fatima continues to initiate additional SHARE programs such as a support group for widows and a day care center where young children can be cared for while their mothers work. In addition, on an annual basis, a lively day of special recreation is planned by and for all MarketPlace artisans. In some years, the artisans held picnics or attended movies. In 1997, artisan groups performed plays for each other as part of their "Our Day" celebration. Under the decentralized organizational structure, bringing all the artisans together for recreation serves a secondary purpose of affirming the mission and values of the larger MarketPlace organization of which the smaller groups are all members.

Leadership Transition

ATOs, most of which were founded by charismatic leaders in the 1960s through 1980s, are at a strategic crossroads in identifying the next generation of energetic and visionary leadership. MarketPlace: Handwork of India is no exception. For the artisans, staff, and management team, Pushpika Freitas and MarketPlace are synonymous. In the early 1990s, Pushpika could oversee much of the company business during several month-long trips to India each year. However, with increasing organizational complexity, an expanding product line, and planning under way for a new interiors catalog, Pushpika's attention is increasingly drawn to marketing issues in the United States. As a result, she is aware of the need for identifying a team of individuals with complementary backgrounds and skills whom she can trust to provide year-round leadership and inspiration in the MarketPlace Mumbai office.

Several recent personnel shifts point to both the opportunities and challenges for leadership transition at MarketPlace. In one case, Fatima Merchant, the new executive director of SHARE, despite extensive experience as a social worker, faced some early resistance to her new problem-solving ideas. She found that producers wanted to be guided by "Pushpika said . . ." directives for giving credibility to the SHARE director's initiatives. In a second example, the new design manager, who brings business skills for overseeing the timely execution of production samples and assessing various shipping alternatives during the production season, has, as Pushpika's sister, the advantage of more culturally sanctioned "family clout" to use, when needed. As MarketPlace leadership progresses from one stage to the next, it will do so within an organizational culture in which experimentation with new models for organizational growth and vitality has been strongly instilled by its founder, Pushpika Freitas.

Conclusions

Under Pushpika Freitas's dynamic and visionary leadership and the work of an intensely dedicated staff and management team, MarketPlace has emerged as an ATO deeply committed to its mission of artisan empowerment. Artisans, many of whom would not be employable in mainstream business, have found work and enhanced self-esteem and dignity (see Box 6.5). Achieving self-sufficiency among the artisans by taking greater responsibility and ownership of their newly decentralized groups is a continuing challenge.

BOX 6.5

Assuming Responsibility

Hasina Seikh, a SHARE artisan, is a Muslim woman whose husband left her not only with their two children but with a host of debts that she knew nothing about. Later she learned that he had married another woman. The debt collectors kept knocking at the door. She was afraid of them, but she did not know how she could provide for herself and her children, let alone pay them back.

After she started working at SHARE, she was able to put her children back in school and began getting her life back together again. Now she says, "My experience has helped me to reach out to other women in trouble. Safiya, for example, is a Hindu who married a Muslim man. Her family disowned her. Later she found out that her husband was already married. She had not worked before and did not know how she would support herself. I took her to SHARE, but there were no vacancies. So I offered to train her myself, and I also started teaching her to read and write. Now she is able to support herself. If we are not able to help other people, life has no importance."

—*Pushpika Freitas, MarketPlace founder, and Hasina Seikh,*
artisan (fall/winter 1994 MarketPlace catalog)

That women are assuming the challenge toward greater responsibility and ownership was evident in two recent stories shared by Pushpika. In one instance, Manisha Pawar asked her sons, ages 13 and 17, to ride across the city in a trishaw (a three-wheeler that is cheaper than a taxi) to pick up 100 jackets that had been sent to a tailor for his final serging of the garment seams. On return to her home, Manisha was distraut to discover that several of the original garments were missing. Together with her two children, Manisha spent 5 hours going all over Mumbai, eventually finding the driver, and retrieving the garments that had become wedged in the trishaw seat. The magnitude of this effort is particularly impressive, considering there are thousands of trishaws in Mumbai. Finding a specific vehicle is like searching for a needle in a haystack.

Pushpika relates a second example of artisan involvement with MarketPlace:

During my last visit to India, I was struck by the strength of the women's commitment to their work. Actually the word *commitment* is inadequate. It doesn't tell you how the women's faces beam with pride when they talk about their lives and their achievements. Gousiya Moiddin Sheik, with eyes twinkling and a big grin on her face, relates, "We do not always deliver on time, or the quality may not always be perfect, but we really try. During the monsoons in July, there was a week when there was knee-deep water in our houses all the time. The electricity was cut off because of the danger of electric shocks and I had to sew and deliver six dresses the next day. If I did not, the entire group would not be able to deliver our order and that would cause problems with cash flow later. I was in such a state because I could not see enough to sew and the machine was halfway under water. Then my husband suggested that I put the machine on top of the bed—it was the only thing that was above water and my machine is a treadle machine, not electric. I had some broken tavdi candles, which were in the spring 1997 catalog, so we put them in cooking vessels and floated them in the water. I got the six dresses done and gave them in the next day."

As Pushpika summarizes, "For these women, it's not really commitment. It's a way of life."

In addition to individual stories of empowerment, group initiative also has expanded. Artisan groups have moved beyond the watch-and-wait mode for future MarketPlace orders (described earlier in the chapter) and, in 1998, collectively formed a company to diversify their production to the Indian market. To fill in during downtimes for MarketPlace orders and to achieve greater consistency in their earnings, the collective group will, with initial MarketPlace technical assistance and financial support for advertising, produce and market a line of apparel to meet the tastes and needs of Indian consumers.

Staying focused on the MarketPlace vision of self-esteem and dignity while also creating self-sufficient, sustainable businesses has not been without its challenges. Pushpika assesses,

Keeping to the mission and the standards and the deadlines dictated by the market is a fine line. Sometimes developing people's self-esteem and maintaining business self-sufficiency are in conflict with each other. When faced with production deadlines, one can often go to the extreme of saying, "I don't care what your problems are; a sick child, family obligations, whatever, the work needs to get done." The goals of running a business are so tangible that the more intangible goals of development can get forgotten. The challenge is balancing the two.

However, as MarketPlace and SHARE move in new directions, Pushpika Freitas remains rooted in her initial vision:

> What excites me the most is seeing the development of the women. I see the changes in the women, very small sometimes and the spark in their eyes when they tell me stories of success they have experienced. This is really what my whole idea was, and the women are telling me that this is happening. This is the biggest success of MarketPlace and SHARE. It is not that we started with 3 women and are now 450 women, or that sales in 1997 were 1.2 million dollars. All that is good but it's what that accomplishes toward the mission—providing women with opportunities and seeing them take those opportunities and making them into something greater.

Insights for Fair Trade

The MarketPlace case analysis provides a holistic assessment of how an ATO learns to solve problems and conduct business. Although set in India, many of the specific solutions and ongoing challenges appear useful for application within the fair trade movement more broadly. More specifically in four areas, the MarketPlace analysis reveals the following:

Production

- ➢ Rich universe from which fair trade businesses can draw for their raw materials and indigenous technologies, including craft skills handed down within families, training offered through school-based programs, discarded materials for recycling, and local markets with a wide array of products for inspiration and adaptation.
- ➢ Importance of a clearly defined market niche to guide product design and thus counter diffusion in product development efforts.
- ➢ Critical role of a designer for establishing a unique "look" that serves as the unifying focus for a small business and the potential conflict of the designer role with business goals for broad-based artisan empowerment.
- ➢ Influence of cultural patterns in deciding on initial product offerings, developing product quality, establishing consistent sizing, and giving and receiving critiques.

Organizational structure

> Value of changing organizational structures for evolving business goals related to group identity, product quality, entrepreneurial risk taking, and market diversification.
> Continuing influences that gendered cultural norms can have as a business evolves, including impacts on types of products produced and on entrepreneurial development.
> Emerging need for more formalized performance evaluation to ensure that the mission is retained as an initially centralized business begins to decentralize.
> Challenge of encouraging artisans, accustomed to the wages and conditions of fair trade, toward developing skills for market diversification and self-sufficiency.
> Value of integrating income generation with other family-related supports in organizations focused on building women's self-respect and dignity.

Customers and volunteers

> Ability to engage customers in the fair trade mission by providing them with opportunities to communicate with artisans.
> Time-limited, project-specific assistance that volunteers and board directors, many of whom are busy professionals, can provide to an ATO.

Leadership

> Importance of an inspirational founder/leader who can bring people together in working toward a common mission while keeping operational costs low so that maximal support goes to the artisans.
> Care with which new leaders must be introduced into an organization and the critical nature that social class and familial ties can play in leadership transition.

MarketPlace Empowerment: From Self-Esteem to Self-Sufficiency

MarketPlace commenced as an organization in which artisans' hopelessness over their personal and family welfare was given primary attention. As the artisans worked together and conversed across religious and ethnic boundaries, they shared first their hardships and later their joys at taking small first steps to improving their personal conditions. Only later, as the business decentralized, was entrepreneurial risk taking given greater priority among the artisans. Assuming responsibility for costing, production planning, and market diversification became the artisans' next step toward achieving self-sufficiency.

MarketPlace's overall mission of achieving artisan empowerment has never wavered; however, measures of its performance in achieving the mission evolved over time. Gauges of self-esteem and dignity at individual artisan levels progressed to indicators of self-sufficiency at group levels. More simply, women had to value themselves and respect each other before they could work toward a common goal of self-sufficiency. Such changes did not come automatically. As the organization matured, self-esteem, dignity, and self-sufficiency have, in progressive order, served as indicators of empowerment.

Based on the MarketPlace: Handwork of India story, we propose that as ATOs mature, the measures and units of analysis for assessing performance in relation to their missions will change as well. What began as personal and social gauges for achieving the MarketPlace mission have now evolved toward economic indicators for assessing artisan empowerment through self-sufficiency. That MarketPlace has been sensitive to and fostered changing indicators for accomplishing its mission illustrates perhaps the greatest strength of MarketPlace organizational culture—its flexibility, innovation, and openness to experimenting with new models for conducting business in a socially responsible manner.

CHAPTER 7

FOCUSED PLAYERS
WITH PRAGMATIC
APPROACHES

What we do is so practical, it's so sensible that I don't see why everybody doesn't do it. That has always been a frustration that people do things either in a pure business way, which isn't life, or a purely do-good way, which is also not realistic. And I just stubbornly don't see why they don't get it because it's so uncomplicated. You just help people to do what they do in a way that they can make a living at it and that's all there is to it. Of course, there's a lot of talent in the middle there, and it's ours and our consultants. It's also willingness of the market and sensible buyers who care about these things—they all mix together.

—Clare Brett Smith, president and CEO of Aid to Artisans

On returning home from work, Anne, a resident of Boulder, Colorado, opens the Internet connection on her computer and types in a Web site address recommended by a colleague. Aware that Anne, a recent university graduate in anthropology, is in the process of outfitting her new apartment, the friend recommended the Web site as a place to find the kinds of ethnic artifacts that she knows Anne likes. A photo of a Guatemalan backstrap weaver welcomes Anne to the home page for the PEOPLink Alternative Trading Organization (ATO).

Choosing next to click on the "electronic catalog" button, Anne is presented with six product options. The "Interior Accessories" option piques Anne's interest. Up springs a series of colorful and functional metal, clay, wax, glass, basketry, and textile items for the home. A handpainted, fruit-covered wall hook for storing keys catches Anne's attention. On further investigation, the next window introduces Anne to a Haitian metal worker from AKOMDEY (Association for Communication and Development) who is in the "process of transforming raw materials into stunning, often haunting, iron sculptures." As Anne further inspects a close-up of the wall piece, she learns that the key rack is made from recycled iron, costs $19.95, and is 11 by 8 inches in size. After clicking to another window where she learns more about the artisans of AKOMDEY, Anne makes her choice and completes the purchase transaction with her credit card.

The ATOs that were profiled in Chapters 3 through 6 are comprehensive, vertically integrated organizations that work with all sectors of the trade system, from producers to final retail consumers. In contrast, other organizations such as PEOPLink, introduced in the opening scenario, focus on a more limited range of from one to three of the functions related to design, production, marketing, or retailing. In this chapter, we examine the approaches and outcomes of three of these more focused organizations. As illustrated by Clare Brett Smith's opening quotation for this chapter, each organization offers what it considers to be a practical and pragmatic approach to its work. It is our assessment that each also offers innovative and cutting-edge ways of accomplishing the business of alternative trade. The three focused players and their pragmatic, innovative approaches are as follows:

> ➤ Aid to Artisans guides and encourages artisans toward marketable designs and then links them to mainstream, commercial markets.
> ➤ PEOPLink creates fast and immediate communication through on-line computer marketing.
> ➤ Traditions Fair Trade expands the retail customer base through a widely visible community presence.

Aid to Artisans: Linking Artisans to the Market

Executive Director Tom Aageson describes the goal of Aid to Artisans (ATA) in two simple words—"creating linkages." From the ATA office in Farmington, Connecticut, he elaborates that Aid to Artisans completes the cycle in the sense that it's not just design or it's not just business training, but it's finally getting into the market. It's that final link that's so essential. We consider ourselves to be a mission-sensitive, market-driven organization.

Although Aid to Artisans elects not to call itself an ATO, we include it because (a) its socially responsible practices exemplify the overall alternative trade mission (see Box 7.1), and (b) its focus and approach are not echoed elsewhere in the alternative trade movement.

BOX 7.1

Aid to Artisans Mission Statement

Aid to Artisans, a nonprofit organization, offers practical assistance to artisans worldwide, working in partnerships to foster artistic traditions, cultural vitality and community well-being. Through training and collaboration in product development, production and marketing, Aid to Artisans provides sustainable economic and social benefits for craftspeople in an environmentally sensitive and culturally respectful manner.

—*From Maker to Market, Aid to Artisans, 1997*

Since ATA's founding in 1976 by Jim and Mary Plaut, artisans in more than 30 countries have benefited from the Plauts' visionary beginnings. ATA's mission of offering "practical assistance to artisans worldwide" comes to life through project-based contracts funded by a variety of corporate, government, and private organizations. A defining characteristic across its many projects is that ATA does not serve as a retailer or wholesaler of the artisans' products. Rather, through a multifaced series of project activities, ATA empowers artisans to reach markets at home and abroad by connecting with wholesale and retail buyers. That accomplished, ATA describes that it "want[s] to get out of the way." Clare Smith, ATA president, shares her thoughts about two Ghanaian ceramic artisans in an ongoing project:

In 10 years, Peter and Happy in Ghana may vaguely remember us and
with some affection say, "Oh yeah, that's right, they did help us a little
bit." But ideally, they'll just be booming along and, if asked, "Who was
your favorite teacher?" we hope that ATA might be one of those favorite
teachers they'll recall from long ago.

Evidence that the ATA approach works for developing artisan expertise,
confidence, and initiative comes from the many ATA producers who
have attracted orders from major U.S. mainstream retailers, including
Pottery Barn, Saks Folio Design, Pier 1 Imports, Sundance Catalog,
Garnet Hill, Gump's, and Smith and Hawken, to name a few.

ATA initiates projects in a variety of ways. ATA's involvement in
Pakistan came through a contact from the Levi Strauss Corporation,
which was interested in investing in the community areas of Lahore,
where their plant was located. ATA was invited to submit a proposal for
an income-generation project focused on children's clothing for the
Pakistani domestic market. A second project in the United States evolved
through contacts that Gaye Ellis, an ATA Trade Network member (see
description later in the chapter), had with Hmong needleworkers in
Minneapolis–St. Paul. Partnering among an ATO, a foundation, and a
local women's association led to a line of silk reverse appliqué products
for the high-end interiors market. The final example illustrates ATA's
strategy for initiating a project in Haiti, an area of the world where they
had long hoped to work. In this case, Tom Aageson went directly to major
government and nongovernmental funders with a proposal outlining a
rationale for investing in Haitian artisans.

Operating almost exclusively from grants through foundations,
government programs, and corporate sponsors, ATA receives funding
from a variety of sources. Grant writing and meeting with potential
funders occupy a large proportion of time for both Clare Smith and Tom
Aageson. Since joining ATA in 1986, Clare Smith, president and CEO, has
worked tirelessly to educate major funders on the importance of artisanal work for social and economic advancement in less-developed
countries. Despite numerous refusals early on, Clare indefatigably persevered. Eventually major funders began to appreciate and adopt Clare's
viewpoints on artisan development. ATA's 1997 budget of $1.8 million
stands as a testament to ATA's persistence, increasingly sophisticated
skills at grant writing, and its impressive abilities to network with

potentially sympathetic collaborators throughout the world. Of their annual budgets, more than 80% goes directly to projects, with less than 20% remaining for headquarters operations.

In recent years, the U.S. Agency for International Development (USAID), Inter-American Development Bank, and World Bank have provided major project funding. In total, more than 36 foundations and 17 corporations have supported ATA projects. In addition to foundation and corporate support, ATA attracts a loyal group of more than 400 individual members who contribute annually in six membership categories, ranging from $35 to $1,000.

ATA projects vary in scope and resources; most last from 3 to 5 years. Smaller projects operate with budgets of $50,000, whereas larger projects range from $100,000 on up to more than $1 million in support. In addition to differences in scope and funding, ATA projects are unlike one another in focus (see Table 7.1). This diversity reflects the ATA perspective of matching artisans' needs with project design and delivery. Tom Aageson describes these differences:

> Our work on a global basis comes under such different circumstances. For example, we're working in central Ghana where they're using a very old traditional bronze-casting technique of lost wax and there's no electricity. All functions are done by hand. And we're also in Central Asia and Eastern Europe where the entrepreneurial background is nonexistent in terms of having several generations without that. It was all done with barter, very little cash. So now they ask, "How do I put a price on something? What do I do?" We're answering different questions from artisans in Eastern Europe than from those in Africa or in Latin America.

Clare Smith continues with insights on how ATA delivers programming:

> We teach in different ways. I took some Hungarians, early in our experience of working in that part of the world, from our Connecticut office to New York City and I drove them there myself to save time. They wanted to learn from me about marketing. That's a 3-hour drive so I talked the whole time and told them everything I know about marketing, and they sounded quite interested. In their evaluation they said, "We never got a marketing lecture." It had just been in the car talking and that doesn't count. Now in Ghana, on the other hand, anytime you say or do something, they understand that's an okay time

TABLE 7.1 Examples of Aid to Artisan (ATA) Projects

Country	Activities
Hungary	ATA worked with felt artisans in Hungary to transform felt greatcoats worn by shepherds into layered, embroidered, and cut felt ornaments, stockings, pillows, vests, jackets, and children's clothing. Old folk designs served as inspiration for fresh and innovative pottery. Publishing of a *Buyer's Guide to Hungarian Crafts*, intended for tourists and retail buyers, was one project outcome.
Romania	In Romania, artisan enterprise development is a project priority with 35 small enterprises representing more than 3,000 artisans. Local marketing to tourists through alliances with Romanian ethnographic museums serves as a marketing strategy. Promising products include flowered carpets, red and white embroidery, and ceramic plates.
Jordan	ATA, the Jordan Design and Trade Center, and Save the Children's Bani Hamide Project teamed to develop marketable lines of embroidered products and woven rugs. American buyers now pursue their own ideas directly with the Jordanian designers.
Honduras	Wreaths and flowers of cornhusk and clay cherubs formed the product core for Amano, a thriving Honduran-owned export trading company that provides employment for more than 500 artisans. Raw materials come from the abundance of cornhusks left after each harvest and clay in nearby clay pits.
Ghana	ATA's model for artisan development has been adopted by a sister organization, Aid to Artisans Ghana (ATAG), with an influential and dedicated board of directors. ATAG has offered product development workshops on textiles, basketry, pottery, and lost wax gold techniques, which have resulted in sophisticated home furnishing collections. As one example of success for ATAG, recycled powder-glass beads and buttons have been successfully marketed to Esprit. Other products include wrought iron and carved wood furniture, kente and batik window treatments, and terra cotta garden accents.

to learn it. So how people learn has been something we've had to learn as well. In Eastern Europe and Russia, we now have all kinds of handouts, descriptions, courses and lecturers, and chalkboards and papers and pencils.

Project Thrusts

ATA maintains a small permanent staff of 15 employees with responsibilities in project management, marketing, grant writing, and development. Almost all have prior mainstream business experience or involvement in international development programming. Projects are coordinated by a member of the ATA permanent staff in conjunction with design, technical, and business consultants who are brought on board related to a project's needs. ATA offers expertise in three areas; any single project may focus on one or a combination of these program thrusts.

Product Development and Design

➤ ATA sends product developers abroad for technical and design assistance offered through hands-on, in-country workshops. Design consultants operate their own well-regarded businesses in the United States, are highly experienced in trend analysis, and are successful in "designing to meet market demand." During these interchanges, consultants work with artisans on technical issues such as producing glaze formulas for ceramics to meet U.S. toxicity standards, developing more efficient equipment or technologies for faster production, or sizing of pillow or table linens for the U.S. market. As an example, bronze workers in Krofofrom, Ghana, were taught to use medical syringes for extruding the many meters of wax tubing needed daily for the lost wax technology. Formerly, the ⅛-inch diameter tubes were laboriously rolled out by hand. Product designs are targeted for a middle- and upper-end mainstream commercial market. At the product level, in some cases, existing items merely need a few adaptations; in other cases, consultants and artisans collaborate on reviving what may be a dying artistic tradition. In still other cases, the partnership may focus on creating entirely new products using local design motifs. Over the years, ATA has cultivated a broad range of experts such that it can effectively match consultants' problem-solving skills to a variety of needs worldwide.

➤ Several times each year, ATA holds product reviews in Farmington, Connecticut, where designers, buyers, and importers are invited to critique products developed through ATA's ongoing projects. Guest consultants, who are active businesspersons in the U.S. market, assess details of product form, material, design, and pricing. Critiques and suggestions for change are then passed back to the artisans for their consideration and application.

Training

➤ ATA offers in-country training seminars of three types. Some address how to organize and run a craft business; topics range from costing and pricing to Internet marketing, quality control, and shipping. Developing a strategy for tourism promotion is a second training focus. Finally,

instruction on organizational development extends to artisan groups hoping to establish their own in-country nongovernmental organizations (NGOs) for small and microenterprise development.
> As part of the semiannual New York International Gift Fair, ATA conducts a comprehensive training program for artisans. Practical information is provided on market trends, how to conduct business in the United States, exhibit techniques, marketing, and packaging.
> ATA conducts feasibility studies and market research, outcomes of which form the basis for training programs or specialized consultation.

Market Link

> The ATA's New York International Gift Fair program introduces artisans, through a multiyear process, to the major U.S. wholesale trade show and its vast system of more than 50,000 buyers. In an initial visit, artisans participate in the ATA training program (see previous section), tour booths, attend trade show workshops offered by other groups, hold appointments with targeted buyers, and visit retail stores in the New York area. Learning how to "work" a trade show and promote their products with buyers are important first steps on the road to marketing in the United States. As artisans become more experienced in designing for the U.S. market, their products are displayed in ATA's visually exciting trade show booth. The booth highlights projects with which ATA is actively involved. Finally, as groups begin to receive orders for their products, ATA encourages them to mount independent booths at the trade show.
> ATA also plans specialized marketing missions for groups of artisans to meet with targeted buyers or to attend other wholesale shows, such as the High Point Market in North Carolina, which focuses on furniture and decorative accessories.
> ATA's Trade Network of approximately 25 socially conscious businesses forms a core of individuals and businesses to which artisans have ready access. These businesses express a special interest and readiness to market products from ATA projects. In addition, Trade Network members often accompany ATA staff and serve as consultants during training workshops abroad. On occasion, a design consultant and Trade Network member collaborate in working with a group of artisans to develop a product line directly for the Trade Network member. Designer Lynda Grose's sweaters, developed in Peru for Indigenous Designs, serve as an example. Likewise, while designing a line of "environmentally friendly" clothing for Esprit, she traveled to Ghana to ensure that powdered glass buttons from an ATA project would meet Esprit's environmental standards for worker protection and raw material sustainability.

In addition to projects organized around the three program thrusts, ATA also administers a small grants program for emerging artisan groups. Hundreds of requests are received each year and reviewed on a biannual basis. The 21 grants awarded in spring 1997 fell within the usual funding range of $400 to $1,500 per project (see Box 7.2). Although some outsiders might question the impact of such small funding, ATA maintains that these grants have a dramatic multiplier effect and some have helped to stabilize or launch now-thriving organizations.

BOX 7.2

Aid to Artisans Small Grants Program

Highlights of the 21 grants made to artisans in spring 1997 include the following:

- The Women's Development Center in **Janakpu, Nepal,** for materials to build a vending cart for the Kathmandu airport to sell decorative crafts based on traditional wall painting techniques.
- Materials to restore and activate a hand-woven hammock factory in **Santarem, Brazil.**
- A materials bank for 11 weavers who are training unemployed youths the art of weaving kente cloth in **Santrokafi, Ghana,** an area no longer fertile enough to support farming.
- Life's Work in **Kingston, Jamaica,** for a kiln, part of a therapy and income project for AIDS and HIV patients.
- Mayan Traditions Doll Project, in **Guatemala,** for a thread project that preserves backstrap weaving traditions of isolated highland communities by making dolls in native costumes.

—*Aid to Artisans News (fall/winter 1997)*

New Directions for Aid to Artisans

Over the years, ATA programs and expertise have continued to expand. As Clare Smith assesses, "We never seem to abandon one of our causes. We just add on." Currently, the ATA staff is directing its attention in yet several more new directions. Perhaps most dramatically, ATA is considering whether it should assume roles as "businesspersons" in the retail market. A proposed move from being a market link to becoming market makers has evolved from the assessment that it is taking too long for artisans to get products into the market. Many U.S. importers are reluctant to take on unproven producers. Accordingly, ATA is developing a marketing system whereby it would work directly with retailers in establishing orders for the artisans with whom it works. In this way, ATA will incubate the lines of new artisan groups until a commercial firm is ready to take them on.

Forming alliances with non-craft-related development organizations is a second initiative under way. As an example, ATA and a development organization in Peru are negotiating an alliance with a focus on alpaca. The development organization would provide technical agricultural assistance to the herders. ATA would contribute well-honed design and marketing expertise for developing a line of products from the alpaca wool. Together the allied organizations believe they could more effectively contribute to a common goal of broad-based community development than could either organization working alone.

In a third new direction, ATA acknowledges the increasingly urgent need to document and communicate project outcomes and impacts, particularly as ATA seeks new funding sources. Potential funders now question, "What is the size of your impact? How many jobs do you create?" Ramifications of working toward larger-scale outcomes are affecting how ATA develops and promotes new projects. Tom Aageson further explains that artisans and development planners must be able to demonstrate measurable return to the funders who invest in them:

> The big challenge in economic development circles is whether crafts can be substantive business, worth investing in. We have to be able to legitimize craft development as truly business, microenterprise development, or small business development. Part of our effort now is to fast-forward and show from the results in Peru that their investment has already produced 3.5 million dollars in new business, 1 million dollars of new business in Ghana, or thousands of jobs created in Peru. Then funders say, "Really now, that's all right. Oh, and they pay okay and people aren't streaming into the city." Funders are really pushing the scale question.

One example of ATA's increased emphasis on communicating "impacts" was evident in its 1996 annual letter to ATA members, excerpts of which follow:

> In Ghana, with your help, income increased by over 400% in the traditional brass-making, rural town of Krofofrom. For every artisan directly employed there are another seven or eight individuals providing materials and labor for the craft production.
>
> In Armenia, with your help, the income for 300 women increased from an average $3 a month to $30, a respectable wage in Armenia.
>
> In Peru, with your help, ATA helped to increase income for over 4000 artisans through the members of an export association called ADEX.

A second illustration of ATA's attention to return from investment comes from its work with exporters in Peru. Although most ATOs strive to eliminate middlemen whom they believe act as a financial drain on return to artisans, ATA boldly initiated such a collaboration with ADEX, an association of craft exporters in Peru. ATA's partnership with ADEX, far different from their more common grassroots point of departure, was formed after careful consideration of both the organization's motives and its potential for large-scale impact with artisans. Clare Smith and Tom Aageson elaborate, respectively:

> I think we are different from the alternate trade organizations in that we think that the organizers, frequently known as the middlemen, can be extremely valuable and very important and we like them a lot. We think middlemen can make the world go around if they are good, honest people. So that's where we have arguments with Pueblo to People and people like that. They get rid of the middleman and we say no, no, no. It depends on the situation.

> They can provide a service that is worth some money. The judgment is not about the work that they do; the judgment is about whether the payment is fair. Because there is a valid need for what they do.

A final example illustrates not a new direction but rather a repositioning for ATA's ongoing program with Artisans and Ecology. Initially, ATA collaborated with its Mexican partner AMACUP (Asociación

Mexicana de Arte y Cultura Popular) to devise environmentally sound businesses; products such as children's blocks, furniture, and embroidered bags and T-shirts evolved. The next stage enlarges the ecology program to a global perspective with a focus on natural dyes, organic cotton, lead-free ceramics, and energy-efficient kilns as cross-country issues of ecological concern. ATA's renewed focus on ecology arises from its observations of threats to the environment from chemical dye products emptied into local water sources, soil contamination from craft-related liquid runoffs, deforestation to meet demand for wood artifacts, and water depletion. Lynda Grose, project director, describes the Artisans and Ecology initiative:

> Normally, ATA projects are *country based*. ATA is involved with a particular artisan group and their products. In contrast, Artisans and Ecology is *ecological issue based*. A particular issue may arise in any country where a similar craft is developed. For example, the toxicological issues of using synthetic dyes may arise in Peru for dyeing wool sweaters, in Central Asia for dyeing felt for rugs, or in India for adding color to wood. For ATA projects, as they are presently set up, when a designer goes into the field, there is no time to address an ecological issue that arises because we are already pressed to accomplish the main objective of developing products and getting them to a marketable point. This is where Artisans and Ecology comes in.

Each ecological initiative will have one or more test sites, such as ceramics in Michoacán, Mexico, and Chulucanas, Peru. Natural dyes on cotton will be centered in Peru, whereas the natural dye and wool interface will occur in Bolkonbaeva, Kyrgystan. Ecological concerns about raw materials, production practices, and packaging will be embraced at each site, where a project will be set up with a primary focus of developing a strategy for addressing issues and creating solutions. A Web site for posting and exchanging "tools of the trade" information in an interactive and exploratory manner will expand project outcomes to a far larger worldwide audience. A second focus central to the program is designing "sensational" products directed to upper-end retailers; a design team has been assembled for action. ATA is counting on these spectacular products to provide the necessary market visibility for attracting both wholesale clients and ongoing project funding.

ATA Organizational Culture

As ATA continues to grow, retaining flexibility remains steadfast in ATA's organizational culture of pragmatism. Clare Smith emphasizes the importance of flexibility to ATA:

> How we answer what's new and different with ATA would likely be different 6 months or a year from now. For example, we have this wonderful project in Romania, and guess what the heart of it is—ethnology museums. We're not working with any museums in Ghana. We're not working with any museums in Peru. But in Romania we're working with museums so that they can become stronger local marketers with their crafts. But in Peru we're working with all these for-profit exporters. We're not working with exporters in Ghana.
>
> We're always presented with different modes for making this happen, and we really have to look at each situation and then work with it, both the craft, the skill, the raw materials, but also the way of doing business. We ask, "What's there? What can you get going? What can happen fast and what's going to take a little longer?" And so if Romania had been our first project, we would probably have said, "One of the principles will be, we'll always check out the local museum." Now we know that isn't going to work everywhere.

In summary, ATA's history is marked by impressive growth and numerous project successes. However, such expansion did not come without vigilant attention to developing and cultivating an important set of pragmatic, reality-based skills. Foremost among these is writing persuasive grant proposals and then tirelessly carrying them through the multiple steps necessary for receiving the funding so integral to ATA operations. Tom Aageson's 30 years of experience managing small domestic and international businesses has contributed much toward incorporating stronger business language in funding discussions. Over time, funders have come to appreciate ATA's day-to-day business savvy, backed by its solid strategic planning and 100% board participation in advisory roles.

Second, expertise at "reading" the consumer market and then transforming those insights into information useful to artisans for the design and production of marketable products is integral to the ATA approach. The ever-elusive "critical eye" and "good taste" are essential to this process. That Clare Smith was a successful craft importer prior to joining ATA is an invaluable asset. As Tom Aageson describes, "It's incredible to watch Clare walk through the trade shows or stores and then suddenly say, 'I'm starting to see things going on in natural fibers and we ought to look at that.' "

Third, willingness to learn from past successes and failures, energy and excitement for trying new strategies, and proclivity toward forming new alliances contribute to ATA's ability to develop vastly different projects for the dramatically different cultural settings in which ATA works.

Finally, central to all ATA activities is its continual assembling of networks among individuals and organizations who actively support, consult, and collaborate in ATA projects. ATA's large and impressive network of designers, technical production experts, international development planners, business leaders, government officials, and fund directors has not emerged overnight. Knowing the right people who can embrace a project and make it work comes from immense time and effort directed by ATA toward deepening ATA enmeshment in the broader craft, business, development, and funding communities in the United States and abroad. In addition, ATA ensures that consultants are reimbursed at levels respectful of their worth in the global market.

PEOPLink: Using the Internet for Global Trade and Democracy

Like ATA, PEOPLink also fosters linkages—in this case, among alternative traders via the Internet. From his office in Kensington, Maryland, Daniel Salcedo passionately describes the mission of PEOPLink:

> PEOPLink isn't just about selling products. More importantly, it's empowering traditional artists with digital tools. We're trying to get the grassroots wired so that they don't get left out of modern commerce. Many concerned individuals fear that globalization and the Internet will only widen the gap between the "haves" and the "have nots." We are committed to ensuring that these dramatic [technological] developments become tools for development and democracy.

Formed in 1995 by the husband and wife team of Dan Salcedo and Marijke Velzeboer, PEOPLink builds on their lifetime of grassroots involvement with the indigenous poor in Latin America. Dan's academic background in operations research and computer programming provides a solid foundation to the emergent enterprise as well. Details of the couple's early international work, including their founding of Pueblo to People (PtP), are chronicled in Chapter 5. With PEOPLink, Dan, Marijke, and a fledgling staff chart still new directions within the alternative trade movement. However, they approach this new endeavor with the same boundless energy, creativity, and respect for input from a variety a quarters as was typical of PtP's early years.

PEOPLink Structure and Activities

Partner Organizations. At a pragmatic, grassroots level, PEOPLink offers totally new modes for artisans to link with potential markets. Partner organizations and a start-up digital imaging package are central to PEOPLink's structure and activities. Partner organizations, currently numbering 28 and located in Africa, Asia, Latin America, and the Caribbean, are nonprofit organizations that provide design and marketing services to a group of artisan associations in their respective countries. Most partner organizations are members of the International Federation for Alternative Trade (see Chapter 1). PEOPLink provides each partner with a basic imaging package; the package, valued at approximately $4,000, includes a computer, color printer, scanner, video cameras, digitizer, and software. For the many groups that already have computers, a $1,000 package includes just the camera, digitizer, and software, which can be repaid in-kind with crafts. Using the equipment, producers capture colored images of their products and then transmit the images via Internet to the PEOPLink Web site in the United States.

As partner organizations acquire additional expertise, they then learn to design and maintain their own Web pages, also linked to the PEOPLink site. Web pages provide a venue for sharing stories of daily life and the traditions surrounding their craft production. PEOPLink adamantly advocates that artisans, and not PEOPLink, control how their products, producers, and their lives are presented to the world. Artisans make decisions on not only what is presented but how it is done. As an example, Dan describes a behavior as simple as smiling:

Whenever I go to take pictures, I'm always sort of cracking jokes, getting people to smile for the camera. Ted [PEOPLink technical coordinator] went to a World Bank conference in Morocco and did a Web page on rugs, and the women weren't smiling much. Maybe it's because they have bad teeth or maybe it's just that they don't want to smile. It should be their choice how they're seen on the Web. We can explain to them that people will probably feel a little warmer, open up to them, and maybe buy more from them if they see smiling faces. But if they choose not to smile, that's the idea.

Although at the outset, PEOPLink staff have been deeply involved in technological setup and training, they hope that producers will train other producers through "south-to-south" technical assistance in the long term.

Web Site Marketing. PEOPLink's Web site offers viewers three purchasing choices (see appendix for Web site addresses). First, the "Global Gallery" option presents one-of-a-kind pieces; once a product is purchased, the image is removed and others added. Second, the "Electronic Catalog" option displays products that can be purchased by larger numbers of customers; these products remain on the site across an extended period of time. A third "Wholesale Catalog" option is similar to the "Electronic Catalog" but available only to wholesale buyers through password entry.

During PEOPLink's start-up period in the late 1990s, orders have been filled from products in stock at the PEOPLink headquarters, a large house in a residential neighborhood of Kensington, Maryland. Eventually, plans call for orders to be received and then transmitted directly to the host group, who will complete all value-added activities in-country. Finally, as groups develop their own Web sites, orders will be placed directly with the group and a 10% finder's fee transferred to PEOPLink.

Marketing issues of break-even points and markup ratios are currently under review. PEOPLink's decisions build on observations that when working with an ATO client, producer groups often focus their attention almost exclusively on ATO production while failing to establish a more diversified market with other clients. Accordingly, PEOPLink is adopting practices from the commercial market. Dan Salcedo explains,

What I was hearing from artisans at the International Federation for Alternative Trade meeting in Asia is that they're going for the commercial markets. And because of that we're going to start off playing by the commercial rules. Basically we're talking about a 6 to 1 ratio. I want people to understand that's the way the market is. It's not just. It's not right. It's not fair but IT IS. The commercial market is large, and if we're really serious about doing this on a large scale, we need to start from that point. So, we're using the standard 3 to 1 for wholesale and 6 to 1 for retail. But the difference here is that we're going to rebate basically 20% back to the artisans above the price for what we sell wholesale and 50% for what we sell retail.

People ask, "Why don't you just pay more at the outset?" It's because we want to set this up on a regular commercial basis for the groups. We want the prices to be in line so if somebody else wants to buy from them, they won't be juggling two sets of books. Now at the same time, we don't want to be paying too low, so this rebate mechanism will be a way to give money back to them, but it'll be after it's sold, a separate transaction.

Designer's Studio. PEOPLink's Designer's Studio capitalizes on Internet capabilities for easy communication across time zones and national borders. Plans, still in their infancy, call for a panel of 15 to 20 designers to access the studio via a password-protected address. On a monthly basis and at their convenience, designers will interactively peruse the designs posted by Partner Organizations, offering critique of and recommendations about techniques, motifs, colors, designs, and products. In addition to the monthly product-specific evaluations, PEOPLink plans, as needs arise, to organize more open-ended discussions among designers, producers, and customers. For example, with the decline in customer demand for Guatemalan products, the question of what to do with Guatemalan fabrics might be the topic for a chat room discussion.

Educational Programming and Fund-Raising. The opportunities for educational programming and outreach through PEOPLink appear limitless. For example, WeCARE, which combines learning modules and fund-raising for an elementary classroom, is being field-tested. Students promote the Web site for selling products in the $3 to $20 range, 30% of which goes back to the school for enrichment activities. In the process, children learn about the countries and producers whose products they are selling. For college students, a variety of internship opportunities are advertised on the Web site. Some projects require that the intern work at PEOPLink offices in Maryland. Other interns could work on-line while also taking coursework on their home campuses.

Maximizing PEOPLink Potential

Because Internet commerce is so new, the business community is unclear how it will evolve. Uncertainty in some quarters and lack of experience in others dramatically affect PEOPLink's potential for start-up and growth. Among the challenges are acquiring start-up funding, attracting clients, and presenting products.

Start-Up Funding. Successfully attracting major outside funding is critical for the development of PEOPLink's full array of projected programs. To date, PEOPLink has received modest but encouraging funding (e.g., USAID, the MacArthur Foundation, and InfoDev, a program of the World Bank and InterAmerican Foundation). PEOPLink's activities qualify as "innovative" or "start-up" projects among some funders; others are unclear where to fit PEOPLink proposals. As with Aid to Artisans, for whom outside funding is of similar urgency, Dan Salcedo directs significant attention to grant writing.

Attracting Clients. Essential to PEOPLink's success is attracting clients to its Web site. To the surprise of PEOPLink's staff, they found producers ahead of wholesale buyers in their readiness to participate in Internet marketing. Dan Salcedo summarizes, "It turned out that mainstream businesses aren't as sophisticated as we thought." Dan goes on to describe his experiences at the 1996 International Federation for Alternative Trade conference in India:

> I pushed PEOPLink to a lot of producer groups and they all liked it. I had expected the First World folks to go, "Yeah Internet, that's the way to go." And I expected the Third World folks to go, "Well, in my country, we. . . ." And I was totally wrong, it was just the opposite. The Third World folks said, "Yes, that's the future; let's go for it; it's professional" and the First World types went, "Well, I don't know, the modems aren't fast enough and the color isn't. . . ." In fact, some of them were outright hostile.

In addition to a general lack of readiness, Dan also assessed that some commercial businesses feel threatened by PEOPLink's commitment to the transparency of business dealings between producers and buyers. Dan Salcedo continues,

> When you talk with someone at a booth at the New York Gift Fair, they'll maybe tell you the country. They'll never tell you the village or the co-op for their producers. Maybe it's because they don't know, but mainly it's because they're afraid that if they tell you, you're going to go and source it directly. And so that means they're blocking off information. It isn't just information about the objects themselves but it's also what's behind the traditions, the colors, the legends, and everything else.
>
> The commercial market really has a difficult time dealing with what we are doing because we're Johnny Appleseeding cameras all over the place. The fact is the world is changing. This is the age of the Internet, of dynamic free-flowing communications. The organizations of the future are the ones that are going to learn how to manage that information. The commercial market will need to go through this huge change in attitude in how they deal with that—this exclusivity and turf stuff is going to have to change, and that's going to take a while. I'm hoping that will give us time to really get solidly in place because this whole area is one of positioning.

The PEOPLink staff conclude that attracting Web site "hits" is a critical first step toward educating potential wholesale and retail customers about Internet marketing. Through an array of approaches, including trade show participation, advertisements in trade publications, and complimentary virtual gift certificates, PEOPLink has launched an aggressive campaign to establish its position and to encourage potential clients and customers to make that critical first hit on the PEOPLink Web site.

Product Presentation. A variety of technical issues also bear on the appeal of Internet marketing to buyers and to members of the Designer's Studio panel. For example, questions remain on how to best use digital imaging for presenting products such that designers and customers have accurate and meaningful images from which to work and make decisions. For designers more specifically, what kind of lighting, camera angles, and distancing is most useful to access product details for critique? Can digital imaging stand alone, or do designers need a few actual samples from which to develop their critiques and recommendations?

PEOPLink is confident that, with additional time and added experience, these and other Internet marketing challenges can be surmounted.
Envisioning PEOPLink's future when the business world is more Internet active has already commenced. Ted Johnson, technical coordinator,
poses the question, "How, 5 years from now, are we going to justify our
existence, when everybody knows how to do e-mail and construct a Web
site?" For the immediate future, PEOPLink is already looking toward
developing tools for facilitating a broad range of business transactions.
Connecting businesspersons across languages and time zones is a critical
part of the equation. As Salcedo muses, "Right now all we're doing is
off-the-shelf technology, nothing fancy. But how we wire it together is
going to be what we'll have to offer . . . our real edge."

Returning to PEOPLink's theme of fostering development and democracy, Dan Salcedo envisions possibilities:

> I can see somebody in Bolivia who is good at photographing textiles
> and somebody in Indonesia who is good at lighting for pottery. Then
> somebody else asks a question on that and we can refer them to the
> expert in Bolivia or Indonesia. We definitely don't want that expertise
> to stay in the States. There's lots of reasons—philosophical, political,
> and economic. And it would just never sustain itself. If we tried to hold
> on to that and become the funnel, we would fall on our faces.

PEOPLink is clearly charting a path toward exciting possibilities for
nearly immediate interchange of ideas, designs, products, and world-
views among individuals from the First and Third Worlds. As PEOPLink
gains additional expertise and exhibits sales success, it is poised for
participation in upcoming international policy debates concerning using
the Internet as a tool for development. PEOPLink will be at the table with
significant pragmatic experience to fuel the discussions.

Traditions Fair Trade: Independent Retailing

In contrast to the nearly 200 retail shops that source products and
receive management direction from Ten Thousand Villages and
SERRV, a smaller group of alternative trade retailers operates in a more
independent fashion. In this section, we explore the strategies and
identify challenges experienced by independent retailer Dick Meyer,

who runs Traditions Fair Trade in Olympia, Washington. Traditions Fair Trade illustrates, in a concrete microcosm, the types of experiences faced by the independent alternative trade retailers we have visited across the United States.

Dick Meyer was drawn to alternative trade retailing as a way to mesh his business acumen with personal values favoring equitable trade relationships. After 24 years as a restaurateur, Dick was ready for new challenges. Since opening in 1994, Traditions Fair Trade's growth has already led to a move to larger quarters. Currently, Traditions occupies a 1,400 square foot floor space for retail sales as well as an additional 1,400 square foot space for a café. Moves have been accompanied by continually expanding sales; revenue in 1996 and 1997 stood at $110,000 and $207,000, respectively. In 1997, the café brought in an additional $70,000 in sales.

With strong grounding in the business world, Dick Meyer chose to incorporate Traditions Fair Trade as a for-profit business; he believes profit and an "ethical value-driven business" need not be incompatible. He is not, however, comfortable with involving volunteer employees, as is integral to much nonprofit alternative trade retailing. It is important to Dick that he "pay people for what they are worth, whether it's in the store or performing as a musician in the café." Accordingly, during the initial years of his business, he has operated with slim margins and has found himself working long hours in the store and café to develop and promote the alternative trade concept in the Olympia area.

Initially, Dick's attendance at several Fair Trade Federation conferences introduced him to a broad range of producer groups from which to source goods. Additional contacts resulted from producers who communicated with him personally, often through visits to the store. Together, these contacts, along with access to products from Ten Thousand Villages and SERRV, provide Dick with the resources to stock products from artisan groups in more than 50 countries in his store.

Dick Meyer applied a number of business strategies for developing Traditions Fair Trade. In a significant decision in 1996, Dick incorporated a small adjoining store as a lunch café/coffee shop and site for evening programs and musical concert performances. Dick describes his retail strategy as striving to become an Olympia "destination" site.

> I decided to expand and try to come up with a number of compatible things that would help the fair trade store support the space. It would

be more of a destination because of a variety of things happening. People are coming to the store, then find out about the café and vice versa. In addition, I make the café available for public events. We had a session on microenterprise lending and also a forum on limited control growth with various public officials attending. Together with the store, this place is viewed as a community resource which obviously ties into being part of the whole world.

Throughout 1997, Dick's strategy for establishing a community presence continued to expand—this time, to local craft artisans. A pine needle workshop not only drew artisans to the store for discussion and experimentation but also exposed them to allied craft traditions from throughout the world.

Other strategies relate more specifically to merchandising the store. Dick Meyer maintains that customers are attracted to an alternative trade store when it is richly stocked with a broad range of products. He works hard to maintain a diverse merchandise mix; product depth in some special niches has proved particularly fruitful as well. For example, with his strong merchandise mix of ethnic musical instruments, Dick assesses he attracts "a different clientele for drums and instruments who wouldn't necessarily come in for other things." Demand for interesting ethnic clothing is also high. However, Dick evaluates that finding fresh, new designs remains a continual challenge, not only for his store but for the alternative trade movement more broadly.

Openness to possible retail partnerships led Dick to yet another merchandising strategy. In this collaboration, Dick joined with another local retailer who was closing her store but wished to remain active in marketing colorful and intriguing toys for children. Dick describes an example of such collaboration:

> They had things like art supplies and wood toys and books. They knew my fair trade criteria. So they went through their suppliers to make sure they fit at least being produced under fair circumstances. Not all of them, like some of the wooden toys from Germany, are from Third World or low-income situations, but they are fairly done. I've taken a stand on boycotting Chinese goods to educate people about human rights issues, so they stopped having Chinese toys, even though they had really nice things. This collaboration was a way for me to vastly increase my supply in the children's section beyond what I could carry from my fair trade suppliers.

Stocking an independent alternative trade store is not without its challenges. Foremost among these are the volumes demanded to place an order with some producer groups. As Dick notes, "I can't order 100 of a particular T-shirt for myself, so then that begs the question of how do I create a market for them in the U.S.?" At times, coordinating a group order from three to six stores has been sufficient to import certain products. However, issues of economy of scale challenge small retailers who want a diverse merchandise mix. In addressing this challenge, Dick Meyer's long-range goal is to make much more tangible the value of an electronic communication network among independent alternative trade retailers. Dick views the retailer network as a conduit for sharing retail strategies and increasing business efficiencies through collaborative buying.

Pragmatic Conclusions

Each of the small, focused organizations described in this chapter contributes uniquely to the alternative trade movement. Each also operates under a specific set of constraints, some of which we have discussed. To end the chapter, we offer several conclusions that draw on the commonality pervading them all: their pragmatic approaches to getting the job of alternative trade done in new and innovative ways.

First, it is clear that foundations and organizations sympathetic to alternative trade demand quantifiable data in language meaningful to their missions. For some, that may mean quantifying the numbers of jobs created. For others, data about increases in household incomes at a villagewide level may be convincing. Historically, alternative traders skillfully communicated their impacts through telling moving and convincing stories about artisans' lives at individual, human levels. Skills for adding quantitative modes of measurement to their already well-honed qualitative repertoire will be in high demand among alternative traders seeking to attract major outside funding for their work in the future. Quantitative impacts may be convincing to retail customers as well, particularly those who value measures of incidence alongside stories of individual impact.

Second, artisan groups in many parts of the world are, with very little training, ready and waiting for Internet communication for design, production planning, and marketing. Quick response (QR) strategies developed by other global industries capitalize on integrated communication systems for the timely interchange along the production and marketing chain. These QR systems warrant careful study by ATOs for their application to the marketing of cultural products.

Third, reaching out to and building alliances with other individuals and organizations that have much-needed business expertise and technical skill contributes to potentially expanding the impacts from alternative trade. For retailers, that may lead to increased visibility and effectiveness as a community citizen acting to address societal issues at both local and international levels. For groups involved in artisan development, alliances may lead to more integrated, community-wide impacts for alternative traders and collaborative partners.

Fourth, the potential for integrating alternative trade into a more mainstream practice is enhanced by promoting extended visions of the fair trade customer. By making connections with mainstream retail gift buyers, community citizens not first thought of as fair trade customers, or the broader range of world customers available through Internet marketing, the three ATOs profiled here extend the possibilities for fair trade to a more global level.

Finally, each of these organizations illustrates that bigger is not necessarily better. Although each organization's challenges are certainly real, it is likely that the diversity of problems is narrower. Change can be effected quickly within a small staff without extended discussions for "bringing people on board." Small organizations with flexible mind-sets and creative organizational cultures position themselves to address new, exciting, and demanding issues as they arise. As illustrated in this chapter, that may be pragmatically designing innovative training programs, critiquing products via the Internet, or integrating a retail store with a café.

PART III

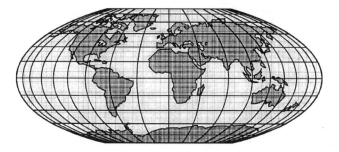

DIVERSE
STAKEHOLDERS
IN THE SYSTEM
OF FAIR TRADE

The Alternative Trade Organizations (ATOs) described in Part II stand in the middle as intermediaries in a system of alternative trade that links diverse stakeholders. Part III examines the values and goals of artisans and consumers involved in the ATO market system and how product development is used to bridge the sometimes diverse perspectives of each group:

Artisans ——— ATOs ——— Consumers

Chapter 8 provides a window into three Guatemalan artisan groups that are connected with North American ATOs. These artisans, intensely impoverished economically, healthwise, and educationally, are at the core of the alternative trade mission. Particularly, in Chapter 8 we reveal important perspectives of artisan stakeholders and ATO approaches to working with them, including

> ➤ how work is focused on meeting dual goals of income generation and nurturing family;
> ➤ the limited job alternatives that are available to artisans and the impact of artisan pay on family needs;
> ➤ how the organizational culture for artisan groups is shaped by cultural norms for who works, when they work, and how they approach their work;
> ➤ the important role of culture brokers in developing an organizational culture that is strategically appropriate for linking with external markets and in encouraging activities that nourish artisan adaptability to change;
> ➤ impacts of working with ATOs that go beyond the direct pay received for the artisan's products, including a flexible and family-friendly work situation, as well as opportunities for personal development, enhanced self-esteem, and cultural identity; and
> ➤ the emotional and business strength provided by group efforts.

Chapter 9 examines the ATO consumer who stands at the other end of the alternative trade system. From surveys of Pueblo to People and MarketPlace: Handwork of India consumers, we reveal important points influencing ATO consumer behavior, including that:

> ➤ the North American market is composed of highly educated baby boomer females who purchase cultural products for the uniqueness and creativity such products add to their lives;
> ➤ ATO consumers are savvy shoppers who are price conscious, quality focused, and not terribly altruistic when purchasing ATO products;
> ➤ although willing to support ATOs, these consumers are not always provided products that satisfy their expectations; and
> ➤ ATO consumers value the world and its people, appreciating opportunities to connect with others through purchasing traditionally produced products and reading ATO editorials.

In Chapter 10, we identify various approaches that ATOs take in product development and the philosophies behind these. Questions that

ATOs ask when developing products for North American consumers are addressed, and factors influencing product development are identified. Ideas of particular importance from this chapter include how:

> ➢ maintaining traditional aspects of design and production while developing products for a contemporary market are basic guidelines under which ATOs operate;
> ➢ approaches to product development differ on the extent of ATO intervention and their orientation toward the producer or market;
> ➢ ATOs are philosophically challenged when they move from a producer- to market-oriented approach to product development;
> ➢ culture brokers are necessary for product development and vary in terms of their insider or outsider status with the culture, their activities as interpreters of ideas or designer of products, and how well they know the culture;
> ➢ a lengthy period of ATO-initiated intervention is necessary for moving artisan groups to a more independent level of product development in which groups use ATOs and a network of others' assistance on an as-needed basis;
> ➢ product development requires a thorough understanding of the culture and how artisan groups define success; and
> ➢ numerous challenges regarding human and physical resources for product development affect the appearance, pricing, assortment, and delivery of products.

Finally, in Chapter 10, a model is proposed that identifies issues that influence product development, selection of artisan groups, and how ATOs work with producer groups for product development.

Sometimes the demands of these diverse constituents are conflicting. We assert that product development is one way by which ATOs act as a bridge between artisans and consumers. Other bridging activities, such as Pueblo to People's strategy of using editorials to educate consumers and the global dialogue initiated by MarketPlace: Handwork of India, have been addressed in the ATO case studies in Part II.

The chapters in Part III examine artisan development, consumer behavior, and product development from the scholarly frameworks presented in Chapter 2. Discussion of these scholarly perspectives is included throughout the chapters. The strength, strategic appropriateness, and adaptability to change of organizational cultures are addressed in Chapter 8 as they relate to artisan groups and in Chapters 9 and 10 regarding the use of product development to meet consumer needs. The competitive business strategies used by ATOs in product development that is focused on their North American customers are discussed in Chapters 8 and 10. Small business performance, from the culturally grounded perspective of Guatemalan artisan groups, is approached in Chapter 8, as is the value of artisan work for development. Finally, how sources of cultural product meaning and authenticity motivate consumers to purchase ATO products are discussed in Chapter 9. The contribution of our research findings to these scholarly perspectives is touched on throughout the chapters but is developed further in Chapters 11 and 12.

CHAPTER 8

ARTISAN PRODUCER GROUPS

"Our Hands Are Our Future"

I came to know about UPAVIM when my children entered the growth monitoring program. Since then I've taught in the preschool and helped out in making crafts. Two years ago the women chose me to work with one other woman in administering the craft project. That was a thrilling time for me. I like my work a lot. I'm learning the computer, accounting, and now some English. Because I'm working as a leader, women confide in me. I'm glad they seek my advice and I listen to them. Unlike the factory where I used to work, we are more like equals here. I live for my children. I ask God to give me help and then I can help the children.

—Angela Bailon, craft project co-manager, UPAVIM

La Esperanza, a squatter settlement filled with houses constructed of cement block, scrap wood, or cardboard, stands on a packed hillside near the outskirts of Guatemala City. Unemployment is high among the 5,000 residents; few hold full-time jobs. Mothers who cross the city to work in factories are forced to lock young children in their homes during the day. Older children skip school to care for their siblings. Alcohol, drug, and physical abuse are common in many households. On the streets, youth resort to robbery and assaults.

As she begins her day at 5:00 a.m., Angela Bailon, a 39-year-old mother of three young children—ages 11, 9, and 3—rises, bathes, washes clothes, makes coffee, and heats the beans in her small home in Esperanza. At 6:30, she awakens her children for breakfast together. By 7:00,

Angela and her younger son leave for UPAVIM, where Angela works as co-manager of the 50-member craft project. Angela's son plays in the nearby UPAVIM day care, where Angela visits him during the day for breastfeeding. Although Angela had childhood dreams of becoming a teacher, she left school at age 17 to help support her family of eight brothers and sisters. Angela's husband, whom she describes as "*el triste de mi vida*" (the sadness of my life), abuses alcohol and drugs and rarely contributes to household income.

Until she found work at UPAVIM 8 years ago, Angela took any job she could get to support her family. These included washing clothes and hauling water containers for people when the water truck delivered the daily supply for the neighborhood in the middle of the night. For hauling 55 gallons of water, Angela received one quetzal or approximately U.S.$.17. At UPAVIM, Angela's daily schedule allows her to return home at noon to eat lunch with her older children and see them off to school. The whole family is reunited when Angela leaves work at 6:00 p.m. and meets her children returning from school. After supper together, the family is in bed by 9:00 p.m.

The poverty and responsibilities for raising young children so salient in Angela's life strike at the core of the alternative trade mission—working with deeply impoverished artisans who have marketable skills but little recourse to commerce outside their communities. In this chapter, we profile three Guatemalan artisan organizations formed in La Esperanza, Chontalá, and Santa Apolonia during the late 1980s and early 1990s. All groups are committed to the fair trade guidelines outlined in Chapter 1. Particularly salient are paying a fair wage in the Guatemalan context; offering equitable employment opportunities; providing safe, healthy workplaces; honoring cultural identity; and encouraging worker advancement. Partnership with North American Alternative Trade Organizations (ATOs) nourished each group at various points in their evolution. ATO partnerships assisted artisans in acting on their belief that "our hands are our future."

In profiling the three artisan groups, we address two objectives. The first is to assess the impacts of ATO-related craft production on artisans' economic and social goals. We also consider whether craft-related earnings provide a living wage. Discussion related to this objective is integrated within the three artisan profiles. A second objective is to identify parameters of artisan organizational culture that have potential applicability to ATO-artisan collaboration within and beyond Guatemala. Our analysis of organizational culture is offered as a separate section at the chapter's conclusion.

ATO Challenges

Although the artisans depicted in this chapter share a common Guatemalan residency, their backgrounds parallel those of artisans in other parts of the world with whom ATOs choose to work. Few artisans have formal schooling; literacy and numeracy skills are limited to a few group leaders. Artisans' first language may not be the language of commerce within, let alone outside, the country. Poor nutrition, hard work, and walking long distances combine to sap energy. Long-established cultural norms subjugate women to decisions made by men; yet, many women provide primary financial support for their families. Not surprisingly, artisans arrive at workshops or group meetings weary and with little hope. Yet, against this backdrop, the three artisan groups in this chapter formed and persevered against tremendous odds.

Our choice of three groups within a single country of Guatemala is purposeful. The groups represent three different responses to life-grinding poverty within a common context of intense civil strife. Each group has approached organizational issues in different ways. As such, they illustrate diversity across a range of variables central to the alternative trade mission of artisan empowerment. More specifically, the groups represent variance in

➤ composition of members related to gender, age, and life stage;
➤ centralization of production;
➤ culturally embedded traditions for production and products;
➤ product and market diversification;
➤ fair prices and living wages;
➤ involvement of a culture broker; and
➤ program diversification beyond craft marketing.

Although we acknowledge that each geographic and cultural area of the world places its own special stamp on the nuances of artisanal work, we believe the issues raised within these three Guatemalan groups illustrate many dilemmas with which ATOs are faced in carrying out their work. As such, they have applicability beyond the Guatemalan context.

❖ Artisan Profile 1: UPAVIM

In urban Guatemala, impoverished mothers flock to "growth monitoring" clinics where their children are weighed once a month and checked for early signs of malnutrition. The mother eagerly watches as her infant's growth is charted in what she hopes will be an upward progression. Barb Fenske, a U.S. nurse who joined the Esperanza growth monitoring clinic in the late 1980s, quickly learned of the many accompanying challenges women confront on a daily basis in rearing their children. Ensuring an adequate diet, maintaining the children's health, and finding a safe place for the children to stay while they work stood paramount in the mothers' minds.

Barb Fenske's first collaboration with the women of La Esperanza came in the form of a dental clinic established to serve the community several half-days a week. A church parish in Bemidji, Minnesota, and dental professionals of Guatemala provided initial financial and technical support. Out of this initial project grew UPAVIM, a solidarity community of 70 Esperanza women joined to improve their lives and the lives of their children. *Unidas para Vivir Mejor* (UPAVIM) translates from Spanish as *United for a Better Life*.

UPAVIM, housed in a three-story building dedicated in 1994, offers an integrated and comprehensive set of services (see Box 8.1). One program evolved from another as UPAVIM members identified needs arising from their lives of poverty. Women, most of whom are in their 30s and 40s, enter the program by initially volunteering 32 hours of service. Some women clean and maintain the building while others run errands. Despite the relatively low initial commitment, some women of Esperanza never find the time to complete the service component required for membership because they must take any job that comes along to support their families. Once accepted, members continue their volunteer contributions of 2 hours per week, all of which assists in keeping overhead costs low. Many of the women find paid employment in UPAVIM's clinics, preschools, or craft program. All members pay reduced fees for UPAVIM services. Day care fees of Q15 for members rise

---

Box 8.1

UPAVIM Programs

- Growth monitoring program in which mothers can bring their children through age 5.
- Dental clinic staffed by a dentist and women from the community trained as dental assistants.
- Medical clinic open 5 half-days a week with a doctor, nurse, pharmacist, and records clerk. All but the doctor are community members.
- Medical laboratory for blood tests and health screenings. Parasite problems among children in the growth monitoring program prompted construction of the clinic.
- Breast-feeding program run by the La Leche League of Guatemala. Other prenatal and postnatal serves are also provided.
- Day care center and Montessori preschool run by teachers trained within UPAVIM. Partial funding provided from the craft program.
- Children's scholarship and tutoring program that pays school registration fees, provides a bag of school supplies, and assists with tutoring for more than 500 community children.
- Craft program offers full- and part-time work to 50 women.

---

to Q30[1] per month for nonmembers. Members pay Q8 for a doctor consultation and Q5 to Q12 for laboratory tests. In a regular hospital, costs for these services could be five times more.

Members organize and run UPAVIM through a series of committees, one for each program (see Box 8.1). An overall president, vice president, secretary, treasurer, and other officers are elected for 2-year terms. The entire membership meets three or four times a year to discuss issues of special concern. A current question revolves around how to better communicate. Barb Fenske, UPAVIM adviser, assesses, "Because UPAVIM has grown quickly, we are experiencing growing pains. We need help in resolving conflicts and communicating more clearly."

The craft program is housed on UPAVIM's top floor. Each morning, a portion of the 50 women in the program arrive at the well-lit and airy workshop to cut fabrics for their sewing projects. Some remain to use the workshop's industrial sewing equipment, and others return home to sew on their own machines or to complete handwork products. School-age children (ages 12-15) are allowed to participate in the sewing but only after they present their report cards as evidence of their regular school attendance and satisfactory performance.

UPAVIM members pride themselves that they will make whatever products their customers want. Most products emanate from typically Guatemalan *jaspé* fabrics (space-dyed yarns used to create intricate patterns when woven) and incorporate machine sewing and handwork. The UPAVIM product mix features a range of bags, notebook covers, kitchen accessories and table linens, simple vests, headbands and bar-rettes, toys and games, jewelry, and holiday decorations. As an example, a holiday wreath, an UPAVIM best-seller, unites 30 colorfully dressed dolls mounted on a circular frame. Always looking for new product ideas, the women recently developed a new tea cozy that encloses a sachet pouch for creating an inviting fragrance while tea is steeping. UPAVIM products are marketed directly to several ATOs; UPAVIM also has a wholesale catalog for distributing to retail stores from an office in Maryland.

Wholesale customers such as SERRV, and formerly Pueblo to People, are attracted to UPAVIM because of the quality of the products and because the project managers work hard to ensure on-time delivery. In addition, the women are willing to develop and refine new products requested from clients such as SERRV. Finally, the bilingual English/ Spanish skills of UPAVIM's adviser Barb Fenske are invaluable for translating what are often very subtle design changes requested from wholesale clients (see Chapter 10 for further discussion of UPAVIM product development and pricing practices).

With this brief organizational description as background, the UPAVIM craft program allows us to examine a variety of cultural issues related to production. We also assess the impact of craft production on UPAVIM artisans' social and economic development. Consideration of Guatemalan women's job alternatives provides a context for our inter-pretation.

Cultural Issues

Several cultural issues surface related to production. First, the fact that UPAVIM members will make whatever their clients want opens them to a potentially broad range of wholesale clients. UPAVIM's products contrast with those of Guatemalan groups whose cultural identities are closely linked to specific production techniques such as backstrap weaving. As Barb Fenske explained,

> I think the women would be sad if they had to sew black and white checks rather than more Guatemalan colors. But most of the UPAVIM women have lived in Guatemala City all their lives, so they don't have the strong ties to traditional textiles that rural women have. Moreover, many of the women have suffered greatly from having no work in the past, so they will be willing to sew new things.

Despite the women's openness to new ideas, each time a new product is introduced, there is some initial reluctance to become involved. When sewing new products, the women's income declines until they can produce up to speed.

A second cultural issue relates to UPAVIM's sewing practices. UPAVIM artisans sew complete products rather than follow assembly-line production. Assembly production might lead to larger volume production for the group overall. However, with complete products, the women believe they have greater control over their income relative to their individual initiative and output. Depending on others for completing products in an assembly process is viewed as risky when women have such desperate need for income. In addition, assembly production would require more women to work on-site at the central workshop, thus reducing the women's flexibility to be with their children.

A third culturally related production issue concerns UPAVIM's commitment to product quality. As the women bring their completed products to the craft office, all products are individually inspected for production details by the project managers. The concept of customers returning inferior products is virtually unknown in Guatemala. Accordingly, the managers initially found it difficult to return substandard products to the sewers for reworking or repair. Over time, the managers surmounted their Guatemalan cultural predilection of "let the buyer beware" as they became firm and consistent inspectors of quality.

Finally, as we assess UPAVIM's production, the following question arises: How important is the role of a bilingual (English/Spanish) culture broker to UPAVIM artisans as they reach out to markets in the United States? Our assessment is that Barb Fenske, who is familiar with and has contacts in the United States, performs many critical communication functions such as grant writing, seeking new wholesale clients in the United States, interpreting the subtleties of product changes requested by wholesale clients, and searching for new product ideas.

Income and Job Alternatives

Issues of job alternatives for poor urban women and assessment of organizational success for UPAVIM are deeply intertwined. Whether craft production contributes to women's dual goals of income generation and nurturance of their children is a complex question. The life story of Angela Bailon, who was introduced in the chapter's opening scenario, aids in understanding and unraveling the complexity.

After leaving school at age 17 and prior to giving birth to her children, Angela worked in a *maquila* (factory) operating a machine for filling cookies. Angela liked the work and was treated fairly by her employers. However, she found the long hours incompatible with rearing a young family. She could not find affordable or dependable child care and was unwilling to leave her children unattended while she worked. Angela is solely responsible for supporting her family of five because her husband is rarely employed.

After joining UPAVIM and advancing to the position of craft program comanager, Angela Bailon now has a steady income of Q14,000 per year ($2,333). The salary represents $871 over the 1997 per capita income of $1,462 in Guatemala. Her workday allows her to be with her school-age children in the early morning, to eat with them at noon, and see them off for school. Her toddler accompanies her to the UPAVIM day care center, as did the other children when they were younger. Through UPAVIM's doctor, Angela arranged free eye surgery; with improved vision, she could complete her hand sewing more accurately and efficiently. Angela likes her work and is motivated to learn computer and language skills (see opening quotation). On several occasions, she has traveled to the United States to participate in Fair Trade Federation conferences where she has observed craft products from throughout the world and learned more about alternative trade. Angela reflects on her experiences at UPAVIM: "I never had the opportunities in my factory jobs that I've had here."

Interestingly, although Angela Bailon and her coadministrator were offered potentially higher salaries of Q7,000 per year plus a percentage of sales, they both declined the offer, preferring instead the possibly lower but stable income. Linking their incomes to sales was too risky for the two women. Besides the comanagers, other workers present a similar picture in terms of earning opportunities versus actual wages. Women working full-time in the craft project can earn between Q40 to Q60 per day ($4.75-$10.00). Monthly averages range from Q500 to Q600 ($83-$100). UPAVIM adviser Barb Fenske assesses that many of the UPAVIM women could earn more. However, they choose to devote time that they could be working to their families, including accompanying their children to and from school and taking them to doctor's appointments.

What job alternatives exist for Angela and the women of Esperanza with their dual goals related to income and family? Angela described several to us, including cleaning for wealthy families, doing washing, and working in *maquilas* (see jobs and typical pay rates in Box 8.2). Washing could bring in up to Q20 each half day, but women must attract and maintain a strong client list to earn close to what can be earned in the craft project. In addition, there can be problems collecting money from employers. Angela also lamented that "the washing machine has arrived for wealthy Guatemalans," thus eliminating this income opportunity for many poor women of Esperanza. *Maquila* work, a second alternative, offers steady employment but requires long workdays, including travel to and from the factory, and holds little assurance of favorable workplace conditions or treatment. In addition, all three job alternatives mentioned by Angela leave little time or flexibility for attending to children.

Artisan Impacts

As noted in Chapter 2, for business performance to be measured, understanding how a firm defines its success is a critical first step. Although sales and profit maximization historically have served as sole indicators of business performance in the United States, entrepreneurs of the 1990s identify personal and family-related motivations for launching and sustaining their businesses. As with many small businesses worldwide, the women of UPAVIM resoundingly identify dual goals of income generation and nurturance of children. Accordingly, along with more profit-oriented goals, addressing what is conceptualized in the business literature as the work-family interface (Kosters et al., 1996;

Box 8.2

Daily Wages in Guatemala (1997)

Minimum wages

Agriculture	Q17.86
Maquila (factory)	Q19.71
Restaurant, entry level	Q19.71

Sample wages

Agricultural work (countryside, seasonal)	Q18-20
Agricultural work (finca-plantation)	Q20-40
Maquila (factory; higher figure includes overtime)	Q18-40
Domestic cleaning, washing	Q20-40
Custodial	Q20-25
Restaurant, entry level (higher figure includes tips)	Q20-45
Sewing (at home)	Q40-50
UPAVIM craft program	Q40-60

1997 per capita income	$1,462
1997 exchange rate	Q6 = U.S. $1.00

Kuratko et al., 1997) is critical for understanding women's attraction to UPAVIM as compared to their other work options.

First, from an economic perspective, the women in the UPAVIM program are earning daily income that is equal to or above many of the job alternatives for minimally educated women in urban Guatemala. For the two managers, income is well above the alternatives. However, as with many of the jobs listed in Box 8.2, income is not always steady. Working at UPAVIM, however, provides the women with some flexibility to be with their children. Mothers breast-feed their babies for several years, which contributes to the infants' health and reduces food expenses. Women's income is further augmented by relatively low costs for health and day care services to which they are eligible at UPAVIM. Members know they will not lose their jobs if they stay home with sick children. In addition, up to three children per family can receive scholarships for school fees and supplies. The Q60 ($10) fee per child, assessed at the beginning of each school year, can be particularly hard for a woman to accumulate at one time when there are many children in a household to enroll in school each year.

Cultural issues also play a part in assessing program outcomes. UPAVIM members take pride that their organization provides a physical and psychological haven where women gain confidence that they can make decisions about their lives and become leaders. Barb Fenske, UPAVIM adviser, elaborates,

> The women who live in Esperanza are totally under the power of men. UPAVIM gives them a *space* to learn how to do things on their own. It shows that women and a women's organization can do the job. It's a major change for women to speak up with their opinions in meetings and to have the self-esteem to say, "I can do it." How they treat their children changes too. There's less beating with belts when the women are less stressed and as they learn more about being a parent.

Although scholars have cited cooperative organizational structures as "safe" venues for learning to express opinions (Eber & Rosenbaum, 1993), Fenske emphasizes the importance of single-gender membership in such organizations for fostering self-esteem among women.

Other evidence of women's empowerment include improved hygiene and increased attention to personal appearance. Several women have gone on to pursue classes on Saturdays at the primary schools their children attend during the day. Some who start out in the craft project take additional training in the day care center to "move up" as teachers with a steady salary and benefits. In a final example, as their Esperanza squatter's plots of 6 by 10 meters became available for purchase, women accumulated the funds and arranged to buy the property in their names. Together, these social and psychological indicators provide further evidence to the expanding body of research suggesting that the measurement of business success should include multiple indicators beyond the purely economic. For women in Guatemala and elsewhere, individual and household-related indicators prove useful in pointing to changes in their lives (Eber & Rosenbaum, 1993; Nash, 1993a; Swain, 1993).

Whether the income from UPAVIM alone is sufficient to qualify as a living wage for supporting a family of four to six in Guatemala City is doubtful. For example, INCAP, a nutrition research institute in Guatemala, estimated that in 1997, a "food basket" to feed minimally a family of five persons required Q27.55 per day (approximately $6.25). For an UPAVIM artisan who earns between $6.67 and $10.00 each day, feeding her family on what is considered a minimal, but not healthy, diet would consume much of her income. No doubt many families get by on much less than a minimal diet. Yet, all the other expenses of clothing, housing, and caring for a family would quickly deplete the remainder of an artisan's earnings. If, however, the artisan's income is combined with that of other family members, her earnings are a significant contributor toward a family's living wage. In addition, UPAVIM's comprehensive health and child care programs further enable her to meet her goal toward family nurturance.

❖ Artisan Profile 2: Ruth and Nohemi

The second producer profile takes us to the highland market town of Chichicastenango and the nearby village of Chontalá. Roots of the artisan group Ruth and Nohemi stem back to the civil strife of the 1980s. In the mid-1980s, Pastor Diego Chicoj Ramos, a Methodist minister, traveled by bus and then foot from Chichicastenango to the village of Chontalá. In search of church members following the mass slayings of families during the civil violence, he found few people he recognized. His former church stood in ashes. Slowly, over the next several years, women emerged from hiding in the hills to share their grief at the loss of husbands and family members. Women pleaded, "Pastor, we need money. We need corn. We're starving."

When approached by the widows of Chontalá concerning their plight for food, Diego Chicoj sought assistance at the regional office of the Methodist church. There he was advised that a charitable offering of corn would only lead to the women's return the following week asking for more. Instead, Diego contemplated alternatives with potential for longer-term self-sufficiency.

The resulting Ruth and Nohemi cooperative integrates the weaving from 16 Chontalá widows with the sewing and schooling of 10 to 12 young boys who work and reside in Chichicastenango at the newly built workshop and dormitory. In discussing Ruth and Nohemi, we consider a producer group that is different from UPAVIM in several ways. Unlike UPAVIM, Ruth and Nohemi provides work for both women and men. The products contrast in that they are deeply rooted in the centuries-old Maya tradition of backstrap weaving.[2] However, similarities abound in that both groups extend diverse economic and social opportunities to members, employ workshop and household-based production, and involve culture brokers in business transactions.

The Women of Chontalá

On meeting with Diego Chicoj in the 1980s, the widows of Chontalá shared their stories of loss and despair; some told of daily contact with members of the civil patrol who had killed their husbands, fathers, and brothers. Others described family members who fled Chontalá out of fear for their lives. Although some of the women had access to small plots of land for growing corn and apples, most had few resources. The women offered their finely honed weaving skills as a base from which to launch a small income generation project. In 1986, the Methodist church provided 100 pounds of yarns, and the weaving began. However, the women quickly learned that with civil unrest, very few tourists frequented the twice-weekly markets in Chichicastenango, where the women hoped to sell their weaving. Sales were virtually nonexistent.

In addition, another problem arose. Due to extreme poverty, many of the women's sons fled to Guatemala City for work. On arrival, the only employment they could find resided in low-paying jobs such as shining shoes and hauling cargo. The mothers feared their sons would "lose their culture, start drinking, and go around with girls." On returning to Chontalá in new jeans and shirts, the boys served as catalysts to other impressionable youth. Lamenting to Diego Chicoj, the mothers shared their suffering: "First we lost our husbands and now we are losing our sons too."

Drawing on his background as a trained tailor, Diego Chicoj was inspired to begin teaching the boys tailoring skills. When asked if they were willing, the boys agreed. Again, the Methodist church assisted the project with a contribution of five second-hand sewing machines. Tailoring lessons 3 days a week commenced in Chontalá. As the boys learned to sew, Diego integrated pieces of the women's exquisite backstrap weaving as focal points for bags, wallets, notebooks, and backpacks.

However, as the project progressed, Diego Chicoj was distressed that the 14- and 15-year-old boys had so little formal schooling. When inquiring among the boys as to why they did not attend school, he was told, "We're too old and would have to give up our tailoring work to go to school." Again, Diego provided mentorship when he shared with the boys that he had only started studying at night school when he was 27 years old.

The Work-Study Program in Chichicastenango

The integrated work-study program moved to Chichicastenango where, since 1990, approximately 10 to 12 boys have learned tailoring during the day and have attended classes at night. In night school, boys can complete the six primary grades in 4 years. Three years of *basico* (middle school) follow. Priority for the work-study program is given to children of widows, orphans, and those living in extreme poverty. Products from the workshop are sold to ATOs and visiting church delegations and through U.S. churches. Profits go toward the boys' food and school supplies. As the boys learn tailoring, some purchase their own machines and seek outside employment. For those who remain at Ruth and Nohemi while finishing school, sliding fees are applied for their food and school expenses. Eventually, through church contacts, a parish in California helped to raise funds for the large, well-lit workshop and dormitory building, which was dedicated in 1994.

Incorporating the women's brightly colored backstrap weaving with indigo-dyed base fabrics is the hallmark of the Ruth and Nohemi product line, which emerged in the 1990s. Bags and small purses, many with shoulder or backstraps, incorporate concealed interior pockets for storing keys or other valuables. Small squares or rectangular pieces of backstrap weaving decorate a bag's surface or provide a colorful accent to a purse's closure flap. The 16 women are provided with thread and weave at their homes in Chontalá. They then take their products to a coordinator who transports the textiles to the Ruth and Nohemi office in Chichicastenango and returns with thread for the next set of weavings. Initially, the women joined together for weaving at one woman's home, but this time commitment led to neglect of their other obligations. Without husbands, the women must also perform men's work of planting and hoeing corn, tending to apple trees, and carrying firewood. Besides income from farming and weaving for Ruth and Nohemi, the women also have some earnings from weaving for area women who have given up producing the distinctive Chichicastenango *huipiles* (women's upper garments) and *fajas* (belts) for their families.

Attracting Clients and Sustaining a Business

The colorful and richly patterned backstrap weaving from Chontalá serves both as a strength and limitation in establishing a wholesale and retail client base for Ruth and Nohemi. Church delegations who visit Chontalá are attracted to the close bond between the women's colorful and richly brocaded clothing and their backstrap woven cloth. Visitors learn of the linkages among women's self-esteem, societal value, and the quality of their weaving. Drawing on the culturally enmeshed weaving practices, Diego Chicoj has worked with the women to modify the width and patterns of their weavings to achieve fabric lengths of 50 inches (five 10- by-10-inch squares) suitable for incorporation in a wide variety of well-sewn, high-quality products. Diego Chicoj also has been highly entrepreneurial in collaborating with a number of ATO-connected designers from the United States and Switzerland on intermittent, short-term consultancies of one day to several weeks. Together they have expanded the product line within the general framework that incorporates brightly colored weavings with indigo or other solid-colored fabrics.

Although the resulting fabrics appeal to church visitors and overseas clients who value a salient "Guatemalan" look, the products hold limited appeal for clients who desire a more subdued "ethnic" appearance. The products also have limited sales potential at times, such as in the late 1990s, when mainstream importers have saturated the global craft market with low-cost, low-quality Guatemalan crafts, and demand for Guatemalan *tipica* (range of Guatemalan products produced from brightly colored fabrics) has fallen to all time lows. Overall decline in the fashionability of saliently ethnic products in U.S. housewares and apparel markets further exacerbates the situation. Unlike UPAVIM, Ruth and Nohemi has not established sustained collaboration with ATOs with whom they might jointly explore whether and how the weaving and sewing skills integral to Ruth and Nohemi products could be modified for broader marketability either through differentiation from other products on the market or by focusing on a select market segment as described by Porter (1980) in Chapter 2.

Beyond attracting customers, Ruth and Nohemi has benefited in other ways from its strong ecumenical, church-based connections. As part of the National Evangelical Methodist church, Diego Chicoj and his pastoral colleagues are dedicated to meeting both the spiritual and material needs in people's lives. Procuring equipment, raising funds for their workshop, and assisting widows with housing and a nutrition center for malnourished children have all been facilitated through support from churches in Guatemala and the United States. In addition, through the Sister Parish program, Diego has joined with the Guatemalan codirectors, a young couple fluent in Spanish and English, to set up Ruth and Nohemi computer records and develop a Web site. Together, these varied church-based connections and Diego Chicoj's leadership lend credence to the critical role that a creative facilitator with connections plays in small artisan business start-up (see Durham, 1996, in Chapter 2).

Income, Job Alternatives, and Artisan Impacts

Like those at UPAVIM, Ruth and Nohemi members hold dual goals of income generation and family well-being. They also acknowledge infused empowerment at economic, social, psychological, and spiritual levels. Economically, women earn Q50 for a five-section piece. When sales are strong, women can average three pieces in a month for an income of Q150 from Ruth and Nohemi weavings. In contrast, if one of the 10" by 10" sections was sold in the market, it would fetch Q5 to Q7. With thread prices as high as Q5, a profit of only Q2 would remain. Income alternatives are few for the women of Chontalá. When asked, the women told us they could do domestic work in the homes of Latinas, for which they would garner monthly earnings of Q200 to Q250. However, domestic work would necessitate the women leaving their homes and children, paying bus fare, and possibly residing at the Latinas' houses. In addition, their farming would not get done.

Beyond direct income, the women cite other economic advantages from their membership in the Ruth and Nohemi cooperative. For several women, their sons learned the tailor's trade and now hold jobs from which they help support their mothers, brothers, and sisters. In addition, all 16 women saved the requisite funds necessary for participation in a house-building project associated with Ruth and Nohemi. By the end of 1997, the 16 women could proudly welcome visitors to their new cement block homes erected in collaboration with project volunteers. With the last house dedication completed, the women helped organize a second group of widows for whom they will serve as mentors in weaving salable products and helping to build homes for each other.

Beyond economic support, the Chontalá women credit Ruth and Nohemi group interactions for supporting them socially and psychologically during their greatest hardships of the civil war. In their own words, the women recount the following:

> I can't imagine not being in the group. It's part of my life now. It's here that I'm comfortable.

> The group has accompanied me when I was on my own and had my young children to support.

> I feel and I see the support of the group. In the beginning we had chickens and we lost out on that project, but I never thought I'd leave the group just because we weren't making money. I'll stay with the group always. As a reward for my persistence, I now have my house to leave to my son.

One elderly woman who has given up weaving because she is unable to see the threads says she feels like she "belongs" in the group; she keeps coming even though she cannot weave. Another younger woman shared that through the group, she learned about the lives of other women as church delegates visit from the United States. She relays, "I'm very happy when visitors are coming. I like to meet people and show them my weaving. I'm very proud of it."

Finally, the women spoke in an almost spiritual sense of the less tangible rewards of income from their weaving:

> When I finish the work, it provides money but it's not just that. When I weave is a time when I feel tranquil.

> Weaving is work that our mothers and grandmothers have passed on to us. My mother wove so it's always been in the family. Through weaving, we can make our clothes, sell some products, and the weaving helps us keep our culture.

For one mother, helping her daughter to learn new and more complex designs means the daughter will be able to weave *huipiles* that command higher prices of Q700 to Q750 while also maintaining the weaving tradition of Chontalá. Tice (1995) assesses that women of different generations are likely to experience the impacts of change in different ways (see Chapter 2). For the mother and daughter of Chontalá, Tice's assessment seems apropos. Although the young widow's income from weaving helped her to rebuild her home and provide basic necessities for her children, she had little time for experimentation toward product development. In contrast, the daughter may be able to significantly increase the family's income if patrons are found for her more intricately woven textiles.

How far do the earnings from Ruth and Nohemi extend? Diego Chicoj explained that Maya people of Chichicastenango "think in terms of corn." For those women in Ruth and Nohemi who do not grow their own corn, a 100 pound bag, costing Q80, would feed a family of six for 9 to 10 days. Beans for 2 days cost the family another Q6. Economically, the income from weaving supplements the women's sales of eggs, chickens, and apples in the market, as well as *fajas* (belts) and other textiles in the village. Because women with access to land may be able to grow some food, their daily expenses for purchased foods are likely lower than for women in Guatemala City. Yet, women clearly could not support their families solely from their weaving. However, without weaving, the widows' ability to feed and care for their children would be dramatically reduced. In support of previous studies, ATO artisanal work, when combined with rural land-based resources, appears once again to offer relatively greater benefits than when carried out in urban areas (Ehlers, 1993; Morris, 1996; Nash, 1993a; Tice, 1995).

❖ ARTISAN PROFILE 3: TEJIDOS DE GUADELUPE

Tejidos de Guadelupe presents yet a third response to the poverty and civil strife of the 1980s. We do not have data from this group for assessing issues of artisan impacts and living wages. However, we include them because the group illustrates how income from crafts can serve an important function for a group at one point during its evolution. When members learn organizational and leadership skills as part of a craft project, these skills can then assist the group in diversifying its activities. Craft earnings become one part of a large group of income generation alternatives.

Located in the Department of Chimaltenango, Santa Apolonia and outlying settlements suffered some of the worst and most persistent hardships during the civil war. Extensive guerrilla and army activity left many children as orphans and women as widows. To provide for the many homeless children, Catholic nuns established an orphanage where they cared for 120 civil war orphans. For older children, workshops provided training in carpentry, cobblery, and sewing. On a weekly basis, widows and young mothers appeared at the orphanage with bundles of backstrap woven textiles. Many walked 6 to 10 miles to deliver the products, hopeful that the nuns could sell them to visitors at their church office in Guatemala. Some mothers took the opportunity to visit children whom they brought to the orphanage when they could no longer afford to rear them at home.

We offer glimpses of Tejidos de Guadelupe at two points in its history, first in 1992 and again 6 years later in 1998. The two visits speak to how artisans' need for and involvement with ATOs can change over time as the participants gain new skills and their life circumstances change.

Along with the Santa Apolonia orphanage, Catholic sisters established a craft project in 1988 to assist widows in selling their weavings. Similar to the women of Chontalá, the women of Chimaltenango weave on backstrap looms. Their distinctive motifs of small animals, birds, flowers, and other geometric motifs on brightly colored fabrics are particularly suitable for coin purses, chicken-shaped pot holders, billfolds, and small table mats. With a strongly humanitarian mission of supporting more than 190 widows, Tejidos de Guadelupe did not wait until orders were received for weaving to commence. Rather, on a continuing basis, yarn was distributed to the women who walked many miles to Santa Apolonia for their supplies. Fabric lengths were woven in the homes and returned to the sewing workshop where the women were paid. The fabric was then cut for sewing by a group of five young women supervised by one of the nuns.

By 1992, a huge inventory backlog lined the cupboard shelves. Despite consistent orders, some product development assistance, and advice from Pueblo to People about reducing inventory, the Catholic sisters' practice of buying as much of the widows' weaving as possible persisted. Soon, supply far outdistanced demand; however, the nuns found it painfully difficult to turn the impoverished women away when they delivered their weavings. The group's humanitarian goals clearly overrode sound business practices. Initially, an international charitable donation to the project provided the cushion that allowed the group to continue weaving purchases; however, the nuns were aware that this practice could not continue in the future. New product development or alternative income generation projects were needed for group sustainability.

Throughout their first 4 years, Tejidos de Guadelupe members and the nuns met regularly as smaller groups in the outlying areas. In addition to discussing orders, women also learned about health, nutrition, and child care issues. As with the women of Chontalá, a group spirit emerged that would carry them into a next phase in the late 1990s.

By 1998, the group of 82 members declined to less than half its original size. Now located in the outlying village of San José Poaquil, the members ran the project themselves; the nuns served as advisers rather than managers. Although the women still needed work, their economic condition was not as desperate as 10 years earlier when the group formed. Some women withdrew from the group because they chose not to walk long distances to pick up supplies for the severely dwindling orders. Many of the women's children were now grown, held jobs, and extended support to the entire family.

Rather than focusing exclusively on craft production, Tejidos de Guadelupe chose to diversify its income-generating projects. It constructed a *molino* (mill) for grinding corn and established a *tienda* (shop) where food commodities were purchased in bulk and sold to members at cost. A markup, which was applied to sales to nonmembers, brought in group income. Finally, their huge inventory from 1992 was virtually eliminated through sales; some products were recut and sewn to enhance their marketability. In 1998, the women produced textiles only when orders were received from a small number of ATO clients in the United States and Germany. Sister Catherine, a longtime manager and adviser for the group, believes that the most important achievement of the project has been "the strong feeling of the group as a way to accomplish goals. By staying together the women can face and tackle challenges." When told that Pueblo to People was closing its doors in 1997, she thanked the organization by saying that "Pueblo to People orders were very important to us at a critical time in the women's lives. Fortunately, now the need is not so critical."

Dhamija (1989) questions whether the promotion of crafts as a strategy for economic development is advisable, given the challenging conditions for craft production in many parts of the world (see Chapter 2). Tejidos de Guadelupe illustrates well the importance of project diversification for a women's group that had little opportunity for acquiring sustained marketing advice to develop their products for export. Instead, as the group members aged and their children began contributing to household income, other projects such as managing a *tienda* and milling corn seemed more appropriate. Both ventures relied on skills long honed by local women through their daily household duties and their participation in the craft projects.

Artisan Group Organizational Culture

ATOs shoulder tremendous challenge from choosing to work with artisans who live in economic, educational, and health-related poverty. Although the challenges are vast, the opportunities for ATOs to jointly explore with artisans how they can reach their goals are unbounded. What can be learned from the three profiles in this chapter that might have broader applicability for ATO collaboration with artisan groups both within and outside Guatemala?

Kotter and Heskett's (1992) model for organizational culture links business performance with cultural strength, strategic appropriateness, and adaptability to change (see Chapter 2). We employ their model for describing parameters of organizational culture among three Guatemalan artisan groups, all of whom achieved a measure of success in meeting members' goals. Through a series of highlighted statements, we first introduce dimensions of organizational culture gleaned from the three artisan organizations. Each section is then followed with our interpretation.

Cultural Strength

Kotter and Heskett (1992) argue that business performance is positively influenced when organizations exhibit strong cultures in which clearly understood values, goals, and normative behavior are broadly shared and persist over time. Parameters of Guatemalan organizational culture related to artisan group values, goals, and normative behaviors follow:

> Artisan group members hold dual economic and social goals of income generation and family nurturance.
> Joining an artisan group often represents considerable risk in time commitment for start-up learning versus eventual income generation.
> A central workshop fosters business goals of quality production, whereas household-based work contributes to family-related objectives.
> Comprehensive group programs (e.g., income generation, health care, preschool, school fees) reinforce and extend the value of artisans' project-generated income.

The three artisan groups clearly illustrate the value of ATO-artisan collaborations and the importance of linking artisan goals with organizational structuring. Without opportunities for women to work at home, nurturance of young children proves difficult in a society where child care is either nonexistent, undependable, or prohibitively expensive. However, we also note that without a central meeting place or workplace for gathering supplies and inspecting completed products, it would be difficult to foster the level of quality control demanded of products destined for the global market. In addition, ideas well beyond those of craft production are exchanged during group meetings. In at least one group, these discussions spawned new projects for local income diversification such that the group was no longer dependent solely on craft production in meeting its goals. Across all groups, the craft programs illustrate how group skills gained through craft production can multiply in their application.

Strategic Appropriateness

Again from the Kotter and Heskett (1992) framework, an organizational culture is considered strategically appropriate for business performance when practices and decisions fit the context in which it is operating. Fit applies to the internal environment of the business itself as well as to the external international business community. Artisan group parameters related to group fit follow:

> ➤ Programs that integrate men's workshop-based work with women's household-based work mesh well with other gendered responsibilities in rural agricultural settings.
> ➤ Product priorities range on a continuum from making quality products that clients want to developing products embedded in Maya textile traditions. Producers in the first group are open to a broader range of wholesale clients than those in the second group.
> ➤ ATO wholesale customers serve as essential intermediaries for new product development.

In our appraisal, internal fit is currently stronger than external fit for Guatemalan artisan groups. In rural Guatemalan society, women's daily life revolves around a series of rarely changing daily duties of grinding corn, cooking, hoeing, caring for children, washing, and carrying water. Men's agricultural responsibilities in the field are more seasonal in nature (Hendrickson, 1995). Artisan groups that offer both workshop venues for men, allowing them greater flexibility to work away from the home for uninterrupted periods of time, and in-home activities that mesh with women's daily routines fit the gendered patterns of life in highland Guatemala.

As noted in Chapter 2, scholars emphasize the importance of establishing work patterns and organizational structures that build on gendered patterns of work and that provide venues for leadership development (Durham, 1996; Eber & Rosenbaum, 1993; Mayoux, 1995; Nash, 1993a; Tice, 1995). For Guatemalan women artisans, the two goals for organizing production appear to be in opposition. If women work exclusively at home, they can care for their children and perform other household responsibilities; however, they have few opportunities to collaborate with other women in formulating quality standards for export or in establishing the group cohesion so important for group empowerment. The example of UPAVIM's production provides a model for accommodating women's needs to work at home in conjunction with a centralized workshop for product evaluation and group discussions.

Turning to external fit, we note two concerns for ATO-artisan collaboration. First, we conclude that ATOs are unrealistic when they assume that artisans can develop products that will effectively cross cultures without extensive and persistent ATO-artisan collaboration. To expect that a Guatemalan widow living in a one-room home set amid a highland cornfield can envision a rapidly changing line of products for

U.S. middle- and upper-class urban homes is asking for the generally unachievable. It is our observation that the prevailing model of intermittent consultant visits for ATO-to-artisan directed product development has limited impact beyond the period of consultation. We propose that models for how ATOs and artisans can collaborate so that ideas flow in both directions are sorely needed and essential for achieving external strategically appropriate fit.

Our second concern relates to ATOs' emphasis on cultural identity as a stimulus for product development and production practices. When a country's culturally embedded products hold limited external marketability, achieving product fit in global markets calls for change that strikes at the core of how producer groups define their craft tradition and for how ATOs address their commitment to cultural products. As noted by scholars in Chapter 2, retaining long-used processes of production appear more critical for preserving a group's traditions than does retention of a full range of product details (Baizerman, 1987; Niessen, 1990; Stephen, 1991c; Swain, 1993; Tice, 1995).

ATO leaders contribute to this debate. Several have argued that Guatemalan products will only be marketable when there is fundamental change at the basic fabric level, as opposed to designing products within the current Guatemalan *tipica* (range of products in brightly colored fabrics) fabric mix. Other ATOs question whether "fiddling" with the distinctive *jaspé* (resist-dyed) and brocaded fabrics destroys the Guatemalan essence. Bringing the artisans as full participants into these discussions will be critical for understanding the subtleties of how they view their dynamic traditions. Scholars (Baizerman, 1987; Niessen, 1990), in pointing to the importance of clearly delineating issues of craft process versus product, suggest a starting point for exploring if and how marketable product development can evolve in ways acceptable to both artisans and ATOs.

Adaptability to Change

Kotter and Heskett (1992) postulate that in strongly performing businesses, leaders adapt organizational practices to the evolving needs of their constituencies. Leaders are entrepreneurial, take risks, and effectively combine an insider's knowledge with an outsider's perspective that is open to new ideas. Artisan group approaches to change are the following:

> Group interactions facilitate skill and initiative for accomplishing economic and family goals.
> Single-gender programs provide women a context in which they have opportunities to gain confidence in their abilities within a male-dominated society.
> Openness to action and change is shaped by economic need, cultural perceptions of training and business practices, and individual artisan initiative.
> Culture brokers with bilingual skills and experience in U.S. society are essential for (a) grant writing, (b) interpreting product development requests, (c) seeking new wholesale clients in the United States, and (d) maintaining networks in support of program goals.

In all three groups profiled in this chapter, achieving adaptability to change manifests itself at two levels. Group interactions, often gender specific, lead to a "I can do it" attitude essential for initiating change. As noted earlier, without these group activities, we question whether artisans would develop the initiative for learning new skills that strengthen a group's performance capabilities from within. Durham (1996) notes that addressing gender-related challenges is critical for moving an organization from its start-up phrase through to longer-term sustainability (see Chapter 2).

Across the groups, the role of a culture broker is essential for guiding a group in its external movement across domestic and international boundaries. As an example, all three groups operated within a network of domestic and international religious organizations that provided varying forms of assistance as the groups evolved. Each group has leaders who are effective at building and drawing on these alliances.

Based on these observations, we believe that enhancing artisan group adaptability to change calls for attention to both internal and externally focused skill building. Within the group, opportunities for artisans to present opinions and contribute to group decisions help them develop a mind-set that change can be accomplished through collaborative efforts. For a smaller number of group members, opportunities to enhance communication skills, shadow existing culture brokers, and visit U.S. ATO offices and markets enhance the group's ability to look outward to new possibilities.

In conclusion, our analysis of the three artisan groups and our identification of common parameters from their organizational cultures combine to offer important instruction for future ATO-artisan collaboration. First, we learn of the importance of understanding artisan goals and values as a prelude to shaping artisan organizational structure for carrying out production and other business transactions. Attention to the work-family interface is essential for assisting artisans to achieve dual economic and social goals. Second, we observe that strategic fit has both internal and external dimensions. Internally, craft production needs to mesh with artisans' other daily and seasonal responsibilities. Externally, models that encourage dual-directional exchange between ATOs and artisans are needed for developing marketable products. Dialogue concerning artisans' criteria for dimensions of cultural identity would provide a context for decisions related to product ethnicity. Finally, enhancing adaptability to change calls for simultaneous attention to activities that foster confidence building within groups and actions that lead to culture brokerage expertise for artisan group leaders intent on ensuring that "our hands are our future."

Notes

1. The exchange rate in 1997 was 6 Guatemalan quetzales to 1 U.S. dollar.

2. Guatemalan women weave on backstrap looms as they produce fabric of approximately 12 to 20 inches in width and 6 to 8 feet in length. To begin, women wind yarns around a set of 6 to 8 wooden sticks; one end is attached to a house post, and the other end is secured with a strap around the weaver's back. Women sit on the floor with their feet tucked under them; their body weight creates the necessary tension to maintain taunt yarns for weaving. When not weaving, the loom is rolled into a small bundle for easy storage. The loom's small size and portability fit well around a woman's daily activities of cooking and caring for children. When not involved in these activities, she unrolls her bundle, sets up the loom, and weaves either in her house or outdoors under a shaded overhang.

CHAPTER 9

ATO CONSUMERS

Creative, Practical, and Concerned

*I think the market will demand that you listen. You will either listen or
will stop doing what you are doing because market forces control fair
trade just like everything else. And you have to listen, you have to be
knowledgeable. . . . What has happened is that fair trade is growing up.*

—Catherine Renno, first president of the Fair Trade Federation

Leafing through the mail that has just arrived at her home in
Columbus, Ohio, Marlene pulls from the stack the most recent Market-
Place: Handwork of India catalog. A unique jacket, embroidered and
dyed in the traditional wax-resist method called batik, adorns the cover,
compelling her to open the catalog. She remembers her favorite dress,
purchased last summer from the retailer. It is easy care and has held up
well in the wash. Plus it is full, with no uncomfortable waistband, made
of soft and comfy cotton, and she has had tons of compliments when she
wears it to school. As a teacher, Marlene also recalls the interest in her
students' faces as she told them about the women who had made the
dress and what they say it is like to live in Mumbai. Smiling to herself,
she looks for something similar—maybe a darker-colored dress for the
upcoming fall season, or maybe she will try one of the jackets this time.
As she thumbs through the catalog, she considers a question raised by
the artisans in an editorial section of the catalog called Global Dialogue.
. . . If she could change one thing in the world, what would it be?

In addition to the artisan groups described in Chapter 8, another important stakeholder group in the alternative trade system is the consumers. As pointed out in Chapter 1, Alternative Trade Organizations (ATOs) have historically prioritized the needs of the producers with whom they work. In marketing terms, the organizations were mission driven rather than market driven. Although little was known about ATO consumers, they were assumed to be very much like ATO founders and employees—extremely devoted to helping the poor in developing countries.

However, as competition from other nonprofit organizations and for-profit craft retailers increased during the 1980s, ATOs began to recognize that the needs and preferences of this important stakeholder group—consumers—must be addressed. This chapter outlines the research we have conducted with 742 consumers from two of the largest ATOs, 376 of Pueblo to People's (PtP's) customers and 366 who purchase from MarketPlace: Handwork of India. We provide demographic and behavioral information about the consumers, clothing preference data, and insights into the consumers' values and attitudes. Due to their unique needs, customized questionnaires were designed for each ATO, but many items were identical or very similar, and the findings from both surveys reveal some marked similarities among ATO consumers. Further details about the research methods and data analysis can be found in Appendix A.

Because of the high proportion of clothing products offered by both PtP and MarketPlace, clothing products are the focus of our consumer research. However, this is not to say that the clothing offered by the two ATOs is similar. Although product offerings from both ATOs might be defined as "ethnic" because of their use of traditional processes of production and traditional motifs and colors, the clothing MarketPlace sells tends to be more creatively styled than that sold by PtP.

Who Are ATO Consumers?

ATO consumers are a demographically homogeneous group. The great majority of PtP consumers surveyed were female (87%). Males were intentionally not sampled in the MarketPlace survey. However, because the ATO's sales focus is on women's clothing, it is anticipated that the base of MarketPlace consumers is also primarily female.

For both MarketPlace and PtP, the typical customer is Caucasian. The little racial diversity there is in the ATO customer base seems to correspond with the ATO's geographic and product foci. A small proportion of PtP customers are Hispanic, whereas a similar proportion of Market-Place customers are African American (see Table 9.1). Perhaps these consumers more closely identify with the products and life struggles of artisans in Latin America and India, respectively.

ATO consumers, most often in their mid- to late 40s, can also be called baby boomers. Yet, PtP has also attracted a good number of the thirty-something customer market as well. This could be due to the popularity of Latin American clothing among younger people and on college campuses during the late 1980s and early 1990s. On the other hand, MarketPlace is popular with older and larger-sized women, perhaps due to the loose-fitting clothing and extra-large size range they offer.

A small majority of ATO consumers are married, and a little under half have children at home. More than three quarters of ATO customers have jobs, an employment rate that is notable because it is 50% greater than the typical U.S. female of the same age (see U.S. Bureau of the Census, 1995). Whether shopping from an ATO catalog or through their work, the ATO consumer is likely to be giving assistance to someone during her daily routines. More than one quarter of ATO customers are teachers. A number of others are health professionals and social workers.

ATO consumers have also spent plenty of time in the classroom. On average, nearly half of ATO customers hold graduate degrees, and 95% have received a high school diploma, which contrasts with similar aged females in the United States, only 75% of whom have high school degrees (Kominski & Adams, 1994). For ATO customers, along with high levels of education comes high rates of pay. Around half of ATO customers' households earn more than $50,000 per year before taxes. All said, rather than being representative of the general population, ATO consumers appear to be much more similar, in terms of age, education, and income, to the cultural creatives population (described in Chapter 2) who are also college-educated women in their 40s with household incomes of around $50,000.

TABLE 9.1 Demographic Characteristics of ATO Consumers

	Pueblo to People	MarketPlace: Handwork of India
Average age[a]	43.0 years	49.0 years
% younger than age 30	10.0	2.6
% ages 30-39	35.0	17.8
% ages 40-49	32.0	43.2
% ages 50-59	10.0	18.4
% ages 60-69	8.0	10.6
% 70 and older	5.0	7.7
Race/ethnic group (%)		
Caucasian	94.4	91.4
African American	0.8	3.2
Other	4.5	5.4
Hispanic	2.8	
Native American	1.1	
Asian American	0.6	
Marital status (%)		
Married	60.2	Not measured
Single, never married	24.5	
Divorced	9.7	
Widowed	3.2	
Alternative	2.4	
Highest level of education (%)		
Elementary school	—	0.3
High school	6.2	3.0
Some college or technical school	14.2	17.0
College degree	22.6	17.6
Some graduate work	17.7	12.4
Completed graduate degree	39.2	49.7
Household income, before taxes (%)		
Less than $10,000	3.6	1.5
$10,000 to $24.999	17.5	10.4
$25,000 to $49,999	38.5	34.5
$50,000 to $74,999	22.4	24.1
$75,000 or more	18.0	29.5
Employment status (%)		
Employed	76.4	76.6
Not employed or retired	23.6	23.4

TABLE 9.1 Continued

	Pueblo to People	MarketPlace: Handwork of India
Occupation (%)		
Education related	26.0	20.1
Artist, writer, performer	9.4	12.6
Health professional	16.6	12.2
Businessperson, manager	8.0	7.7
Social worker, counselor	6.0	11.4
Computer, clerical	11.4	8.5
Lawyer, engineer, journalist, scientist	8.9	8.5
Other	14.4	8.9
Population of community residence (%)		
Farm or less than 2,000 residents	9.6	7.1
2,000 to 9,999	14.6	13.6
10,000 to 49,999	24.5	17.8
50,000 to 99,999	7.2	13.3
100,000 to 249,999	12.7	11.0
250,000 to 749,999	8.8	11.3
750,000 or more	22.6	25.8
Households with at least one child at home	38.1	44.0
Traveled in region/country where ATO's products are made[b]	56.4	8.2

a. Data on Pueblo to People customers were collected in 1993, whereas data on MarketPlace customers were collected in 1996. Therefore, average age for comparison purposes would be 46.0 for Pueblo to People customers and 49.0 for MarketPlace's customers.
b. Latin America for Pueblo to People customers, India for MarketPlace customers.

What is it about ATOs, their products, and message that have attracted highly educated, well-off, 40-ish Caucasian women? Is there something in their backgrounds that can be encouraged in other consumers who are not familiar with or interested in alternative trade? The high level of education provides ideas for tapping the younger generation of consumers who can be reached at colleges and universities across the country. Schools of higher learning encourage diversity and provide opportunities for contemplation of individual and societal differences and for increased interaction with international students. Consumers who have spent more time in an academic environment may have a broader and more accepting view of the world and its people. This could plausibly lead to an increased likelihood of purchasing through ATOs that champion the needs of others in diverse societies. But whether this younger generation of potential customers will take an interest in alternative trade is uncertain, given their very different life experiences as compared with their parents.

Born in the early 1950s, ATO customers came of age in the mid- to late 1960s, a period marked by protests and civil unrest. During the early 1960s, the civil rights movement gripped the nation as society came to terms with equality for all persons regardless of race. High school age at the time, many ATO consumers would have been old enough to understand and grapple with the issue of equality. Growing up at the right time may have nourished caring and concerned attitudes for different others, attitudes that are now influencing helping behaviors such as purchasing from ATOs.

Shopping

Given the large share of catalog space that both PtP and MarketPlace devote to clothing, we wanted to know to what extent these consumers included ethnic clothing in their wardrobes. It appears that ethnic apparel is a part but not the majority of most ATO consumers' wardrobes. Instead of filling their closets with ethnic-styled garments, there appears to be more focus on classic wardrobes. Seven out of 10 PtP customers buy classic- or basic-styled garments along with some ethnic clothing. A third of MarketPlace's customers' wardrobes are ethnic-styled garments. Six out of 10 MarketPlace customers center their wardrobe around black, highlighting this classic color with shades of purple, blue, and green.

Catalog purchasing is not uncommon for ATO customers. More than 60% of PtP's customers purchase clothing through the mail; one third buy the majority of their wardrobes from catalogs. Four out of 10 clothing purchases made by MarketPlace customers are from a catalog. Given their tendencies to purchase from catalogs, it is not surprising to find that ATO customers perceive little risk in catalog shopping.

What types of information do ATO consumers weigh when shopping? Almost undoubtedly, price. It seems that ATO consumers are somewhat price conscious. MarketPlace consumers pay attention to prices; some are hoping to save a lot of money by shopping for bargains. PtP consumers are also price sensitive. When asked how much they would be willing to pay for a jacket, pair of pants, and shirt, often the prices indicated were lower than the moderate prices actually charged by PtP for the merchandise. When PtP raised its prices on many long-standing garments in 1996 and introduced a variety of new, higher-priced garments, sales dropped.

What Are ATO Consumers Looking for in a Product?

ATOs long suspected that their consumers might be altruistic, meaning they behave in a way that benefits others (see Kohn, 1991; Rushton, 1980). As such, we had expected that the consumer might be willing to make some sort of sacrifice, either in price paid for a product or in quality or styling requirements, to provide monetary support for the artisans. However, ATO consumers were not altruistic in ways that we had anticipated. ATO consumers would buy products only if they liked them. Furthermore, ATO consumers clearly indicated that they would not lower their quality expectations just to buy from an ATO. These firmly held product expectations, along with the sensitivity to price noted by PtP staff when they attempted to make minor changes in their price structure, lead us to believe that ATO consumers do not buy simply out of altruistic support for the artisans. As Lynda Grose, director for the Artisans and Ecology project for Aid to Artisans (ATA), noted at the February 1998 Fair Trade Federation conference, "The product can carry the message, but the message cannot carry the product."

Quality Requirements

No matter the taste or style preferences of the consumers, high quality is the most valued feature for ATO products (see Table 9.2). ATO consumers defined quality in terms of workmanship, characteristics contributing to product longevity, and a garment's fit and appearance on the body. The following features are most important to both PtP's and MarketPlace's consumers:

TABLE 9.2 Clothing Characteristics With Most Highly Rated Desirability

MarketPlace Customers	Rating	Pueblo to People Customers	Rating
Clothing that is comfortable to wear	6.71	Clothing that is comfortable to wear	6.67
Clothing that feels good when I wear it	6.61	Fabric that feels good	6.61
Good-quality clothing	6.60	Clothing that is sewn well	6.56
Clothing that does not shrink when washed	6.59	Colors that do not run when laundered	6.55
Clothing that is sewn well	6.53	Good-quality clothing	6.55
Colors that do not run when washed	6.49	Clothing that fits me properly	6.48
Clothing that fits well	6.42	Durable clothing	6.47
Durable clothing	6.40	A size range that meets my needs	6.38
Clothing that is easy to care for	6.38	Clothing that is easy care	6.33
		Clothing that resists shrinking during laundering	6.28

NOTE: Identical questionnaires were not used for the MarketPlace and Pueblo to People studies. Clothing characteristics varied slightly across the two questionnaires. In addition, MarketPlace rated clothing characteristics using a scale ranging from 1 = *strongly disagree* to 7 = *strongly agree,* whereas Pueblo to People customers rated clothing characteristics using a scale ranging from –3 = *strongly disagree* to +3 = *strongly agree.* For easier understanding, the scales for Pueblo to People ratings were changed to match the MarketPlace scales.

> clothing that is comfortable, feels good when worn, and fits;
> good-quality clothing;
> clothing that is easy-care and does not shrink or have colors that bleed when washed; and
> clothing that is sewn well and durable.

Differing Market Segments for Uniqueness and Ethnicity

Although ATO consumers strongly desire quality products, they also look for ethnicity and uniqueness in ATO clothing. However, different market segments seem to exist among the ATO consumers; in particular, there seem to be two distinct market segments for both PtP and MarketPlace. Across each market segment, quality criteria continued to be the most desired characteristics. However, beyond that styling preferences emerge (see Tables 9.3 and 9.4).

Seven out of 10 PtP customers fall in a category we named *creative ethnic*. These customers prioritize high-quality garments that create an individual look through their traditional colors and fabrics. The creative ethnic group enjoys receiving information about the producers and techniques. As fans of the traditional bright colors of Latin America, it is not surprising that this group is less interested in pastel colors or earthtones that artisan producers sometimes adhere to as they try to tap the North American market.

Plain and simple describes a second group of nearly 30% of PtP's customers. Although prioritizing high quality and enjoying information about other cultures and producers, plain and simple customers stand out for their interest in simple, solid-colored fabrics in neutral gray, black, and white; these fabrics are far removed from what can be considered traditional in Latin America. These customers have little interest in traditional fabrics and techniques or in fashion.

As for MarketPlace customers, *creative/culturally focused/hedonic* describes 46% who are focused on quality and personal attractiveness. These customers use traditionally embellished garments to create a dramatic, yet fashionable look. Authenticity of garment details to the producing culture is important. Simple, loose-fitting garments that camouflage the body are preferred.

The 54% of MarketPlace customers described as *classic/pancultural* focus on quality and design characteristics that will assist them in creating an attractively individual, non-fashion-dictated appearance. A more pancultural ethnic look is desired; strict cultural authenticity is not demanded. Information about the ethnic culture of their producers, although of interest to classic/pancultural customers, takes a backseat to individuality and personal attractiveness.

Now comparing across the four groups, for both market segments of MarketPlace customers (creative/culturally focused/hedonic and classic/pancultural) and the largest segment of PtP's customers (creative ethnic), traditional techniques and colors that are combined in complex fabrics are preferred. These styling characteristics allow the wearer to showcase her uniqueness and creativity in a personally attractive

(Text continued on p. 237)

TABLE 9.3 Characteristics Most Desirable to Market Segments

Pueblo to People 1: Creative Ethnic (71%)	Pueblo to People 2: Plain and Simple (29%)	MarketPlace 1: Creative, Culturally Focused, Hedonic (46%)	MarketPlace 2: Classic, Pancultural (54%)
• **High quality** Clothing that is comfortable to wear (M = 6.79) Colors that do not run when laundered (6.68) Durable clothing (6.67) Clothing that is sewn well (6.60) Clothing that fits properly (6.51)	• **High quality** Clothing that is comfortable to wear (M = 6.39) Colors that do not run when laundered (6.31) Durable clothing (6.12) Clothing that is sewn well (6.34) Clothing that fits properly (6.38)	• **High quality (M = 6.70)** Clothing that is sewn well Colors that do not run when washed	• **High quality (M = 6.35)** Clothing that is sewn well Colors that do not run when washed
• **Individuality** (M = 6.30) Unique/different styles (6.21) Clothing that allows me to express creativity with my appearance (6.17) Bright colors (5.98)	• **Simplicity** Neutral colors such as black, white, or gray (M = 5.24) Solid colors with no print or surface design (5.18)	• **Personal attractiveness** (M = 6.63) Looks good on body type Helps me look attractive	• **Personal attractiveness** (M = 6.01) Looks good on body type Helps me look attractive
• **Ethnicity** Prints, embroidery, or other surface designs traditional to Latin American producers (M = 6.27) Colors traditional to Latin America (6.00) Fabrics made with traditional techniques (5.93) Prints or surface designs all over the garment (5.49)	• **Information for cultural connection** (M = 5.12)	• **Information for cultural connection** (M = 6.48)	• **Individuality** (M = 5.75) Allows me to create a unique look Allows me to be creative Differs from mainstream fashion Interesting or unusual colors Fun to wear

- **Information for cultural connection** (*M* = 5.95)

- **Individuality** (*M* = 6.43)
  Allows me to create a unique look
  Allows me to be creative
  Differs from mainstream fashion
  Interesting or unusual colors
  Fun to wear

- **Ethnicity/Indian surface design** (*M* = 5.93)
  Fabrics made with techniques traditional to India
  Handmade qualities evident in fabric prints or surface decoration
  Interesting or unusual surface decoration

- **Camouflage** (*M* = 5.84)
  Clothing that hides my figure/body type
  Loose-fitting clothing

- **Simplicity** (*M* = 5.63)
  Solid colors
  Simple garment styles
  Neutral colors such as black, gray, and navy

- **Fashionability** (*M* = 5.34)
  Currently fashionable colors
  Fashionable styles

- **Information for cultural connection** (*M* = 5.50)

- **Ethnicity/Indian surface design** (*M* = 5.41)
  Fabrics made with techniques traditional to India
  Handmade qualities evident in fabric prints or surface decoration
  Interesting or unusual surface decoration.

- **Camouflage** (*M* = 4.98)
  Clothing that hides my figure/body type
  Loose-fitting clothing

- **Simplicity** (*M* = 4.76)
  Solid colors
  Simple garment styles
  Neutral colors such as black, gray, and navy

NOTE: MarketPlace rated clothing characteristics using a scale ranging from 1 = *strongly disagree* to 7 = *strongly agree*. Pueblo to People customers rated clothing characteristics using a ranging from −3 = *strongly disagree* to +3 = *strongly agree*. For easier understanding, the scales for Pueblo to People ratings were changed to match the MarketPlace scales.

TABLE 9.4 Characteristics Less Desirable or Not Desirable to Market Segments

Pueblo to People 1: Creative Ethnic (71%)	Pueblo to People 2: Plain and Simple (29%)	MarketPlace 1: Creative, Culturally Focused, Hedonic (46%)	MarketPlace 2: Classic, Pancultural (54%)
• **Nonethnic colors** Pastel colors (M = 4.37) Natural or earthtone colors such as tan, beige, or brown (4.79) • **Simplicity** Solid colors with no print or surface design (M = 4.76) Neutral colors such as black, white, or gray (4.93)	• **Ethnicity** Prints, embroidery, or other surface designs traditional to Latin American producers (M = 4.63) Colors traditional to Latin America (4.30) Fabrics made with traditional techniques (4.84) Prints or surface designs all over the garment (3.88) • **Fashionability** Fashionable styles (M = 3.87) • **Colors** Pastel colors (M = 3.78) Bright colors (3.35) Natural or earthtone colors such as tan, beige, or brown (3.12)		• **Fashionability (M = 3.82)** Currently fashionable colors Fashionable styles

NOTE: MarketPlace rated clothing characteristics using a scale ranging from 1 = *strongly disagree* to 7 = *strongly agree*. Pueblo to People customers rated clothing characteristics using a ranging from –3 = *strongly disagree* to +3 = *strongly agree*. For easier understanding, the scales for Pueblo to People ratings were changed to match the MarketPlace scales.

manner. Thus, for the largest proportion of consumers who buy ethnic apparel from ATOs, concentrating on using traditional colors, techniques, and styles indigenous to a particular culture is an appropriate design strategy. Adherence to textile traditions in the artisans' culture can vary, with some products conveying a general ethnic feel and others an exacting authenticity. None of the ATO consumers surveyed desires pastel- or natural-colored clothing (see Table 9.4).

However, catering to this large majority of consumers may not tap the entire market for ethnic apparel. The small proportion of PtP's customers, labeled *plain and simple*, were very averse to the visually complex *jaspé* fabrics that are created with a mix of bright-colored yarns that are carefully measured and dyed to form intricate patterns. In contrast, this group preferred more simple clothing in solid neutral colors. This group of PtP's customers is also averse to fashionable styles.

Although the preference for unique ethnic clothing is widespread among many ATO consumers, a complex array of cultural meaning and authenticity in the products motivate these consumers' preferences. In Chapter 2, we outlined the variety of influences these factors have for motivating the purchase of cultural products (see Figure 2.1). The preferences of four segments of ethnic clothing consumers from ATOs support this complex model. First, ATO consumers, particularly the creative ethnic, creative/culturally focused/hedonic, and the classic/pancultural, are motivated in self-directed ways toward creating an aesthetic experience by the traditional workmanship and handmade characteristics of the products.

These same three market segments enjoy connecting with others through the traditional products of culturally diverse artisans and the stories ATOs tell about these artisans. These products and stories motivate ATO consumers by tapping their interest in the world and its people. Motivations for establishing self-identity are evident among the creative ethnic and creative/culturally focused/hedonic consumers who seek individuality through ethnic styles that are not common to the apparel market. Classic/pancultural consumers are motivated toward establishing self-identity because of individually offered by antifashion styles.

Finally, ATO consumers' motivations toward managing daily life are evident in the seamless manner in which they have incorporated ethnic clothing into their wardrobes. Consumers in all four market segments own some ethnic apparel, although the greatest majority of their wardrobes is nonethnic. This represents the functional value and daily contrast that are available to them when buying ethnic clothing. Furthermore, MarketPlace customers like this ATO's clothing for its functional ability to provide personal attractiveness and camouflage their bodies.

Are ATOs Offering Products With the Desired Quality and Appearance?

Once we knew what ATO consumers were looking for in ethnic clothing, we asked, "How do the products offered by ATOs fare in terms of their quality and appearance?" MarketPlace customers perusing the clothing offered in the catalog tend to describe it as unique, creative, and comfortable to wear. Interesting surface decorations, unusual colors, and handmade qualities are present and welcomed (see Table 9.5). The quality of the clothing, in terms of fit, care, and durability, is rated thumbs-up by MarketPlace customers (see Table 9.6). Thus, it would seem that, in many ways, MarketPlace's clothing is living up to the expectations of its customers.

PtP's clothing also stood up reasonably well under the scrutiny of its customers, who tend to view the clothing as comfortable to wear and somewhat unique due to its colors and surface decorations. However, PtP's customers suspect that the garments may not fit properly, and they seem to be looking for better garment construction (see Table 9.7). Furthermore, PtP's customers fear the garments will require extra time and effort to care for and may not hold up well in the laundry. With what PtP's customers are looking for in quality and creativity in styling, it seems that PtP's clothing comes up a bit short.

Overall, then, how are ATOs meeting their customers' high demands for quality? MarketPlace certainly fared better on its customers' assessment of quality. However, there is room for improvement on characteristics related to workmanship, ease of care, and durability. PtP garments were assessed somewhat similar to MarketPlace garments in terms of workmanship and ease of care, but improving the care and

TABLE 9.5 Desired Characteristics That Are Present in ATO
            Clothing

Present in MarketPlace Clothing	Rating	Present in Pueblo to People Clothing	Rating
Clothing that differs from mainstream fashion	6.64	Clothing that is comfortable to wear	6.17
Ethnic clothing	6.53	Bright colors	6.13
Handmade qualities evident in fabric printing or surface decoration	6.41	Prints, embroidery, or other surface decorations that are traditional to the Latin American producer's culture	6.08
Clothing that allows me to create a unique look	6.38	Ethnic styles	6.07
Interesting or unusual surface decorations	6.37	Unique colors	6.04
Clothing that is comfortable to wear	6.33		
Clothing that feels good when I wear it	6.28		
Interesting or unusual colors	6.31		
Loose-fitting clothing	6.30		
Clothing that allows me to be creative	6.13		
Clothing that allows me to create a dramatic appearance	6.12		
Good-quality clothing	6.05		

NOTE: MarketPlace rated clothing characteristics using a scale ranging from 1 = *strongly disagree* to 7 = *strongly agree*. Pueblo to People customers rated clothing characteristics using a ranging from –3 = *strongly disagree* to +3 = *strongly agree*. For easier understanding, the scales for Pueblo to People ratings were changed to match the MarketPlace scales.

durability of garments is important for long-run retention of ATO customers. If the garments do not hold up well over time, any hopes of maintaining a long-term relationship with the customers will be dashed. ATOs may be losing customers due to quality imperfections or perhaps never attracting consumers who are initially suspicious of quality levels. In fact, PtP customers who had previously made a clothing purchase from the ATO believed the clothing to be higher quality than those who

TABLE 9.6 Desired Characteristics That May Be Present in ATO Clothing

May Be Present in MarketPlace Clothing	Rating	May Be Present in Pueblo to People Clothing	Rating
Clothing that is sewn well	5.97	Colors that are traditional to the Latin American producer's culture	5.89
Pockets in skirts or pants	5.96	Clothing that allows me to be creative with my appearance	5.83
Durable clothing	5.70	Fabrics made with techniques that are traditional to the Latin American producers	5.83
Simple garment styles	5.63	Fabric that feels good	5.73
Clothing that does not shrink when washed	5.63	Unique or different styles	5.73
Classic styles I can wear for a long time	5.33	Good quality clothing	5.65
Clothing that is easy to care for	5.27	Clothing in the blue color range—navy, blue, etc.	5.65
Colors that do not run when washed	5.17	Interesting surface decorations created with brocade or embroidery	5.63
Clothing that fits well	5.03	Durable clothing	5.59
		Ability to create a dramatic look with my clothing	5.51
		Clothing that is sewn well	5.45
		A variety of styles in lighter-weight fabrics	5.15
		A size range that meets my needs	5.13
		Clothing that is easy care	5.11

NOTE: MarketPlace rated clothing characteristics using a scale ranging from 1 = *strongly disagree* to 7 = *strongly agree*. Pueblo to People customers rated clothing characteristics using a ranging from –3 = *strongly disagree* to +3 = *strongly agree*. For easier understanding, the scales for Pueblo to People ratings were changed to match the MarketPlace scales.

had not tried the products. ATO catalog retailers must take particular note of the quality requirements and inform and assure their customers of the quality of their products because the customers cannot examine the garment prior to purchasing.

TABLE 9.7 Desired Characteristics Not Present in Current Clothing

Not Present in MarketPlace Clothing	Not Present in Pueblo to People Clothing	Rating
All desired characteristics are at least slightly agreed to be present.	Colors that do not run when laundered	4.74
	Clothing that fits me properly	4.67
	Clothing that resists shrinking during laundering	4.39
	A variety of styles in heavier-weight fabrics	4.83

NOTE: MarketPlace rated clothing characteristics using a scale ranging from 1 = *strongly disagree* to 7 = *strongly agree*. Pueblo to People customers rated clothing characteristics using a ranging from –3 = *strongly disagree* to +3 = *strongly agree*. For easier understanding, the scales for Pueblo to People ratings were changed to match the MarketPlace scales.

Are ATOs meeting the styling needs of the four market segments identified earlier? MarketPlace seems to satisfy its two market segments' desire for ethnicity and creativity and, in doing so, creates a nonmainstream fashion look that likely satisfies classic/pancultural customers. In contrast, PtP may not have satisfied its creative ethnic customers in terms of the originality and uniqueness of the styling and surface characteristics; attempts should have been made to add more flair and drama to the styles geared toward this market segment. Most of the apparel was Western styled, with traditional aspects of the producers' culture evident only in the *jaspé* fabric. Creative ethnic consumers may have enjoyed garments that were styled much like the producers' own clothing, incorporating brocade, embroidery, and backstrap woven cloth. In addition, in merchandising these more unique styles, PtP might have considered photographing the garments in stylish combinations that make a statement about the wearer. Showing the garments with blue jeans may have given a less inspired look than would satisfy the creative ethnic. Overall, it seems that PtP's clothing may not have been as ethnic or as unique as the majority of its customers desired.

Desired characteristics of the plain and simple customers were certainly not met. Few solid garments were offered by PtP, and when they were, they seemed to be overwhelmed and lost in the catalog that featured more unique and visually complex products.

How Do ATO Consumers Feel About the World, Its People, and the Contributions ATOs Are Making?

Values and Attitudes Toward the World

Values are centrally held beliefs that affect and guide human behavior throughout life (Rokeach, 1973). Values provide a basis for individuals to determine whether situations are good or bad and to motivate their actions (Feather, 1982). Values and attitudes help consumers form their purchasing decisions. The most important guiding principles in the lives of both MarketPlace's and PtP's customers are values that focus away from the self and toward society (see Table 9.8). ATO consumers are interested in equality and educational opportunity throughout a peaceful, beautiful, and environmentally secure world. These societally directed values are more highly prioritized than values that are more individually centered, such as self-respect or inner harmony. Clearly, the global and societally directed nature of the values will have some influence on ATO consumers as they read the messages provided by ATOs about life in developing countries and make decisions regarding the support they will provide people throughout the world.

Although values are more abstract sets of beliefs that influence human action, attitude "refers to an organization of several beliefs focused on a specific object or situation" (Braithewaite & Scott, 1991, pp. 663-664). Unlike values that are most central to an individual's self-concept and fairly resistant to change, attitudes are less central and more conducive to change (Smith, 1982). Given the importance ATO consumers placed on societally focused values, it is not surprising that these consumers have strong feelings about conditions in developing countries (see Table 9.9). PtP's and MarketPlace's customers take critical views of many social conditions in Latin America and India. In these countries, distribution of wealth; access to basic health care, education, land, and jobs; adequacy of housing; and opportunities for political expression are unacceptable to North American consumers.

How ATO consumers arrived at these beliefs is uncertain. More than half of PtP's customers had traveled to one or more Latin American countries, but their travels may not have taken them off the tourist path

TABLE 9.8 Importance Ratings on Values

Life-Guiding Value	MarketPlace	Pueblo to People
Outer- /societally directed		
Equality (brotherhood, equal opportunity for all)	87.19	87.94
Environmental security (balanced coexistence of people and their environment)	86.06	86.99
A world at peace (free of war and conflict)	86.51	86.44
An educated society (equal educational opportunities for all)	86.50	84.40
A world of beauty (beauty of nature and the arts)	82.91	82.55
Inner-directed		
A sense of accomplishment (lasting contribution)	80.49	81.81
Happiness (contentedness)	80.85	81.22
Pleasure (an enjoyable, leisurely life)	73.39	65.50
A comfortable life (a prosperous life)	68.02	62.11
Social recognition (respect, admiration)	59.18	54.17

NOTE: 1 = not at all important, 100 = extremely important.

TABLE 9.9 Issues in India or Latin America and ATO Concerns

Social Attitudes	MarketPlace	Pueblo to People
Issues and conditions in India/Latin America		
People feel safe to express their political views	2.53	1.73
People have access to basic health care	2.37	1.85
Children have access to basic education	2.10	1.97
Enough land is available for people who want to farm	1.91	2.34
Enough jobs are available for people who want to work	1.90	1.82
Enough adequate housing is available	1.89	1.81
Wealth is fairly evenly distributed	1.56	1.44
ATO concern		
I am concerned about issues affecting people in less-developed countries around the world.	6.12	5.90
I am concerned with issues affecting people in India/Latin America.	5.80	5.72

NOTE: 1 = strongly disagree, 7 = strongly agree.

where they could observe firsthand what life was like for the poor in these countries. Not even 1 in 10 MarketPlace customers had traveled to India. Thus, their views were unlikely to be a result of firsthand knowledge. However, 9 out of 10 MarketPlace customers read the editorial features in MarketPlace's catalog. The informative features in the catalog would give greater familiarity to the issues affecting quality of life for the artisans in India. Thus, we believe that the information on artisans and their lives provided by ATOs in editorials and on hangtags is important to the consumer experience.

Attitudes Toward ATOs

When looking more specifically at the attitudes ATO consumers have toward the work and mission of the ATOs themselves, we find a very supportive group of consumers (see Tables 9.9 and 9.10). The mission of ATOs to assist the poorest artisans in developing countries is clearly compatible with the values and worldview of ATO consumers. ATO consumers expressed clear solidarity in the efforts made by ATOs. Perhaps even more important, these consumers are also willing to support this work through purchases. All in all, the values and attitudes of ATO consumers, along with the demographic characteristics noted earlier, closely parallel the cultural creatives described in Chapter 2. Like this segment of the population, ATO consumers value the world and its people and are interested in understanding global issues through detailed accounts of human conditions. Buying products from ATOs can provide connection to artisan producers.

What Will Influence ATO Consumers' Future Purchasing?

Knowing the strong values and attitudes ATO consumers have toward the world and people in developing countries and the solidarity expressed toward ATO work, it might be tempting for ATOs to continue their producer-directed marketing while addressing consumer product needs as an afterthought. This approach would be misguided. Figure 9.1 shows how values, attitudes, and product characteristics

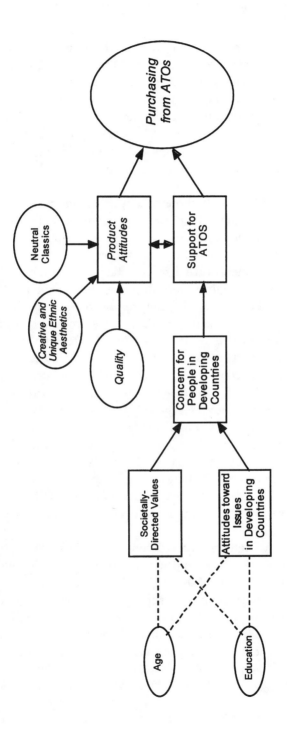

Figure 9.1. Factors Motivating ATO Consumer Behavior

influence plans to purchase from an ATO. The italicized portions in the figure represent what most influences ATO consumer behavior.

How ATO consumers feel about the products offered is critical as consumers contemplate buying from an ATO. First and foremost, products must be high quality and durable. For many consumers, high priority is also placed on unique, ethnic-styled products that allow the purchaser to express her creativity. If ATO products do not meet the expectations of the consumer for quality and styling, they will simply not be purchased.

The high product expectations held by consumers have implications for ATOs as they consider adapting their organizational cultures to the changing business environment. As noted in Chapter 2, Kotter and Heskett (1992) equate strong business performance with a fit between the market environment and a firm's practices. The current highly competitive business environment for cultural products demands that ATOs provide products that are strategically appropriate for their customers' wants and needs. In particular, product development strategies aimed at creating Porter's (1980) competitive edge of differentiation and focus seem warranted, particularly as they focus on quality and styling requirements of ATO consumers. For example, in retrospect, PtP might have focused on the large creative ethnic consumer group by expanding offerings of garments more closely styled to traditional Latin American garments. Most of PtP's apparel was Western styled, with traditional aspects of the producers' culture evident only in the *jaspé* fabric. Creative ethnic consumers may have enjoyed garments that were styled much like the producers' own clothing, incorporating brocade, embroidery, and backstrap woven cloth. This would also have created greater differentiation between PtP's offerings and clothing sold by mainstream retailers.

However, the high priority ATO consumers place on the quality and styling of the product does not mean that they are not amenable to supporting the work of ATOs. High levels of support for ATOs also directly improves the chances consumers will buy ATO products. Consumers may receive an ATO catalog, read some of its editorials on life in a developing country, and decide they are interested in supporting the work. However, if they examine the retailers' offerings and find nothing they like or believe will meet their quality or styling expectations, they will not buy just to support the ATO's mission. On the other hand, if they wish to support the ATO and find the products interesting and of high enough quality, then they will likely buy.

Because purchasing from ATOs is based on more than just product-related characteristics, it behooves us to ask what influences a consumer to be supportive of ATO work. First, they are concerned about the people in developing countries who live in an environment of poverty, inequality, and oppression. The greater their concern for people, the greater their support for alternative trade. Concern is fostered by ATO consumers' societally directed values and how unacceptably they view issues in developing countries. They are very conscious of and place high priority on all the world's needs for education, peace, environmental security, and beauty. ATO consumers also understand the issues in the developing world, realizing the harsh conditions that the producers of ATO products face. Last, many ATO consumers fall in the highly educated baby boomer group.

The essential messages from this model of ATO consumer behavior are the following:

> ➢ Values and attitudes concerning the world provide a foundation of support for ATOs.
> ➢ The more supportive consumers are of alternative trade, the more likely they will be to buy ATO products.
> ➢ Consumers will not buy ATO products if they do not meet their quality and styling requirements.

Influencing ATO Consumer Behavior

Understanding how values and attitudes are linked with ATO consumer behavior helps us determine how to encourage consumers to purchase from ATOs. The best strategy to increase purchasing is to provide higher-quality products.

However, there are also opportunities to encourage purchasing by garnering greater customer support for alternative trade. How might this be done? We know that when people believe that conditions in developing countries are unacceptable, they tend also to have greater concern for the people who reside in these countries and are more supportive of ATO work. This would suggest that a fundamental way to influence consumer behavior, at least a bit, is by helping the consumer

TABLE 9.10 Support for Alternative Trade and Willingness to Make Product Sacrifices

Attitudes Toward Alternative Trade	MarketPlace	Pueblo to People
ATO support		
I am supportive of/believe in the type of work that ATOs are doing.	6.74	6.58
If exactly the same product were available at the same price from an ATO and a non-ATO, I would make an extra effort to buy the product from an ATO.	6.51	6.36
I like the idea of having a direct link to the producers of my clothing.	6.48	5.78
I make a point of purchasing as many products as possible from ATOs.	5.27	4.28
ATO trade-offs		
I would not buy from an ATO unless I really like the product.	5.53	5.83
If I found the same product at a cheaper price from a non-ATO, I would buy it from the non-ATO.	3.74	4.06
I would buy products from ATOs just to help support the craft producer.	3.61	3.86
I would settle for a lower-quality product in order to buy something from an ATO.	3.10	2.71

understand the deplorable conditions in the region of the world where the products are made. The editorials in ATO catalogs, the brochures offered in ATO stores, and other educational materials used by ATOs are of great importance. These educational materials provide an opportunity to educate consumers and thus may also increase their support to these producers.

Conclusions

From what we know about MarketPlace's and PtP's customers, we believe that, overall, purchasers of ATO products exemplify socially responsible consumers who value the world and its people. ATO consumers hold strong values related to the world and its people and exhibit heartfelt concern for citizens of developing countries who reside in bleak and unacceptable conditions. These values and attitudes lend support to ATOs and their products and reflect a strong belief in and support for a manner of trade geared toward providing direct support to craft producers. Yet, product purchase does not appear to be viewed as an altruistic act because purchasers are unwilling to sacrifice product quality for the sake of purchasing. Expectations for a high-quality product may reflect a nonpaternalistic view and respect for the artisans' capabilities in Latin America and India.

In terms of the product itself, two very important points emerge. First, ATO consumers demand high-quality products, yet do not always perceive that ATO clothing meets their quality expectations. If ATOs are indeed offering high-quality products that are well fitting, comfortable, sewn well, easy care, and do not bleed and shrink during care, then they must convince potential consumers of these advantages. If an ATO's products have any shortcomings related to quality, they must be addressed at the product development level.

Second, the great majority of ATO consumers seem to like ethnic apparel offered by ATOs for their unique and ethnic characteristics. Traditional colors and weaving techniques can provide the outlet for creativity desired by many ATO consumers.

Finally, ATOs should be encouraged that the messages they have been sending about artisan groups in developing countries address the genuine concerns their consumers have for the poor in developing countries and are well suited to the beliefs and needs of ATO customers. ATOs should continue to provide new and updated information on artisan producers and their cultural environment, in addition to pursuing product development aimed at satisfying ATO consumer needs and encouraging repeat purchases.

CHAPTER 10

CHALLENGES IN
PRODUCT DEVELOPMENT

I think up until 10 years ago, we [SERRV] didn't sell crafts—we sold fair trade. Our customers didn't care so much what the product was. What they were buying into was the concept. And I think that was one of the reasons why we could get away with doing practically no product development. And in fact we had the same products year after year.

—Bob Chase, SERRV

Docey Lewis scans the preliminary sales report from the recent SERRV catalog. She sighs in relief when she sees that the brooms she worked on with the group in Peru are selling. Although she has years of experience in product development, a keen eye for trends, and well-honed skills in analyzing sales and market reports, she is not comfortable that she and a group have arrived at the right product until it is successfully marketed. She had pressured SERRV to include the brooms in its catalog, partially because she considered the makers to be a worthy group. Yet, she also had a good feeling about these functional but decorative brooms because the piasaba palm fiber was a unique color that gave inherent interest to the product. Also, the group members had some experience working with the materials. But as Docey explains, "I don't start waving the flag until I know there is a market for the product."

The brooms are one of many products Docey Lewis has worked on recently as a product development consultant with Alternative Trade Organizations (ATOs). Docey admits having years of good luck in developing products that suit their intended market. For example, rugs developed with Bedouin carpet weavers in Jordan in 1989 are still selling in 1998. High-volume sales of a birchbark nativity made by a group in Russia with whom Docey has worked are especially meaningful. The group's efforts stem from an Aid to Artisans project for which funding ended 3 years ago. The continued ability of the group to make salable products shows Docey that the Russian group is achieving the long-term sustainability she had hoped for.

However, not all projects are as successful. On a recent trip, Docey admired beautiful products in a Nepal showroom. She could tell from the products that the producers had exciting materials available to them along with well-developed skills. However, they lived and worked in an isolated location that would require more than 2 days of walking to reach the community. The group's isolation and limited communication capabilities made extended product development improbable. In addition, sometimes despite having wonderful skills, the available materials limit product development. Docey expresses frustration when considering the talented Guatemalan weavers who work with "the same old cotton" that has saturated the market. Docey's extensive interaction with the market tells her that something new in the way of materials is needed to bring retail buyers' attention back to Guatemala.

In 1998, Docey's travels took her to one country per month, sometimes more. She never experiences jet lag anymore, even on a trip to Nepal that takes 35 hours of travel. She typically works with a group 2 or 3 weeks before heading to SERRV headquarters in Maryland or to her home in Connecticut, where she has a studio well stocked with research materials and volumes of ideas from past projects. Docey enjoys having an outlet for her creativity that allows her to "leverage her talent in a way that benefits others." She recalls the reward that comes with opening a catalog and seeing a product she has developed, knowing that she is helping a village from its sales.

As is explained in this chapter, ATOs are increasingly using experienced consultants such as Docey Lewis in product development efforts to mesh a group's skills and available materials with market trends. Product development carried out by ATOs and their consultants links the needs of the artisan producers (Chapter 8) and consumers (Chapter 9) who are at the two end points of the alternative trade system. From a market-oriented, mainstream business point of view, product development is an essential business strategy in the marketing mix (i.e., the four Ps of marketing—product, price, place, and promotion; Kotler, 1988). Product development influences the characteristics of the product itself, the minimum price that must be charged to profit from its sale, and where and how the product is best promoted. Strategies for product development are an integral part of a successful business plan because sales of current products will almost certainly decline at some point in the future, making replacements necessary (Kotler, 1988). For artisans, product development conducted under the guidance of skilled professionals can also assist them in developing design and production skills necessary for the export market.

This chapter outlines the product development approaches used by a number of ATOs. Three major topics are covered: (a) the focus on maintaining traditional aspects of a culture in product development, (b) types of product development approaches and the differing philosophies on which they are based, and (c) the day-to-day factors influencing product development decisions. At the end of the chapter, we present a model summarizing key issues influencing product development decisions. We focus primarily on product development of textile and apparel items because these are the products about which we have the most research-based data. However, our observations of other product categories suggest that a number of the ideas put forth in this chapter apply across media and product types.

Focus on Tradition

Developing products for a contemporary market while maintaining the traditions of the artisan group is basic to the assumptions from which ATOs operate (see Chapter 1). Sometimes, tradition is emphasized to provide continuity and enhance cultural identity for the producer and the products they make. Other times, tradition represents a marketing strategy of product differentiation or a way to accommodate trade restrictions. In an example of cultural continuity, Ron Spector and the women of Asociación Maya have chosen to work solely with the traditional backstrap weaving of Guatemala. All the group's efforts in product development have focused on creating different fabrics within the parameters of this traditional loom. Regarding his decision to prioritize tradition, Ron explains,

> There is a project in a nearby village teaching the women how to tie fish flies. These are other options that are presented when people begin to understand the obstacles in the marketplace to success for these weavers. And to me it would be fine for them to involve themselves in other activities. But backstrap weaving is at the center of their life. These women we work with traditionally have woven their own blouses, their own sashes, their own head coverings.

Ron credits interest displayed by the women during recent product development workshops to the close connection maintained with their tradition:

> It worked because first of all, everything that we were doing in terms of new designs was something that grew out of their own experience. This [motif] that came off their *huipil,* the only change was making a little space in between.

In a second example, MarketPlace: Handwork of India artisans focus on a niche market through emphasizing trading in their unique styles created for customers wanting to develop a personal image. Toward reaching their goal, MarketPlace emphasizes an ethnic look that maintains ties with the producers' indigenous culture and also creates a unique look desired by its customers. According to Pushpika Freitas,

> Partly what we wanted to do was to produce or design clothes that didn't alienate the producer. So what we've done is take traditional garments and change them around. Like the pants are very traditional, but we put pockets in them. The tops are basically from the traditional Indian garment style. I think also the Eastern clothes have been designed to not waste as much fabric as possible. Every small piece of fabric is used so then you're really working in straight lines, which helps the producer. We wanted to work directly with the producers and use the skills that they're already used to, like the tie dye or block print. By definition then you're talking ethnic clothes, because that's what your raw materials are, but at the same time wanting to adapt it to the customer.

Focusing on traditional garment styles provides MarketPlace with an added business advantage in that its clothing is categorized as handcrafts and thus is exempt from quota restrictions. The amounts of cotton textile products that can be exported to the United States from India are restricted by quota that are arranged through bilateral agreements falling under the Multi-Fiber Arrangement. Typically, products that represent traditional handcrafts for the exporting country are exempt from quota. For example, to be defined as a handcraft and thus not subject to restrictions on the number of garments imported into the United States, MarketPlace includes a drawstring rather than elastic in the waist of their skirts. Jackets must overlap at the front, have tie closures, and be a specific length. Scarves must be rectangle like traditional ones, and pants must be handwoven or have a certain amount of handwork. By choosing to make products falling under the definition of handcrafts, MarketPlace artisans retain a level of control over their export business that would otherwise be influenced by government bureaucracy.

Despite consumer preference for traditional ethnic fabrics, styles, and embellishment (see Chapter 9), the ATO focus on tradition can constrain product development and actually create problems, especially if a country's distinctive products are out of fashion in U.S. markets. In concurrence with Docey Lewis's views on Guatemala expressed in the opening section of this chapter, we heard repeatedly in Guatemala that the products incorporating the traditional bright and intricately dyed *jaspé* fabrics had reached peak export sales in 1995 and now were difficult to market. As a result, Barb Fenske stated that UPAVIM's product development was focused on making "anything that does not look Guatemalan." Rather than clinging to cultural ties in product development, Barb identifies two primary questions for UPAVIM product development, including (a) what will sell? and (b) can we make it? Barb credits the group's growing success with its reputation for high quality. In addition, buyers know UPAVIM will work with them to develop just the right product.

We believe that a focus on tradition is a valid and competitive strategy for ATOs to differentiate themselves in the craft market. However, as discussed in Chapter 2, there are differing opinions of whether cultural traditions are maintained in product aesthetics and form or in the processes used to create products. At issue is how and why craft traditions evolve and whether cultural identity is lost as a result. The concern of some Western artists and scholars focuses on whether products straying from their traditional form and appearance can be valid for expressing and maintaining cultural identity. On the other hand, other scholars focus on how cultural identity is embodied in the production of products using traditional technologies passed down through the generations. Our observations suggest that placing too great a concern on how cultural products look could ultimately inhibit artisans' maintenance of cultural identity. Ignoring consumer demand for change in product styles and features will make it impossible for an artisan group to continue production for business purposes. Many artisans recognize that the product they make will change as the market demands; however, the love of creating a product retains a cultural link to their parents and ancestors. For example, when asked what weaving represents to them, one women who works with Ruth and Nohemi stated,

> It is important because it is a job that our mothers and grandmothers taught us. My mother didn't make *huipiles* but did other weaving. It was different weaving, but there was always weaving in the family. It is important for my daughter to learn to do more complicated *huipiles* so that she can get larger amounts of money, 300 quetzales for your time versus 150. Also, we can make our own clothes, as well as keeping our culture.

Diverse ATO Approaches for Product Development

Beyond common underlying assumptions about tradition, ATOs employ a number of different approaches to their product development. These approaches vary widely, ranging along a continuum representing differing levels of intervention. On one end of the continuum is a no-intervention, "shop-the-market" approach in which ATO employees simply select products that the artisan groups are producing (see Figure 10.1). Little time is spent with the artisans other than to determine who has the desired products. With this approach, ATO staff or design consultants make little or no attempts to change the product in ways that might influence salability in the North American market. When designer-artisan interactions do occur, they are often intermittent or one-shot consultancies with little or no follow-through from the

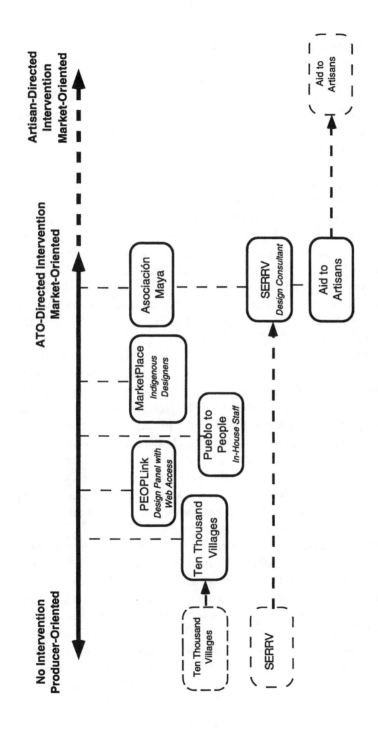

Figure 10.1. ATO Approaches to Product Development

ATO to the artisans. Philosophically, respect for the producers' culture and traditions underlies this producer-oriented approach to nonproduct development. ATOs embracing this approach view outsider intervention as tampering with traditional skills and design. They fear that through external input, a neocolonial relationship of dependency will be created. Accordingly, care is taken not to intervene in product development so that producers do not become dependent on ATOs for success.

The one-sided view of product development just described seems to be an approach from which many ATOs have moved away. Increasingly, ATOs are realizing the need to create products for an overall product mix that caters to their customers' preferences. As such, an ATO-directed intervention, market-oriented approach distinguishes the other end of the product development continuum. Under this approach, ATOs use culture brokers to collaborate with artisan producers in developing products for current consumer tastes. A culture broker works with the artisans on a sustained basis, seeking their input, but at the same time nudging them toward higher skill levels.

As seen in the matrix in Figure 10.2, culture brokers are insiders or outsiders to the culture and may work in design or interpretation capacities. The culture broker may be an employee of a North American ATO, such as Teresa Cordón, a Guatemalan who worked with Pueblo to People (PtP) for 5 years, helping to translate the producers' unique skills and abilities into desirable export products. On the other hand, the culture broker may be a local artisan with special design skills and market experiences such as MarketPlace's former designer Kirit Dave. Some ATOs hire highly skilled design consultants, often American or European, to act as culture brokers. Docey Lewis, introduced in the opening scenario, works with SERRV in this capacity.

Another type of culture broker may be a Peace Corps representative or some other outsider who volunteers to work closely with a group; Barb Fenske, adviser for UPAVIM, would fit this classification. Whoever the culture broker, there is a talented individual providing at least some understanding of the consumer on whose assistance an artisan group may rely. Indeed, executives with SERRV partially credit a recent financial turnaround to their design consultant, Docey Lewis, who had valuable product development experience in an international business context.

	DESIGNER	INTERPRETER
INSIDER	MarketPlace Kirit Dave	Pueblo to People Teresa Cordón
OUTSIDER	SERRV Docey Lewis	UPAVIM Barbara Fenske

Figure 10.2. Matrix of Culture Brokers

Like ATOs adopting a no-intervention, producer-oriented approach for product development, ATOs using a culture broker are sensitive to creating dependency among the artisans and ATO staff. However, ATOs adopting a market-oriented approach for product development place greater importance on a culture broker's input in helping the artisans succeed in the competitive world market than they do on worrying about creating dependent relationships.

Examples of Differing ATO Approaches

Since the mid-1990s, many ATOs have begun to move away from the no-intervention approach to development. In a first example, Ten Thousand Villages' employees have traditionally prioritized the producer over the consumer, focusing on finding rather than developing new products. For much of its history, Villages' product development approach would have fallen under the no-intervention end of the continuum presented in Figure 10.1. But according to Villages' Rachel Hess, "It has become increasingly difficult to just go shopping with them." Villages' staff recognizes that those producer groups providing the newest and most creative products either have benefited from an outsider's input on product development or have group members who are more experienced in the market. In contrast, less successful artisans have focused on copying what others in their area are doing; increasingly, these groups are asking Villages for help on product development. As such, Villages is in a transitional period in which it is moving into an approach that provides more sustained product development assistance.

One essential aspect of Villages' move toward greater intervention in product development is an understanding of the context and environment in which work takes place. The purchasing manager, marketing manager, and director make several international trips each year to familiarize themselves within the context that they're working in and come back with a better understanding of what they can continue to work on. These trips help clarify miscommunications that may have arisen through nonpersonal faxes or phone calls and also help to establish an understanding of the producers' production limitations.

As Villages expanded its product development assistance, the organization received criticism from those within and outside who believe the ATO is straying from its fundamental beliefs that craftpersons' needs and traditions should override market forces. Likewise, as the merchandise team starts to develop product lines, they worry about how their intervention will be perceived by the producers. According to one Villages staff member,

> What does it mean to [the craftspeople] when we send them a swatch with our order? What kind of gymnastics do they have to go through to try and match that? It's always so hard when I write a letter—I try to think about what does this sound like on the other end. I try to hear the tone.

While Villages staff members have long been very hesitant about intervening in the process of product development, another ATO leader behaves exactly opposite. Ron Spector's design work with Asociación Maya in Sololá, Guatemala, probably differs most extremely from Villages' product development. In this second example of product development, Ron's strategy typifies an ATO-directed intervention, market-oriented approach (see Figure 10.1). Ron's strategy for product development focuses on actively developing transferable skills that artisans can use for creating innovative products for the export market. Ron spends a great deal of time communicating and sharing ideas with the artisan members of Asociación Maya while also taking the time to learn from them. For example, Ron became particularly interested in learning the constraints and limitations of backstrap weaving. A production issue that arose from using backstrap woven fabric serves to illustrate. Fabric was pulling apart and separating at the seams of a U.S.-destined garment, even when the seams were finished with a sturdy French seam technique. This problem would not have surfaced when the women created their traditional clothing since their own clothing fits rather loosely in less tailored styles; the garments do not receive the stress at the seams as a more tailored garment might endure. The problem was resolved when Ron hosted two Mayan women in Oregon for 7 months working on design, studying the U.S. market, and problem solving.

Ron has also spent considerable periods of time in Guatemala, where he learned even more about backstrap weaving and the possible fabric textures and appearances that could be achieved. Once he mastered a basic understanding of backstrap weaving, Ron and the weavers started to experiment more. For example, he put together an intense weaving workshop in which eight Mayan women resided at the workshop for several weeks, working solely on new design ideas and ultimately coming up with some exciting tradition-based weaving.

Skill levels of both the artisan producers and those North Americans helping with product development influence product development. Ron's philosophy on product development is to involve the producers while not letting their inexperience in product development limit innovation. Regarding his work with Mayan women, Ron notes,

> Their experience in many ways is quite limited to village life, and when asked to look at doing something differently, their first response might be no [to trying a new product]. You know if one is going to be sort of stopped at that point and say, "Well, the weavers have said they can't do it," then one would inevitably be limited to certain ways of doing things, certain ways of producing cloth, certain designs in cloth that would also have their limited ability to be sold in the market place. Wouldn't help weavers put food on their table, wouldn't help anybody. So you have to keep going further.

However, Ron acknowledges that pushing the product development abilities of the producers is time-consuming and labor intensive, conditions that are difficult for many ATOs and producers whose business foci center on survival. ATOs do not always have staff with the necessary skills to provide input on product development. If a design consultant is hired, his or her charges are generally quite high—especially to the producers in developing countries. For example, a woman from Ireland worked with Pop Atziak, a marketing organization in Guatemala that works with seven artisan groups, giving them some ideas for new products and showing them several more efficient production techniques. However, to continue training members of the group, the specialist wanted compensation at $450 per day.

In a third ATO example of product development, SERRV is rapidly changing its philosophy toward product development and has moved from a no-intervention, producer-oriented approach to an ATO-directed intervention, market-oriented approach (see Figure 10.1). In the past few years, SERRV has greatly increased its product development efforts, bringing in an outside consultant to provide assistance. But like Villages, SERRV staff is also concerned with the ramifications of this practice. Brian Backe, marketing director at SERRV, comments on product development:

> Philosophically I struggle with this, as I think there are times when it's very hard to not go over the line—sending Santa Claus designs to India. . . . I think one of the challenges with product development is [when] you've come in and you've imposed a design that has no reflection on that culture—versus adapting a design. And from the short-term point of view [the producers] want sales from us and they want product design—"Forget it, we're not concerned. Give us stuff that will sell." But from the long-term point of view, I worry greatly that if we get too much product development going and we're too successful, we could take away what is unique about our products.

Still other ATOs use product development approaches falling between the two extremes shown by Villages and SERRV and Ron Spector's views. Particularly regarding clothing, PtP made most of its clothing design decisions in Houston because the group members in Guatemala (where most of their clothing was made) had virtually no exposure to U.S. customers. Consistent with their values of providing new skills to the producers, PtP's product development staff was very concerned with not creating a dominant-subordinate, neocolonial relationship with the groups. Nor did the staff have professional expertise for evaluating market trends. Thus, PtP did not take on a full ATO-directed product development approach (see Figure 10.2). In attempts to avoid a dependent relationship and to move toward decentralization of design decisions, the product development team worked closely with the artisan groups on design ideas by incorporating the group members' ideas with their own. For example, members of Las Girasoles had tried embroidering their traditional flower motifs on T-shirts. However, the embroidery ended up looking very heavy and puckered on the soft T-shirt fabric. PtP staff took the initial idea and changed the base to a stiffer woven fabric, creating a shell blouse of 100% cotton with flowered embroidery.

In addition, PtP employees' design ideas were always suggestions, not mandates; the final decision on whether to make a product was made by the craft producers. Joan Stewart recalled one situation in which she had requested that the members of Artesanas de San Juan develop a duffel bag from their backstrap woven cloth. However, despite repeated requests to see a sample, the group did not send one and seemed uninterested in making the bag. Joan thought that the disinterested attitude might be due to the lack of originality to the product, which is frequently seen in the Guatemalan markets, and to the producers' well-founded beliefs that making such a bag would not differentiate them from others in the area.

For most of its early years at MarketPlace: Handwork of India, product development was conducted by a Mumbai-based designer who took direction from the founder in the Chicago office. Thus, MarketPlace occupies a position midway between the no-intervention and ATO-directed portion of the continuum presented in Figure 10.1. The designer worked hard to balance customer preferences with producer skills. While the designer was employed with MarketPlace, Pushpika Freitas noted,

> We have a full-time designer at Share who is Indian and really great. He can move from medium to medium. He doesn't only look at what the customer wants, but also what the skills are of the people. He really works with the people. He doesn't just sit at his drawing board, he's at their level and will sit down with the person and work on the design depending on how that person is progressing.

The input of the Indian women who sew and embroider the clothes was attained by asking their opinions on designs and color schemes. Kirit Dave, former head designer in Mumbai, comments,

When I work with the craftpersons to develop new fabric designs, we experiment together, making mistakes but also developing some winners. This collaboration is important because it encourages their creative abilities, something they have come to believe is the responsibility of the "designer."

A particularly innovative but somewhat less direct product development approach is one used by Dan Salcedo in his Internet marketing firm, PEOPLink. In a World Wide Web site called Designers' Studio, artisans present digital pictures of their products and fabrics. A panel of U.S. designers can then access the Web site and contribute feedback on the Web. Comments are stored on the Web site so that others on the panel of designers can respond to each other. Artisans are then free to use the feedback if they desire; thus, PEOPLink is placed in the mid-portion of the product development approach continuum (see Figure 10.1).

Across all approaches to product development currently used by ATOs, we see evidence of an organizational culture that is shifting from a producer/product orientation to one much more focused on the demands of consumers in the market. Increasingly, ATOs are making use of a culture broker who can assist with the extensive communication and product development work required as an artisan group creates unique products for export. All these activities suggest a competitive business strategy focused on differentiation in the market (see Porter, 1980, in Chapter 2).

Creating Sustainable, Self-Sufficient Businesses for the Highly Competitive World Market

As noted earlier, many ATOs are greatly concerned that the artisans groups with whom they work become sustainable and self-sufficient in the world marketplace. This philosophy leads some ATOs to adopt a no-intervention, producer-oriented approach, thinking that absence of intervention early on will increase sustainability. However, under a no-intervention approach, artisans' skills likely remain static because there are no extra demands that might push artisans beyond their present skill levels. What is most likely needed is an initial period of time under an ATO-directed intervention approach and then movement toward a producer-directed intervention approach once the artisans have developed product development skills for an export market. Under the latter approach to product development, producers will have developed the necessary skills and networks to seek out design assistance on an as-needed basis. Thus ideally, in the long-term, most ATOs would find their product development efforts passing through the central portion of the continuum shown in Figure 10.1 to occupy a position under the extreme right-hand side of the model.

On the ATO-directed intervention end of the product development continuum, care must be taken by ATO staff to give an artisan group plenty of learning time. Many ATOs adopting a market-oriented approach for product development still retain a fear of creating dependency, thus pushing the artisans too quickly toward what appears to be self-sufficiency. For example, a new trend among ATOs and consultants is to provide the types of information typically used by North American designers to their counterparts in developing countries. Villages' Rachel Hess describes this strategy:

> Right now a lot of ATOs have been using storyboards and general trend information about the market and sending it to producers. And I can see it could be an awfully confusing picture. I've seen those storyboards used in ways that indicate to me they don't quite understand what to do with them. And I must admit, some of them have quite a bit of market jargon in them. And some of them have very little text . . . it's all these images and what is one really to learn from them?

Although Villages is moving away from its antiproduct development stance, staff members are thinking carefully about how best to assist the producers. According to Rachel Hess,

> We are working with people with so many different levels of their own thinking process that sometimes it [storyboards and market information] doesn't work and it doesn't make sense, and it would be better to send them a very specific sketch with very directive instructions.

Villages' staff believes that you must understand the skills of the producers and then consider the type of information that would be helpful to producers, in addition to showing them how to use it.

It is probably realistic to view the goal of artisan self-sufficiency as a long-term one that involves a difficult transition. Extensive communication and work with a culture broker allows artisans to develop their skills as they are increasingly exposed to the world market. For example, Barb Fogle, purchasing director at SERRV, remembers an experience in Bangladesh:

> We asked them to make us some trellis and we wanted them six foot high and four foot wide. And so they faxed us and said, "This can't be correct—this is as large as a human person." So I said, "No, it's true, it's right, and we expect people to put them in their garden and they'll grow their roses up over them, so go right ahead and make them. You haven't made a mistake." But they couldn't conceive that anyone would want this thing because they had never seen it before.

Over time, artisans will generally prefer to make established products because they can be produced more efficiently and seem, to the artisans, to offer more of a money-making prospect. Ron Spector explains,

> Their thinking is, well it has been good for 7 or 8 years, why can't it still be good? I mean why do we have to change? Look, we sold our stuff in the past, why does it have to change? There is no understanding of the speed of development of design in this marketplace.

What seems essential for ATO leaders to realize is that their philosophical ideal that product development will occur without outsider intervention is unrealistic for artisan groups with little export experience. Which approach an ATO adopts should be guided by how strategically appropriate it is for the prevailing market environment (see Chapter 2). Currently, the market for cultural products is highly competitive; thus, an ATO-directed intervention approach that uses some sort of culture broker seems most appropriate at this time.

Day-to-Day Factors Influencing Product Development

Once ATOs have decided to intervene in product development, they take into consideration many human and physical resources influencing day-to-day design and production. The following questions are addressed in this section:

> What will be made, and what will the product look like?
> How are product form and appearance influenced by the artisans involved?
> How much should the product cost?
> What product mix is best for the ATO sales venue?
> What factors may prevent an ATO from receiving products?

What Will Be Made, and What Will the Product Look Like?

What types of products will an ATO carry? What styles? What colors? Answers to these questions will depend on an ATO's attitudes toward tradition, discussed earlier in this chapter, and a number of other factors such as the availability of raw materials and components, quality control programs, equipment a group uses in production and its maintenance, space available for production, available skills, and special considerations according to product type.

Domestic Sourcing

Sustainable Peace Corps craft projects have tended to use readily available local materials as component parts (see Durham, 1996, in Chapter 2). Likewise, Docey Lewis considers locally available materials as a key ingredient for successful product development. We also observed evidence of this in ATO product development. The first products that MarketPlace artisans made were patchwork quilts. Fabric scraps were obtained from tailors and mills at little or no cost. Then the scraps were pieced together by hand, so no investment in sewing equipment was necessary. A later product development idea involved recycling worn or damaged jute bags used in shipping and storage throughout India by unraveling the jute yarns, redyeing them in fashion colors, and then crocheting them into new bags.

Although Ron Spector has toyed with the idea of importing alpaca or hemp for the Guatemalan women to use in their backstrap weaving, he finds it more appropriate and reliable to experiment with locally available cotton fibers, using lighter-weight yarns. Ron notes,

Guatemala is a cotton-producing country. To be able to go down the road and purchase what you need versus being dependent on all the difficulties that could erupt bringing fiber in a timely manner from another country [makes it] sort of hard to make the change.

Despite giving priority to the use of locally available materials, obtaining these component parts can still prove difficult. Particularly for women, being away from their households is difficult as cultural norms demand that they take daily responsibility for the time-consuming activities of food preparation, overseeing their children's travel to and from school, and supervising their after-school studies. In addition, in some households, husbands are reluctant to let their wives travel.

Level of Quality

Achieving and maintaining higher levels of quality is becoming a focus of many ATOs and their consumers. As a result, producer groups have implemented extensive quality control programs—often carefully examining every product before approving it for export. This practice of 100% inspection is highly unusual as compared with the mainstream apparel industry that performs random checks of a limited number of garments and only considers conducting full inspections when there is a significant problem. In many artisan groups, individual members take responsibility for ensuring the quality of each piece they make; each artisan puts his or her name on the product he or she makes. When the product is deemed unacceptable for export, usually by an individual or group of individuals responsible for quality control, the product goes back to the maker for repair. Barb Fenske at UPAVIM says that all the fuss about quality control is unusual to Guatemalan business culture that says "let the buyer beware."

Despite the extensive quality control checks performed by producer groups, some products that arrive in the United States may not be up to the quality expectations of ATOs. This stems from differences in how the producers and ATO employees define quality. For example, we encountered producers in Guatemala who prided themselves on their high-quality work, as evidenced by their extensive use of handsewing. However, to ATOs and their North American consumers, some of the hand stitches give garments a "loving hands," homemade look that is not desirable. Defining and communicating quality standards presents a significant challenge to ATOs and also illustrates the important role of a culture broker. Pushpika Freitas of MarketPlace comments,

> At the meetings with the producers, they felt our quality expectations were much too high. So we went into this whole thing about perception. You can't really blame the artisans because price in India is such an important factor, and in many cases it is more important than quality. Producers have to cut corners. You can cut corners by using cheaper fabric and by doing the work fast. If the person is selling it even $.05 cheaper than you, he has an edge. We've had to go on and on saying we are ready to pay the price. Quality is the most important thing.

Substandard equipment also can make attaining a high level of quality difficult. Groups completing large clothing orders often sew on machines intended for household use. Las Artesanas de San Juan, a vertically integrated group of weavers and sewers located on Lake Atitlán in Guatemala, were particularly ill equipped. The very heavy fabric and fairly large volume of production were extremely wearing on their treadle and electric home sewing machines, half of which were already broken and piled against the wall. Las Artesanas had been given two home sergers, but no one knew how to use them. Industrial overlock machines, intended for round-the-clock sewing, would be very useful and offer superior finishing to the heavy handwoven fabric that easily unravels with just a zigzag stitch. In addition, although previous research on Peace Corps projects showed the value of donations for business sustainability (Durham, 1996), equipment donations made to ATOs may be of little use unless the machines are in good repair and a training period is included with them.

Limits in the workspace also influence both product quality and form. Some groups come to a central location to work, and others work at home. Communication within the groups seems to be enhanced when members work in a central location. In Guatemala, groups that worked together or that met frequently to discuss business had more definite goals and standards of quality than did groups that worked primarily in their own homes or met infrequently. For example, the women of UPAVIM, when working in the central location, had an opportunity to benefit from the quality control staff and a sewing teacher's input as they worked. Soila, an experienced Guatemalan seamstress, comes to the workshop for 2½ days per week to help the craft producers solve production and sewing problems with products they are making. When we met Soila, she was working with the group to determine the best place to stitch a functional trim on children's slippers. However, for many groups, this type of in-house training support is uncommon because it is too costly for the groups to pay an instructor.

Other factors inhibiting product development included how many people a workspace can accommodate and the type of support equipment it holds. La Esperanza seamstresses worked in a small Guatemalan church and had only one table, approximately four by six feet, for cutting products and preparing them for shipping. The table, when combined with their limited space for sewing machines, had influenced the decision to produce only small items.

Special Problems With Clothing

Besides the trade regulations specific to textile products mentioned earlier, clothing presents other particular challenges for product development. Ten Thousand Villages sold clothing for a while but pulled apparel from its product mix because it took extensive resources for product development. Likewise, UPAVIM has discontinued a number of clothing items because the wholesale prices were too high. Not surprising, given ATO consumers' high priority for well-fitting clothing, sizing is a recurring problem. For PtP, whose clothing sales accounted for a large proportion of total product sales, fit or sizing problems were the most frequent reasons for customer returns. An example of sizing problems is also seen in the Mumbai office of MarketPlace, where the patterns were made from slopers (standard pattern shapes) based on patterns intended for home sewing in the United States. The sloper measurements did not correspond to sizing charts found in U.S. catalogs, thus creating difficulties for consumers as they selected their size. As a result of employing U.S. consultants to help with their sizing problems, MarketPlace now offers four sizes and makes generally loose-fitting garments.

Environmental Regulations

Finally, environmental concerns are emerging as a factor in product development. In Guatemala, groups have begun to experiment with naturally colored cottons. This stems from recent actions of the European

Union, which boycotts the import of textile products containing a commonly used class of dyes called Azo because of fears that they are carcinogenic. This chemical is widely used in Guatemala because it is economical and provides bright and fast colors for cotton. Although many of the producer groups we talked with have no or very little business with European ATOs, they fear that the boycott might spread to the United States and will greatly restrict the use of dyes that provide the traditional bright-colored fabrics. It is hoped that the Artisans and Ecology project from Aid to Artisans, discussed in Chapter 7, will help identify and solve environmental problems encountered by the artisans.

How Are Product Form and Appearance Influenced by the People Involved?

The appearance of a product is also affected by who makes the product, their skills and training needs, and the expertise of the ATO staff and consultants who contribute product development ideas. An example of how product appearance is influenced by who makes the product is seen with the Ruth and Nohemi group in Chichicastenango, Guatemala (see Chapter 8), where newly developed products must incorporate both the women's backstrap weaving and the men's sewing skills. The bulk of the indigo fabrics used in sewing is purchased from foot loom weavers who are not a part of the group, and the backstrap weaving is put to use only for decorative accents. The group's founder, Diego Chicoj Ramos, described one situation in which a design consultant developed a backpack that only used the foot-loomed fabric. Although Diego's group agreed to make this bag, which used only the labor of the sewers, for the U.S. ATO, Diego has since adapted a similar bag for sale to others that also incorporates the women's backstrap woven cloth. MarketPlace employees use a similar strategy of involving multiple workers when designing products. To employ adequate numbers of employees, each season's product line must employ the work of three embroiderers for each sewer involved.

The age of the artisan also potentially influences what products will be made and the division of labor among group members. Ron Spector has found that women in Sololá prefer to make traditional products but realize that the export market requires change. The older women have more trouble than the younger ones with the precisely measured and specifically placed new designs that have been developed with Ron's assistance. When orders are available, these older weavers are given the task of weaving more traditionally styled cloth.

Gender norms also influence what is made by any particular producer group, as well as their potential for growth in product development. Among the women of Las Artesanas de San Juan, backstrap weaving was traditional; however, smaller floor looms also were developed to make weaving quicker for the women. This is significant because floor loom technology goes against Guatemalan norms for gender-specific roles and family responsibilities. In rural Guatemala, women are responsible for food preparation and a number of other household-based tasks. When these time-consuming tasks are complete, women will then weave on portable backstrap looms that can be easily set up on patios while looking after their children and animals. It is more common for men to use the large stationary floor looms housed inside the home or in central workshops.

Finally, sometimes for men who have had more formal education than women, more advanced skills of sewing and pattern making are taught. This is problematic for women who, without an opportunity to learn these techniques, will not have the necessary skills for producing complete garments.

Artisan Skills and Availability of Training

The level of artisans' technical skills affects whether a product can be made, as well as flexibility for switching production to a new product. Skills of the producers are sometimes rather limited, and training is expensive. The most common type of training we saw in Guatemala was geared toward teaching artisans how to make a new product. However, at least in Guatemala, there seemed to be little transfer of skills from one type of product to another.

For example, women in La Esperanza, a small group in a squatter area of Guatemala City, learned to sew from a group of young university women who volunteered to help the group. The baby booties they made required fairly advanced sewing skills; the booties were small, had tight curves, were lined, and had an elastic casing around the ankle. Yet despite the precise and intricate sewing required for the booties, the women were not readily able to transfer their skills to another product, such as children's shorts, that would require similar sewing skills. In general, the groups seemed very open to making new products, but their potential for action was limited by their skill level or perceptions of what they could produce.

The inability to break down production into tasks that can be used for other products may be due to the way artisans learn their skills. For example, we have been told that young girls in Guatemala learn to weave by watching their mothers as they set up the loom and produce an entire length of fabric. This contrasts with U.S. training that often segments learning into units or production skills. Barb Fenske recalled an attempt made by a man who volunteered to help train women at UPAVIM. The training was viewed as unsuccessful because he did not show them how to make a product but instead talked in general terms that related only to portions of a product. This strategy did not work because the women needed to make money right away, even if they could only make one product. Ultimately, at early stages of their development, most groups' training needs for product development will likely require that attention be directed to making a specific product.

ATO Staff Skills

Finally, product development is also influenced by the skills brought to the task by the North American ATO staff and their design consultants. For example, PtP's product development staff had very limited skills in pattern making, sample making, and fitting for mass markets. PtP staff would first collect fabric samples from Guatemala. Ideas for new designs were then gathered from U.S. magazines, catalogs, and other nonindustry sources. Next, a commercial pattern approximating the design idea was purchased. A sample was made and sent to PtP's in-country representative in Guatemala. If a chosen group liked the idea, they would make up a sample. Because of limited sewing skills at the Houston office, PtP sometimes asked a Guatemalan group to make the product with better workmanship than the sample. This practice was problematic because it established unclear expectations; the artisans were not sure of the quality level required by PtP. Ultimately, for ATOs adopting a market-oriented approach to product development, not retaining a highly skilled culture broker is a disservice to the producers. As some ATOs move toward using design consultants, this type of problem should be reduced. However, care must be taken to ensure that the consultant understands the context and constraints in production faced by the artisans.

How Much Should the Product Cost?

Determining the cost of a product is an essential part of the product development process and involves two important decisions: (a) What will the producer be paid in terms of the wholesale cost of a product? and (b) What final retail price will be charged to the customer? For ATOs, it seems that pricing is handled rather unscientifically. PtP's design staff considered how the retail pricing of each product compared with pricing of similarly styled ready-to-wear garments in the U.S. mainstream market. PtP prices were not set higher to reflect the uniqueness of their products, nor were they set lower to compete with prices the garments would bring if sold in the Guatemalan market. When setting retail prices, care must also be taken to cover the tariffs that will be assessed on the product during importing. Ten Thousand Villages works with artisan producers in countries, such as India, that have most favored nation (MFN) trade status with the United States; thus, the tariffs for products coming from these countries are relatively low. However, Villages also works with artisans in countries, such as Laos, that do not have MFN status, and tariffs for importing these countries' products can be extremely high. Failing to take into consideration the tariffs and other import expenses that will accrue on the product prior to it being sold would result in setting retail prices that are far too low.

In general, ATOs have tried to pay producers more than the local market value for their products. For example, the money paid for approximately one foot of backstrap woven fabric made by Ruth and Nohemi is 10 quetzales, and the weavers are provided the yarn for the weaving. In the local market, the same piece would bring 5 to 6 quetzales, and the expense of raw materials would be the weaver's own.

For Villages, usually the price paid for a product is whatever the producers ask. In-country Mennonite Central Committee staff, with their in-depth understanding of local conditions, serve as valuable resources in assessing fairness within local contexts. If the final retail price seems too high for the product to be competitive in Villages stores, negotiations in price paid to the producers may occur. However, as one Villages staff member explains,

> We would prefer to simplify a product so the price constraint can be taken out of the cost of production—so the producer doesn't end up having the same investment in labor and getting a lower cost for it.

Diego Chicoj Ramos, of Ruth and Nohemi, described just this type of situation for a bag that would require 30 quetzales (approximately U.S.$5.00) for his weavers and sewers to make. A representative from one ATO for which the bag was planned worked out the retail price the ATO would be required to charge if the producers were paid their requested 30 quetzales. The ATO determined that its customers would not pay such a high price. As a result, Ruth and Nohemi was offered 25 quetzales for the bag. Fearing that the ATO would go elsewhere if he did not agree, Diego accepted the price and subsequently found ways to make production more efficient. However, increasing productivity may be particularly difficult if the artisans cannot clearly isolate the cost of production, including the cost of materials, the value of their time, and their overhead.

Producer groups vary in their pricing sophistication. Bob Chase of SERRV recounts,

> They'll show you this item and they'll say $17.50—and you just saw it down the road or in another country, almost identical, for $2.95. And then you get into these issues—they don't have enough work, enough orders—so they are only making three per week. So they try to get a full week's pay out of three products.

In contrast, UPAVIM in Guatemala has a more formal pricing process that takes into account its desire to cover some expenses of their day care and other social programs. The following formula is used for product pricing:

1. Direct costs of production are calculated: Cost = cost of components + actual labor + $\frac{1}{6}$ labor (for a government required bonus paid twice yearly) + 10% tax.
2. A charge for overhead is included: Total cost = cost * (.26).

3. A percentage is factored in for the costs of social projects. The percentage is determined by the size of the product—say, 10% for a vest and 30% for small items that take a lot of sales to make any money: Wholesale price = total cost * (.10, .20, or .30).

4. Finally, the wholesale price is converted to U.S. dollars.

Although this formula includes a larger percentage for lower-priced products, even this strategy may need to be carefully considered. Teresa Cordón, former Guatemala in-country representative for PtP, cautions that the percentage attached to each product to pay for social programs needs to vary. Smaller products may require a smaller markup percentage for social programs because of the limits on retail prices that can be charged.

An observation about pricing that became increasingly evident throughout our research was ATOs' philosophies that they can pay producers a fair wage, maintain relatively low markups because they are eliminating middlemen, and survive as a business on the remaining low margins. This thinking assumes that because there are fewer levels of business in an ATO, there are also lower operational expenses, and this seems to be an attempt to distance ATOs from what they believe have been excessive markups charged by middlemen. This thinking may be dangerously flawed. Jimmy Pryor of PtP points out,

> The prices that other people are selling stuff for are not all that unreasonable. There's not very much profit in it really. And to think that you can go in and just because you're doing something direct or whatever, that you're going to be able to cut the cost in half, or reduce it by 25%, is totally unreasonable. Especially if you think at the same time you're going to pay the producers more. . . . I know that [in handcraft channels] there are excessive numbers of middlepeople adding a lot onto [the price]. But there are also some functions going on. Looking at hats, for example. We've been cultivating this production for 18 years now, but you have odd stuff—the crown's too high, the brim's too short, the braid's too thick. Somewhere along the way, somebody's got to be doing some filtering. And I'm sure that some middlemen have done a lot of that in non–fair trade channels. . . . So we had a big illusion. We were basically subsidizing it all through low wages [in the United States].

ATOs may be misleading themselves and not realizing the markup they need to successfully develop and market artisan products. Because of the important role that pricing has played for success in small businesses in the United States, we believe that this aspect of product development needs more careful attention by ATOs.

What Product Mix Is Best for the ATO Sales Venue?

In Chapter 9, we revealed the importance consumers place on having garments that can be purchased as mix-and-match coordinates or will work with classic attire in their current wardrobes. Having an appropriate product mix also plays a role in the success and failure of small businesses in the United States (Gaskill et al., 1993). A growing trend among ATOs is to consider product development not only in terms of individual products but also the mix or line of products they will offer for sale. One of PtP's more successfully selling garments, a black blouse with flowered embroidery, was shown in the catalog with a hat, jewelry, and blue jeans. The complete look was attractive, and all but the jeans could be purchased from the catalog.

According to Paul Myers, Villages has, over the past few years, recognized the need to attend to product lines. Rachel Hess describes events that precipitated bringing in a consultant for advice on their product mix:

> Although we had worked quite a bit on developing our home accents collection of products, you still could walk into the Ephrata store and not know that we had things for tabletops.

The consultant brought to their attention the need to think about the sales venue and how the products will be combined for visual promotion. Some of the product development needs were as simple has having napkins that coordinated with the placemats. Ultimately, Villages' analysis of its product mix led staff members to focus on six major product categories: home accessories, holiday, personal accessories, musical instruments, cards/stationery, and plant and garden. For each season, Villages' staff decide on the focus and colors of their product lines. Then the buyers are responsible for finding the products that fit these predetermined needs while not duplicating each other in the process.

PtP's product development and merchandising staff also were faced with product development challenges specific to catalog marketing.

Because of a very lean budget that strictly limited catalog space, each new product that PtP employees wished to put in the catalog required the removal of another product. Maintaining the mix of producers, as well as products, was very important to PtP because pulling a product from the catalog that was the only item a group made could be devastating to the group. Ultimately, having a more focused product mix may move away from the ATO desire to have long-term relationships with several groups. One product development staff member at Villages questions,

> How many different kinds of products can we manage, and what does that mean for how many different kinds of people we can work with? How many jewelry makers in how many different countries? How many different jewelry looks do we need?

Villages worries that working with product lines tends to involve a few key suppliers at a higher volume level and reduces the opportunities for some small producer groups.

What Factors May Prevent an ATO From Receiving Products?

Once ATO staff have decided which products to buy, numerous factors may prevent or delay their production and shipment. The production capacity of a group and various difficulties in day-to-day living in a developing country can all slow down or stop production and delivery.

Production Capacity

Many craft producers lack the necessary production capacity for large orders, and ATO representatives must decide whether a group can produce enough of an item to make the business relationship worthwhile. In the case of catalog retailers, this issue becomes even more critical because the catalog can expose the product to a very large number of customers. Whether the group has the necessary labor power to complete an order by the deadline is an issue.

Yet, production capacity should not be viewed as a static condition. Some ATOs are providing assistance to artisan producers on techniques that allow for quicker assembly. Increases in production efficiency concomitantly increase production capacity. Sometimes, large orders can be filled by small producer groups who locate additional workers, often family members, who can help meet the deadlines. However, these temporary workers may not be as skilled as the "full-time" producers with whom the order is made, a situation that has led to problems for the success of U.S. small businesses (Littrell et al., 1991).

Is it appropriate to ask a small group to grow to meet an order? Sometimes a producer group working with an ATO may be in a position to expand production due to consumer demand for its products. However, to do so may push a group out of the household and toward a factory or industrial approach to production. In some cases, this change may be successful, as explained earlier in this chapter when discussing quality; however, in other cases, significant expansion may not necessarily be in the best interests of female producers who mesh their income-generating activities with other household tasks. In addition, increasing production/orders for one successful product may be misleading to the craft producers. For example, the women of La Esperanza expressed an interest in adding more members; however, most were afraid that if orders were to decrease, all the members would suffer from lack of work. As the group has since gone out of business, this concern was a valid one; temporarily bringing in family members when a big order arrived was a reasonably workable solution.

Production capacity is also linked to a group's equipment, access to raw materials, and the number of employees or members they have available to work on the product. For example, sometimes electricity in developing countries is intermittent, and for groups that use electric sewing machines, production is slowed. Heavy use of home sewing machines leads to more frequent breakdown of equipment, and workers do not always have the means for repair.

Even when functioning as they should, certain types of technology can also slow the production process. Ron Spector believes that backstrap weaving is the slowest weaving technology and thus adds considerably to the expense and labor value of the product. Likewise, SERRV staff explained how certain wood products require time to dry the wood so as to prevent cracking. These processes cannot be rushed.

Of course, production capacity is not always an issue, and some producer groups have much more capacity than an ATO can possibly use. Tejidos de Guadelupe, a group of weavers and sewers organized by nuns in Santa Apolonia, Guatemala, felt the need to keep their weavers working and continued to make products for which they had no market. This resulted in a tremendous oversupply of products that eventually had to be taken apart and remade into other products before they could be sold.

Other Influences

Simply understanding where work is occurring and how it is balanced with other responsibilities provides insights on production timing as well. Even when they work away from home in a central workplace, women prioritize the needs of their families. For example, Angela of UPAVIM segments her work time around a lunch break when she goes home to attend to her children's needs. Likewise, at La Esperanza, older siblings brought babies to their mother's workplace periodically during the day for feeding.

Weather can also create havoc in production. Timely production for Las Artesanas de San Juan was made difficult by the occasional unavailability of *jaspé* (resist-dyed) yarn. The process of dyeing *jaspé* requires that the yarn be strung outside to dry; accordingly, dyeing comes to a halt during rainy periods. Likewise, the monsoon season in India slows production because fabric cannot dry under these very wet conditions. Furthermore, bad weather can divert craft producers' attention away from meeting order deadlines. For example, workers who reside in makeshift houses of cardboard and plastic typical of the slums around Guatemala City must rebuild their houses after heavy storms. In addition, lack of potable water in residential areas means that workers must stand in line for long hours to obtain the needed drinking water for their families. Flexibility in scheduling work, as well as flexibility in meeting deadlines, can be a necessity for craft producers.

Once the production is complete, there still may be delays before the North American–based ATO receives the products. The infrastructure of developing countries is often inefficient for reaching rural areas. For example, when transporting their products for shipment, members of the cooperative Las Artesanas, located approximately 90 miles from

Guatemala City, must first take their products across Lake Atitlán on a 1-hour boat ride and then catch a bus for a 3-hour trip into the city. This problem expands proportionally to the bulk and weight of the order.

Trade Regulations

Although an artisan producer group may have had every necessary skill and production and delivery occur in its favor, trade regulations established between the United States and its trading partners may ultimately influence whether the ATO will actually receive the products. Cathie Chilson recalls a beautiful decorative product carved from dried lemon and orange rinds that PtP wanted to sell. When samples arrived in Houston, the U.S. Department of Agriculture blocked their entry because the product was perishable. Karla Buch, Villages' international accountant, describes how their customs broker must obtain certification for the U.S. Fish and Wildlife Department that the Capiz shells they import are not endangered species. Even with the certificate, delivery is slowed because these products must enter through the busy New York port.

Earlier in this chapter, we explained MarketPlace artisans' interest in maintaining control of their business by staying out of the heavily monitored export of cotton clothing. Villages' Karla Buch provides examples of the bureaucracy that might otherwise result. Some of the groups have not been able to obtain quota at the time their products were ready for shipping because the quota were closed for the month. Thus, shipping delays were created as the groups waited for the next month when quota reopened. A group in India was required to show that they had been paid for their order before they could receive permission to export. However, Karla admits that these delays do not happen frequently because the groups are well aware of what the government requires of them and they prepare in advance. In addition, although trade regulations can sometimes create extra red tape and slow down delivery, Villages staff are undaunted by them and believe that their work with producers in developing countries merits the extra effort. Finally, as the Multi-Fiber Arrangement that allows countries to restrict the import of textile products with quota is phased out early in the 21st century, exporting these products should become simpler for countries that are members of the World Trade Organization.

Conclusions

The approaches ATOs currently use for product development range from limited intervention to an ATO-directed intervention strategy in which ATO staff or consultants work with the producers to develop products aimed at satisfying North American consumers. Choice of a product development approach is guided by either a producer-oriented, nondependent philosophy in which foreign intervention should be avoided or a market-oriented philosophy in which outsider intervention is viewed as essential for successful business. Unless producer groups have extensive understanding of the export market and know how to use market-related information to inform product development, it is unlikely that they can improve their skills without some sort of culture broker. Finally, no matter what type of culture broker directs product development, numerous challenges affect the appearance, pricing, and assortment of products and their eventual delivery to North America. In addition, consumer preferences for a high-quality and well-fitting ethnic product that allows creativity in dress (see Chapter 9) must be considered.

We envision that a next point on the continuum of product development approaches will be one in which intervention is more artisan directed (see Figure 10.1). As producer groups, through intensive ATO-directed product development, learn more of the skills necessary for creating products for the export market, they will be able to act independently from the ATOs. As producer groups gain additional skills, ATOs will begin to serve more as a resource to be called on as necessary, rather than a constant presence in the group's business decisions. However, we do not anticipate this happening quickly.

Programmatic Recommendations for Product Development

This chapter focused on the decisions involved with product development and the challenges an ATO will face as it does so. In this last portion of the chapter, we integrate the information on ATO consumers and producers in a model of key issues that must be attended to when working in product development (see Figure 10.3). The model draws on

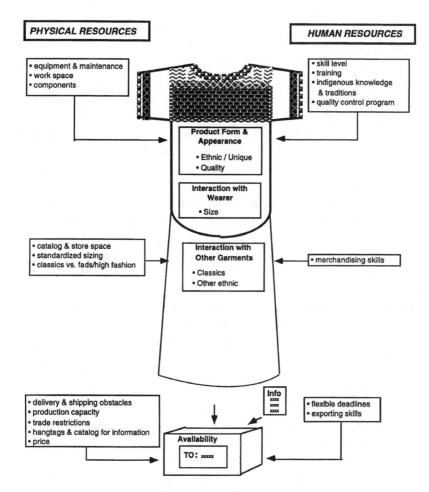

PHYSICAL RESOURCES

- equipment & maintenance
- work space
- components

HUMAN RESOURCES

- skill level
- training
- indigenous knowledge & traditions
- quality control program

Product Form & Appearance
- Ethnic / Unique
- Quality

Interaction with Wearer
- Size

- catalog & store space
- standardized sizing
- classics vs. fads/high fashion

Interaction with Other Garments
- Classics
- Other ethnic

- merchandising skills

- delivery & shipping obstacles
- production capacity
- trade restrictions
- hangtags & catalog for information
- price

Info

Availability
TO: xxxx

- flexible deadlines
- exporting skills

Figure 10.3. Key Issues for Product Development

findings from our research on ATO product development and the challenges artisans face in creating a sustainable business. The model is intended as a product development guide for ATO staff and design consultants as they work with artisan producers. The model is focused on achieving three-way balance among the cultural needs and labor patterns of producers, ATO needs and specifications, and design preferences of U.S. consumers. As such, the model reinforces our belief that product development requires multidirectional communication across cultures through networks that include ATOs, culture brokers, and artisan producers.

The center portion of the model in Figure 10.3 outlines three broad categories of consumer needs that were discussed in Chapter 9, including (a) product form/appearance, (b) interaction of product with the wearer and wearer's other apparel (both located within the garment diagram), and (c) availability and extrinsic characteristics (located in the center of the figure below the garment). The outer portions of the model detail key physical and human resources influencing each category of consumer need.

A number of factors discussed earlier in this chapter have the potential to affect the form and appearance of ethnic apparel and should be considered for how they support and inhibit product development to meet consumer needs. These are separated into physical resources on the left and human resources on the right. Examples of physical resources influencing product development include factors such as equipment and its maintenance, space, and components. Factors such as staff skills, training, indigenous knowledge, attitudes, and quality control programs are some of the human resources affecting product development.

Some key variables influencing interaction of ethnic apparel products with wearers and other garments include retail or catalog space available for showing the merchandise mix, sizing specifications, garments with which ethnic apparel is to be coordinated, and merchandising skills of retailers and producers. Availability of the products may be affected by key variables such as delivery and shipping, production capacity, trade restrictions, deadline flexibility, and exporting skills. Extrinsic characteristics relate primarily to the information provided to the consumer about the producer group.

The product development model identifies key variables ATOs need to consider as they commence an ATO-directed intervention style of product development in developing countries. The model is not meant to be used in any particular hierarchical fashion; however, an ATO may want to begin product development activities by investigating the markets available for craft products and what retailers in these markets require. A next logical step might be to determine what the producers can and are willing to do. This will be based on both what the producers profess they wish to do and a realistic assessment of what their situation allows them to do. The model should also provide useful ways to consider group selection by focusing on which resources the artisans bring to the business relationship.

A highly skilled culture broker can help ATOs and artisans as they adopt and implement this model for product development. We anticipate that a significant amount of time will be spent in this type of product development intervention before an ATO can move toward the next stage in the product development continuum, in which product development is artisan directed.

PART IV

CHALLENGES
AND OPPORTUNITIES
FOR MAXIMIZING
SOCIAL RESPONSIBILITY
THROUGH FAIR TRADE

CHAPTER 11

STRATEGIC
APPROPRIATENESS
FOR THE GLOBAL MARKET

*We provide our Third World brothers and sisters a spot in our marketplace.
In the process of doing that, I would like for our customers to learn as
much about these people and why they need a spot in our marketplace.
I want the customer to be able to say, "I think this craft is a beautiful
piece not only for its aesthetic value but because it was made by someone
who has learned the skill through generations." The artisan is doing it
because they need to and it's their way of feeding their family.*

—Paul Myers, director, Ten Thousand Villages

In Chapter 11, we return to two of the three questions guiding our
analysis of the alternative trade movement. In the first question, we look
back in time and ask how Alternative Trade Organizations (ATOs) developed viable business while their organizational cultures focused on
producers. In answering the initial question, we address how ATOs have
succeeded despite shunning the commonly accepted market orientation
in which customer demand drives business decisions. In the second
question, we ask whether ATOs have accomplished the fair trade mission
of empowerment and improved the quality of life for artisan producers.

289

Question 1: Past Viability With an Artisan Focus

The first research question posed in Chapter 1 inquired, How have U.S.-based ATOs developed viable organizational cultures that focus on support for producers while giving limited attention to customers? In answering the question, we address four interrelated issues. First, we identify how a large labor supply of artisans affected their early interactions with ATOs. Second, ATO organizational culture is explored for its early strengths and weaknesses. Third, product strategy is elaborated for how ATOs met consumers' purchasing motivations. Finally, we explore retail competition for promoting ATO cultural products. We end the discussion of each issue by offering a set of strategic implications from past alternative trade practices that we believe have applicability to future ATO viability.

Artisan Issues

A fundamental component of ATO success in the global market was a large number of artisans in desperate need of income. ATOs follow Kotter and Heskett's (1992) assertion that strategically appropriate businesses are compatible with labor supply. For many years, larger ATOs received requests for employment from new producer groups on a near-daily basis. Artisans consistently and strongly voiced their need for more work. With ready access to essential raw materials, creative spirit, and willingness to innovate, artisans met and exceeded ATO demand for a broad range of cultural products.

ATOs were attractive to artisans for reasons beyond that of income generation alone. Impacts were particularly pronounced for women artisans. In India, women learned to speak their opinions openly for the first time and interacted with people from different religions. In Guatemala, women credited their experiences for providing them with the strength and determination to join regional and national organizations focused on improving women's lives. Still other women noted changes in gendered interactions. For some, their husbands, who were initially reluctant when the women left home for group meetings or to gather supplies, now assisted in child care and even did some cooking so the women could complete their orders.

For many artisans, craft production was appealing due to the ease with which work could be integrated in their daily patterns of life. For Latin American women, opportunities to carry out artisanal work at home allowed them to nurture young children during their formative years. In Guatemala, men performed a variety of agricultural tasks in distant fields during planting and harvesting seasons. When not in the fields, they joined other men at central workshops. In India, women devoted 4 to 6 hours a day to sewing, interspersed with another 5 to 6 hours collecting water, cooking, and taking children to and from school. Despite these daily responsibilities, artisans resourcefully found ways to complete their work, often pooling their efforts, enlisting additional family members with appropriate skills, and working long hours to meet a deadline.

Adding to the strategic appropriateness of the workforce was artisans' willingness to develop new products. However, despite numerous requests and significant artisan interest, ATOs devoted little attention in their early years to systematically working with artisans on new product development. Rather, with an abundant supply of products from which to choose, ATOs adopted a "shop-the-market" approach to sourcing a broad product mix.

For some ATOs, their resistance to product development was more purposeful; among these groups, product development was equated with outsider intervention in local cultural patterns. Yet, listening to artisans' perspectives suggests that product development can occur in ways that meet producers' expectations. Artisans who we questioned consistently linked their craft traditions with the "hows" of production. As examples, Guatemalan weavers cited intimate associations between the backstrap loom and their gender and cultural identities. Indian embroiders spoke of mother-daughter bonding through intergenerational teaching and learning of needle arts. In contrast, the detailed "whats" of production (i.e., specific colors, motifs, products) were infrequently mentioned as essential for the long-term maintenance of a craft tradition. A Guatemalan weaver clearly voiced this perspective at a mid-1990s Fair Trade Federation conference, imploring ATO attendees to cease equating tradition with permanence in object form and aesthetics. As she movingly noted, "Our traditions are alive. They have always been changing. We like to make new things as a way of keeping our work interesting."

In summary, in their early years, ATO goals of supporting artisans matched demand for work from an ever-expanding artisan workforce. Artisans employed flexible work patterns and developed products to attract attention from the limited number of ATOs in the world marketplace. ATO wholesale buyers regularly located new products during their international travels or from samples submitted to ATO headquarters by artisan groups around the world. Artisans who needed work, met ATO criteria, and contacted an ATO with a potentially salable product of acceptable quality often received ATO orders. Beyond providing cash for the immediate order and some feedback to artisans on sales figures and quality issues, ATOs did little more to invest in longer-term artisan development.

However, as the marketplace for cultural products became highly competitive in the 1990s, previously established patterns of limited artisan-ATO interaction were ill suited for the new environment. First, to compete, ATOs required rapidly changing, integrated product lines. In looking to artisans, ATOs found them poorly equipped to carry out product development. Beliefs among ATO leaders that artisans could "figure out" product development by extrapolating from past "bestsellers" were not supported. Second, as profit margins narrowed, ATOs also needed strategies for increasing artisan production efficiency so ATOs could continue paying fair wages to artisans. Knowing that they would soon have to be more selective in groups with whom they worked, ATOs had few criteria to fall back on for identifying artisans with whom best to collaborate on product development and capacity building.

Finally, over time, many artisan producer groups became solely dependent on ATO orders, rather than working toward self-sufficiency. The ATO commitment to fair wages appears to have contributed to some groups' reluctance to adopt a more entrepreneurial approach to establishing a diversified market at local, regional, and international levels. Instead, these groups assumed a watch-and-wait mode for the next ATO order to appear. This pattern was particularly acute in 1997 among some groups who had depended solely on Pueblo to People's (PtP's) orders. ATO lack of past investment in artisan development and limited understanding of issues related to capacity building left many artisan groups with few skills for developing a diversified market for their products at a time when they needed them most. However, Tejidos de Guadelupe (as reported in Chapter 8) was able to transfer skills learned through its interaction with PtP to other business ventures of a small retail store and a grain mill.

Artisan Implications

In looking to the future, ATOs, while continuing to assist craft groups, will need clear criteria for initially assessing group skills and motivation that will lead to group sustainability beyond a period of initial ATO support and development. Training programs that encourage artisans to creatively explore their indigenous environments for design inspiration and to develop skills for product development will be crucial for self-sufficiency. As craft producers expand to markets outside their communities, changes in gender roles and work patterns are likely to evolve that could significantly affect family and community traditions. Because of their grassroots involvement with artisans, ATOs seem well positioned to work with producer groups on addressing potential impacts that such change may bring.

ATO Organizational Issues

Organizational issues related to strategic appropriateness center on early ATO leadership, the far-reaching use of volunteers in many ATO functions, and cooperative strategies employed by ATOs for inter-ATO teaching and learning.

ATOs were founded and led in their early years by several generations of charismatic founders and subsequent managers who were involved in the exciting but often difficult stages of initiating and building organizations around clearly articulated values of developing individual potential worldwide. These leaders approached the founding of alternative trade as a social and spiritual quest. As inspirational leaders, they attracted employees who shared the values and vision of the organization. As strong leaders, they infused their particular visions of alternative trade throughout the organizations.

Most remarkable to us across our 6 years of interacting with hundreds of ATO managers and employees was their singular understanding of and ability to clearly articulate their organization's mission. In many cases, employees were so committed to the mission that they made personal sacrifices, usually in terms of pay levels, or they volunteered their services during peak holiday sales. In the late 1990s, expectations that future employees will not only retain strong values of social responsibility but also continue a pattern of willingness to live on a limited income remain salient in some but not all ATOs.

Personal rewards came to employees through the broad-based sharing of stories about artisans' difficult lives, their creative energies, and their willingness to work long hours and travel great distances to deliver goods on time. Over time, a "story-telling" culture evolved in ATOs as a way of recording their accomplishments in working with artisans. Qualitative indicators of incremental change in artisans' lives formed the basis for telling the story of impacts from ATOs' different ways of conducting business.

By the mid-1990s, preparing a next generation of leadership was a concern among all current ATO directors and managers with whom we spoke. Most believed, however, that the next generation of leaders would be different from the current leadership. Visionary individuals who founded organizations or took them through their early years often have different skills, goals, and motivations than leaders who move those organizations forward through later periods of growth and change (Novelli & Tullar, 1988; Scott & Bruce, 1987).

In addition to visionary leaders, ATO performance also was linked to their extensive involvement of volunteer employees. ATO reliance on volunteers as store managers, church sale organizers, sales associates, and warehouse employees proved to be strategically appropriate for maintaining low operational costs, given the strong commitment among U.S. citizens to provide a service to society by volunteering their time to nonprofit organizations.

For Ten Thousand Villages, the largest North American ATO, volunteers were essential for establishing and operating its 200 retail shops, many of which had only a store manager as a paid employee. Likewise, SERRV's church-based channel for distribution relied on an active volunteer constituency. Although many ATO volunteers worked year-round, other volunteers assisted on a seasonal basis. As examples, professional models volunteered their skills and time for the production of MarketPlace's catalog and then used the photo shoots for developing their professional portfolios. In addition, throughout the alternative trade community, volunteers assisted in receiving and processing orders at peak seasons.

During the early years of ATO activity, many volunteers were selected based on altruistic motives rather than on specific skills needed by the ATO. Not surprisingly, volunteers involved in day-to-day activities sometimes held jobs unrelated to their areas of expertise. Lack of a match between ATO tasks and worker expertise led in some cases to intense frustration and in other cases to lack of interest or boredom. Over time, some in this initial wave of volunteers from the 1970s and 1980s lost their initial energy and enthusiasm, but little ATO effort was placed on their revitalization.

In the 1990s, a "new breed" of volunteers has emerged that fits volunteer activities into an already full work and family schedule. This contrasts with early years when many ATO volunteers, particularly within stores and at church sales, were female full-time homemakers rather than career professionals. In contrast, the new volunteers want flexible volunteer activities, goal-directed work that uses their expertise, meaningful activities that address social problems and provide clientele services, and opportunities to build skills, provide leadership, or make contacts (Aburdene, 1992; de Combray, 1987; Mergenhagen, 1991). Faced with a variety of organizations from which to choose, volunteers are in a position to associate with those groups that hold the most potential for meeting their individual volunteerism goals (Sundeen, 1992). As Betty Beene, a nonprofit leader, stated, "Volunteers want to fundamentally change lives. The challenge for us in the nonprofit sector is to figure out how to enable them to make a real difference in a short period of time" (O'Neal, 1998, p. D1).

A final organizational issue centers on the propensity among ATOs to broadly share their expertise and to nurture each other's growth and development. Because their work was new and groundbreaking, there were few others in the business world with whom to share visions and experiences. Rather, ATO leaders regularly discussed strategy by telephone, exchanged customer lists, and traveled to each other's places of business. In addition, they were frequent presenters of workshops at Fair Trade Federation conferences on topics such as starting a catalog, pricing for fair trade, and working with producer groups. Together, they shared a cooperative strategy in which they taught and learned from each other as they attempted to establish a presence for ATOs in the world market.

ATO Organizational Implications

In considering future ATO leadership, it is our assessment that future ATO leaders will need to combine an insider's perspective of strong focus on artisans with a more finely honed outsider's perspective of attention to demographic, economic, social, and business changes in a competitive international marketplace (Kotter & Heskett, 1992). In considering volunteers within the highly competitive marketplace of the late 1990s, ATOs will need volunteers who have marketing, sales, and promotions expertise to create a strong business presence in the retail market. Accordingly, knowledge of individuals' values, motives, leisure time activities, personal goals, and other demographic characteristics will be critical for ATOs to effectively recruit volunteers (Heidrich, 1990; Sundeen, 1992). Once volunteers are attracted, using their skills will be important for establishing and maintaining volunteer loyalty. To use a business analogy, individual volunteers are in a buyers' market within their communities; a host of organizations are eager to "employ" volunteers' expertise. Rethinking how they use volunteers, clearly describing skills needed to match particular volunteer roles, and delineating short-term and long-term activities should assist in tapping new volunteers for meeting an ATO's mission.

Product Issues

Up until the mid-1990s, promoting the ATO cause by providing quality products with cultural identity was sufficient to build and sustain the emerging ATO business alternative. Given limited competition, there was little urgency for examining customers' motivations beyond the general assumption that they were supporters of the ATO quest. We believe that several reasons account for ATO past "success" with customers. The dual competitive strategies of product differentiation and focus on customer-to-artisan linkages meshed well with ATO customers' product criteria and purchasing motivations. A no-intervention, producer-oriented approach in which ATO buyers shopped the market of available products was sufficient for attracting and maintaining customers.

During the 1970s and 1980s, ATOs' focus on cultural products was fresh and unique to the consumer market. Consumers had few opportunities to purchase crafts and ethnic apparel, and often the cultural products available were sold as art and priced accordingly. Offering functional and decorative ethnic crafts at low to medium prices provided ATOs a business strategy of differentiation; these unique products distinguished ATOs from their competitors. Through their unique ethnic products and their promotional messages of solidarity toward artisans around the world, ATOs tapped a niche market, the forerunners of cultural creatives (Ray, 1997), thus also creating a business strategy of focus.

ATO success with the consumer market may have been purely accidental, a function of good timing in terms of both the fashion life cycle for cultural products and the extensive media coverage given to problems in developing countries during this time. Because cultural products were new to the market, almost any product or style seemed unique. U.S. government involvement and support for anticommunist military and rebel groups in Central America were hotly contested by North Americans who watched television reports detailing massacres of religious leaders and civilians. Whether their successes in linking the producer with the consumer were by luck or not, ATOs' choice of products and promotional messages proved to be successful business strategies.

Through their strategies of differentiation and focus, ATOs created a satisfying link between producers and consumers. In some cases, ATOs capitalized on these linkages through direct global dialogue between artisans and consumers; other ATOs developed and regularly updated their educational leaflets, posters, and videos for in-store use and distribution to customers. More specifically, PtP's mission statement invited the customer to join "in a partnership which sustains, rather than exploits the rich craft heritage and natural abundance of Latin American." In these ways, ATOs hoped to gain customer loyalty by helping "customers cross a philosophical bridge where meaning is attached to something someone has made" (Villages staff member).

From our ATO consumer research, we gained expanded understanding of consumer motivations for purchasing that reveal how ATOs were able to satisfy consumers, without directly making them the focus of their marketing plans. We detail this link by expanding Figure 2.1 (see Chapter 2), which outlined consumers' motivations for purchasing cultural products. In the expanded model, we have added a column on the far right titled "Bases of ATO Support," which delineates predictors of ATO purchases as described in Chapter 9 (see Figure 11.1). From the ATO data, we find continuing support for four of the originating motivations in the center of the figure. In addition, a new "other-directed" motivation has been added. The ATO data support our assertion put forth in Chapter 2 that consumers' motivations for purchasing cultural products go beyond the commoditization of ethnicity as asserted by other researchers.

For the self-directed motivations, we note how traditionally produced cultural products satisfied consumers' self-interests for *creating an aesthetic experience* (see Figure 11.1). Consumer motivation aimed toward *managing daily life* took on a wider conceptual definition for ATO consumers who drew on new bases of ATO support. Practical product characteristics related to quality, versatility in a wardrobe comprising primarily nonethnic apparel, and simple, attractive, and figure-friendly appearance characteristics all contributed to an expanded functional concept of managing daily life. Individuality and uniqueness of ethnic garment styles were desirable to consumers interested in *establishing self-identity.*

Turning to other-directed motivations, information on hangtags and stories in catalogs that focused on the creator of the cultural product appealed to consumers who focused outward toward *connecting with artisans.* In addition, a new motivation for purchasing, *affirming social responsibility,* was evident among ATO purchasers of ethnic apparel. Consumers supported the ATO practice of providing information on world issues affecting those in developing countries. Likewise, ATO consumers' strong societally centered values and attitudes, as well as their great concern for people around the world, served as a basis of ATO support and motivation for affirming social responsibility. Thus, through the ethnicity, uniqueness, and functional characteristics of their products and their messages about the developing world and its artisans, ATOs provided fundamental bases of patronage that motivated consumers to purchase for varying and complex reasons.

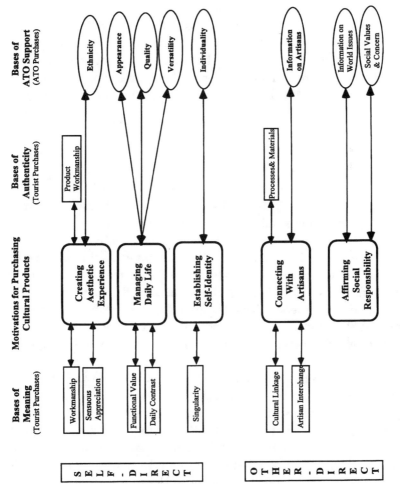

Figure 11.1. Expanded Model of Consumer Motivations for Purchasing Cultural Products

Product Implications

This expanded model of consumer motivations for purchasing craft products provides a guide for ATOs as they move toward a purposive, market-oriented business focus. Competition demands that ATOs place greater attention on identifying and targeting niche consumer markets. Some consumers may buy only because of self-directed motivations, some may buy for other-directed reasons, and still others may be motivated by a combination of self- and other-directed motivations. ATOs must determine whose demands they will meet and continually adjust their products to maintain differentiation and focus within the changing market.

Retail Issues

ATO strategic appropriateness can also be credited to their retail distribution practices. In the 1970s and 1980s, Ten Thousand Villages specialty store retailers had little competition, particularly in small-town America. Accordingly, offering international crafts at moderate prices through a competitive strategy of differentiation was sufficient for creating a distinctive presence in locales across the United States. Pueblo to People and MarketPlace: Handwork of India offered their goods primarily through mail-order catalogs. These catalogs, established well before the mid-1990's glut of consumer products catalogs mailed to U.S. homes, also effectively employed a differentiation strategy in what was then a thinly tapped sales channel.

In building its retail channel, Ten Thousand Villages worked closely with its stores by distributing a monthly newsletter, providing resources for business management, and conducting workshops for store managers and volunteers. Staff retained little control, however, over what happened on a day-to-day basis in the stores, making communication of a clear and consistent corporate identity difficult. Despite these challenges, ATO stores expanded in number and location well into the 1990s.

However, the 1990s heralded competition from emerging mainstream importers and increased numbers of mail-order catalogs promoting imported handcrafts. Pier 1 Imports, the nation's largest specialty retailer of imported decorative household furnishings, strengthened its market position as an ATO competitor with a strong customer focus. Forty percent of Pier 1 Imports merchandise is newly designed each year to meet changing customer demand. Company insiders assess that the firm has "grown up with the tastes and income levels of its targeted baby boomer market" (Rosenthal, 1989, p. 11; see also Brookman, 1991). In 1996, new store layouts were designed to enhance customers' shopping pleasure (Pier 1 Imports, 1996). In the 5-year period from 1992 to 1996, Pier 1 Imports sales expanded by 38%, from $587 million to $811 million (Pier 1 Imports, 1996).

As ATO retailers moved into urban settings, they also faced competition from mainstream retailers who promoted their products through messages that could easily appear to consumers to have some commonality with fair trade practices. For example, several countrywide mass merchandisers commit a percentage of their profits to local programs for disadvantaged children in the communities where the businesses operate. These practices, as we noted in Chapter 1, position social responsibility as an outside-firm contribution to local communities in the United States. This form of social responsibility differs from an inward, within-firm commitment to social responsibility on a day-to-day basis as ATOs source products and assist artisans in establishing sustainable businesses. Despite these differences, the increasing attention to either form of socially responsible business should enhance consumer awareness of the issues, a fact that could be beneficial to ATOs. However, our research on socially responsible apparel consumers suggests that although consumers are willing to make an extra effort to shop with socially responsible businesses, they will do so only if the product is high quality, competitively priced, and suitable for their wardrobes.

In addition to competition from specialty stores, the number of mail-order catalogs specializing in international crafts also expanded in the 1990s. Prominent in this group were Peruvian Connection, featuring knitted apparel from South America, and Sundance Catalog, with southwestern U.S.-flavored apparel and household goods produced around the globe. Our comparative analysis of 13 ATO catalogs and 13 mainstream catalogs specializing in international handcrafts reveals differences in product mix, promotional narratives, and product presentation; however, the divergence apparent in the early 1990s narrowed by the later 1990s (Paige & Littrell, 1995).

Retail Implications

In the future, the increased presence of mainstream apparel retailers in the arena of socially responsible business may serve to lessen the contrast, in the eyes of the consumer, between fair traders and mainstream apparel retailers, making it difficult for ATOs to differentiate themselves. To maintain their differentiation strategy, ATOs will need to clearly communicate those aspects of the fair trade mission, such as their day-to-day decisions regarding product sourcing, employee treatment, and working conditions, as well as on broader approaches to artisan support, business sustainability, and community development in ways that differentiate their businesses and attract customers.

Question 2: Accomplishing the Mission

In our second research question, we asked the following: Do ATOs foster empowerment and improved quality of life for artisan producers? Many artisan groups with whom ATOs work are only in early stages of evolution toward becoming sustainable businesses involved in international commerce. Accordingly, assessing impacts first at individual, household, and business levels seems appropriate at this time. Only later will the measurement of broader community-level impacts be in order as a unit of analysis.

In addressing the question of whether ATOs foster empowerment and improved quality of life for producers, the artisans would probably answer yes. ATOs respected and appreciated artisans' skills and their indigenous knowledge concerning local aesthetics and production practices, such that a favorable grassroots context for development occurred. ATOs provided much-needed income, and day-to-day life was made easier for many people as a result. New skills for business management, pricing, quality control, shipping, and fax and Internet communication were passed on from ATOs to the artisans. As skills were acquired, artisan self-esteem and confidence rose. Not only were the new business and management skills appropriate for managing artisan enterprises, but many skills transferred to household problem solving as well. In contrast, however, few product development skills have been passed on to the artisans.

Whether ATOs were able to offer living wages is more debatable. Although ATOs worked hard to decipher and pay fair wages in the local context, it is unlikely that the wage for a single artisan was sufficient to support his or her family. However, the income of several family members, particularly when combined with agricultural resources, would go a long way toward household sustainability, particularly in rural areas.

As ATOs seek to more clearly distinguish and communicate their impacts to the U.S. buying public, greater systematic estimation of what is meant by "fair" and "living" wages will be in order. As consumers become more aware of socially responsible buying, sweatshop working conditions, and living wages, it is likely they will demand concrete evidence of a company's accomplishments. Within the international development community, the phrase "social audit" appears more frequently, indicating the clear need to assess project impacts. Based on our work with ATO-connected artisans, we recommend the following parameters as a minimal list to consider when figuring the value of work in local contexts: costs of school fees and supplies, health care, day care, transportation, housing, clothing, and food. United Nations "bread basket" studies also provide useful comparative data, as do wages from potential income alternatives for artisans, many of whom have limited educational backgrounds.

Because ATO culture fostered storytelling as a tool for describing artisan change at individual and household levels, the range or scope of ATO impacts with artisans is unclear. Measures to date have been primarily qualitative. As foundation funders and consumers seek evidence of a return on investment, ATOs will need to more systematically monitor and collect quantitative data on business sustainability and on individual, household, and community impacts. Together with qualitative, in-depth case studies of selected artisans and their families, data on the number of jobs created; changes in household income; domestic, tourism, and export sales; and new business start-ups will be critical for addressing whether ATO involvement in crafts is a viable investment for international development.

THE FUTURE FOR ALTERNATIVE
TRADE ORGANIZATIONS

I think for all of us in the alternative trade area—we're in a period of transition. It's clear to me that the way we used to do things doesn't work anymore. The world has changed. People's understanding of the issues has changed. Our customers of 20 years ago had a much more superficial understanding of fair trade than many of them do today. And so we really need to be in conversation with lots of people about these issues and to learn from what they are doing. Not only from our own network of customers and producers, but from others who have experience in this area as well.

—Robert Chase, executive director, SERRV

Chapter 12 brings us to the final question concerning the future of fair trade: How will Alternative Trade Organizations (ATOs) continue to be viable in the increasingly competitive international market for cultural products? In answering the question, we are reminded that ATOs have long valued a "small is beautiful" approach to planning that honored grassroots initiatives for affecting change in artisans' lives at household and community levels. However, how a grassroots and a people-oriented approach to achieving the ATO mission can be retained and supported, in concert with an expanded marketing approach with its focus on customers, will call for new forms of integrated, systemic planning. Balanced attention to all constituencies, including artisans, ATO management and employees, retailers, and consumers, will be central to the planning. Using the distinction between fair trade philosophy and practice as introduced in Chapter 1, we assess that although the philosophy of artisan empowerment will remain for the future, we also agree with Robert Chase's opening quotation that many of the practices for how ATOs conduct business will change.

Chapter 12 is in three parts. First, we discuss issues for future ATO viability as they work with artisans, manage their organizations, and design and promote products to meet consumer demand. Future research questions on fair trade are proposed in boxes accompanying each topical section. Second, we identify core conditions that we believe to be critical for the ATO system to work and the ATO mission to be realized. Finally, we offer a model that graphically summarizes essential tasks and skill requirements that various segments in the system of fair trade must undertake for future efficient and effective functioning in the global market for cultural products.

Future Viability for ATOs

In Chapter 11, we offered our interpretation for reasons behind successful past ATO performance. In addition, we identified implications for ATOs as they engage in a more competitive market for cultural products. In the following sections, our more concrete suggestions are intended to provoke thinking on new strategies for working with artisans, managing ATO organizational culture, and developing and promoting products to consumers.

Working With Artisans

As ATOs work to assist artisans in establishing sustainable businesses, it is likely that their collaboration will occur within a new set of parameters. First, artisans will be called on to contribute items to an ATO's integrated product line in what are likely to be more focused and perhaps fewer product categories. Second, artisans will be expected to develop adequate capacity for more quickly producing new products in larger volume than in the past to meet changing customer demand. Finally, for the foreseeable future, ATOs will need to be more direct in intervening with artisans to develop marketable products that cross cultural boundaries between producers and consumers. Together, these parameters suggest that ATOs will work with artisans in new ways as they go about selecting producer groups, developing training formats for teaching and learning, and assisting artisans in diversifying their products and markets.

In looking to the future, will ATOs work with more or fewer groups than in the past? Each approach has its advantages. A larger number of groups allows the ATO greater flexibility to develop the ever-changing product lines needed for maintaining and expanding sales in a competitive market. However, if there is limited ATO to artisan group involvement in working toward artisan development and business sustainability, the question of whether ATOs differ from mainstream importers begs answering. In contrast, a smaller number means greater depth of involvement for collaborative product development. However, with this approach, far fewer artisans will be reached, and the quantitative outcomes used in obtaining future project funding may be limited. What does seem clear is that there are some artisan groups that, due to their limited potential for expanding capacity related to product quality, volume, and timely delivery, cannot be accommodated, despite their desperate need for income. Such groups are poor candidates for achieving the ATO mission of business sustainability; supporting groups who are late with their delivery of questionable quality products does not prepare the group for domestic diversification or for eventual operation in the broader mainstream market.

Several strategies for group selection have been proffered. In one strategy, an ATO would rank the skills of various groups with whom it works, attempting to maintain a balance among three types of groups: First are groups that already produce the types of products desired by the ATO and can relatively easily expand their volume and switch production to new products. A second category includes artisans who have well-developed skills but require greater attention for new product development. A final group, likely far smaller in number and just starting out, require more extensive training before income is generated. Maintaining a three-part strategy meets the ATO's demand for dependable production at necessary volume levels while also addressing the mission of adding new groups in need of income.

Like the first approach, the second strategy acknowledges that ATOs have limited time to devote to intensive artisan development among all groups with whom they work. In this strategy, most groups would have relatively well-developed skills. Each would follow a strategic plan of cycling in and out of intensive involvement with the ATO and outside designers on issues of product development and business management.

Once groups are selected, ATOs will need to devote greater attention to indigenous patterns for teaching and learning to increase the efficiency of their training activities. Consulting with in-country educators on local learning styles offers a valuable resource for designing culturally appropriate training. In particular, exploring how learning is transferred across teaching situations within the culture should prove useful for assisting artisans in transferring skills and creative ideas from one product to another.

For ATOs to maintain fresh and ever-changing product lines, it is likely they will not be able to work with artisan groups for as long or place orders of a similar magnitude as in the past. Some ATOs may choose to work primarily with a few key accounts that offer great flexibility in product offerings. Accordingly, placing greater focus by ATOs on market diversification that better prepares groups for working with other clients is critical for assisting groups in reaching sustainability. For dependency relationships to be minimized, ATOs will need to explicitly explain at the outset and continue reminding groups with whom they work that groups will find it hard to establish a sustainable business based solely on ATO orders. Although an outside designer may always be essential as a culture broker for product development to external markets, artisans are the market experts in their own societies. Sharing with artisans explicit details for how to analyze and assess their own domestic markets is a valuable skill for market diversification with local clientele.

A project that is currently under way by MarketPlace: Handwork of India illustrates ATO guidance toward market diversification. The 11 MarketPlace producer groups planned a 4-day sale to local Mumbai clients. In committees, artisans discussed and developed a sales target, designed and sourced products from each of the 11 groups, identified necessary inventory, and developed an advertising plan to reach local customers. With guidance from MarketPlace Mumbai staff, the artisans are transferring skills from the international to domestic situation. Following the sale, a federation of the 11 groups was formed as a structure for continued local market diversification.

Although training for market diversification is laudatory, it is but another responsibility to add to an already full plate of activities for comprehensive ATOs such as Ten Thousand Villages, SERRV, and MarketPlace. Yet, without such programs, it is likely that ATOs will continue to foster unwanted dependency, and artisans will assume unrealistic expectations about the contributions of ATO orders to group sustainability. Likewise, without focus on artisan development, ATOs will find it hard to answer the question of whether ATOs do anything beyond what mainstream commercial enterprises that focus on safe and clean workplaces do in sourcing their products.

BOX 12.1

Research Needs for Working With Artisans

Regarding the artisan workforce, case studies of exemplary, sustainable artisan groups are needed to document strategies employed in group development across time. Illuminating macro-level group dynamics as well as micro-level artisan experiences of empowerment seems critical for guiding ATOs toward achieving sustainable, people-centered development. In addition, strategies for encouraging market diversification, such as that under way by MarketPlace, warrant documentation for unraveling what does and does not work in encouraging artisans to attract local clientele rather than being caught up in viewing exports as the sole avenue to business sustainability.

In recognition of the need for greater attention to product development, ATOs have initiated various models for more intensive ATO to artisan interactions directed to product development and capacity building. PEOPLink's Designers Studio, SERRV's use of gift fair reports and product specifications, and ATA's Artisans and Ecology project are just a few of the product development approaches that warrant monitoring for their effectiveness in transferring an artisan group's culturally embedded practices, forms, and aesthetics to marketable products in the United States.

ATO Organizational Issues

A variety of organizational issues call for attention as ATOs plan for the future. Among these are strategic and incremental planning; organizational culture and leadership; boards of directors, volunteers, and nonprofit status; hiring practices; and efficient use of organizational resources.

Planning

Although ATOs have used qualitative and, to some extent, quantitative measures to predict and arrive at artisans' impacts, they have on the whole neglected to carefully monitor and strategize for their own success. However, if they are to achieve their mission, ATOs must stay in business long enough for artisans to put them out of business, rather than the other way around, as for Pueblo to People. Although ATOs seem to have considered incremental steps toward change as applied to their involvement with artisans, they did not seem to employ the same incremental planning strategy for their own internal operations. Perhaps ATOs wanted to accomplish too much too quickly. In setting a goal of creating an "ideal" trading alternative, most failed to strategically outline steps for achieving the goal.

Likewise, although a balance of both economic and social impacts was considered important for assessing artisan empowerment, ATOs themselves did not achieve that balance in their own social and economic goals. In fact, most did not have economic goals, such as sales targets, early in their histories. However, achieving the ATO social mission is dependent on survival of the business. In the highly competitive market of cultural products, organization-wide strategic planning with well-identified and incrementally achievable economic and social goals will be essential for survival.

Organizational Culture and Leadership

In moving to issues of organizational culture, we repeatedly observed the strength of commitment to mission across all levels of ATO personnel. However, we wonder if, in some ways, ATO culture has been almost too strong, such that cultural inflexibility, rather than agility and adaptability, evolved. ATOs have long been intensely introspective and have frequently limited the exchange of ideas to other like organizations. Perhaps shared values and norms were taken to the extreme, making ATOs insular in their thinking and preventing them from pursuing a strategically appropriate culture necessary for the changing environment. In some cases, strong commitment to mission led ATOs to either turn away from outsiders or to actively avoid mainstream businesspersons whose professional expertise could have helped the organizations.

ATOs' attention to the next generation of leadership seems particularly timely in relation to our concern about cultural insularity. To survive in the future, ATOs will need leaders who are open and flexible to change, have the vision to arrive at decisive conclusions, and can effectively guide organizations in modifying their organizational culture for a changing business environment. Interacting with and drawing from the experiences of mainstream business leaders related to quick response sourcing and replenishment strategies, Internet communication capabilities, and methods for achieving organizational flexibility and agility are just some of the practices from which ATOs could learn and then adapt to their particular ATO organizational missions and cultures.

Strong leadership, along with broad-based networking in the business and international development communities, will be increasingly important as ATOs adopt a stronger marketing approach to their work. The next generation of ATO leaders will clearly need an insider's perspective of alternative trade focus on producers combined with a finely honed outsider's perspective on demographic, social, economic, and business changes that affect consumer decisions in a competitive market for cultural products.

Boards of Directors, Volunteers, and Nonprofit Status

One resource central to being a nonprofit organization is ATOs' mandated advisory boards or boards of directors. With the exception of Aid to Artisans, we found that ATOs made limited use of their advisory boards in guiding the organizations toward achieving their missions. In some cases, board members, although sympathetic to the ATO mission, had limited business, design, or international development expertise to offer the ATOs. Positioning board membership as a "volunteer" activity for which mainstream business and community leaders can combine their professional expertise with their interests in social responsibility opens potential for drawing board members from a broad range of business executives and community service personnel useful to ATO functioning. In addition, these board volunteers may be particularly helpful in assisting ATOs to attract additional full-time corporate and professional employees for other ATO volunteer assignments at retail store and headquarters levels.

Furthermore, strategic choice of board members can also assist ATOs in exploiting their nonprofit status in a greater variety of ways. Carefully selecting board members who manage their own businesses or with strong networks in the business community can help ATOs secure pro bono or reduced costs for business space and necessary operational services, such as advertising, printing, and shipping.

Hiring Practices

Because ATOs have tended to draw on each other's experiences in learning how to do business and have often hired from within, they frequently have failed to bring in fresh ideas from the outside and, in some cases, placed individuals in positions for which they were ill suited. The result has been a lack of skilled professionals to focus on the business aspects of the ATO. For the future, skill-oriented hiring practices with an emphasis on bringing in new employees with expertise in design, marketing, finance, and international development will be critical. In the case of the business community, ATOs will need to reach out to potential business professionals of all sorts, sell them on the ATO mission, and then draw on their knowledge and experiences for achieving the mission.

Greater emphasis on recruiting skilled professionals likely will require ATO management to carefully evaluate their pay structures. Skilled professionals are also sought for positions in mainstream businesses. Offering too low a salary may force a potential ATO employee who has great interest in working for an ATO to accept a mainstream business opportunity.

Organizational Resources

As comprehensive ATOs grew, they added new programs, many of which were directed toward helping consumers understand the ATO focus on artisan development. As financial margins tighten and competition increases, ATOs will need to carefully assess, as did SERRV, all aspects of their organizations. Asking tough questions of how each activity contributes directly or indirectly to sales, although anathema to some in the ATO movement, is crucial for ensuring that healthy sales do in fact occur. Only then is the mission of artisan support fulfilled. Asking this question should assist in focusing energy and resources on those activities that are most useful in expanding sales and in achieving the mission.

Box 12.2

Research Needs Addressing Organizational Issues

Better understanding of how to attract appropriately skilled volunteers will be critical for maintaining low operational costs such that ATOs can compete in a tight market. Research is needed to determine whether ATO volunteers exhibit a unique set of characteristics or are similar to volunteers more generally. Whether interests in artisans and handcrafts, concerns for children and families, commitment to community development, or interest in socially responsible practices lead to ATO volunteerism is worthy of study. Such research would provide insights for designing programs aimed at volunteer recruitment, retention, and revitalization.

In a second research example, the 1997 renaming of SELFHELP Crafts to Ten Thousand Villages offers an opportunity for a "revelatory" case study of a unique, one-time experience (Yin, 1994). A case study of Ten Thousand Villages would provide insights on how a company that has been previously based in small communities establishes an urban presence and how the fair trade mission can be effectively promoted among retail specialty stores in urban North America.

In some cases, ATOs may, with limited staffs, be attempting to accomplish too much either by offering too many product lines, operating in too many different distribution channels, expecting too much of employees, or simply participating in too many diverse activities across the ATO system. Across our 6 years among ATO employees, although we witnessed immense dedication to the movement, we also observed high levels of employee stress that led to burnout, particularly when financial renumeration is low. If an ATO is attempting to be involved in all aspects of fair trade marketing, it must also carefully monitor this complexity to ensure that adequate resources, including capital, employees, pay scales, and expertise, are in place.

Developing and Promoting
Products for Consumers

The ATO competitive strategy of differentiation from competitors by offering unique products warrants reexamination so that ATOs can more effectively deal with changing consumer demand. Consumer interest in fairly traded products may be on the increase as customers become more knowledgeable about and demanding of products produced under humane conditions. However, customers will not all want products with a strongly cultural appearance. In fact, our discussion with ATO consumers suggests that some want high-quality items that coordinate with their existing wardrobes or that function well in their homes; cultural distinctiveness is not a priority. In addition, ATOs that focus solely on cultural products face a highly saturated market of similar but often lower-priced goods and a market in which strongly cultural products cycle in and out of fashion. The problem can be particularly acute when an ATO focuses on ethnic products from a single country or region. The bottoming out of sales for Guatemalan *tipicá* (garments and accessories in vivid Guatemalan colors) in the mid-1990s serves as an example of both market saturation for Guatemalan products along with the simultaneous decline in fashion for ethnicity in apparel and home decor more generally.

The following question then arises: How do ATOs who wish to honor artisans' indigenous craft traditions work with artisan groups when demand for their products is down and cultural products generally are out of fashion? Artisans with whom we visited provide guidance for answering the question when they more strongly associate their craft traditions with the processes of production than with the resulting products. In Guatemala in 1997, some artisans were experimenting with weaving softly hued cottons, using traditional backstrap weaving technology. The result is what some scholars would call a nontraditional product because it does not contain the vivid colors common to Guatemala; however, the process of production was one passed down over hundreds of years. Accordingly, focusing on cultural embeddedness of production processes, although acknowledging the need to alter some aspects of product aesthetics, seems a workable solution for the dilemma of wanting to build on tradition while also needing to make product changes for a competitive market. In addition, interpreting tradition as process, while making product changes, should allow for longer-term involvement between an ATO and artisan group when demand for their strongly cultural products declines.

Approaching the ATO-artisan collaboration as one in which artisans are the experts in process and ATOs bring expertise related to market-driven product development holds promise for creating cooperative rather than neocolonial approaches to business so abhorrent by ATOs. Continual sharing of information from the ATO to artisans about changing consumer demand in the U.S. market is vital for avoiding what Stewart (1991) calls a differential "opportunity structure" in which individuals in a business system are not privy to a common set of knowledge on which to base decisions.

Producing and selling high-quality products will remain an essential ingredient for reaching all types of ATO consumers. Due to the importance that consumers place on product quality, sharing perceptions about quality among producers, ATOs, and consumers related both to processes of production and final product features will be critical for avoiding misunderstanding on what quality means in various cultures. ATOs that most effectively address quality issues will retain staff and design consultants who are also experts on quality. These professionals must be readily available so that artisan producers can use their skills as questions and problems arise. Short visits by consultants who offer quick fixes for current production problems will be less valuable than having committed staff who are on call to address problems as they arise throughout production.

In achieving truly collaborative product development, special care must be taken in selecting consultants who not only are knowledgeable about consumer taste, market demand, and product design but who are also aware of indigenous craft processes and the conditions under which artisans work. In visiting with artisans, we repeatedly heard the plea, "Don't send us consultants who know nothing about us and what we can do." Such a plea suggests that culture brokers are needed who can provide a variety of expertise, including market-driven product design expertise as well as cultural interpretation related to local practices for artistic production. Consultants who are available to work with artisans for several weeks or months at a time, rather than those who drop in every 6 months or yearly for a half-day of working with artisans, will prove more effective for the long-term transfer of product development skills.

Whether consultants are insiders or outsiders bears on their potential for offering advice on marketable designs and on application in local contexts. Both are needed. In achieving this balance, it behooves ATOs to build a knowledge base about indigenous production processes from which future design consultants and culture brokers can draw. The Internet database on natural dyes and other ecological production practices, under development by the Artisans and Ecology project from Aid to Artisans, serves as an example from which to draw for designing other databases.

In the late 1990s, potential ATO customers have more product options; thus, retaining and expanding the customer base will demand greater attention than in the past. Customer criteria for product type, quality, aesthetics, and everyday functionality need further refinement for effective differentiation in the market. Conducting both informal and formal market research on consumer lifestyles, product preferences, and shopping practices will be vital for monitoring changing consumer demand for products offered by ATOs. Informally, ATO staff will benefit from staying attuned to market offerings through regularly attending major U.S. trade shows for gifts, apparel, and home furnishings and through "shopping the market." Although it is unlikely that ATOs, small and large, will have staff time or expertise to commit to more formal consumer profiling, linking with university marketing departments in locations where ATOs are located provides a promising network for research collaboration at a minimal cost to ATOs.

Beyond carefully attending to the competitive strategy of differentiation through offering unique and high-quality products, assessing whether ATO promotional messages are appropriate to attracting ATO customers also is in order. For those ATO customers who are more self-directed in their purchase motivations (see Chapter 11), it seems clear that distinctive, high-quality, usable products must carry the ATO message, rather than the other way around. In fact, these customers may have little interest in the ATO story of artisan support. Buying products to meet personal needs is their primary goal. On the other hand, what sets ATOs apart from their competitors is their opportunity to tell stories about real changes that are evolving in artisans' lives due to craft production. Certainly, the telling of stories continues to hold promise as an avenue for reaching other-directed customers (see Chapter 11). Due to ATO in-depth involvement with artisan producers, ATOs are in a position to continue monitoring impacts. However, by being more systematic and employing tools for collecting both qualitative and quantitative data, ATOs can expand and lend greater credibility to their stories of impact. Expanding the knowledge base with empirical data will be critical for developing creditable promotional messages that help ATOs to communicate to customers how their distinctive form of social responsibility focuses on systemwide commitment to artisan business sustainability.

In acknowledging that the "product must carry the message," ATOs will need new strategies to assist consumers in easily understanding product quality and functionality, accessing the "mission," and making the connections across cultures that they desire. Some ATOs may wish to focus only on promoting products that assist customers in managing daily life with the understanding that through selling products, they are achieving the organization's mission of artisan support. Others may choose to focus on promoting both the product and the mission. For the latter group, communicating cultural dimensions of craft production calls for greater resource commitment to educational programming than with the first approach. More ATOs may want to follow the lead of MarketPlace, People to Pueblo, and SERRV by offering global dialogues and travel opportunities that directly link producers and consumers.

Core Conditions for ATO Performance

In drawing conclusions about the future viability for ATOs, we assess that the initial premises undergirding the fair trade philosophy remain valid for the future (see Chapter 1). First, indigenous products can be commercialized in ways that honor artisan traditions. Second, production and trade can transpire in socially responsible ways. Finally, a customer base exists for culturally embedded goods. However, in looking forward, we asked ourselves the following: With artisan em-

BOX 12.3

Research Needs Addressing Product Issues

In the area of product characteristics, profiling product preferences among ATO consumers will provide insights for the refinement of a *differentiation* competitive strategy. Our evolving model of market segmentation for ethnic apparel consumers, based on analysis of Pueblo to People and MarketPlace consumers, serves as a point of departure for such research. In addition, studies are needed that compare perceptions of quality among all members of a marketing system, including producers, retailers, and consumers. The research would alert ATOs when definitions of quality do not coincide across cultures and would be particularly useful for ATOs working in a variety of countries.

Three areas of research on social responsibility would improve understanding of linkages between individuals' propensity to consume ethically and their interest in ATO products. First, testing the predictive model of ATO consumer values, motivations, and preferences that lead to purchase intention (presented in Chapter 9) would be useful. Second, cause-related marketing studies that explore interactions among consumers' attitudes toward products, a firm, and its cause are needed. Questions arise as to whether marketing that engages consumers in the ATO cause of supporting artisans in developing countries is similar to other types of cause-related marketing. Finally, as mainstream and ATO catalogs have become increasingly similar in format and presentation in the past 5 years, saliency of the ATO message needs further scrutiny.

powerment as the overriding mission, what are the critical core conditions for ATO systemwide sustainability in a highly competitive market for cultural products in which profit margins are increasingly slim? We propose the following set of conditions, any one of which, if removed, we believe renders the system vulnerable.

The ATO system of artisans, managers and employees, retailers, and consumers can be sustainable when

➤ Artisans are committed to capacity building, quality production, and product development, which foster a dynamic craft tradition.
➤ Artisans' indigenous production processes, rather than product form and aesthetics, make up the embedded cultural base from which new products are developed and cultural traditions are honored.

➢ A program of product development draws on indigenous methods for teaching and learning, leads to marketable products, and provides income for empowering artisans at individual and household levels.

➢ Flexible and agile leaders mesh insider and outsider perspectives in strategic planning, management, and decisive decision making.

➢ Management and employees share a strong, united value system of social responsibility across the organization. Organization members "walk the talk" as they assume a balanced relationship between their level of renumeration and the less tangible rewards gained from working toward the ATO mission.

➢ Networking outside the organization and other ATOs serves to continually infuse new ideas for interpretation and application within the context of the fair trade approach to conducting business.

➢ Management and employees, selected through skill-based hiring, provide balanced expertise in grassroots development and in business management and marketing.

➢ A significant base of volunteers assists ATOs in taking advantage of their nonprofit status as a means of maintaining low operational costs. Volunteers provide business and development expertise at a variety of levels, including boards of directors, stores, church and community sales, warehouses, and management.

➢ Distinctive, high-quality, usable products address consumers' self- and other-directed motivations for purchasing and using cultural products.

➢ Sales venues promote product features (uniqueness, quality, function) as well as opportunities for consumers to connect with artisans and act on their commitment to socially responsible business practices.

Modeling the Fair Trade System

Throughout this book, we have approached fair trade as a holistic system involving many facets of business and social development. The goal of the system is to provide a nonexploitative trade alternative to impoverished artisans in developing countries so that they can gain socially and economically from export trade with North American consumers. Many business and development functions take place in this system. ATOs work with artisans to hone their skills for developing independent and sustainable businesses. ATO management and employees gear their operations toward customer sales; these acts are often performed under conflicting market- and producer-oriented circumstances. Activities intended to link the artisan and consumer in a personal and satisfying way are part of the alternative trade system as well. Finally, fundamental to the ATO practice of social responsibility, the system includes efforts made by ATOs to bring social and economic change to the developing world at household, community, and regional levels.

Although we drew much of the data in this book from large, comprehensive ATOs that perform many or all of the tasks described earlier, we also provided examples of smaller, more focused ATOs that choose to specialize in a limited set of functions within the trade system. As ATOs increasingly face the need to tighten their business focus and make more effective use of their resources, we believe that examination of the alternative trade system as a series of independent but related business objectives is valuable. Although some ATOs will continue to perform many of the tasks, there is also a place in the ATO system for those who, with more limited resources, wish to specialize.

Central to the model outlined in Figure 12.1 is the idea that, for alternative trade to be successful, the system must generate sales at a magnitude that satisfies consumers and producers in a continually evolving and competitive global market. The ATO mission simply cannot be met unless business success is attained at all levels. In Figure 12.1, we outline four key functions of the alternative trade system and identify the major business objective, specialized skills essential to meeting the objective, and direct outcomes that can be measured as quantitative evidence of success for each function. The center of the model represents core requirements that were outlined in the previous section of this chapter and that we believe are fundamental to the ATO system. The model is not intended to cover every activity that must occur within each function of alternative trade. Rather, it is designed to assist ATO personnel as they refine their business focus, search for appropriately qualified employees, and efficiently direct their resources to meeting their primary objective. By focusing on the most pressing needs for reaching their major business objectives, ATOs will be less likely to spread themselves too thin.

The first portion of the model, shown in the upper-left quadrant, identifies the major business objective of connecting artisans to the ultimate consumer. To meet this objective, product and line development that draws on a sound understanding of consumer preferences, market directions, and competitors' offerings is a primary activity. Resources

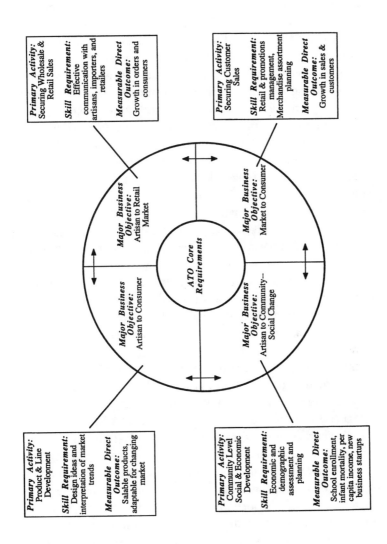

The circular diagram contains the following text:

Center circle: **ATO Core Requirements**

Top-left quadrant:
Major Business Objective: Artisan to Retail Market

Top-right quadrant:
Major Business Objective: Market to Consumer

Bottom-left quadrant:
Major Business Objective: Artisan to Consumer

Bottom-right quadrant:
Major Business Objective: Artisan to Community— Social Change

Upper-left box:
Primary Activity: Securing Wholesale & Retail Sales

Skill Requirement: Effective communication with artisans, importers, and retailers

Measurable Direct Outcome: Growth in orders and consumers

Upper-right box:
Primary Activity: Securing Customer Sales

Skill Requirement: Retail & promotions management, Merchandise assortment planning

Measurable Direct Outcome: Growth in sales & customers

Lower-left box:
Primary Activity: Product & Line Development

Skill Requirement: Design ideas and interpretation of market trends

Measurable Direct Outcome: Salable products, adaptable for changing market

Lower-right box:
Primary Activity: Community Level Social & Economic Development

Skill Requirement: Economic and demographic assessment and planning

Measurable Direct Outcome: School enrollment, infant mortality, per capita income, new business startups

Figure 12.1. ATO Essential Objectives and Skill Requirements

must be directed to design consultants and culture brokers who understand culturally embedded craft production and who can collaborate with artisans in developing products for the North American market. A measure of success will be product sales that grow or are maintained over time in the changing market. This segment of alternative trade is sometimes performed by individuals who wish to work closely with artisans in the development of their business; however, all the comprehensive ATOs reviewed here perform this function to a certain extent.

The arrows connecting this portion of the model to others suggests logical next steps for those ATOs wishing to develop a more comprehensive business. Expansion could be approached as a process of forward integration in which ATOs adopt business activities that facilitate movement of products toward the consumer market, or as a backward integration process in which ATOs pick up business activities that occur before their present activities. However, expanding into another segment of the alternative trade system should not be done without ascertaining whether resources needed to do so are available.

Taking a forward integration perspective, the next step after the product development phase occurs in the upper-right portion of the model; the major business objective involves connecting the artisan to the retail market. Securing sales at wholesale and retail levels is the responsibility of experts who have a vast network of business connections and can communicate effectively across cultures. Success is measured by growth in orders and customers.

A third major business objective in the alternative trade system, located in the lower-right quadrant, is focused on promoting artisan products, telling artisan stories, and communicating artisan impacts from ATO sales to the consumer through a variety of retail formats. Growth in sales and customers must be tracked to determine how well an ATO is doing in its primary business activity of securing customer sales. Experts in retail and promotions management, as well as those who are highly skilled in merchandise assortment planning, will best contribute to success in this portion of the alternative trade system.

Finally, in the lower-left quadrant, the connection is made within the alternative trade system between artisan business development and the social and economic development of their greater communities. This portion of the alternative trade system represents the ultimate social responsibility mission of ATOs but should be viewed as a separate component of the system. Attaining social and economic development at the community level will be a direct offshoot of success reached at all other levels of the alternative trade system. This activity should be directed by experts in economic and development assessment and planning and can be tracked through a variety of quality-of-life measures.

Within the circular model, arrows are intentionally dual directional between quadrants. ATOs tend to begin in a particular quadrant and then expand either in a forward or backward integrative manner. For example, Ten Thousand Villages' historic focus has been in the right-hand artisan-to-retail market and market-to-consumer quadrants. However, as they expand more into product development, they move counterclockwise into the artisan-to-consumer section of the model. On the other hand, Aid to Artisans seems to have been primarily in the artisan-to-consumer section with product development and the artisan-to-retail section with their market connection programs. However, Aid to Artisans is expanding its artisan-to-retail scope and perhaps eventually could go into the retail-to-consumer section if it acts as its own wholesaler. Finally, Dick Meyer, with the retail shop Traditions Fair Trade, is in the retail-to-consumer section; however, he could expand into the artisan-to-retail section as he develops a plan for cross-retail store-buying collaboration.

In closing, we present this model in hopes of assisting the ATO community in achieving success within a holistic system of alternative trade. The model recognizes the increasingly competitive business environment in which alternative trade exists. Its aim is to help ATOs and individuals interested in joining the ATO movement direct their energies and resources to achieve alternative trade success, both economically and socially. The model guides artisans and ATOs toward attaining competitive advantage as they carry out the unique, daring, and often difficult work of alternative trade.

APPENDIX A

Methods

Research emerges and unfolds in many ways. Describing our methods in some detail has several purposes. First, the methodological details provide readers with background on the rich body of data from which we drew our interpretation. Second, the various studies illustrate the power of having at our disposal a range of quantitative and qualitative methodological expertise for application to diverse settings and for answering different kinds of research questions. Finally, the description offers insight into the value of conducting market research from a holistic, systemic perspective. Study of each stakeholder in the system informs understanding of other system members and of the complex interactions involved in marketing products across cultures.

To begin our research journey, in the spring of alternate years, Mary Littrell leads a study tour to Mexico for Iowa State University's graduate students in textiles and clothing. Students visit indigenous entrepreneurs in Oaxaca and Chiapas who are attempting to tap tourist and export markets. Marsha Dickson, a participant in the 1991 trip, came away especially unsettled by the juxtaposition of artistic beauty and poverty among the Maya Indians in Chiapas. A new Ph.D. student at the time, Marsha was thinking about ideas for her dissertation research.

Shortly after returning home from the 1991 study tour, Mary Littrell received a mail-order catalog from Pueblo to People (PtP). Initially, the catalog caught Mary's eye with its Latin American crafts. However, she soon realized that there was more to the organization than just the products and standard commercial practices. Excitedly, she shared the catalog with Marsha. Over the next few months, we initiated plans for a multiphase research program focused on attaining a holistic under-standing of the alternative trade system.

The earliest research ideas focused on consumers who buy from Alternative Trade Organizations (ATOs). Particularly, we were inter-ested in surveying PtP's customers to see if there were market segments with differing interests and preferences for ethnic products. We wanted to be able to share a greater understanding of PtP's customers with the artisans in Latin America so that they might have opportunities for expanded sales and thus increased livelihood from their craft sales. However, we realized that for our "advice" to be relevant to ATOs and the artisans, we first needed to understand the needs and business practices of all stakeholders in the alternative trade system, including artisans, ATOs, and consumers. Over the next few years, we pieced together grants from a variety of sources to support a research program that would include studies of artisan groups in Guatemala and India, ATO organizations and movement leaders across the United States, and consumer studies with PtP and MarketPlace: Handwork of India.

Establishing Rapport in the ATO Community

Our initial entry to the ATO community was by letter and then a subsequent site visit paid by Mary Littrell during autumn 1991 to PtP's headquarters in Houston. Basic information on the mission and scope of operations was attained at this time. During her visit, Mary ap-proached PtP with the idea that Marsha Dickson would like to conduct her graduate research on PtP's customers; Jimmy Pryor, Sandy Cal-houn, and Joan Stewart were receptive of the idea. Shortly after the Houston trip, similar background information was sought by mail from other ATOs.

From our initial contacts with ATOs and continuing throughout the 6 years of research, the ATO community responded freely and enthusiastically to our requests for information. We were given open access to headquarters, managers, and staff during on-site field research. A core of ATO leaders served as key informants and collaborators throughout the project. As our interpretations emerged, we readily provided them with the results of our work. As reports, research manuscripts, and chapters of this book were written, drafts were shared with ATO members so that accuracy was validated. To place the case studies within the broader context of the U.S. ATO movement, over the years that followed, we participated in four national conferences of the Fair Trade Federation (FTF). During the conferences, we presented and received feedback on papers that offered early interpretations of our research findings. By sharing our ongoing research with various ATO leaders and FTF members, their responses served as "member checks" in providing feedback on our emerging interpretation of the research findings (Lincoln & Guba, 1985, p. 314; Miles & Huberman, 1994).

The diversity of methods used for our research parallels the diversity of people we studied. In the next three sections, we outline the approaches employed for each major phase of the research, including that conducted with artisans, ATOs, and consumers.

Artisan Research

The artisan research initially focused on Guatemalan groups. We traveled to Guatemala for field research in 1992 and returned in 1997. The research was designed to inductively describe and analyze the organizational cultures of artisan groups who work with ATOs as grounded in the explanations and behaviors of the managers and employees (Lincoln & Guba, 1985). Multiple case studies with theoretical replications formed our research design (Yin, 1994).

During the 1992 trip, we visited nine Guatemalan groups from the population of 22 cooperatives that worked with PtP. The choice of groups was purposeful; we wanted to capture multiple realities based on an array of business experiences (Lincoln & Guba, 1985). Criteria for sampling included a range of business sizes (6-member cooperative to an organization with 190 members), gender composition (all women, all men, both women and men), geographic location (mountain hamlet of five households to the capitol city of 1.2 million residents), production sites (in-home production, centrally located workshop), products (household products; men's women's, and children's apparel; textile accessories), and success achieved (limited market for products to marketing through multiple outlets). Teresa Cordón, who was PtP's in-country representative in Guatemala, helped select the groups and traveled with us as we collected data. The groups we visited in 1992 included the following:

> Asociación San Lucas and La Esperanza in Guatemala City
> Las Girasoles in Patzun
> Tejidos de Guadelupe in Santa Apalonia
> Artesanas de San Juan in San Juan la Laguna on Lake Atitlán
> Artexco, a federation of cooperatives in Quezaltenango
> Cooperative de Desarrollo do Occidente (CDRO), a development group in Totonicopán
> A group of sewers called Impuladora Mercederia and an unnamed group of weavers in rural Totonicopán who worked through CDRO

Traveling with the ATO representative, we were better able to understand the content and dynamics of interactions between ATO managers and artisan producers. In addition, because Teresa was well respected by the artisans, she provided us entry into each group and lent credibility to our efforts.

The 1992 Guatemala field research took place over a 3-week period with one day spent with each group. Interviews were conducted in Spanish and lasted from 15 minutes to 1 hour with each person interviewed; observations were made over several hours during the day. The field research was guided by interview and observation schedules developed based on the organizational culture literature. Questions for the interviews were phrased in a manner to avoid shaping the direction in which informants responded (Miles & Huberman, 1994). An overall goal was to "step into the mind of another person, to see and experience the world as they do themselves" (McCracken, 1988, p. 9). Through interviews with 29 managers and employees and observations in a variety of production workshops, we were privy to how product decisions were made and business was conducted. Interviews centered on topics related to the group's history, organizational structure, and leadership; member participation; product decisions and new product development; local textile traditions; interactions with retail and wholesale customers; community involvement; and future goals.

At each research site, while Mary conducted interviews, Marsha used an observation schedule for guiding her focus among employees as they made products, inspected them for quality, and prepared products for shipping. Across the nine businesses, 134 employees were observed. Observations focused on workplace layout and conditions, work patterns, equipment, materials, and product range, quality, sizing, and aesthetics.

Trustworthiness of the data was established using several techniques incorporated throughout research design, data collection, and interpretation (Lincoln & Guba, 1985). To enhance credibility and dependability, we used triangulation of methods (interviews, observations), sources of data (multiple individuals, multiple businesses), and multiple investigators (Huberman & Miles, 1994; Lincoln & Guba, 1985). At the end of the day, we independently wrote up field notes and identified emerging themes. Data analysis began while we were in the field; open coding was applied to the interviews, observations, and field notes. Each new theme and subtheme was compared to previous themes for similarities or differences. Then, we exchanged notes, and themes were discussed and negotiated. During these daily debriefings, we acted as independent judges for each other's work. In addition, emerging insights were shared on a daily basis with Teresa Cordón as a form of audit on our evolving interpretation of organizational culture.

Upon return to the United States, we continued comparative refinement and elaboration of themes that formed the profile of organizational culture for textile and apparel artisan businesses in Guatemala. At this stage, Marsha used deductive analysis to compare themes elaborated during the field research with dimensions of organizational culture identified in previous research literature. With inductive analysis, she also allowed unique dimensions to emerge that were not identified in previous research on organizational culture. After Marsha concluded interpretation, Mary examined the interpretation for agreement.

During a second trip to Guatemala in September 1997, we revisited some of the groups interviewed in 1992 to learn how their conditions had changed. In addition, we were introduced to several groups we had not met before. Our initial stop during the 1997 trip was with UPAVIM in

Guatemala City, a group with whom Mary had made contact through Barb Fenske, their North American adviser (mentioned in Chapters 8 and 10). At UPAVIM, we interviewed the 4 managers and observed 30 employees involved in craft production.

Kerry Evans, then in-country representative for PtP, was our initial contact in setting up the PtP portion of the trip, and she provided information about the groups that were still in business since our 1992 visit. Because Kerry was unable to accompany us to see the groups, Teresa Cordón once again traveled with us. We made return visits to Las Girasolas, Tejidos de Guadelupe, and Artesanas de San Juan. In addition, Teresa accompanied us on our visit to the group Ron Spector founded in Sololá, Asociación Maya. Here we interviewed 6 managers and employees, including a U.S. intern, and observed 10 employees. The 1997 trip with Teresa was particularly insightful because she delivered a letter to the artisan groups that PtP's Guatemala office would be closing. We were able to observe and discuss firsthand the impact PtP's anticipated closing had on the artisans.

In addition, during the 1997 trip, Jackie Arreaza, a Scottish expatriate who lives in Guatemala and works with Sister Parish and SERRV, made arrangements and accompanied us to meet several other groups with ATO involvement. Through Jackie's efforts, we visited Ruth and Nohemi in Chichicastenango, staying 2 days at the group's dormitory and traveling with its leader, Diego Chicoj Ramos, to the small community of Chontalá, where the weavers reside. This connection afforded us the opportunity to interview and observe six more artisans in a household context. Data collection and analysis techniques, similar to those used in 1992, were applied to gather and interpret data on our second trip to Guatemala.

To broaden the geographic and cultural perspective for ATO artisans, in 1996 Mary conducted field research in India at the time of an intense 2-week design and product review for a forthcoming catalog of MarketPlace: Handwork of India. Organizational decentralization described in Chapter 6 was under way at that time. Following similar procedures to those in Guatemala, household-based workshops were observed, and interviews were conducted with 10 artisans, the head designer, and 7 managers. In Mumbai, interviews focused on business management and product sizing issues. Participation in the design workshop held in Bhavnigar afforded many opportunities to experience the concentrated activities surrounding the evolution of a MarketPlace apparel line. On a near-daily basis, Mary was invited to return home with artisans to meet their families, discuss daily routines, and observe first-hand the conditions in which women embroider and sew MarketPlace products.

ATO Research

Our research with ATOs first focused on PtP, but we quickly expanded to include two other comprehensive ATOs: MarketPlace and Ten Thousand Villages. As with the artisan research, we sought to inductively describe and provide emic analysis of ATO culture and behaviors (Lincoln & Guba, 1985; Strauss & Corbin, 1990; Yin, 1994). The first three ATOs were selected for their variety in the size of a U.S.-based office (6 to 100 employees), level of annual sales ($1 million to $6.8 million), years in operation (10 to 50 years), retail distribution (specialty store, mail-order catalog), and geographic focus for product sourcing (worldwide, regional, and country specific). Later, we added SERRV to our research because of its distinctive channels for distribution and its financial turnaround in recent years.

To initiate the case studies, field interviews were conducted with 30 managers and employees in human resources, marketing, product development, sourcing, catalog design, and promotion functions. Interviews lasted from 30 minutes to 2 hours, depending on the range of topics relevant to the employee's job. Open-ended "grand tour, example, and experience" questions (Spradley, 1979, pp. 85-90) allowed us to understand ATO employees' views of alternative trade. Topics, identified a priori from the organizational culture and competitive strategy literature, were posed as a form of anticipatory conceptual exploration but were carefully worded to avoid leading the informants' responses (Miles & Huberman, 1994). Interviews addressed company history, organization, and management of the U.S. office (leadership, employee structure, communication, finances), products (mix, development), market (target, competition, pricing), personal satisfaction and support, and organizational accomplishments, challenges, and goals. In addition to interviews, employees were observed as they received and filled telephone orders, participated in meetings, and made product and catalog decisions. Printed materials, including mission statements, newsletters, and catalogs, served as sources for confirming and augmenting interviews and observations.

Since our initial field research in 1992 and 1993, we have remained in close touch with each ATO on a semiannual or annual basis. In 1997, we returned to Ten Thousand Villages, Pueblo to People, and Market-Place for follow-up, in-depth interviews and discussions with managers concerning our analysis of ATO past performance and future viability. In addition, as the book unfolded, we went back to key informants with additional questions that arose from our writing.

Trustworthiness of the data was established using a variety of techniques (Lincoln & Guba, 1985). Credibility of the research findings was instituted through prolonged (6 years) and repeated engagement (two to six interviews) with key leaders at each ATO and through our presence at their workplaces and conferences. Triangulation, a form of convergent validation, involved multiple techniques for data collection (interviews, observations), multiple data sources (transcripts, documents, conference notes), and multiple researchers (Denzin, 1978; Lincoln & Guba, 1985; Yin, 1994). To understand ATO promotional strategies, observations of visual merchandising and product mix were also made in more than 20 U.S. shops that feature ATO products. Through triangulation, each method, data source, or researcher provided a different "line of sight" on a substantive picture of ATO business performance (Berg, 1995, p. 5).

A grounded theory approach was used to analyze the data in a manner that was not specified a priori, revealing the "reality under investigation" (Glaser, 1992; Strauss & Corbin, 1990, p. 24). Derived categories of meaning are said to fit when they are "readily . . . applicable to and indicated by the data under study" (Glaser & Strauss, 1967, p. 3). Open coding was applied by both Mary and Marsha to field notes, transcribed interviews, observations, and documents. Open coding involves careful examination of the data for inductively discovered themes and subthemes of meaning (Strauss & Corbin, 1990, p. 62). As the coding evolved, each new narrative unit was compared to previous units for its similarity or differences. This process of "constant comparing" led to continual refinement of individual themes and to the evolution of broader patterns and expanded conceptual insights (Glaser & Strauss, 1967, p. 101). During the coding process, differences in interpretation were negotiated until consensus was achieved between the two researchers.

In addition to case studies with the larger, comprehensive ATOs, as we learned more about ATOs and became committed to a holistic understanding of the ATO system, we sought out some of the smaller, more focused ATOs and prominent leaders in the North American ATO movement. Case studies and interviews were conducted with Claire Smith and Tom Aageson at Aid to Artisans; Daniel Salcedo, Elaine Bellezza, and Ted Johnson at PEOPLink; Ron Spector, who founded Asociación Maya; FTF board member Dick Meyer, who owns the retail store Traditions Fair Trade; Marilyn Clark at Paraclete Society; and Catherine Renno, longtime ATO participant and former president of FTF. Similar data analysis methods were used for these new data as had been used in the earlier case studies.

Consumer Research

Methods used for market research with PtP's and MarketPlace's customers depart dramatically from the qualitative field research methods used in the artisan and ATO case studies. Our goal with the market research was to gather a large amount of data from as many ATO consumers as we could affordably reach. Thus, we used survey research methods and quantitative data analysis techniques.

Pueblo to People Consumer Research

The PtP consumer study was conducted in 1993. The population of interest was the approximately 94,000 persons throughout the United States who had purchased or had the opportunity to purchase ethnic clothing from PtP. To facilitate comparison between groups with differing past purchase behavior, PtP's mailing list was stratified into three groups from which 1 in k systematic random samples were selected (Scheaffer, Mendenhall, & Ott, 1986). The groups included (a) persons who had purchased clothing and possibly other products within the last 2 years (clothing purchasers), (b) persons who had purchased some products but no clothing from Pueblo to People within the last 2 years (other purchasers), and (c) persons who had requested the catalog during the last 6 months of 1992 but had not purchased any products (nonpurchasers). We sampled 296 names from each of the two purchaser groups and 333 names from what we anticipated was the less committed non-purchasing group. An anticipated returned sample size of 200 from each group (total returned, $N = 600$) was based on the response rate achieved in research using similar telephone screening and mailing procedures (Abraham, 1992; Dillman, 1978).

In attempts to increase response rate, telephone screening to encourage participation was conducted with persons from the two purchaser lists for whom there were telephone numbers. Mailings took place in spring of 1993 and followed the first three steps of Dillman's (1978) four-step mailing. Distribution of the 788 questionnaires included 233 to clothing purchasers, 230 to other purchasers, and 325 to nonpurchasers. Of 433 returned questionnaires, 376 were usable (49% response rate); the distribution of usable questionnaires by group was the following: clothing purchasers = 160 (68% response), other purchasers = 124 (54% response), and nonpurchasers = 92 (29% response).

Instrument

The questionnaire mailed to each participant was a 12-page booklet similar to that recommended by Dillman (1978). The topics included were suggested through focus groups interviews with U.S. consumers that took place prior to questionnaire development. A table of specifications aided in determining the content areas to be measured and the number of items appropriate for measuring each major variable (Touliatos & Compton, 1988). Five researchers familiar with the study examined the questionnaire for its appropriateness and ability to discriminate among content areas. Pretests of the questionnaire led to several changes in content, length, and format.

The values section of the questionnaire comprised 18 terminal values from the Rokeach Value Survey (RVS) (Rokeach, 1973) plus three new items related to environment, education, and human welfare. Rokeach defines terminal values as those end goals in life for which people strive. The 21 values items were measured on a 99-point rating scale (1 = *not at all important to me. Nothing I do is ever based on this guiding principle* and 99 = *an extremely important guiding principle in my life. Everything I do is based on this principle*), as developed by Rankin and Grube (1980).

Attitudes toward issues in Latin America and alternative trade were measured with two sets of attitudinal items. All items in this section were rated on a 7-point scale (1 = *strongly disagree* to 7 = *strongly agree*).

To gather more detailed information on ethnic apparel preferences and perceptions, a clothing evaluative criteria section included 53 items falling within the categories of aesthetic, usefulness, performance and quality, expressive effect, and extrinsic criteria described in previous research with apparel customers (Abraham-Murali & Littrell, 1995; Eckman, Damhorst, & Kadolph, 1990). Additional evaluative criteria were based on previous studies of textile craft consumers (Littrell, 1990; Littrell, Casselman, & Johnson, 1990; Littrell et al., 1992; Slaybaugh et al., 1990). Two questions were asked for each of the 53 evaluative criteria items. The desirability of evaluative criteria was measured by asking respondents to "tell us how *desirable* each of the characteristics would be to you, whether or not they describe the clothing currently available from PtP." Possible ratings included 7 points ranging from –3 (*very undesirable*) to +3 (*very desirable*). A second question asked participants to rate how well they thought the item described the clothing sold by Pueblo to People (7-point scale, with –3 = *strongly disagree* to +3 = *strongly agree*). The question referred specifically to clothing currently available from Pueblo to People, and instructions directed participants to refer to the current catalog, mailed with the questionnaire, as they answered the questions.

Nine items, all of which were measured on a 7-point scale (1 = *strongly disagree* and 7 = *strongly agree*), were used to measure risk perceived in making mail-order purchases of apparel. The items were adapted from previous studies that included the types of risk most relevant to the purchase of ethnic clothing from PtP, including general risk, psychological, social, financial (Jacoby & Kaplan, 1972), time (Roehl & Fesenmaier, 1992), and performance or satisfaction risk (Jacoby & Kaplan, 1972; Rucker, Ho, & Prato, 1989). Reliability ratings of .71 to .78 had been achieved using scales that included several types of perceived risk (Brooker, 1984; Roehl & Fesenmaier, 1992).

To measure behaviors and demographics, we developed a variety of items. We affirmed the dependent variable, past purchase behavior, with one item that asked participants to state whether they had purchased any product from Pueblo to People. A follow-up question for those answering in the affirmative asked participants to indicate the variety of product categories from which they had purchased. One item, "How likely is it that you will buy clothing from Pueblo to People in the next 12 months?" measured consumer behavior intentions (1 = *very unlikely* and 7 = *very likely*). We also asked participants to list the Latin American countries to which they had traveled and to identify if they had ever volunteered in the Peace Corps or other similar institutions. Demographic variables included race, sex, education and income levels, and amount of ethnic clothing owned.

Data Analysis

Data were analyzed in multiple stages. First, common factor analysis, using the principal factor method of extraction and varimax rotation, was used to examine relationships among items and to aid in the creation of summated scores of variables that would reduce the number of items carried into further analyses (Cliff, 1987; SAS Institute, 1990). Factor analysis provided a basis for determining whether items developed for the study were conceptually unified. Factor analysis was run separately on groups of variables measuring all major topics—values, Latin American involvement, altruism, evaluative criteria that described clothing sold by PtP, evaluative criteria that were desirable when purchasing clothing from PtP, and mail-order risk. Inter-item correlation was calculated as a measure of internal reliability, and all were well within the acceptable range (.50 to .60 or greater) for new instruments (Nunnally, 1967).

In the second stage of data analysis, multiple discriminant analysis (MDA) was conducted as a sample-descriptive technique to determine the relative contribution of variables explaining differences between the three purchasing groups: clothing purchasers, other purchasers, and nonpurchasers (Churchill, 1991; SPSS, Inc., 1988). MDA attempts to develop weighted linear combination of variables or canonical discriminant functions that maximally separate categorical groups. MDA "thinks" much like the purchaser would; it simultaneously considers a number of variables.

In a third stage of data analysis, cluster analysis, using Ward's clustering criterion (SAS Institute, 1990), allowed formation of clusters based on similarities in ratings of desirability for the clothing evaluative criteria. Ward's criterion for clustering minimizes within-cluster variance, thus allowing for more homogeneous groupings (SAS Institute, 1990). The number of clusters was determined by examining how groups differed on their ratings of desirability for clothing evaluative criteria as well as the most significantly different criteria. Emphasis was placed on practical as well as significant differences to ensure that the resultant market segments could be targeted for meaningful product development. In addition, the relative ratings of evaluative criteria within each cluster were examined. Clusters were named to reflect the dominant characteristics of the market segments.

After segmentation, the clusters were further described by running univariate and chi-square tests of significance on descriptive variables, including personal values, attitudes regarding interest and involvement in issues pertinent to the producers of ethnic apparel, beliefs concerning benefits currently offered by PtP clothing, and consumer behavior regarding ethnic apparel. In addition, a number of demographic variables were examined to provide information on reaching a given market segment.

During a fourth stage of examining the data, we used path analysis to examine empirically a series of theoretically grounded causal relationships among variables. Ordinary least squares regression was used to obtain path coefficients (direct effects) and total effects (Pedhazur, 1982). Direct effects are a measure of the influence one variable has on another after controlling for all other variables that influence the dependent variable. The total effect for each independent variable on a particular dependent variable indicates the change that would occur in a dependent variable due to a unit change in the particular independent variable. An indirect effect is the amount of influence of a cause variable that reaches the effect variable by way of an intervening variable (Pedhazur, 1982). This analysis revealed the variables having the most influence on consumers' likelihood of buying ethnic clothing from PtP in the future.

MarketPlace Consumer Research

Market research with MarketPlace: Handwork of India consumers was conducted during 1996 and followed very similar procedures to the PtP study. Two Ph.D. students at Iowa State University, Jennifer Ogle and Soyoung Kim, provided assistance in questionnaire design, data collection, and analysis. The nationwide survey of MarketPlace consumers focused on a sample of 477 individuals drawn from a stratified mailing list of 90,000 individuals receiving the catalog. The resulting stratified sample comprised five mutually exclusive subsamples: (a) females who had not made a purchase from the MarketPlace catalog, (b) females who had made one to two purchases from the MarketPlace catalog, (c) females who had made three or more purchases from the MarketPlace catalog, (d) females who had participated in MarketPlace's Global Dialogue program by writing personal letters to the artisans whose products are featured in the MarketPlace catalog, and (e) females who had participated in a child sponsorship program by donating money to support a child in India. Questionnaires were returned by 367 for a response rate of 77%, again quite high as with the PtP study.

The questionnaire used for the PtP study was adapted for MarketPlace customers. A few new items were added to the clothing evaluative criteria section, and all items in this section were scored on a 1 to 7 scale rather than the –3 to +3 scaled used for the PtP survey. As a means of customizing the questionnaire to the specific needs of the ATO, some additional sections were also included, such as shopping confidence, catalog shopping involvement, patronage commitment, and a series of items related to respondents' height, weight, and garment size.

Data analysis was generally similar to that done with PtP data. Principal components analysis reduced the large number of items into a few key variables, many of which were identical to those variables found in the PtP data. Similar to the PtP analysis, cluster analysis was conducted with the MarketPlace data. However, for clustering the MarketPlace data, variables created through principal components factor analysis, rather than individual items regarding desired clothing evaluative criteria, served as a basis for clustering.

Causal relationships among variables were investigated with a maximum-likelihood estimation procedure using LISREL VII (Jöreskog & Sörbom, 1989). Analysis of the proposed model was conducted in three steps. First, a measurement model was examined for appropriateness of the indicators included. Second, the proposed model was tested for its overall fit to the data. The last step involved examining the parameter estimates associated with the research hypotheses proposed in the model.

Although we performed many theoretically driven statistical tests with sophisticated quantitative techniques, our interpretation of ATO consumers, reported in Chapter 9, draws from some of the more basic analyses of central tendency and an assessment of the meaning of average scores according to the scales used. In addition, a qualitative assessment of key findings from the discriminant, path, and LISREL analyses of PtP and MarketPlace data was conducted to pull together the two data sets for a broader understanding of ATO consumers. The model of factors motivating ATO consumer behavior is compiled from the results of these various analytical techniques on the responses of MarketPlace and PtP consumers (see Figure 9.1). Any variable that is connected with an arrowed line has an influence on the variable to which the arrow points. Increasing or decreasing the strength of the attitude or value from which the arrow extends will have a subsequent increase or decrease on the attitude it influences. Those variables not connected by an arrow do not influence each other.

The model may have limited generalizability. It was created using data from consumers, most of whom already buy from ATOs and may only be applicable to PtP and MarketPlace customers. In addition, it may not include all factors that would influence purchase likelihood. For example, whether consumers have discretionary money to spend on ATO products was not taken into consideration. This and other variables may interfere with the purchase intentions.

An Assessment of 6 Years of Research

As we began writing this book, we marveled at the great amount of data we had to draw from. Not only did we have rich information on each stakeholder in the alternative trade system (artisans, ATOs, and consumers), but we also had an understanding of how stakeholders view each other and work together within the system. Although it is easiest to talk about the research methods from the standpoints of artisans, ATOs, or consumers, we stress that the research with stakeholders was conducted simultaneously. Our study of each stakeholder group was shaped by and continuously informed our research on each of the other stakeholder groups. Throughout our research, we were mindful of our dual goals of offering applied interpretations to ATOs from our findings as well as identifying long-term conceptual and theoretical implications arising from our 6 years of study.

APPENDIX B

Contact Information for ATOs and Artisan Producers

ATOs

Below is contact information for the Alternative Trade Organizations (ATOs) profiled in this book, as well as the North American organization of ATOs.

Organization	Address	Contact Persons/ Officers
Aid to Artisans	14 Brick Walk Lane Farmington, CT 06032 Tel: (860) 677-1649 Fax: (860) 676-2170 E-mail: atausa@aol.com Web site: www.aid2artisans.org	Clare Brett Smith, president Tom Aageson, executive director

Organization	Address	Contact Persons/ Officers
Fair Trade Federation	P.O. Box 3754 Gettysburg, PA 17325 Tel: (717) 334-3583 E-mail: ftfok@fairtradefederation.com Web site: www.fairtradefederation.com	Cheryl Musch, executive director
MarketPlace: Handwork of India	1455 Ashland Avenue Evanston, IL 60201-4001 Tel: (847) 329-4011 Fax: (847) 328-4061 E-mail: market@wwa.com Web site: www.marketplaceindia.com	Pushpika Freitas, president
PEOPLink	11110 Midvale Road Kensington, MD 20895 Tel: (301)-949-6625 Fax: (301) 949-8693 E-mail: peoplink@peoplink.org Web site: www.peoplink.org	Dan Salcedo, president
Pueblo to People	No longer in business	
SERRV International	Box 365 500 Main Street New Windsor, MD 21776-1365 Tel: (800) 723-3712 E-mail: SERRV.parti@ecumet.org Web site: www.serrv.org	Robert Chase, director
Ten Thousand Villages	704 Main Street P.O. Box 500 Akron, PA 17501-0500 Tel: (717) 859-8100 Fax: (717) 859-2622 E-Mail: inquiry@villages-mcc.org	Paul Myers, director
Traditions Fair Trade	300 5th Avenue SW Olympia, WA 98501 Tel: (360) 705-2819 Fax: (360) 705-0747 E-mail: dmeyeroly@aol.com	Dick Meyer, owner and president of the Fair Trade Federation

Artisan Producers

The following artisan producers currently work with MarketPlace: Handwork of India or worked with Pueblo to People and may be contacted directly. To reach artisan groups working with the other ATOs, contact the ATO headquarters listed previously.

Organization	Address	Contact Persons/Officers
Aj Quen	Carretera Panamericana km. 56 Chimaltenango, Guatemala Tel: 502-9-839-1725	José Victor Pop Vol, executive director Alda Beatrice Fernández, commercial coordinator
Asociación Centro Cultural y Artesanal Pop Atziak	17 Calle, 10-63 Zona 1 Guatemala Guatemala Tel: 502-2-251-8288 E-mail: popatzia@infovia.com.gt	Virginia Ajxup, president Máximo Terráza, Internet specialist
Asociación de Artesanas de San Juan	San Juan la Laguna Sololá, Guatemala Fax: 502-9-762-2387	Caterina Hernandez Ramirez, president Noemi Ixtamer, vice president and legal representative Juana Cholotio, secretary Micada Juarez Morales, treasurer Micada Tue Cholotio, vocal 1 Nicolosa Perez Ujpan, vocal 2 Maria Virginia Mendoza, vocal 3
Asociación Maya de Desarrollo	K'amolon K'i K'ouejel 8 Avenida 13-21 Zona 2 San Bartolo Sololá, Guatemala Tel: 502-9-762-3367	Juana Cuc Ben, manager
Asociación de Cooperación para el Desarrollo Rural del Occidente (CDRO)	Paraje Tierra Blanca Totonicapán, Guatemala Tel: 502-9-766-2177 E-mail: cdro@pronet.net.gt	Andres Hernandez, director of Artisan Program

Organization	Address	Contact Persons/Officers

Las Girasoles	Florenda Chavajay
	Canton Oriente
	Mancana #11
	Patzun
	Chimaltenango, Guatemala
	Tel: 502-9-839-8328
		Florenda Chavajay, president
		Valentina Xulu, vice
		  president
		Josefina Canux, secretary
		Reyna Ixen, treasurer
		Maria Cristina Ejcalon,
		  vocal 1
		Silvia Suyuc, vocal 2
		Victoria Guanta, vocal 3
		Estela DeLeon Mucia,
		  Commission for Discipline
		Cecilia Can, Commission for
		  Discipline
		Ana Upun, member
		Blanca Suyuc, member
		Paula Jochola, member
		Maria DeLeon Marcroc,
		  member
		Rosa Canux, member
		Ana Mucia, member
		Vitalina Sayuc, member

Ruth y Nohemi	Colonia 10 de Julio Casa No. 41 Chichicastenango, Quiché Guatemala Tel: 502-9-756-1170 Fax: 502-9-756-1051 E-mail: rnohemi@gua.net Website: www.geocities.com/ MadisonAvenue/3959	Reverend Diego Chicoj Ramos

SHARE
(Support the
Handicapped's Rehabili-
tation Effort)
	16A Adarsh Apartments
	Golibar Road
	Santa Cruz (W)
	Mumbai 40055
	India
	Tel: 91-22-618-3385
	E-mail:
	sharemp@bom5.vsnl.net.in
		Fatima Merchant, executive
		  director
		Producer groups:
		Ghar Udyog
		Udaan Mandal
		Women's Artisans
		  Rehabilitation Effort
		  (WARE)
		Community Outreach
		  Program (CORP)
		Ekta Vikas Mahila Mandal
		Sahara
		Aaraaish
		VGS—Bhavnagar
		VGS—Mandvi

Organization	Address	Contact Persons/Officers
Tejidos Guadelupe	Maria del Rosario Otzoy Pichiyá San José Poaquil Chimaltenango, Guatemala	Maria del Rosario Otzoy Pichiyá, head of Sewing Project
	Hermanas Excolares de San Francisco Ave Simeon Canás 8-35 Zone 2 Guatemala Guatemala	
UPAVIM (Unidas Para Vivir Mejor)	Calle Principal, Sector D-1 La Esperanza, Zona 12 01012 Guatemala Guatemala Tel/Fax: 502-2-479-9061 E-mail: upavim@guate.net	Barb Fenske, adviser

REFERENCES

Aageson, T. H. (1997, October). *Investing in the artisan sector*. Paper presented at the International Symposium on Crafts and the International Market: Trade and Customs Codification, organized by the United Nations Educational, Scientific and Cultural Organization, Manila, Philippines.

Abraham, L. (1992). *Consumers' conceptualization of apparel attributes and apparel quality*. Unpublished doctoral dissertation, Iowa State University, Ames.

Abraham-Murali, L., & Littrell, M. A. (1995). Consumers' conceptualization of apparel attributes. *Clothing and Textiles Research Journal, 13*(2), 65-74.

Aburdene, P. (1992). *Megatrends for women*. New York: Villard.

AT&T. (1993, August). *AT&T small business study* (Prepared by David Michaelson & Associates). Holmdel, NJ: AT&T Bell Laboratory, Holmdel Library Internal Technical Document Service.

Baizerman, S. (1987, March). *Textile tourist art: Can we call it traditional?* Paper presented at the symposium, Current Issues in Ethnographic Costume and Cloth: Middle America and the Central Andes of South America, Haffenreffer Museum, Providence, RI.

Baligh, H. H. (1994). Components of culture: Nature, interconnections, and relevance to the decisions on the organizational structure. *Management Science, 40*(1), 14-27.

Bartol, K. M., & Martin, D. C. (1991). *Management*. New York: McGraw-Hill.

Basu, K. (1995). Marketing developing society crafts: A framework for analysis and change. In J. A. Costa & G. J. Bamossy (Eds.), *Marketing in a multicultural world* (pp. 257-298). Thousand Oaks, CA: Sage.

Belk, R. W. (1986). Generational differences in the meanings of things, products, and activities. In J. Olson & K. Sentis (Eds.), *Advertising and consumer psychology* (pp. 199-218). New York: Praeger.

Belk, R. W. (1988). Possessions and the extended self. *Journal of Consumer Research, 15*, 139-167.

Benjamin, M., & Freedman, A. (1989). *Bridging the global gap*. Washington, DC: Seven Locks.

Berg, B. L. (1995). *Qualitative research methods for the social sciences*. Boston: Allyn & Bacon.

Berlo, J. C. (1991). Beyond *bricolage:* Women and aesthetic strategies in Latin American textiles. In M. Schevill, J. C. Berlo, & E. B. Dwyer (Eds.), *Textile traditions of Mesoamerica and the Andes* (pp. 437-479). Austin: University of Texas Press.

Braithewaite, V. A., & Scott, W. A. (1991). Values. In J. P. Robinson, P. R. Shaver, & L. S. Wrightsman (Eds.), *Measures of personality and social psychological attitudes* (pp. 661-753). San Diego, CA: Academic Press.

Brooker, G. (1984). An assessment of an expanded measure of perceived risk. In T. C. Kinnear (Ed.), *Advances in consumer research* (Vol. 11, pp. 439-441). Provo, UT: Association for Consumer Research.

Brookman, F. (1991, January). Re-inventing Pier 1. *Stores, 73,* 76-80.

Buell, R. (1987). Grassroots development: A question of empowerment. *Cultural Survival Quarterly, 11*(1), 34-37.

Buttner, E. H., & Moore, D. P. (1997). Women's organizational exodus to entrepreneurship: Self-reported motivations and correlations with success. *Journal of Small Business Management, 35*(1), 34-46.

Carroll, T. F. (1992). *Intermediary NGOs: The supporting link in grassroots development.* Hartford, CT: Kumarian.

Chambers, R. (1983). *Rural developing: Putting the last first.* New York: Longman.

Charvet, S. R. (1997). *Words that change minds* (2nd ed.). Dubuque, IA: Kendall/Hunt.

Churchill, G. A., Jr. (1991). *Marketing research: Methodological foundations* (5th ed.). Chicago: Dryden.

Claxton, M. (1994). Culture and development: A symbiotic relationship. *Culture Plus,* (12/13), 5-9.

Cliff, N. (1987). *Analyzing multivariate data.* San Diego, CA: Harcourt Brace.

Cohen, E. (1988). Authenticity and commoditization in tourism. *Annals of Tourism Research, 15*(3), 371-386.

Csikszentmihalyi, M., & Rochberg-Halton, E. (1981). *The meaning of things: Domestic symbols and the self.* Cambridge, UK: Cambridge University Press.

de Combray, N. (1987, March). Volunteering in America. *American Demographics, 9,* pp. 50-52.

Denzin, N. K. (1978). *The research act.* New York: McGraw-Hill.

Dhamija, J. (1989). Women and handicrafts: Myth and reality. In A. Leonard (Ed.), *Seeds: Supporting women's work in the Third World* (pp. 195-211). New York: Feminist Press.

Dickson, M. A. (1999). U.S. consumers' knowledge of and concern with apparel sweatshops. *Journal of Fashion Marketing and Management, 3*(1), 44-55.

Dillman, D. A. (1978). *Mail and telephone surveys: The total design method.* New York: John Wiley.

Donckels, R., & Lambrecht, J. (1997). The network position of small businesses: An explanatory model. *Journal of Small Business Management, 35*(2), 13-25.

Durham, D. E. (1996). *Performance factors of Peace Corps handcraft projects.* Unpublished master's thesis, Iowa State University, Ames.

Eber, C., & Rosenbaum, B. (1993). "That we may serve beneath your hands and feet": Women weavers in highland Chiapas, Mexico. In J. Nash (Ed.), *Crafts in the world market* (pp. 155-179). Albany: State University of New York Press.

Eckman, M., Damhorst, M. L., & Kadolph, S. J. (1990). Toward a model of the in-store purchase decision process: Consumer use of criteria for evaluating women's apparel. *Clothing and Textiles Research Journal, 8*(2), 13-22.

Ehlers, T. B. (1993). Belts, business, and Bloomingdale's: An alternative model for Guatemalan artisan development. In J. Nash (Ed.), *Crafts in the world market* (pp. 181-196). Albany: State University of New York Press.

European Fair Trade Association. (1998). *Fair trade yearbook: Toward 2000.* Maastricht, Belgium: Author.

Fair Trade Federation. (1997a). *Consumer's guide to fairly traded products.* Barre, MA: Author.

Fair Trade Federation. (1997b). *Retailer's guide to fair trade.* Barre, MA: Author.

Feather, N. T. (1982). Human values and the prediction of action: An expectancy-valence analysis. In N. T. Feather (Ed.), *Expectations and actions: Expectancy-value models in psychology* (pp. 263-289). Hillsdale, NJ: Lawrence Erlbaum.

Ferraro, G. P. (1994). *The cultural dimension of international business* (2nd ed.). Englewood Cliffs, NJ: Prentice Hall.

Fincham, L. H., & Minshall, B. C. (1995). Small town independent apparel retailers: Risk propensity and attitudes toward change. *Clothing and Textiles Research Journal, 13*(2), 75-80.

Gartner, W. B. (1985). A conceptual framework for describing the phenomenon of new venture creation. *Academy of Management Review, 10,* 696-706.

Gaskill, L. R., Van Auken, H., & Kim, H. (1994). Impact of operational planning on small business retail performance. *Journal of Small Business Strategy, 5*(1), 21-35.

Gaskill, L. R., Van Auken, H., & Manning, R. (1993). A factor analytic study of the perceived causes of small business failure. *Journal of Small Business Management, 32*(4), 18-31.

Glaser, B. G. (1992). *Emergence vs. forcing: Basics of grounded theory analysis.* Mill Valley, CA: Sociology Press.

Glaser, B. G., & Strauss, A. (1967). *The discovery of grounded theory: Strategies for qualitative research.* Chicago: Aldine.

Graburn, N. H. H. (1976). The arts of the fourth world. In N. H. H. Graburn (Ed.), *Ethnic and tourist arts* (pp. 1-32). Berkeley: University of California Press.

Graburn, N. H. H. (1977). Tourism: The sacred journey. In V. Smith (Ed.), *Hosts and guests: The anthropology of tourism* (pp. 17-32). Philadelphia: University of Pennsylvania Press.

Graburn, N. H. H. (1983). The anthropology of tourism. *Annals of Tourism Research, 10*(1), 9-33.

Halvorson-Quevedo, R. (1992). The growing potential of micro-enterprises. *OEDC Observer, 173,* 7-11.

Hamada, T. (1994). Anthropology and organizational culture. In T. Hamada & W. E. Sibley (Eds.), *Anthropological perspectives on organizational culture* (pp. 9-54). Landam, MD: University Press of America.

Hamerschlag, K. (1985). *Indigenous women's craft groups in the Guatemalan highlands: Constraints and opportunities for empowerment through organization.* Unpublished master's thesis, University of California, Berkeley.

Hamerschlag, K. (1994, July). *The missing link: The role of a local intermediary non-governmental organization in the promotion of successful handicraft development in Guatemala.* Paper presented at the annual conference of the Fair Trade Federation, Washington, DC.

Heidrich, K. W. (1990). Volunteers' life-styles: Market segmentation based on volunteers' role choices. *Nonprofit and Voluntary Sector Quarterly, 19*(1), 21-31.

Henderson, H. (1991). *Paradigms in progress: Life beyond economics.* Indianapolis, IN: Knowledge Systems, Inc.

Hendrickson, C. (1995). *Weaving identities: Construction of dress and self in a highland Guatemala town.* Austin: University of Texas Press.

Herald, J. (1992). *World crafts.* London: Charles Letts.

Hess, I. (1996). *SELFHELP Crafts of the World: The first 50 years.* Akron, PA: SELFHELP Crafts of the World.

Hill, H. (1995). Small-medium enterprise and rapid industrialization: The ASEAN experience. *Journal of Asian Business, 11*(2), 1-31.

Holstein, W. J. (1996, December 16). Santa's sweatshop. *U.S. News & World Report,* pp. 50-60.

Huberman, A. M., & Miles, M. B. (1994). Data management and analysis methods. In N. K. Denzin & Y. S. Lincoln (Eds.), *Handbook of qualitative research* (pp. 428-444). Thousand Oaks, CA: Sage.

International Trade Centre UNCAD/GATT. (1991). *Handicrafts and cottage industries: A guide to export marketing for developing countries.* Geneva, Switzerland: Author.

Iyer, P. (1993). *Falling off the map.* New York: Knopf.

Jacoby, J., & Kaplan, L. B. (1972). The components of perceived risk. In M. Venkatesan (Ed.), *Association for Consumer Research proceedings* (pp. 382-393). College Park, MD: Association for Consumer Research.

Jöreskog, K. G., & Sörbom, D. (1989) *LISREL VII: A guide to the program and applications.* Chicago: SPSS.

Kadolph, S. J., Gaskill, L., Littrell, M. A., & Heinicke, J. (1997). Advancing scholarship through sister-state collaborations. In N. J. Owens (Ed.), *ITAA proceedings* (pp. 17-20). Monument, CO: International Textile and Apparel Association.

Kohn, A. (1991). Cooperation: What it means and doesn't mean. *World Futures, 31*(2-4), 107-115.

Kominski, R., & Adams, A. (1994). *Educational attainment in the United States: March 1993 and 1992.* Washington, DC: Government Printing Office.

Kosters, P., Damhorst, M. L., & Kunz, G. I. (1996). Organizational culture of small retail firms. *Small Business Strategy, 7*(3), 29-52.

Kotler, P. (1988). *Marketing management* (6th ed.). Englewood Cliffs, NJ: Prentice Hall.

Kotter, J. P., & Heskett, J. L. (1992). *Corporate culture and performance.* New York: Free Press.

Kuratko, D. F., Hornsby, J. S., & Naffziger, D. W. (1997). An examination of owner's goals in sustaining entrepreneurship. *Journal of Small Business Management, 35*(1), 24-33.

Leander, B. (1994). The forgotten dimension of development. *Culture Plus,* (12-13), 10-12.

Liedholm, C., & Mead, D. (1987). *Small scale industries in developing countries: Empirical evidence and policy implications* (MSU International Development Paper No. 9). East Lansing: Michigan State University, Department of Agricultural Economics.

Lincoln, Y. S., & Guba, E. G. (1985). *Naturalistic inquiry.* Beverly Hills, CA: Sage.

Littrell, M. A. (1990). Symbolic significance of textile crafts for tourists. *Annals of Tourism Research, 17,* 228-245.

Littrell, M. A. (1994). "My hands are our future": Artisans, retailers, and consumers in global dialogue. In C. M. Ladisch (Ed.), *ITAA proceedings* (pp. 5-8). Monument, CO: International Textile and Apparel Association.

Littrell, M. A. (1996). Shopping experiences and marketing of culture to tourists. In M. Robinson, N. Evans, & P. Callaghan (Eds.), *Tourism and culture: Image, identity and marketing* (pp. 107-120). Northumbria, UK: Centre for Travel and Tourism.

Littrell, M. A., Anderson, L., & Brown, P. J. (1993). What makes a craft souvenir authentic? *Annals of Tourism Research, 20*(1), 197-215.

Littrell, M. A., Casselman, M. A., & Johnson, J. S. (1990). Tourists' perceptions of authenticity in textile crafts. In P. E. Horridge (Ed.), *ACPTC proceedings* (pp. 149). Monument, CO: Association of College Professors of Textiles and Clothing.

Littrell, M. A., Reilly, R., & Stout, J. (1992). Consumer profiles for fiber, clay, and wood crafts. *Home Economics Research Journal, 20*, 275-289.

Littrell, M. A., Stout, J., & Reilly, R. (1991). In-home businesses: Profiles of successful and struggling craft producers. *Home Economics Research Journal, 20*(1), 26-39.

Littrell, M. A., Wolff, N. H., & Blackburn, V. (1999). *Mentoring for the global market: A case study of craft marketing in Ghana.* Ames: Iowa State University (available from the authors).

Local Weaving Development Project. (1995). *Weaving for alternatives!* Bangkok, Thailand: WAYANG.

Loker, S., & Scannell, E. (1992). The unique nature of textile and craft home-based workers: A comparison. *Journal of Family and Economic Issues, 13*(3), 263-277.

MacCannell, D. (1976). *The tourist: A new theory of the leisure class.* New York: Schoken.

Mayoux, L. (1995). Alternative vision or utopian fantasy? Cooperation, empowerment and women's cooperative development in India. *Journal of International Development, 7*(2), 211-228.

McCormick, J., & Levinson, M. (1993, January 15). The supply police. *Newsweek, 121,* 48-49.

McCracken, G. (1986). Culture and consumption: A theoretical account of the structure and movement of the cultural meaning of consumer goods. *Journal of Consumer Research, 13,* 71-84.

McCracken, G. (1988). *The long interview.* Newbury Park, CA: Sage.

McLeod, J. R., & Wilson, J. A. (1994). Corporate culture studies and anthropology. In T. Hamada & W. E. Sibley (Eds.), *Anthropological perspectives on organizational culture* (pp. 279-291). Landam, MD: University Press of America.

Mergenhagen, P. (1991, June). A new breed of volunteer. *American Demographics,* pp. 54-55.

Mikkelson, L. H., Goldmark, L., & Hagen-Wood, M. (1997). *IDB support to the handicrafts sector 1965-2001.* Washington, DC: Inter-American Development Bank.

Miles, M. B., & Huberman, A. M. (1994). *Qualitative data analysis.* Thousand Oaks, CA: Sage.

Miller, D., & Toulose, J. (1986). Strategy structure, CEO personality and performance in small firms. *American Journal of Small Business, 10,* 47-62.

Mitchell, R., & Oneal, M. (1994, August 1). Managing by values. *Business Week,* pp. 46-52.

Moreno, J. M. (1995). *Retailers as interpreters of textile traditions in Antigua, Guatemala.* Ph.D. dissertation, Iowa State University, Ames.

Morris, W. F., Jr. (1991). The marketing of Maya textiles in highland Chiapas, Mexico. In M. Schevill, J. C. Berlo, & E. B. Dwyer (Eds.), *Textile traditions of Mesoamerica and the Andes* (pp. 403-433). Austin: University of Texas Press.

Morris, W. F., Jr. (1996). *Handmade money: Latin American artisans in the marketplace.* Washington, DC: Organization of American States.

Nash, J. (1993a). Introduction: Traditional arts and changing markets in Middle America. In J. Nash (Ed.), *Crafts in the world market* (pp. 1-22). Albany: State University of New York Press.

Nash, J. (1993b). Maya household production in the world market: The potters of Amatenango del Valle, Chiapas, Mexico. In J. Nash (Ed.), *Crafts in the world market* (pp. 127-153). Albany: State University of New York Press.

National Labor Committee. (1998). *The people's right to know campaign: A call for corporate disclosure.* New York: Author.

Niessen, S. A. (1990). Toba Batak textile inventions. In *Textiles in trade: Proceedings of the Textile Society of America Biennial symposium* (pp. 223-232). Washington, DC: Textile Society of America.

Novelli, L., Jr., & Tullar, W. L. (1988). Entrepreneurs and organizational growth: Source of the problem and strategies for helping. *Leadership and Organizational Development Journal, 9*(2), 11-16.

Nunnally, J. C. (1967). *Psychometric theory.* New York: McGraw-Hill.

Nyoni, S. (1987). Indigenous NGOs: Liberation, self-reliance, and development. *World Development, 15*(Suppl.), 51-56.

O'Neal, G. (1998, March 30). Volunteers eager but want time well spent. *USA Today,* p. D1.

O'Neill, H. M., & Duker, J. (1986). Survival and failure in small business. *Journal of Small Business Management, 24,* 30-37.

Page-Reeves, J. (1998). Alpaca sweater design and marketing: Problems and prospects for cooperative knitting organizations in Bolivia. *Human Organization, 57*(1), 83-93.

Paige, R., & Littrell, M. A. (1995). Ethnic product marketing: Analysis of catalog promotional strategies. In C. Ladish (Ed.), *ITAA proceedings* (p. 101). Monument, CO: International Textile and Apparel Association.

Pedhazur, E. J. (1982). *Multiple regression in behavioral research* (2nd ed.). New York: Holt, Rinehart & Winston.

Pier 1 Imports. (1996). *Passport: Pier 1 Imports 1996 annual report.* (1996). Fort Worth, TX: Author.

Popelka, C. A., Fanslow, A. M., & Littrell, M. A. (1992). Profiles of success: Mexican textile handcraft entrepreneurs and their businesses. *Home Economics Research Journal, 20*(4), 235-253.

Popelka, C. A., & Littrell, M. A. (1991). Influence of tourism on handcraft evolution. *Annals of Tourism Research, 18*(1), 392-413.

Porter, M. E. (1980). *Competitive strategy: Techniques for analyzing industries and competitors.* New York: Free Press.

Price, S. (1989). *Primitive art in civilized places.* Chicago: University of Chicago Press.

Pye, E. (1988). *Artisans in economic development: Evidence from Asia* (IDRC Monograph 262e). Ottawa, Canada: International Development Research Centre.

Rankin, W. L., & Grube, J. W. (1980). A comparison of ranking and rating procedures for value system measurement. *European Journal of Social Psychology, 10,* 233-246.

Ray, R. H. (1997). The emerging culture. *American Demographics, 19*(2), 29-34, 56.

Reynierse, J. H., & Harker, J. B. (1986). Measuring and managing organizational culture. *Human Resource Planning, 9,* 1-8.

Roehl, W. S., & Fesenmaier, D. R. (1992). Risk perceptions and pleasure travel: An exploratory analysis. *Journal of Travel Research, 30,* 17-26.

Rokeach, M. (1973). *The nature of human values.* New York: Free Press.

Rosenbaum, B. (1993). *With our heads bowed: The dynamics of gender in a Maya community.* Albany, NY: Institute for Mesoamerican Studies.

Rosenbaum, B., & Goldin, L. (1997). New exchange processes in the international market: The re-making of Maya artisan production in Guatemala. *Museum Anthropology, 21*(2), 72-82.

Rosenthal, T. (1989, January). Pier 1 Imports: Taking care of business. *Global Trade, 109,* 10-11.

Rucker, M., Ho, H., & Prato, H. (1989). Consumer evaluation of the mail order apparel market. In C. N. Nelson (Ed.), *ACPTC proceedings* (pp. 43). Monument, CO: Association of College Professors of Textiles and Clothing.

Rushton, J. P. (1980). *Altruism, socialization, and society.* Englewood Cliffs, NJ: Prentice Hall.

SAS Institute. (1990). *SAS/STAT user's guide* (Version 6, 4th ed., Vol. 1). Cary, NC: Author.

Scheaffer, R. L., Mendenhall, W., & Ott, L. (1986). *Elementary survey sampling* (3rd ed.). Boston: PWS-KENT.

Schein, E. H. (1985). *Organizational culture and leadership.* San Francisco: Jossey-Bass.

Scott, M., & Bruce, R. (1987). Five stages of growth in small business. *Long Range Planning, 20*(3), 45-52.

Slaybaugh, J., Littrell, M. A., & Farrell-Beck, J. (1990). Consumers of Hmong textiles. *Clothing and Textiles Research Journal, 8*(2), 56-64.

Smircich, L. (1983a). Concepts of culture and organizational analysis. *Administrative Science Quarterly, 28,* 339-358.

Smircich, L. (1983b). Studying organizations in cultures. In G. Morgan (Ed.), *Beyond methods: Strategies for social research* (pp. 160-172). Beverly Hills, CA: Sage.

Smith, M. J. (1982). *Persuasion and human action.* Belmont, CA: Wadsworth.

Soldressen, L. S., Fiorito, S. S., & He, Y. (1998). An exploration into home-based businesses: Data from textile artists. *Journal of Small Business Management, 36*(2), 33-44.

Spradley, J. P. (1979). *The ethnographic interview.* New York: Holt, Rinehart & Winston.

Spradley, J. P. (1980). *Participant observation.* New York: Holt, Rinehart & Winston.

SPSS, Inc. (1988). *SPSS-X user's guide* (3rd ed.). Chicago: Author.

Steiner, C. B. (1994). *African art in transit.* Cambridge, UK: Cambridge University Press.

Stephen, L. (1991a). Culture as a resource: Four cases of self-managed indigenous craft production in Latin America. *Economic Development and Cultural Change, 40*(1), 101-130.

Stephen, L. (1991b). Export markets and their effects on indigenous craft production: The case of the weavers of Teotitlán del Valle, Mexico. In M. Schevill, J. C. Berlo, & E. B. Dwyer (Eds.), *Textile traditions of Mesoamerica and the Andes* (pp. 381-402). Austin: University of Texas Press.

Stephen, L. (1991c). *Zapotec women.* Austin: University of Texas Press.

Stephen, L. (1993). Weaving in the fast lane: Class, ethnicity, and gender in Zapotec craft commercialization. In J. Nash (Ed.), *Crafts in the world market* (pp. 25-57). Albany: State University of New York Press.

Stevenson, H. H., & Gumpert, D. E. (1985). The years of entrepreneurship. *Harvard Business Review, 85*(2), 85-94.

Stewart, A. (1991). A prospectus on the anthropology of entrepreneurship. *Entrepreneurship Theory and Practice, 16*(2), 71-92.

Stoesz, E., & Raber, C. (1994). *Doing good better!* Intercourse, PA: Good Books.

Strauss, A., & Corbin, J. (1990). *Basics of qualitative research.* Newbury Park, CA: Sage.

Stromberg-Pellizzi, G. (1993). Coyotes and culture brokers: The production and marketing of Taxco silverwork. In J. Nash (Ed.), *Crafts in the world market* (pp. 85-100). Albany: State University of New York Press.

Sundeen, R. (1992). Differences in personal goals and attitudes among volunteers. *Nonprofit and Voluntary Sector Quarterly, 21*(3), 271-291.

Swain, M. B. (1993). Women producers of ethnic arts. *Annals of Tourism Research, 20,* 32-51.

Tice, K. E. (1995). *Kuna crafts, gender, and the global economy.* Austin: University of Texas Press.

Touliatos, J., & Compton, N. H. (1988). *Research methods in human ecology/home economics.* Ames: Iowa State University Press.

U.S. Bureau of the Census. (1995). *Population profile of the United States: 1995.* Washington, DC: Government Printing Office.

U.S. Department of Labor. (1996). *Protecting America's garment workers: A monitoring guide.* Washington, DC: Author.

Vesper, K. H. (1990). *New venture strategies.* Englewood Cliffs, NJ: Prentice Hall.

Wallendorf, M., & Arnould, E. (1988). "My favorite things": A cross-cultural inquiry into object attachment, possessiveness, and social linkage. *Journal of Consumer Research, 14,* 531-547.

Walter, L. (1981). Social strategies and the fiesta complex in an Otavaleno community. *American Ethnologists, 8*(1), 172-185.

Warren, M. D. (1991). *Using indigenous knowledge in agricultural development* (World Bank Discussion Papers No. 127). Washington, DC: World Bank.

Watkins, D. G. (1986). Toward a competitive advantage: A focus strategy for small retailers. *Journal of Small Business Management, 24,* 9-15.

Whitehouse, B. (1996, Summer). Fair trade. *World View,* pp. 31-35.

Wijewardena, H., & Cooray, S. (1995). Determinants of growth in small Japanese manufacturing firms: Survey of evidence from Kobe. *Journal of Small Business Management, 33*(4), 87-92.

Willmott, H. (1993). Strength is ignorance, slavery is freedom: Managing culture in modern organizations. *Journal of Management Studies, 30,* 515-552.

Wong, B. (1987). The role of ethnicity in enclave enterprises: A study of the Chinese garment factories in New York City. *Human Organization, 46*(2), 120-130.

Yin, R. K. (1994). *Case study research.* Thousand Oaks, CA: Sage.

Zorn, E. (1987). Encircling meaning: Economics and aesthetics in Taquile, Peru. In B. Flemenias (Ed.), *Andean aesthetics: Textiles of Peru and Bolivia* (pp. 67-80). Madison: University of Wisconsin, Elvehjem Museum of Art.

Other Publications by the Authors on Alternative Trade Organizations

Dickson, M. A. C. (1994). *Consumers of ethnic apparel and textile crafts from alternative trading organizations.* Ph.D. dissertation, Iowa State University, Ames.

Dickson, M. A., & Littrell, M. A. (1996). Socially responsible behaviour: Values and attitudes of the alternative trading organisation consumer. *Journal of Fashion Marketing and Management, 1*(1), 50-69.

Dickson, M. A., & Littrell, M. A. (1997). Consumers of clothing from alternative trading organizations: Societal attitudes and purchase evaluative criteria. *Clothing and Textiles Research Journal, 15*(1), 20-33.

Dickson, M. A., & Littrell, M. A. (1998). Consumers of ethnic apparel from alternative trading organizations: A multi-faceted market. *Clothing and Textiles Research Journal, 8*(1), 1-10.

Dickson, M. A., & Littrell, M. A. (1998). Organizational culture for small textile and apparel businesses in Guatemala. *Clothing and Textiles Research Journal, 16*(2), 68-78.

Kim, S., Littrell, M. A., & Ogle, J. L. (in press). Social responsibility as a predictor of purchase intentions for clothing. *Journal of Fashion Marketing and Management.*

Littrell, M. A. (1996, April 3). Trading with a difference: Boom in nonprofits promoting Third World products. *USA Today*, p. A8.

Littrell, M. A., & Dickson, M. A. (1997). Alternative trading organizations: Shifting paradigm in a culture of social responsibility. *Human Organization, 56*(3), 344-352.

Littrell, M. A., & Dickson, M. A. (1998). Fair trade performance in a competitive market. *Clothing and Textiles Research Journal, 16*(4), 176-189.

Littrell, M. A., Ogle, J. P. O., & Kim, S. (1999). Marketing ethnic apparel: Single or multiple consumer segments? *Journal of Fashion Marketing and Management, 3*(1), 31-45.

INDEX

Aageson, Thomas, 5, 172-173, 174, 175, 180, 181, 183-184, 333
ADEX, 181
Advisory boards. *See* Boards of directors
African Version, 41
Aid to Artisans (ATA), 5, 59, 98
    Artisans and Ecology project, 181-182, 271, 316
    board of directors, 183
    budget, 174-175
    development of artisan expertise, 174, 175-176
    funding, 174, 175, 180, 183
    goals, 172-173, 179-182, 323
    grants, 179
    members, 175
    mission, 173
    organizational culture, 183-184
    product development, 177
    projects, 173-174, 175-176, 252
    staff, 176-177
    success, 174-175
    training, 175-176, 177-178
Aid to Artisans Ghana, 13, 176
Aid to Artisans Trade Network, 174, 178
AKOMDEY (Association for Communication and Development), 172
Alfadon, 37, 46
Alternative trade. *See* Fair trade
Alternative Trade Organizations (ATOs), 4
    associations, 18-19, 139
    behavioral norms, 22-23
    business operations, 13-16
    business strategies, 35, 296-297, 302, 314, 316-317

changes in marketplace, 292-293
employee commitment, 293-294, 310-311
expenses, 276, 294
factors in past success, 290-292
financial goals, 310
for-profit, 16
functions, 4-5, 320
future challenges, 23, 306-314
future performance, 317-319
goal of creating sustainable businesses, 14-15, 264-266, 293, 302-303, 306, 308-309
history, 16-17
leaders, 139, 147, 293, 294, 296, 311
mainstream competitors, 17, 19-20, 23, 134, 226, 246, 292-293, 300-302
marketing practices, 15, 17-18, 19-20
measurement of success, 15-16, 20, 180-181, 193, 303, 317
mission statements, 19-20
networking among, 139, 147, 295-296, 311
organizational cultures, 19, 310-311
organizational issues, 293-296, 309-314
organizational structures, 23
planning, 310, 312-314
pragmatic approaches, 193-194
product delivery problems, 22, 278-281
production guidelines, 14-15
profit margins, 276-277, 292
research methods, 331-333
sales, 17
selection of producer groups, 14-15, 19, 99-100, 125-126, 278, 307-308
values, 19-22, 64, 66, 322-323

See also Customers; Fair trade; *and specific organizations*
AMACUP (Asociación Mexicana de Arte y Cultura Popular), 181-182
Apparel. *See* Clothing
Arrafin, W. M., 45-46
Artesanas de San Juan, 263, 269, 272, 280-281, 328
Artisans:
  as focus of alternative trade organizations, 5, 20-22
  backgrounds, 201
  benefits of working with ATOs, 207-210, 214-216, 290-291
  direct relationships with customers, 51, 317
  evolution of culture, 11-12, 40, 46-48, 255-256, 271-272
  generational differences, 271-272
  income alternatives, 10, 149, 206-207, 214
  incomes, 37, 149, 206-207, 208, 209-210, 216, 274
  interest in expanding craft production and markets, 10-11, 290-291
  linking to retail market, 185-186, 322
  number supported by alternative trade organizations, 15
  poverty, 201
  research methods, 327-331
  rural and urban residents, 37
  training, 175-176, 177-178, 223, 269-270, 272-273, 293, 308
  See also Cultural products; Gender issues; Producer groups; Wages; Women
Artisans and Ecology project, 181-182, 271, 316
Asociación Maya, 4-5, 253-254, 260-261, 330
ATA. *See* Aid to Artisans
ATOs. *See* Alternative trade organizations

Backe, Brian, 98, 103, 104, 105-106, 107, 262
Backstrap weaving, 210, 212, 217, 253-254, 260-261, 272, 279, 291
Bailon, Angela, 199-200, 206-207, 280
Bali, 48
Bangladesh, 82, 101-102
Beene, Betty, 295
Boards of directors:
  Aid to Artisans, 183
  expertise, 46, 311-312
  Pueblo to People, 136, 138
  roles, 46
  Ten Thousand Villages, 79
  Ten Thousand Villages retail stores, 71-72
Bolivia, 47
Bombay. *See* Mumbai; SHARE

Brazil, Aid to Artisans grants, 179
Brunette, Jane, 147
Brunson, Doug, 129
Buch, Karla, 281
Burkholder, Joyce, 74, 82
Business performance, 35
  failure rates, 36-37
  financial measures, 35-36, 169
  in developing countries, 37-39
  quantifying results of ATO projects, 180-181, 193, 303, 317
  relationship to organizational culture, 32, 33
Business strategies, 33-35
  differentiation, 34, 253, 296-297, 300, 302, 314, 316-317
  focus, 34, 296-297
Byler, Edna Ruth, 62

Calhoun, Sandy, 119, 126-128, 130, 131, 132, 138, 139, 140
Canada, Alternative Trade Organizations, 16
Catalogs. *See* Mail-order catalogs
Catholic Church, 104, 217-218
Catholic Relief Services, 90, 147
Cedi Beads, 34
Center for Global Education, 109
Central America:
  politics, 119-123, 131
  See also specific countries
Chase, Robert, 90-93, 95, 97, 99, 106-107, 108-109, 110, 251, 275, 305
Chemical dyes, 182, 270-271
Chet, Celia, 119-120
Chichicastenango (Guatemala), 210, 211, 212
Chicoj Ramos, Diego, 210, 211-212, 213-214, 216, 271, 275, 330
Chilson, Cathie, 119, 120-123, 126, 130, 133, 134-135, 136, 281
Chontalá (Guatemala), 210, 211-212
Christian Children's Fund, 17-18, 90, 104
Church of the Brethren, 16, 93-95, 106-107
Churches:
  Catholic, 104, 217-218
  Mennonite, 16, 64
  Methodist, 211, 213-214, 215
  SERRV sales, 17-18, 89-90, 103
  See also Religious organizations
Clothing:
  consumer concerns about sweatshop conditions in manufacturing, 9-10
  demand for ethnic, 192, 230, 237-238, 298
  Guatemalan products, 13, 124, 127, 131, 218-219, 246
  MarketPlace designs, 146, 148-149, 150-154, 254-255, 270

Pueblo to People products, 13, 124, 131, 218-219, 246, 262, 270
quality, 270
sizing, 270
See also Textiles
Coffee importers, 16
Competition, between mainstream businesses and Alternative Trade Organizations, 17, 23, 134, 174, 226, 246, 292-293, 300-302
Consultants. *See* Design consultants
Consumers. *See* Customers
Cooperatives:
producer groups, 44
Pueblo to People as, 118, 136-137
Cordón, Teresa, 124, 125, 258, 276, 328, 330
Craft businesses. *See* Producer groups
Crafts. *See* Cultural products
Cramer, Tracy, 126, 127
Cultural creatives, 52, 54, 227, 244
Cultural products:
adaptations of, 101, 221-222, 255-256, 314
appealing to outsiders' tastes, 46, 48-49, 256, 314-315
as core products of Alternative Trade Organizations, 13, 297
authenticity, 51-53
concerns about commercialization, 11-12, 40, 47, 255-256, 291
customers' motivations for buying, 49-51, 52-54
definition, 4
evolution of traditions, 11-12, 40, 46-48, 255-256
generational differences among artisans, 271-272
importance of production processes compared to product designs, 47, 222, 255-256, 291, 314-315
mainstream retailers, 17, 174, 300-302
meanings to consumers, 48-54
volatility of consumer demand, 46, 48-49, 256, 314-315
See also Clothing; Product development; Production processes
Culture, definition, 30
Culture brokers:
advantages of involving, 273-274, 285, 315-316
at UPAVIM, 205-206, 258
need for, 11
product development assistance, 252, 258, 264, 308
roles, 205-206, 223, 265-266, 315-316
Customers:
attitudes toward Alternative Trade Organizations, 244, 246-247

attitudes toward world, 242-244, 298
cultural creatives, 52, 54, 227, 244
demographic characteristics, 226-230
direct relationships with artisans, 51, 317
ethnic clothing in wardrobes, 230, 237-238, 298
expanding base, 194
factors in purchasing decisions, 244-248
future research questions, 318
market segments, 232-238, 241, 318
motivations, 27, 49-51, 52-54, 237-238, 296-300, 316-317, 318, 339
price sensitivity, 131, 231
product preferences, 231-238, 246, 256, 284, 296-297, 314
quality expectations, 231-232, 238-240, 246, 247, 298, 318
research methods, 333-339
retaining, 316
satisfaction of expectations, 238-241
shopping behaviors, 230-231
surveys, 226-249, 326, 333-339
values shared by, 20, 242-244, 298, 318
views of developing countries, 242-244, 298
See also Education of consumers

Dave, Kirit, 158, 159-160, 258, 263-264
Design consultants, 110
at MarketPlace, 158, 159-160, 263-264
at SERRV, 97-99, 251-252
costs, 261-262
quality issues, 315-316
roles, 45-46, 258, 315-316
Development programs:
assistance to producer groups, 40, 123-125
debate over crafts businesses as, 40, 41, 48, 219
failure of top-down, 39-40
grassroots, 40
links with Alternative Trade Organizations, 180
of SHARE, 156-157, 163
Differentiation strategy, 34, 253, 296-297, 300, 302, 314, 316-317
Djaba, Nomoda E., 34
Dominican Republic, 37, 46

Education of consumers:
ATO efforts, 15, 248, 317, 322
by MarketPlace, 160-162
by PEOPLink, 187-188
by Pueblo to People, 115, 123, 140, 297
by SERRV, 90, 104, 108, 109
by Ten Thousand Villages, 76-78, 86
Fair Trade Federation efforts, 19

Ellis, Gaye, 174
Employees of ATOs:
    commitment to organization, 293-294,
        310-311
    hiring practices, 312
    product development expertise, 273-274
    salaries, 129-130, 136, 312
Environmental issues:
    Artisans and Ecology projects, 181-182,
        271, 316
    chemical dyes, 182, 270-271
    in production processes, 182, 270-271,
        316
Esperanza, 270, 272-273, 279, 280
Esprit, 178
Europe, Alternative Trade Organizations, 16
European Union, 270-271
Evans, Kerry, 124-125, 132-133, 330

Fair trade:
    leaders, 26
    model of system, 319-323
    need for study of, 7-9
    philosophy, 5-6, 90-92
    practices, 6-7
    scholarly perspectives on, 29-30, 54-55
    See also Alternative Trade Organizations
        (ATOs)
Fair Trade Federation (FTF), 18-19, 139, 206,
    291, 295, 327
Fenske, Barb, 202, 203, 204, 205-206, 207,
    209, 255, 258, 268, 273, 330
Focus markteting strategy, 34, 296-297
Fogle, Barb, 95, 99, 100, 101, 102-103, 266
Food products, 16, 126
Freinluch, Paul, 147
Freitas, Pushpika, 139, 147, 269
    as social worker, 26, 143-144
    leadership of MarketPlace, 147, 152, 155,
        157-158, 159, 164, 165-167
    letters in catalogs, 161, 165
    MarketPlace products, 148-149, 150-151,
        254, 263
FTF. See Fair Trade Federation

Gandhi, Mahatma, 66-67
Gender issues among artisans, 12, 38-39,
    42-43, 201
    division of work, 13, 42, 44, 156, 221,
        272, 290, 291
    empowerment of women, 144-146, 149,
        164-166, 168-169, 209, 290-291
Ghana:
    Aid to Artisans grants, 179
    Aid to Artisans projects, 173-174,
        175-176, 177, 178
    cultural products, 13

producer groups, 30-31, 32-33, 34, 41
Global Exchange, 117
Glomski, Tracy, 163
Golibar (India), 144, 154
Grose, Lynda, 178, 182, 231
Guatemala:
    Aid to Artisans grants, 179
    Artesanas de San Juan, 263, 269, 272,
        280-281, 328
    Asociación Maya, 4-5, 253-254, 260-261,
        330
    clothing, 13, 124, 125-126, 127, 131,
        218-219, 246, 314
    cotton produced in, 252, 267-268, 270-271
    effects of Pueblo to People closing,
        109-110, 132-133, 292
    gendered division of work, 290, 291
    growth monitoring clinics, 202
    hats, 115
    jaspé fabrics, 124, 204, 222, 255, 280
    market demand for tipica products, 48,
        132, 213, 222, 255, 314
    peace accord, 131
    Pop Atziak marketing organization, 262
    poverty, 199-200, 202
    problems of small cooperatives, 38
    producer group organization, 44
    producer groups, 200, 201, 272, 327-330
    producer groups working with Pueblo
        to People, 119-120, 123, 124, 127, 204,
        217, 218-219, 327
    product quality issues, 268
    Pueblo to People founded in, 26, 114-115
    Pueblo to People representatives,
        119-120, 124-125, 125, 132-133, 258,
        328, 330
    Tejidos de Guadelupe, 216-219, 280,
        292-293, 328
    violence, 119, 210, 211, 217
    weavers, 127-128, 215-216, 256, 260-261,
        273
    weaving groups, 39, 41, 210, 211, 217,
        252, 253-254, 256
    See also Ruth and Nohemi; UPAVIM

Haiti:
    Aid to Artisans project, 174
    metal workers, 172
Handcrafts. See Cultural products
Hess, Rachel, 69, 70, 81, 259, 265, 277
Hmong, 47, 174
Honduras:
    Aid to Artisans projects, 176
    producer groups, 115
Hungary, Aid to Artisans projects, 176

IFAT. *See* International Federation for
    Alternative Trade
Imports. *See* Trade regulations
India:
    exports to United States, 153-154, 255
    gendered patterns of work, 13, 156, 290,
        291
    madras cloth, 46
    monsoons, 152, 280
    price consciousness, 269
    producer group organization, 44
    product development, 45
    recycling, 151
    traditional needlework, 13, 291
    See also MarketPlace: Handwork of India
Indonesia, 45, 47, 48
InfoDev, 188
Inter-American Development Bank, 175
Internal Revenue Service, 138
International Federation for Alternative
    Trade (IFAT), 18, 185, 188
Internet. *See* Web sites
Iowa State University, 62

Jamaica, Aid to Artisans grants, 179
Jaspé fabrics, 124, 204, 222, 255, 280
Java, 48
Johnson, Ted, 190, 333
Jordan, Aid to Artisans projects, 176

Kenya, 100
Kufe, Happy, 30, 33
Kuna *mola* makers, 11, 43, 47
Kyrgystan, 182

Lepinski, Beth, 89, 90
Levi Strauss Corporation, 174
Lewis, Docey, 98-99, 100-103, 110, 251-252,
    258, 267

MacArthur Foundation, 188
Mail-order catalogs:
    competitors of ATOs, 17, 134, 301
    differentiation marketing strategy, 300
    MarketPlace: Handwork of India,
        147-148, 150, 159, 161, 165, 244, 294,
        300
    Pueblo to People, 116, 117, 123, 128,
        131-132, 140, 277-278, 300
    purchases by ATO customers, 230
Mainstream businesses:
    competition with Alternative Trade
        Organizations, 23, 226, 246, 292-293,
        300-302
    mail-order catalogs, 17, 134, 301
    marketing, 252-253
    mission statements, 19-20

product development, 252-253
retail stores, 17, 300-302
social responsibility in, 7, 108, 140, 301
Malaysia, 45-46
Market diversification, for producer groups,
    46, 103, 166, 292-293, 308-309
Marketing:
    Aid to Artisans projects, 178, 180
    Aid to Artisans staff expertise, 183-184
    by alternative trade organizations, 15,
        17-18, 19-20
    by mainstream businesses, 252-253
    by producer groups, 34, 36, 43-46
    differentiation strategy, 34, 253, 296-297,
        300, 302, 314, 316-317
    focus strategy, 34, 296-297
    in future, 316
    need for culture brokers, 11
    Web sites, 185-186, 188-190
    See also Design consultants; Product
        development; Product preferences
MarketPlace: Handwork of India, 59,
    167-168
    achievements, 164-167
    child sponsorship program, 162
    clothing designs, 146, 150-154, 254-255,
        270
    communication with artisans, 153
    customer survey, 226-249, 337-339
    customers, 152-153, 233, 237, 241
    decentralization, 154-158, 163
    designers, 158, 159-160, 258, 263-264
    education of consumers, 160-162
    effects of trade regulations, 153-154, 255
    employees in United States, 149-150
    global dialogue, 160-163
    goal of empowering women in India,
        144-146, 149, 150, 164-166, 168-169
    goals, 20-22
    history, 144-147
    leadership, 163-164
    mail-order catalog, 147-148, 150, 159,
        161, 165, 244, 294, 300
    market segments, 233, 237, 241
    offices in India, 144
    organizational structure, 146-147,
        154-158, 163
    problems, 152
    product development, 150-154, 158-160,
        263-264, 271, 330-331
    product quality issues, 269
    products, 144-146, 148-149, 255, 267
    sales, 18, 147-148
    volunteers, 168, 294
    wages paid, 149
    wholesale customers, 146, 148
    See also SHARE

Max Havelaar Foundation, 16
Maya weavers:
    backstrap weaving, 210, 212, 217,
        253-254, 260-261, 272, 279, 291
    floor looms, 272
    in Guatemala, 127-128, 210, 215-216, 217,
        253-254, 256, 260-261
    in Mexico, 45, 47
MCC. *See* Mennonite Central Committee
Memorial Presbyterian Church (Appleton,
    Wisconsin), 89-90
Mennonite Central Committee (MCC), 62,
    64, 65, 69-70, 80, 274
Mennonite Church, 16, 64
Merchant, Fatima, 161-162, 164
Methodist church, 211, 213-214, 215
Mexico:
    Artisans and Ecology projects, 181-182
    Maya weavers, 45, 47
    pottery villages, 43
    rug weavers, 11, 42-43, 47
    wood carvers, 13
Meyer, Dick, 5, 15, 190-193, 323, 333
Middlemen, 11, 181, 276
Monteiro, Lalita, 144
Muchina, Joseph, 100
Multi-Fiber Arrangement, 255, 281
Mumbai (Bombay), India, 143-144
    See also SHARE
Myers, Paul, 23, 66, 70-71, 76, 77-78, 82-83,
    277, 289

National Council of Churches, 95
Nepal, Aid to Artisans grants, 179
New York International Gift Fair, 102, 178
Nicaragua, 115, 131
Noor Arfa Batek, 45-46

Opoku-Ampomsah, Nanasei, 41
Organizational cultures:
    adaptability to change, 222-223
    goals, 31-32
    of Alternative Trade Organizations, 19,
        310-311
    of producer groups, 30-31, 219-224
    relationship to business performance,
        32, 33
    strategic appropriateness, 220-222
    study of, 30-33

Pakistan, Aid to Artisans project, 174
Panama:
    Kuna *mola* makers, 11, 43, 47
    producer group organization, 44
Paule, Marty, 147
Pawar, Manisha, 165

Peace Corps, 38, 267, 269
PEOPLink, 5, 59
    activities, 185-188
    Designer's Studio, 187, 189, 264
    educational programming, 187-188
    funding, 188
    mission, 184-185
    partner organizations, 185-186
    pricing decisions, 186-187
    Web marketing, 188-190
    Web site, 171-172, 185, 186, 187, 189, 264
Peru:
    Aid to Artisans projects, 180, 181
    Artisans and Ecology project, 182
    cultural products, 178, 180, 181, 301
Peruvian Connection, 301
Pier 1 Imports, 17, 174, 300-301
Plaut, Jim and Mary, 173
Politics:
    focus of Pueblo to People, 119-123, 131
    views of ATO customers, 242-244, 297
Pop Atziak, 262
Pricing decisions:
    import expenses, 274
    of PEOPLink, 186-187
    of producer groups, 274, 275-276
    of Pueblo to People, 129-130, 131, 231,
        274
    of SERRV, 95, 98, 102
    of Ten Thousand Villages, 70-71, 274-275
    price sensitivity of ATO customers, 131,
        231
    retail prices, 231, 276-277
    See also Wages, fair
Producer groups:
    assistance from religious organizations,
        211, 213-214, 215, 217-218, 223
    ATO selection of, 14-15, 19, 99-100,
        125-126, 278, 307-308
    benefits to local economies, 10, 47
    business strategies, 34
    capacities, 278-280, 306
    central workshops, 12, 42, 154, 205,
        269-270
    class issues, 42-43
    collaboration with ATOs, 221-222, 224,
        315
    communication with ATOs, 82, 101-102,
        153
    cooperatives, 44, 155
    dependence on ATO orders, 292
    development assistance to, 40, 123-125
    equipment, 177, 269, 270, 279
    future relationships with ATOs, 306-309
    future research questions, 309

information needed on demand for products, 13-14, 316
international associations, 18
local sales to tourists, 34, 36, 46
market diversification, 46, 103, 166, 292-293, 308-309
marketing by, 43-46, 185-186
measurement of success, 37-38, 39
obstacles to success, 40-41
organizational cultures, 30-31, 219-224
organizational structures, 155, 157
production organization, 43-45
risks assumed by Alternative Trade Organizations, 128, 129, 134
social goals, 39, 207-210, 220
sustainability, 14-15, 38-39, 264-266, 293, 302-303, 306, 308-309
Web sites, 185-186, 194, 214
See also Artisans; Cultural products; Product development
Product delivery, potential problems, 22, 125-126, 152, 278-281
Product development:
adaptation of cultural products, 101, 221-222, 255-256, 314
artisan interest and skills, 252, 266, 271-273
at MarketPlace: Handwork of India, 150-154, 158-160, 263-264, 271, 330-331
at Pueblo to People, 123, 124, 126-129, 131, 262-263, 273
at Ruth and Nohemi, 213
at SERRV, 97-103, 110, 111, 262, 266
at Ten Thousand Villages, 79-83, 86, 259-260, 265
based on indigenous aesthetics and production practices, 98, 150-154
by Aid to Artisans, 177
by artisans, 47-48, 102, 221-222, 265-266, 282, 291
collaboration between ATOs and artisans, 13-14, 45-46, 221-222, 256-264, 260-261, 284-285
concurrent efforts to create sustainable businesses, 264-266
day-to-day factors in, 266-267
design trend information provided to artisans, 102, 110, 265
focus on customer demand, 264
future research questions, 309
in future, 306
in mainstream businesses, 252-253
key issues model, 282-285
quality issues, 268-270

respect for cultural traditions, 6, 253-256, 291
scheduling issues, 101
skills of ATO staff, 273-274
technical assistance from outsiders, 45
See also Culture brokers; Design consultants
Product preferences:
of ATO customers, 231-238, 246, 256, 284, 296-297, 314
volatility of market, 46, 48-49, 256, 314-315
See also Quality
Production processes:
Aid to Artisans projects, 177
capacity, 278-280, 306
central workshops, 12, 42, 154, 205, 269-270
cultural importance, 47, 222, 255-256, 291, 314-315
environmental issues, 182, 270-271, 316
increasing efficiency, 275, 279
indigenous, 98
raw materials, 150, 151, 182, 267-268, 279
weather problems, 152, 280
Pryor, Jimmy, 116, 118, 119-120, 121-122, 128, 134, 135, 137-138, 139, 140, 147, 276
PtP. *See* Pueblo to People
Pueblo to People (PtP), 58, 113-114, 140-141
achievements, 138-140
board of directors, 136, 138
closing of, 110, 114, 132-138, 218-219, 292
clothing products, 13, 124, 131, 218-219, 246, 262, 270
competition, 134
customer survey, 226-249, 326, 333-337, 339
customers, 27, 130-132, 237
development assistance for producer groups, 123-125
education of consumers, 115, 123, 140, 297
financial problems, 134-136
financial structure, 118, 135
goals, 20, 115, 128, 138, 297
history, 26, 114-119
inventory management problems, 126, 128-129
mail-order catalog, 116, 117, 123, 128, 131-132, 140, 277-278, 300
market segments, 233, 237, 241, 246
organizational culture, 120
organizational structure, 118-119, 136-137
political focus, 119-123, 131
pricing decisions, 129-130, 131, 231, 274

product categories, 116, 277
product development, 123, 124, 126-129,
    131, 262-263, 273
representatives in Guatemala, 119-120,
    124-125, 125, 132-133, 258, 328, 330
retail stores, 117-118
sales, 116
selection of producer groups, 125-126
staff, 115, 118, 119, 120-123, 273
staff salaries, 129-130, 136
volunteers, 136
Web site, 137-138

Quality:
    at UPAVIM, 204
    expectations of ATO customers, 231-232,
        238-240, 246, 247, 298, 318
    varying definitions, 268-269, 315, 318

Religious organizations:
    assistance to producer groups, 211,
        213-214, 215, 217-218, 223
    financial assistance to Alternative Trade
        Organizations, 147
    partnerships with Alternative Trade
        Organizations, 90, 93-95, 104
    See also Churches
Renno, Catherine, 14, 225, 333
Retail stores:
    business strategies, 35, 191-193
    community involvement, 191-192, 194
    competition from mainstream
        businesses, 17, 174, 300-302
    electronic communication network
        among, 193
    failure rates, 36-37
    independent, 190-193
    MarketPlace clothing sold in, 146, 148
    product displays and promotion, 80, 277
    product mix, 192 193
    Pueblo to People, 117-118
    SERRV products sold in, 90, 104, 191
    Worldly Goods (Ames), 61-62
    See also Ten Thousand Villages retail
        stores; Traditions Fair Trade
Romania, Aid to Artisans projects, 176
Russia, producer groups, 252
Ruth and Nohemi, 330
    benefits to artisans, 214-216
    clients, 213
    goals, 214
    history, 210, 211-212
    house-building project, 214-215
    income alternatives, 214
    incomes, 216, 274
    Methodist church assistance, 211,
        213-214, 215

product pricing, 274, 275
products, 212, 213, 271
weavers, 211, 256
work-study program for boys, 211-212,
    214

Salcedo, Dan, 137
    at PEOPLink, 5, 15, 184-187, 188-189,
        190, 264, 333
    at Pueblo to People, 26, 114-115, 116, 119,
        123, 125, 135, 139
El Salvador, 131
San José Poaquil (Guatemala), 218
Sanders, Fran, 113, 133
Santa Apolonia (Guatemala), 217
Seikh, Hasina, 165
SELFHELP Crafts of the World. See Ten
        Thousand Villages
SERRV, 58
    Church of the Brethren support, 93-95
    church sales, 17-18, 89-90, 103
    communication with producer groups,
        101-102
    customer base, 95, 104
    design consultant, 97-99, 251-252, 258
    distribution channels, 90, 103-106, 191
    education of consumers, 90, 104, 108, 109
    financial problems and recovery, 92-93,
        96-97
    future challenges, 111-112
    goals, 95-96
    grants program, 96
    history, 93-95
    independence from Church of the
        Brethren, 106-107
    mission, 94, 106
    partners, 17-18
    philosophical issues, 107-110, 111
    philosophy, 90-92
    pricing decisions, 95, 98, 102
    product development, 97-103, 110, 111,
        262, 266
    product mix, 108-109
    purchasing decisions, 92, 102-103
    relations with producer groups, 95,
        109-110, 204
    sales, 18
    selection of producer groups, 99-100
    staff reductions, 96-97
    strengths, 110-111
    volunteers, 105, 109, 294
SHARE (Support the Handicapped's
        Rehabilitation Effort), 146-147, 149,
        156, 164
    development programs, 156-157, 163
    local marketing efforts, 308
    See also MarketPlace: Handwork of India

Small businesses. *See* Business performance;
  Producer groups
Smith, Clare Brett, 5, 171, 173-174, 175-176,
  179, 181, 183-184, 333
Social responsibility:
  as value of Alternative Trade
    Organizations, 19, 322-323
  future research questions, 318
  in mainstream businesses, 7, 108, 140,
    301
  of ATO customers, 298
  practices, 6-7
Spector, Ron, 4-5, 124, 253-254, 260-261, 266,
  267-268, 271-272, 279, 330, 333
Stewart, Joan, 119, 128, 137, 138, 139, 263
Stores. *See* Retail stores
Sundance Catalog, 174, 301
Sweatshops, concerns of U.S. consumers,
  9-10

Tejidos de Guadelupe, 216-219, 280,
  292-293, 328
  craft projects, 216-218
  educational programs, 218
  empowerment of members, 218-219
  products, 217
Ten Thousand Villages, 58
  approach to change, 64-66
  board of directors, 79
  distribution channels, 76, 191
  education of consumers, 76-78, 86
  future challenges, 78, 85-87
  goals, 20, 23, 68
  history, 62, 63-67
  integration of mission and business, 66,
    79, 85, 87
  Mennonite values of, 64, 66
  mission, 62, 68-71, 323
  name change, 66-67, 79, 313
  organizational culture, 23, 78
  organizational structure, 64
  pricing decisions, 70-71, 274-275
  principles of operation, 68-69
  product categories, 80, 270, 277, 278
  product development, 79-83, 86,
    259-260, 265
  promotional materials and activities, 61,
    77-78, 86
  purchasing decisions, 69-70, 74, 79-83, 86
  relationship with artisans, 62, 82, 84
  sales, 18, 62
  selection of producer groups, 278
  strategic planning, 66, 68, 85
  strengths, 84-85
  volunteers, 68, 74-76
Ten Thousand Villages retail stores, 71-74, 85
  boards of directors, 71-72

competitors, 23, 300
displays, 80
future challenges, 86
in urban areas, 73, 83-84
number of, 17
SERRV products sold in, 90
types, 72
volunteer staff, 71, 73, 75-76, 86, 294
Textiles:
  chemical and natural dyes, 182, 270-271,
    316
  cotton, 267-268, 314
  Ghanaian batiks, 34
  Indian madras cloth, 46
  Malaysian batiks, 45-46
  production in India, 13
  See also Backstrap weaving; Clothing;
    Jaspé fabrics; Trade regulations;
    Weavers
Thailand, 43
Tidwell, Monte, 119
Trade regulations, 281
  content labeling, 124, 125-126
  Multi-Fiber Arrangement, 255, 281
  tariffs, 274
  U.S. import quotas on textiles, 153-154,
    255, 281
  U.S. import regulations, 281
Traditions Fair Trade (Olympia,
  Washington), 5, 59, 190-193, 323
Trevino, Diane, 126-127
Trinity Jewellery, 100
Turkey, 38, 45

Unique Ceramics, 30-31, 32-33
United Nations, 303
U.S. Agency for International Development
  (USAID), 175, 188
U.S. Department of Agriculture, 281
U.S. Fish and Wildlife Department, 281
U.S. government:
  investigations of conditions in clothing
    manufacturing, 9
  See also Trade regulations
UPAVIM (Unidas para Vivir Mejor),
  199-200, 329-330
  craft program, 202, 203-206, 221, 255,
    268, 269-270, 273, 275-276
  culture broker role, 205-206, 258
  customers, 204
  empowerment of women, 209
  goals, 207-210
  history, 202
  incomes of members, 206-207, 20⁹
    209-210
  organizational structure, 203
  products, 204-205, 255, 270

programs, 202-204
quality control, 268, 269-270
USAID. *See* U.S. Agency for International
    Development

Values:
    of Alternative Trade Organizations,
        19-22, 64, 66, 322-323
    of ATO customers, 20, 242-244, 298, 318
Velzeboer, Marijke:
    at PEOPLink, 184-185
    at Pueblo to People, 26, 114, 115, 125
Volunteers, 294-295
    at MarketPlace: Handwork of India, 168,
        294
    at Pueblo to People, 136
    at SERRV, 105, 109, 294
    at Ten Thousand Villages national
        organization, 68, 74-76
    at Ten Thousand Villages retail stores,
        71, 73, 75-76, 86, 294
    in future, 296, 312, 313

Wages, fair:
    commitment of ATOs to pay, 15, 303
    decision-making process of Pueblo to
        People, 129-130
    decision-making process of Ten
        Thousand Villages, 70-71, 274-275
    paid by mainstream businesses, 7

setting, 274-276, 303
Wal-Mart, 9
Walt Disney, 9
Weavers:
    in Guatemala, 39, 41, 211, 252, 256, 273
    in Thailand, 43
    Mexican, 11, 42-43, 47
    See also Maya weavers
Web sites:
    challenges of marketing on, 188-190
    for producer groups, 185-186, 194, 214
    PEOPLink, 171-172, 185, 186, 187, 189,
        264
    Pueblo to People, 137-138
Women:
    business goals, 38
    empowerment of, 144-146, 149, 164-166,
        168-169, 209, 290-291
    family responsibilities, 32, 42, 156,
        207-208, 220, 221, 272, 280, 290, 291
    See also Gender issues
Wood carvers, in Ghana, 41
World Bank, 175, 188
Worldly Goods (Ames, Iowa), 61-62

Yeary, Megan, 152-153
Yoder, Kristen, 69

ABOUT THE AUTHORS

MARY ANN LITTRELL is Professor in the Department of Textiles and Clothing at Iowa State University. She conducts research on ethnic product marketing, with a special focus on artisans' lives, impacts from participation in the global marketplace, and strategies for product development. Tourism research linking travel styles, shopping behavior, and product authenticity forms a second research focus. Over the past 10 years, teaching, research, and development projects have taken Dr. Littrell to Ghana, Malaysia, Guatemala, Mexico, South Africa, Nigeria, and India. She is currently developing three documentary films and accompanying business case studies that chronicle entrepreneurial firms in Malaysia, Ghana, and Guatemala that have successfully developed export markets for their cultural products. Her research has been published in *Human Organization, Annals of Tourism, Journal of Travel Research, Clothing and Textiles Research Journal,* and the *Journal of Fashion Marketing and Management.* Her Ph.D. is from Purdue University.

MARSHA ANN DICKSON is Associate Professor in the Department of Consumer & Textile Sciences at The Ohio State University. Her research program focuses on balancing the needs of all constituents in the apparel marketing system (producers, retailers, and consumers) to create a fair and beneficial system for all involved. Her research has taken her to the People's Republic of China, Guatemala, and Puerto Rico. Recent research projects have focused on consumers' knowledge of sweatshop issues and how they take this knowledge into consideration when shopping for clothing. Prior to her academic career, Dr. Dickson was a clothing designer for various apparel manufacturers in Dallas, Texas. She has published her research in the *Clothing and Textiles Research Journal*, the *Journal of Fashion Marketing and Management*, *Sociology of Sport Journal*, and *Human Organization*. She has a Ph.D. from Iowa State University.